G NIGHT
STORY OF
ION CAMPS

Nev

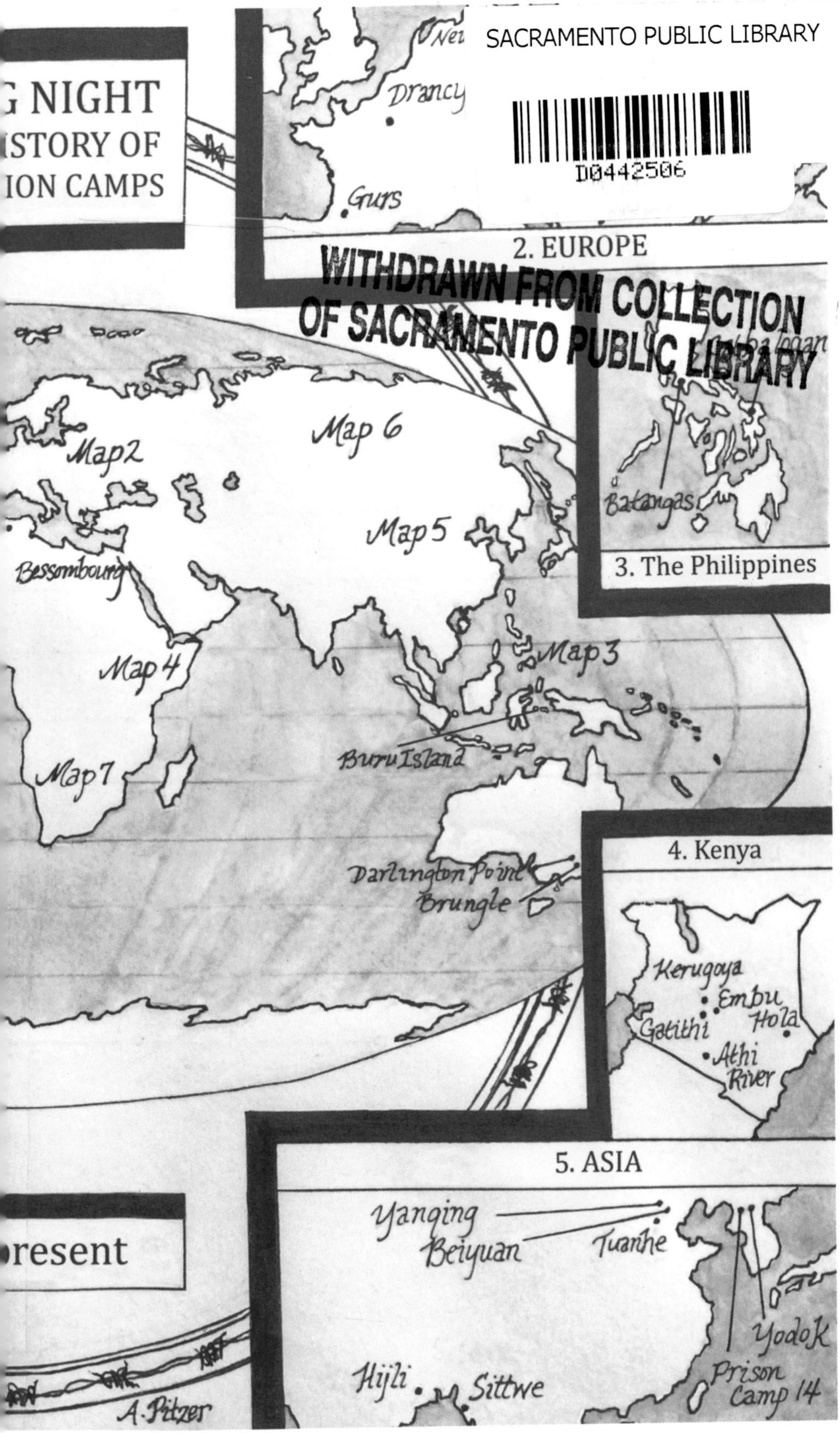

Drancy

Gurs

2. EUROPE

Map 6

Map 2

Map 5

Bessombourg

Batangas

3. The Philippines

Map 4

Map 3

Map 7

Buru Island

Darlington Point
Brungle

4. Kenya

Kerugoya
Embu
Gatithi
Hola
Athi
River

5. ASIA

resent

Yanging
Beiyuan
Tuanhe

Yodok

Hijli
Sittwe
Prison
Camp 14

A. Pitzer

One Long Night

Never shall I forget that night, the first night in camp,
that turned my life into one long night seven times sealed.
— ELIE WIESEL, *NIGHT*

It can happen, and it can happen everywhere.
— PRIMO LEVI

One Long Night

Sailing to Guantánamo

1. A DOUBLE-DECKER FERRY CARRIES visitors to the windward side of Guantánamo Bay naval base and drops them off at the bottom of a hill just short of Camp Justice. A handful of current and former detention sites with names like Camp Echo and Camp Delta cluster near the southeastern corner of the base, tucked behind chain link fences topped with loops of razor wire. Those facilities still in use hold a small number of detainees awaiting proceedings, as well as others who will never see their cases presented at Camp Justice.

The ferry docks at a utilitarian parking lot on Fisherman's Point, but the lot's bare pavement fails to reflect its storied history. In 1898, the US Marines landed here during the Spanish-American War, coming ashore the morning of June 10, setting fire to a seaside village and capturing the Spanish blockhouse perched above it before lunchtime. The hill became a wartime camp, then a permanent base, and US forces never left.

A bronze plaque embedded in a cairn of white stones by the water's edge commemorates an even earlier invasion. On Christopher Columbus's second voyage to the West in 1494, he visited Fisherman's Point, too, having already claimed Cuba for Spain. The plaque states that Columbus and his men were hunting for gold, but "not finding likely prospects they left the next day."

For more than four hundred years after Columbus's expedition, Cuba remained a Spanish colony. But in the 1890s, Spain created the world's first concentration camps on the island. The death toll unleashed by that decision eventually led to the loss of the colony, with US Marines coming ashore on the same spit of land where Columbus had stood centuries before.

Until a few years ago, I had no thought of traveling to Guantánamo. My interest lay in writing a history of concentration camps. Twenty-first-century detention at Guantánamo might have seemed disturbing, but it had not occurred to me to think of it as a concentration camp. The more time I spent researching mass arrests and detention, however, the more Guantánamo kept creeping back into view.

I couldn't imagine writing about the place without going there. And so in 2015, I made two visits. The first gave me a chance to observe pretrial hearings in the case of the five 9/11 defendants, who make an appearance in the last chapter of this book. Not being obliged to file a story on deadline, as other journalists on the trip were expected to, I opted to fill in for the absent sketch artist and absorb as much as possible in a courtroom custom-built for prisoners in the war on terror. Having arrived in the fifteenth year of an ongoing story, I wanted to catch up.

My second trip took me to the detention camps, or at least the ones that I was permitted to see. In both cases, setting foot on Guantánamo was like entering another world. The thousands of personnel and dozens of buildings that made up the machinery of detention for what was then a little over a hundred prisoners felt overwhelming. The issue that most troubled me — the legitimacy of holding untried suspects for more than a decade — was not the minute-to-minute concern of the soldiers and sailors who were busy doing their jobs. The big questions had been decided elsewhere. There the detainees sat, and there they would remain as long as those orders stood.

Yet after September 11, 2001, the US consecration of Guantánamo as an ideal site for extrajudicial detention had been greeted with the same international dismay elicited by Spain's inauguration of *reconcentración*—mass civilian detention—in 1896. In crucial ways, the twenty-first-century American detention camps at Guantánamo are descendants of the nineteenth-century Spanish camps. But there are many generations between them, each iteration carrying elements of the old while evolving into something new.

The history of concentration camps circles from Cuba around the world and back, visiting six continents and nearly every country along the way. Camps have been in existence continuously somewhere on the globe for more than a hundred years. Barracks and barbed wire remain their most familiar symbols, but a camp is defined more by its detainees than by any physical feature. A concentration camp exists wherever a government holds groups of civilians outside the normal legal process—sometimes to segregate people considered foreigners or outsiders, sometimes to punish.

If prisons are meant for suspects convicted of crimes after a trial, a concentration camp holds those who, most often, had no real trial at all. A detainee is the most specific term for those held in this way, but for the purposes of this book, they can also be considered prisoners or captives. Sometimes, as at Guantánamo, the naming of categories of detainees is bound up with specific legal protections. "Prisoner" might imply the granting of rights due to prisoners of war under the Geneva Conventions, so camp staff tend to refer to them only as detainees.

Concentration camps house civilians rather than combatants—though at many points, from World War I to Guantánamo, camp administrators have not always made an effort to distinguish between the two. Detainees are typically held because of their racial, cultural, religious, or political identity, not because of any prosecutable offense—though some states have remedied this flaw by making legal existence next to impossible. Which is not to say that all detainees are innocent of criminal actions against the government in any given system; rather, the innocent and the guilty alike may be swept up without distinction or recourse.

Concentration camps are established by state policy or, less frequently, run by a provisional government during a conflict or civil war. They represent the exercise of state power against citizens, subjects, or others for whom the government holds some degree of responsibility. Unlike prisons, camps often detain prisoners without a scheduled date of release. Where a date exists, it has generally been set arbitrarily and is changed without warning.

Detention in a handful of camp systems has been framed as protective, ostensibly guarding an unpopular group from public anger—and sometimes they really have offered protection. More commonly, detention is announced as preventative, to keep a suspect group from committing potential future crimes. Only rarely have governments publicly acknowledged the use of camps as deliberate punishment, more often promoting them as part of a civilizing mission to uplift supposedly inferior cultures and races.

If mass civilian detention without trial is the defining feature of a camp, then it becomes possible to look at a whole host of categories of camps, many of which have interrelated histories over time. In internment camps, people are detained for a fixed or indefinite period of time, usually in the wake of a crisis. Transit camps generally deport people to another camp or region. Labor camps require work from detainees, usually on behalf of the state. And detainees in extermination camps are completely cut off from sustenance or murdered outright.

Political philosopher Hannah Arendt described concentration camps as divided into Purgatory, Hades, and Hell, moving from the netherland of internment to labor camps of the Gulag and Nazi death factories. But nearly all concentration camps share one feature: they extract people from one area to house them somewhere else. It sounds like a simple concept, but both elements are distinct and important. Camps require the removal of a population from a society with all its accompanying rights, relationships, and connections to humanity. This exclusion is followed by an involuntary assignment to some lesser condition or place, generally detention with other undesirables under armed guard. Of these afterworlds, Arendt writes, "All three types have one thing in common: the human masses sealed off in them are treated as if they no longer existed, as if what happened to them were no longer of interest to anybody, as if they were already dead and some evil spirit gone mad were amusing himself by stopping them for a while between life and death."

The concentration camp experience rarely begins and ends inside barbed wire. It is part of a process—usually one that starts with arrest and interrogation, continues via a journey of minutes, days, or weeks to a camp, and persists in exile or continued threat of punishment after release. The worst moments of detention tend to define the entire experience. As Resistance fighter and Auschwitz survivor Jean Améry wrote, "Whoever was tortured, stays tortured."[1]

A typical concentration camp includes communal living among hundreds or thousands of people, though in some cases, particularly in the last decades of the twentieth century, detainees have also been held in small groups, in an attempt to keep them hidden. There are few hard lines in classification, as concentration camps can bleed into other categories of camps, giving them dual identities. At some sites, convicted prisoners ended up comprising a measurable percentage of the population, and were brought in to supervise and police political detainees. At other times convicts were sent to camps after serving their legal sentences, instead of being released into the general population.

Elsewhere, refugee camps built to deal with massive immigration—often due to war—have sometimes transformed into hybrid refugee-concentration camps. For more than a century, countries have established refugee camps to coordinate food and shelter during crises. But where the camps exist predominantly to isolate refugees and relegate them to dangerous or inhospitable terrain, serve as de facto detention areas to discourage border crossing, or become permanent purgatory for detainees unable to return home, they begin to take on characteristics of concentration camps. With refugee populations, a clear line does not always mark the peripheries of concentration camp definitions.

Differences between the earliest camp systems and the later Nazi concentration camp model have led historians like Andreas Stucki to ask whether such varied settings and results even belong together under the category "concentration camp."[2] But examination of the entire range of camps reveals that while they developed differences in tactics as well as tremendous variability in outcomes due to limits that culture and governments imposed on them, most systems arose from similar political crises and possessed parallel early goals.

2. Unlike war, murder, and the baroque tortures of antiquity, concentration camps do not stretch back across millennia. Criminal statutes in the ancient world more often called for exile, execution, or physical punishment—such as branding or flogging—than detention. The Mesopotamian Code of Ur-Nammu, a legal code dating back more than four thousand years, designates murder as the sovereign punishment for a range of crimes, from robbery and deflowering married virgins to murder itself. Detention, on the other hand, necessitates feeding and sheltering prisoners, obligations that offer a partial explanation for the late debut of jails and camps alike.

While some later camp phenomena, such as permanent tattoos to identify prisoners, made an appearance in the Roman Empire, authorities there resisted sentencing subjects to incarceration.[3] Mass imprisonment as a societal tool arrived in the era of factories and public schools, when having an assigned role in a large hierarchical group with a supervisor to enforce order or efficiency became part of daily life.[4] Yet forced labor does have deep historical roots. The Romans condemned subjects to hard labor on infrastructure projects, or in mines—*damnatio ad metallum*—through sentences handed down to those convicted of criminal offenses.[5] During the same era, Chinese dynasties instigated a system of corvée labor, in which every adult was expected to work for the state one month each year.[6] Corvée servitude, however, was not imposed as punishment but was part of an individual's obligations to the emperor.

Imperial Russia made similar use of peasant conscription at the beginning of the eighteenth century for the construction of St. Petersburg, where tens of thousands of Russian peasants died driving wooden piles into the swampland upon which the city would be built. Later, tsars established penal labor, in which convicts were sent thousands of miles from home to *katorga,* working in bitter Siberian settings under a nebulous legal status. Traveling eleven weeks to see prisoners working on Sakhalin Island in 1890, Anton Chekhov detailed the suffering he witnessed in a camp there. He described children falling asleep in piles of prisoners alongside their fettered convict parents and complained that no legal definition of *katorga* or its purpose existed.[7] The legacies of corvée labor and *katorga* would shape the local evolution of concentration camps as they made their way into Russia and China in the twentieth century.[8]

History's most direct precursors of concentration camps, however, appeared in the wake of Columbus's 1492 voyage. The Spanish Empire led the way, authorizing a system of religious missions in New Spain that began a year after Columbus's arrival and continued into the 1800s. The timing of campaigns varied, but from California to Peru, a policy of *reducción* reigned. Native communities were burned, and millions were forcibly relocated out of the countryside into new villages or into mission compounds. Fortress garrisons enforced the plan, while Jesuits, Franciscans, and Dominicans "civilized" their wards, converting them to Christianity, teaching them to read, and socializing them as Europeans.

In the midst of this process, Spanish authorities conducted the Valladolid Debate of 1550, a formal argument over whether Indians were human beings or "natural slaves."[9] After the close of the debate, both sides claimed victory, as Spain pressed on with *reducción.* Concentrated together in the missions, many of which were crude and filthy, natives had little chance for survival in the face of devastating European epidemics such as typhus and smallpox.

The United States' removal of native populations in the eastern half of North America began later than the Spanish efforts but was similarly brutal. A series of conflicts that would come to be known as the Indian Wars raged intermittently from the American Revolution into and across the whole of the nineteenth century. Using bribery and coercion to co-opt some leaders, the US government attempted to extricate whole Native American nations from their own territory in the Southeast during the 1830s. In a series of forced relocations that would come to be known as the Trail of Tears, Cherokees were held in detention at transit camps rife with dysentery before being forced farther west to reservations in present-day Oklahoma.[10]

Many tried to escape, only to find themselves captured. The officer in charge of Fort Hetzel, Georgia, reported to army headquarters in May 1838 on his efforts to track fleeing Indians prior to departure: "I commenced on the 26th securing the Indians. I have made prisoners of 425 or perhaps 450. I think by the time I get in the outstanding members of the families that I have broken up I will have as many as I can manage.... They run in every instance where they have the best opportunity."[11] Some four thousand Cherokee died en route, and more than ten thousand Native Americans from all the relocated tribes did not survive the march.

Canada, too, pinned its indigenous peoples down on reserves and in some regions forced residents to apply for travel passes to leave their designated territory—despite the fact that the pass system had no legal foundation under the Indian Act or the Criminal Code.[12] Lacking only more effective technology to enable complete detention on such a massive scale, nineteenth-century Native American reservations and earlier Spanish missions prefigured concentration camp systems to come.

3. The spark that ignited imperial willingness to commit to concentration camps at the end of the nineteenth century can be found in the US Civil War, a watershed conflict that forever transformed the treatment of civilians in combat. The brutality of the Confederate prisoner-of-war camp at Andersonville, Georgia, where some thir-

teen thousand US soldiers died, is sometimes considered a harbinger of the civilian concentration camps that soon followed. But the establishment of camps later in the century owes as much or more to the Union Army's theoretical approach to the war, as well as the actual tactics it employed to win.

The Lieber Code of Conduct, written by jurist Francis Lieber in 1863 and adopted by the US Army, tried for the first time to modernize the rules of war. The code explicitly rejected torture and laid out a plan for humane treatment of noncombatants, but loopholes meant to deal with guerrilla fighters and concerns about binding the military's hands too tightly left room for brutal tactics. In a war of rebellion, the code authorized commanders to expel or imprison "disloyal civilians," even those "known to sympathize with the rebellion without positively aiding it."[13] Commanders were also authorized to administer loyalty oaths, with a wide range of punishments permitted against those who refused. Though every attempt should be made to protect loyal citizens during the rebellion, Lieber wrote, the burden of war should be made to fall disproportionately on civilians deemed disloyal.[14] All these elements would become key in the creation of concentration camps.

The Lieber Code's effects were limited during the Civil War itself but provided a foundation for US military conduct going forward. Lieber's ideas introduced a clever approach to forbidding specific war crimes, such as torture and poison, while legitimizing almost everything else. Shortly after the war, Germany adopted the code almost wholesale. Its balance of limited humanitarian assurances and broad authorization of military powers during wartime inspired similar regulations in more than half a dozen other countries.[15] The code also served in subsequent decades as the basis for the development of international laws of war, first at The Hague in 1899 and then at the Second Geneva Convention in 1906. Embracing the common ground they had suddenly discovered, nations worldwide failed for decades to adequately address the fate of civilian noncombatants or to foresee the extensive role that civilian detention camps would come to play in war.

The Civil War legitimized camps in other ways. Orders from

Major General William Tecumseh Sherman in 1864 advised his cavalry on its way through Virginia to hold all male civilians under the age of fifty "as prisoners of war not as citizen prisoners," setting in place a dichotomy that directly subordinated civilians to battle strategy.[16] Sherman further institutionalized total war, in which everything under the sun, including civilians and their possessions, could be used as means to the military's desired end, with personal possessions destroyed alongside strategic assets.

During the last year of the war, General Philip Sheridan laid waste to the Shenandoah Valley in Virginia, and General Sherman went on his March to the Sea through Georgia and South Carolina. In both cases, troops burned and sacked not just military matériel, but also the homes, businesses, and crops of civilian residents. One officer from Ohio on Sherman's March observed, "The country behind us is left a howling wilderness, an utter desolation."[17]

The willingness to destroy everything was a revelation; the two generals' tactics would amaze and inspire generations of generals around the world. Five years after the end of the Civil War, Sheridan encouraged Prussian forces to adopt harsher methods in dealing with enemy civilians. As a guest of Prussian statesman Otto von Bismarck during the Franco-Prussian War in 1870, he advocated a strategy of "causing the inhabitants so much suffering that they must long for peace, and force their Government to demand it. The people must be left nothing but their eyes to weep with over the war."[18]

While many have argued the necessity of embracing cruel strategies in pursuit of one of history's most noble causes—an end to slavery in America—the widespread adoption of Sherman and Sheridan's methods meant that the same tactics would soon be embraced around the world for a whole range of lesser objectives. Demanding devastating victory without concession or negotiation became the goal, and strategic punishment of civilian populations to break the back of enemy forces occurred again and again.

Historian Jonathan Hyslop has analyzed how an increasing professionalization of the officer corps in militaries around the world during the nineteenth century seems to have had the paradoxical effect of heightened brutality against civilians, fostering the rise of concentration camps. He also references the concept of *Ausnahme-zustand* ("state of exception") described by General Julius von Hartmann in the 1870s to explain how a state of war served to remove all legal restraints in place during peacetime.[19] I would go further and argue that this normalization of extreme measures made punishing civilians appear not only permissible but necessary for any campaign truly committed to victory.

4. The final elements making concentration camps possible came from innovations in the second half of the nineteenth century. Public health, census taking, and bureaucratic efficiencies all played their part, as did inventions such as barbed wire and automatic weapons.

In the public health arena, governments began to take a role in maintaining public sanitation and disease-free communities, and of "numbering the people" in order to track them toward that end. The germ theory of disease revealed the nature of contagion and how illnesses spread—a triumph of rational discovery. But the same Enlightenment rationality and efficiency could be mixed in a stew with irrational fears and ignorance to assault those seen as inferior. For decades, American sociologists studied an extended family they named the "Jukes," at first showing the role that environment and poverty played in fostering criminal behavior but eventually claiming that the research vindicated theories of inherited feeblemindedness and degeneracy. Public health measures further introduced the idea that the state had a sometimes punitive role to play in protecting citizens through monitoring the spread of disease and enforcing health codes.

Industrial innovations included barbed wire, patented and put into mass production in the 1870s, which immediately found use in military campaigns. Ditches, trenches, and fortified buildings surrounded by barbed-wire mazes changed battlefield tactics, slowing cavalry charges and delaying the progress of soldiers on foot. The new invention was, however, not just effective at keeping the enemy out; it could also be used to keep prisoners in.

In 1898, Hilaire Belloc composed a couplet about the might of the British Empire in Africa as part of a children's treasury, writing "Whatever happens, we have got / The Maxim gun, and they have not." With barbed wire to trap people in camps, automatic weapons would soon make it possible to assert precise and devastating control over them. In time, barbed wire and automatic weapons together would make it simple for a small guard force to hold a tremendous number of detainees indefinitely. War strategies had already made civilian detention permissible; suddenly it also became feasible. By this point, the brutalization of civilians had not only been practiced on indigenous groups around the globe but employed against white American southerners and Europeans as well.

In hindsight, it seems almost inevitable that concentration camps would emerge. Yet hindsight also brings with it a moral clarity generally lacking in the moment. Concentration camps perpetually offer the illusion of a simple solution available to the malicious and myopic alike. If it were easy to understand in real time the threat represented by the camps, at least the myopic might be less inclined to keep resurrecting them.

Concentration camps are at heart a modern phenomenon and belong in the company of the atomic bomb as one of the few advanced innovations in violence. Just as other kinds of bombs existed before nuclear devices were developed, concentration camps also had precursors, but nonetheless represented a deliberate escalation and transformation of previous tactics. In both cases, observers realized that some dangerous genie was being released from a bottle, but in neither instance would it have been possible to imagine everything that would follow.

5. Literary scholar Leona Toker writes that Alexander Solzhenitsyn's achievement in writing about the Soviet Gulag is that "he has provided

a broad basis for polemic that comes closest to a substitute for the Nuremberg Trials."[20] Where no trial is expected, an author can make a case of his or her own. I have tried to acknowledge those cases in which camps have intentionally or inadvertently played some kind of protective role for detainees, at least for a while, such as some internment camps from the First World War, which preserved mostly military-age males from conscription and the higher risk of death in combat. Even in those cases, however, the evidence in this book adds up to a brief for the prosecution against the very idea of concentration camps.

In recent years, wars have filled refugee camps on several continents. From Calais and Nauru to vast Syrian refugee camp complexes, as well as American and Israeli immigrant detention centers, the world's most vulnerable citizens often end up pinned without recourse in quasi-concentration-camp conditions. Even without the relocation aspect intrinsic to concentration camps, ghetto-like conditions in the West Bank—not for extermination but for long-term isolation and control—are similarly problematic. All of these, along with staggering mass incarceration rates in the United States, particularly of African Americans, are important subjects that are beyond the scope of this book.

It is easy to demonize countries that have resorted to camps and to judge their citizens as unrecognizable monsters. But a close look at history reveals that nearly every nation has used camps at some point, though the degree to which their populations have embraced them and the devastation wreaked by each camp system have varied wildly. Their worst effects tend to be dampened in freer societies, where legal systems and legislatures have an opportunity to act. Yet a relatively healthy democracy is just as capable of instituting camps as the most corrupt Communist society or military dictatorship, sometimes with horrific results.

With few exceptions, camps are generally created to address real crises. They rarely succeed, more often trailing such damage in their wake that the original crisis is eclipsed. Nevertheless, the mechanics of many camps are similar in the first years. Even the most grotesque and deliberate detention-based genocide—the camp system of the Third Reich—began much like many others.

I have no wish to excuse the leaders and followers who perpetrated war crimes or peacetime atrocities; rather, I mean to suggest that it is worth paying attention to the historical moments in which concentration camps appear. Camps have fallen into disgrace only to be embraced again. Like a cunning virus, they evolve to survive. But at root, the use of mass civilian detention in any of its forms is a temptation as counterproductive as it is inhumane.

Philosopher Giorgio Agamben has written that concentration camps serve as a place to exile those recognized as possessing "bare life" but not meaningful, valuable lives—humans not entitled to legal recognition or due process. Concentration camps, he claims, have come to replace cities as the dominant sociopolitical structure of the modern era.[21] Solzhenitsyn used the cancer metaphor of metastasis to describe the growth of the Soviet Gulag, and even today, camps and the ideas behind them continue to spread and multiply. Without recognizing how concentration camps came to infest the twentieth century, the impulses that led to them will only generate additional detention in the twenty-first. By seeing the whole story of camps from their birth to the present and tracing their various evolutions, perhaps future observers will discover how camps might be averted. It is too late for those countries and peoples whose stories are told here.

This account spirals out from Cuba and southern Africa at the turn of the twentieth century and traverses the globe, fated to land back on the shores of Guantánamo Bay a century later, where shackled detainees in orange jumpsuits and blackout goggles are brought off the ferry at Fisherman's Point and driven, unseeing, past the Christopher Columbus monument, past the landing area for the Marines in 1898, past the cacti, coral reefs, and iguanas the size of small dogs, off the road to the chain link, concrete-floor cages of Camp X-Ray.

The story continues as it began, the latest chapter in the biography of a bad idea.

CHAPTER ONE

Born of Generals

1. The *Alfonso XIII*, a half-finished cruiser known for its instability, sailed into the port of Havana on February 10, 1896. After a week at sea, General Valeriano Weyler y Nicolau, Marquis of Tenerife, had come to take command. With a fierce gaze and flared muttonchop sideburns, the trim Weyler stood just five feet tall, meeting the army's height requirement only due to a general dispensation made for the diminishing stature of the Spanish Empire's recruits.[1]

Forty-seven years old and on the cusp of worldwide fame, he had set out from Madrid, traveling four thousand miles to lead Spanish forces into a second year of war against Cuban insurgents. The ship arrived well after sunrise. As the general and his entourage sailed by the weathered white stone of Morro Castle, guns fired off a salute to their new governor. Inside the harbor itself, the artillery at La Cabaña Fortress sent up an answering volley, while nearby vessels dipped their flags in greeting.

In the company of two generals and a marquis who had made the voyage with him, Weyler disembarked in the heat of the day. Met by Havana's civil and military authorities, Spain's newest champion strode two blocks inland to the governor's palace. Garlands and streamers hung everywhere, with red blankets hoisted from the windows of private homes to show loyalty to Spain. People lined the streets and crowded into the greenery of the Plaza de Armas facing the palace to cheer for their new viceroy and to hope for a bright Cuban future under Spanish rule, or perhaps just an end to the war. On arrival at the palace, Weyler took his oath of office and became governor and commander in chief of Cuba.[2]

Before leaving Europe, he had reviewed the reports of his predecessors and absorbed lessons from veterans of recent offensives. He had met with the minister of war in Madrid, to lay out exactly what he would do. Weyler had thought through his strategy and knew that the tactics involved would be controversial, but he believed that he would win the war for Spain in less than two years.[3]

With decades of military service behind him, he was hardly a cipher. As he stepped onto Cuban soil, newspapers on both sides of the Atlantic were already making dire assessments of what would happen under this new governor-general, predicting bloodshed and mayhem. And so it happened that both the world and Valeriano Weyler had some idea—yet no idea at all—what he was about to unleash.

2. Before Nazi extermination factories rose in Europe, before the first prisoner entered the Soviet Gulag, before the twentieth century had even begun, concentration camps found their first home in the cities and towns of Cuba. The modern experiment in preemptively detaining groups of civilians without trial was launched by two generals: one who refused to bring camps into the world and another who did not.

A year before Weyler's arrival, Cuban rebels had declared independence from Spain. While the government in Madrid collapsed in the face of anxiety over yet another war, rebels spent the spring of 1895 harassing Spanish forces, occasionally seizing rifles, bullets, and food.[4] Representatives of the Cuban junta had lived in exile in America for years, organizing their resistance, raising money, and ginning up sympathy stateside. Choosing their moment, rebel leaders in exile returned to the island to fight.

The first general Spain sent to lead the campaign, Arsenio Martínez Campos, knew Cuba well. He had fought for five years in the last Spanish war there, concluding a peace as governor that sparked the eventual abolition of slavery on the island. He had since commanded Spanish forces in Mexico and Morocco, led a coup that restored the monarchy in Spain, and survived an assassination attempt. By the time he returned to Cuba he was fifty-three years old, a round man with a Van Dyke beard gone white, a mixture of progressive ideals and atavistic honor, known for the judicious use of both warfare and negotiation.

But during Martínez Campos's first months back on the ground, nature appeared to favor the rebels. Cuba in high summer was a heatstroke-ridden swamp of malaria and yellow fever. Some locals had immunity through prior exposure, but few Spaniards did. Illness decimated imperial forces just as profoundly as any rebel stealth attack.

On the insurgents' side, dynamite and ambush proved effective tools for stalling the forward progress of Spanish troops or stealing their supplies. A small number of snipers, even with outdated weapons, could instill terror in a whole column of troops. Able to disappear into the countryside at will, the rebels could pick and choose their encounters, leaving Spanish forces plotting how to draw them into traditional battle.

The insurgents spent their first months making strategic raids or capturing undefended towns. That July, Martínez Campos went into the field to provoke a decisive fight, only to see his troops forced to flee the field by superior rebel tactics. Even given the insurgents' superior intelligence networks, it was a staggering humiliation for Spain.[5] Faced with escalating measures on the part of the rebels and pressured by a new government overseas less inclined toward concessions, Martínez Campos began to consider desperate means to end the uprising.

Days later, he wrote to the Spanish prime minister, giving a stark assessment of the challenges facing his troops. As for what could be done in the future to improve Spain's position, he explained that it would be possible to "reconcentrate" hundreds of thousands of rural Cubans into Spanish-held towns behind trenches and barbed wire, but he would need significant forces to hold them there. He felt certain that emptying the countryside to isolate insurgents would be effective, but the price to be paid in misery and hunger would be horrible.[6]

History is full of moments in which hindsight provides the only clear view. This is not one of them. During the final months before *reconcentración* became official policy, as his own troops and the rebels both adopted harsher tactics, Martínez Campos explained to the Spanish prime minister that he had already authorized shooting armed rebel commanders captured in battle and those caught setting fires to homes and crops. Though Martínez Campos found Cubans dangerous and unconventional fighters, he described how they had nursed Spanish wounded who fell into their hands and returned prisoners of war unharmed. He could not, he telegraphed to Spain, raise the stakes in brutality against an opponent he felt to be honorable.

After years fighting the rebels in multiple campaigns, Captain General Arsenio Martínez Campos offered to surrender his imperial post governing the island rather than embark on a policy of deliberate atrocity. The man who thought concentration camps the only road to victory refused to embrace them.

Martínez Campos could hardly have imagined the gas chambers and the killing fields that would bloom in the debris of the Cuban experiment; yet he understood the suffering inherent in mass executions and clearing the countryside of inhabitants. "I cannot," he wrote, "as the representative of a civilized nation, be the first to give the example of cruelty and intransigence."[7]

3. As Spain pondered what to do, the insurgents adopted more extreme measures, with rebel general Máximo Gómez issuing an

order in November 1895 declaring that "all plantations shall be totally destroyed."[8] But Martínez Campos had made his position clear, laying out his unwillingness to launch full *reconcentración* as the result of principles he held above everything. Months later, he was recalled to Spain in disgrace, sailing across the Atlantic to a homecoming of crowds gathered at each stop to insult him as he rode the train from the coast to Madrid.

No such reservations existed for the man Martínez Campos recommended to take his place—Captain General Valeriano Weyler. Knowing Spain was set on adopting more severe measures, Martínez Campos wrote his superiors and said that among the Spanish generals willing to carry out the new battle plan, "only Weyler also has intelligence, valor, and an understanding of war." But Cuban rebels already had their own view of Weyler, giving him the title "the Butcher."

Weyler's father, a doctor in the Spanish army, had risen to direct the medical corps, and as a child Weyler had been fascinated by surgeries and autopsies. Just after his eighteenth birthday, he had entered officer school, graduating first in his class. In 1863 he sailed to Cuba for the first time, where he secured a fortune by winning the national lottery but then promptly caught yellow fever. After a full recovery, he joined the battle over Santo Domingo, learning jungle warfare and winning the military's highest combat medal, even as Spain surrendered Santo Domingo itself.[9]

Weyler returned to Cuba in 1868 for the beginning of the insurrection that would come to be known as the Ten Years' War. Now immune to yellow fever, he headed up a band of volunteers composed of Havana's pro-Spanish loyalists. Earning respect for his fearlessness in the countryside, he also revealed a brutal streak, encouraging his troops to savagery, killing civilians along with enemy soldiers, and imposing his own rules of combat. Stories of beheadings, rapes, and executions he left in his wake were never forgotten. He left Cuba as a brigadier general.

Returning home to Spain, Weyler fought rebels within the country, defending the new republic. Sent to Catalonia, he decimated insurgents there and stunned the public with his slaughter of civilians. In the imperial era, it was one thing to kill noncombatants in a distant colony, but entirely another to kill Spanish subjects within Spanish borders. He was reprimanded for his conduct and plummeted further into disfavor due to political infighting.

But a general with Weyler's experience was a tempting weapon. Recalled to service, he sailed off to secure the empire's far-flung possessions, from the Canary Islands to the Philippines.[10] Three years later, he was brought back to Catalonia, where he put down anarchists and unionists and earned the gratitude of the wealthy in the region, restoring his reputation in and outside Spain.

Before heading to Cuba a third time for the defining command of his career, Weyler met with the minister of war in Madrid to lay out his assessment of the Cuban crisis. If the enemy was reluctant to meet in open battle, preferring to dissolve into the anonymity of rural communities, then perhaps, as Martínez Campos believed, the only way to win was to remove civilians from the countryside. The heart of Weyler's plan was to drive the process of destruction started by the insurgents to its logical end, isolating rebels by forcing all noncombatants into towns where Spanish forces could control them. If his predecessor did not feel he could in good conscience unleash *reconcentración* on civilians in Cuba, Weyler was prepared to embrace concentration camps to break the back of the rebellion.

The new governor-general would now have a chance to implement strategies he had previously only flirted with in the Philippines and Cuba. Perhaps recalling the censure he had faced over his extreme tactics in earlier decades, Weyler demanded—and received—the authority to impose whatever measures he wanted.[11]

4. Even before Weyler's return to Cuba, America had identified with the Cuban revolutionaries and their quest for independence. Yet when Weyler was selected as governor-general, rebels launched a

public relations offensive against him in the United States. "Weyler believes in a policy of terror," the insurgents' spokesman in New York said, predicting that Spain would return to a system of warfare from the dark ages. Accusing him of atrocities against women, machete murders, and midnight executions during his earlier stint in Cuba, they claimed that if Weyler returned to Cuba, "the very dead will rise out of their graves to fight him."[12]

When Weyler disembarked from the *Alfonso XIII* on February 10, 1896, to take command of the island, he was escorted to the palace by local officials. A boy stepped forward to offer wildflowers in welcome and kissed the general. After he was sworn in, Weyler went out on the balcony of the palace to reveal himself to the crowd waiting below. In his first address to the inhabitants of Cuba, he announced, "My honorable mission now is to end the war."[13]

The next day, Weyler made clear that he blamed civilians for the success of the insurgents. Women and children across the countryside had no neutrality, he argued, but were spying on Spanish forces and alerting the rebels. Observers quickly pinpointed the direction that the Spanish offensive would take under Weyler, expecting savagery: "If he cannot make successful war on the insurgents, he can make war on the noncombatants."[14] Responding to his critics, Weyler made a show of meeting with reporters on arrival. "Notwithstanding the reputation which has been built up for me...you can tell your people that whatever I may do the United States would do under similar circumstances."[15]

Days later, Weyler issued three proclamations. The first defined more than a dozen categories of people newly subject to trial by court-martial, among them those who "belittle the prestige of Spain," as well as anyone who praised the rebels. All categories of offenders could be subject to the death penalty after summary judgment. The second proclamation introduced *reconcentración* on a limited basis. All inhabitants of the countryside around the city of Sancti Spiritus and the eastern provinces of Puerto Principe and Santiago were required to present themselves with identification papers to military authorities in cities. Henceforth, they would not be allowed to live in and move through the countryside without express permission. The third proclamation made clear that anyone captured in battle could be subject to execution. The very steps that Martínez Campos had seen as the road to victory but had been unwilling to take were now being laid out as law.

Residents who were required to clear the countryside in the eastern regions had eight days to comply. Many military-age noncombatants in these sectors had already abandoned their civilian status to join the insurgency, and most Spanish loyalists had already fled into the cities for safety. Under the new orders, the rest of the population—predominantly women, children, and ill or elderly men—were expected to relocate into garrison towns. Eager volunteer companies began to impose informal *reconcentración* in other areas, but in rebel-held areas it remained impossible for the time being to enforce a civilian exodus across the board.

The response from US newspapers was sweeping and merciless. The *New York Times,* far from the most hysterical of the papers covering the Cuban drama, trumpeted the headline "Weyler's Draconic Laws."[16] The rebels piled on in press releases: "A butcher of men, women, and children he was before, and such he is now, and will remain to the end of his days."[17] Spurred on by a circulation war in New York, other newspapers showed less restraint. Nellie Bly, a reporter for the *New York World* who had gained fame with her trip around the world six years before, announced she would head up a regiment of women officers and lead troops into battle.[18] That summer, the satirical magazine *Puck* ran an illustration of a helpless maiden wearing a Cuban flag kneeling in supplication before a gaudy Uncle Sam, as a mustachioed Weyler crouched nearby in a black cape.[19]

By the time Weyler sailed past Morro Castle into the port of Havana, US involvement in the Cuban conflict was a many-headed creature. American businesses supplied matériel to the Spanish government in Havana, while ships ran dynamite, guns, rifles, and more than a million bullets to the revolutionaries in illicit *filibustero* expeditions. The US Secret Service wandered the docks of south Florida trying to intercept the gunrunning, as Pinkerton detectives monitored the Cuban junta in New York.[20] Meanwhile, former officials of the United States—which was in theory still neutral—promoted the Cuban cause and encouraged impetuous young men to run off and join the insurgency.

US senators debated American interests in Cuba from a business and a humanitarian perspective, with members describing conditions on the ground in terms of murder, reprisals, and "a sea of blood." Damning Weyler's policies as a plan of extermination, Massachusetts senator Henry Cabot Lodge compared Cuban suffering to that of the Armenians, who had just undergone slaughter by the Ottoman Empire. Lodge wondered whether America, like Europe, would fail to defend civilization in its hour of crisis. Politicians debated whether to recognize the rebels as legitimate belligerents in the conflict rather than terrorists undeserving of humanitarian treatment.[21]

Europe, used to managing colonies, watched American handwringing over human rights in Cuba with skepticism and amusement. US senators, with no apparent sense of hypocrisy, condemned Spain for "her extermination of the Indian."[22] Accusations against Weyler were read into the record, detailing how, during his previous campaign in Cuba, he had ordered his troops to butcher men by machete in front of their families, then wielded a whip to force widows and daughters to strip and dance; that he had branded women on the breast; that he had suffocated the wounded in hospitals and executed them in their homes; that he had promised exile to captives who were then shot along the road; and that his policy was to give over wives and daughters of slain insurgents to be raped by troops.[23] Some of these accusations later proved dubious or hard to link directly to Weyler. But the truth was unsettling enough. When asked directly about one Cuban battle from which he was said to have returned carrying the heads of his enemies, Weyler did not deny it.[24]

While politicians and journalists from the yellow press drew attention to the plight of the rebels, Cuban representatives in the United States managed by 1895 to generate additional support among a motley coalition of socialists, unions, business interests, and church communities.[25] The American public was not yet calling for war with Spain, but demands grew for greater support of the rebels, and rumors of war began to appear. The possibility echoed in the Spanish press, which had a very different view of the Cuban crisis, depicting the insurgents as bandits set on pillage.[26] Amid public outrage over Washington's wish to recognize the rebels as legitimate belligerents, Spain shuttered its universities to reestablish calm in the face of student riots.[27] The government at Madrid railed bitterly against the attacks on Weyler and Spain delivered by representatives of the US government.

5. Meanwhile in Cuba, on the brink of the deadly summer season, Weyler surrounded himself with officers capable of brutality. "One does not," he said to critics, "make war with bonbons."[28] A mid-May order gave farmers in the western provinces twenty days to deliver all of their grain to the army in nearby towns, with criminal prosecution as the penalty for refusal.[29] Four days later, officials called for the confiscation of all cattle and announced that two months of rations would be provided for civilians in the towns, except for the wives and children of insurgents, who would get nothing.[30]

US newspapers were filled with accounts of rebel victories. In reality, the insurgents' public relations offensive was far more effective than its military strategy, as they lost battle after battle, even those they should have been able to win. Scavenging or stealing food from locals, revolutionaries found the terror of stepped-up Spanish reprisals had struck fear into the hearts or minds of civilians, who became less willing to help them. Short on food and shorter on bullets, they made more frequent recourse to dynamite and machetes.

If the rebels had started with a plan to damage the economy, Weyler would go them one better and lay waste to the island. As they swept through the prairies and hills of the countryside, Spanish troops began destroying everything in their path that the rebels had not already burned. Having previously blocked the production and export of tobacco, Weyler moved in September to shut down sugar production, the heart of the Cuban economy.

With insurgents militarily weakened, Weyler then turned his attention back to *reconcentración*. On October 21 he expanded his earlier decree, announcing,

1. That all the inhabitants of the country districts, or those who reside outside the lines of fortifications of the towns shall, within a delay of eight days, enter the towns which are occupied by the troops. Any individual found outside the lines in the country at the expiration of this period, shall be considered a rebel, and shall be dealt with as such.

2. The transport of food from the towns, and the carrying of food from one place to another, by sea or by land, without the permission of the military authorities of the place of departure, is positively forbidden. Those who infringe upon this order will be tried and punished as aiders and abetters of the rebellion.

Civilians had to move, on penalty of death, behind the barbed wire of fortified towns. Those transporting food without permission were likewise subject to execution. The first concentration camps were formed out of a battlefield strategy and collective punishment, and it took less than two weeks to transform rural Cubans into a new class of prisoners.

The October edict went into effect for the westernmost province of Pinar del Río. In January, it was imposed for the adjoining provinces of Matanzas and Havana, as well as all of Santa Clara. As with the announcement in the eastern provinces the prior spring, hundreds of thousands of rural families were given almost no notice to move, and many learned of the order only after this window had closed.

As he broadened his policy, Weyler censored the press more aggressively, with troops seizing issues of papers that voiced opposition, and forbidding offending articles to be sent by telegraph.[31] Meanwhile, troops appeared at homes, giving a few hours' notice to the lucky. At bayonet point, adults, children, and the elderly alike began the journey to their assigned destinations.

They marched toward garrison towns that had become closed worlds. Entering exterior gates at an outer perimeter of barbed wire, they walked through a cascade of mazes and entanglements that made even friendly approach difficult—and a charging attack impossible. Inside the barbed wire sat trenches, with excavated dirt piled high toward the interior. Another layer of wire surrounded key defensive structures, with earthen redoubts buttressing churches and taverns that had been transformed into fortifications.

The businesses of the United States, still neutral, took money from both sides for the time being. A flow of munitions to the rebels continued, while Oliver Brothers, a Pittsburgh company, won a contract to supply two million additional pounds of barbed wire to the Spanish government just as *reconcentración* was implemented.[32] Outside the fences, soldiers burned crops and confiscated livestock, rooting out and killing those hiding or staying behind without permission.[33] One traveler through the desolate countryside described it almost entirely in terms of its absences: no banana trees, no sugarcane, no houses, no humans, not even dogs.[34]

Not counting the vast influx to Havana, some three hundred thousand civilians were driven into makeshift camps in Spanish-held cities on Cuba, an island the size of the state of Tennessee. And behind the entanglements, mazes, and interior rings of barbed wire lived the original residents of the city, who were not inclined to welcome the peasant refugees. In theory, local authorities were to build accommodations for newcomers—the *reconcentrados*—and set aside parcels of nearby land for cultivation zones where they could grow their own food. In reality, the land was often unusable, and only a small minority of *reconcentrados* got access even to these substandard parcels.[35] No tools, seeds, or oxen were provided, and new arrivals were expected to produce enough food to become self-sustaining within weeks.

Refugee quarters lay in designated areas on the outskirts of towns. Some camps offered shoddy, overcrowded barracks or requisitioned buildings, but the housing that was supposed to have been built was more often nonexistent. Families crafted lean-tos from palm leaves, scouted out abandoned shelters, or slept on the ground.

They had carried with them what they could, and what they could not carry was burned or butchered by the soldiers that swept behind them. Even the items they had managed to keep might not remain theirs for long. Townspeople, resentful over having to provide space for the newcomers—and suspicious about their sympathies—sometimes confiscated possessions on arrival as payment for the largesse of shelter. As summer came on, a *Harper's* dispatch described the *reconcentrados* as "penned up in starvation stations," sleeping in "narrow, filthy lanes," and exposed to mosquitoes, not yet recognized as carriers of malaria in Cuba's fetid summers.[36]

The unwilling pilgrims herded into camps remained at liberty inside the barbed-wire perimeters of the cities that held them, but rarely found a way to earn a living. They had few skills of use in the towns, and residents suspected them as carriers of disease, with the wealthy setting up "disinfectant stations" to decontaminate them.[37] Sentries in the watchtowers of the blockhouses were authorized to shoot not only unwanted intruders but also anyone leaving without permission.

Rumors proliferated of daily executions of *reconcentrados* who tried to crawl beyond the fences to find food, but at least some of the lurid tales of massive Spanish violence inside the garrison towns appear to have been exaggerations. In truth, once detainees had been corralled into miniature citadels of suffering, bullets did not top the list of threats to them. Before long, things Weyler had said or done decades ago or how he conducted himself on the battlefield in the present moment mattered less and less. Events had been set in motion with consequences that would rival the bloodshed of all the battles of the war combined.

6. Standing on a hill overlooking the city of Matanzas that May, one journalist saw "three great fires burning to the right and to the left of me, and before me. Everything was on fire except the sea, which cannot be made to burn, even by royal decree." The military governor, he wrote, had reserved a cultivation zone for the *reconcentrados* but decided to burn it instead. The western provinces were ash heaps. Shocked by the lack of efforts by the *reconcentrados* to file grievances or organize for revolt, he observed that with no concerted uprising, "each family starves alone."[38]

What began with overcrowding and hunger turned to disease. As Spanish and American journalists visited Cuban cities, they reported townsfolk attempting to go about their daily business during wartime, while *reconcentrado* adults and children wasted away in their huts and in the streets. Advances in photo reproduction allowed newspapers to run startlingly clear black-and-white images for the first time.[39] Papers not yet equipped with the new technology ran illustrations of dying women and skeletal children on their front pages.

Richard Harding Davis, an American journalist admired for his reporting on the execution of a Cuban insurgent by firing squad, made his way to concentration camps in three cities. Along with widespread smallpox and yellow fever, he found claustrophobic rows of huts built in unwalkable slums that were ankle-deep in filth. Elsewhere, hundreds of *reconcentrados* huddled inside warehouses that straddled pools of sewage, with fungus growing up their walls. Dead bodies lay by the roadside. He saw babies "whose bones showed through as plainly as the rings under a glove," covered in sores that made their mothers' touch excruciating.[40]

Weyler, confident of quick victory, had initially relaxed censorship, only to find himself drowning in negative publicity. The *New York Journal* declared him "the prince of all cruel generals this century has seen," while the *New York World* dubbed Weyler "the most sinister figure of the nineteenth century."[41] The yellow press, always seeking maximum drama, delighted when Weyler deigned to respond, using even his complaints to sell more copies under headlines such as "Baffled Weyler Rages at The Journal."[42]

Other stories took the facts of the unfolding tragedy and added to them with hallucinatory fever: "Blood on the roadsides, blood in the fields, blood on the doorsteps, blood, blood, blood! The old, the young, the weak, the crippled, all are butchered without mercy."[43] Realizing that he was losing the media war, Weyler protested bitterly. "The Cubans are fighting us openly, the Americans are fighting us secretly.... The American newspapers are responsible. They poison everything with falsehood."[44]

Spanish ambassador to America Enrique Dupuy de Lôme countered the charges made by rebel newspapers and yellow journalists from the United States, dismissing them as rumors. Spain, he noted, was not doing anything that other countries at war had not already done, and the descriptions of Weyler's cruelty were either misleading or entirely false.[45] But Dupuy de Lôme could hardly keep ahead of the yellow press, and the fact that some of the most horrific descriptions turned out to be true made his job impossible.

A report by the US Senate's Committee on Foreign Relations released that spring asserted that hundreds of American citizens had been swept up in Weyler's *reconcentración* strategies and were stuck in Cuba, known to be "starving and wretchedly clothed."[46] Senator John Sherman of Ohio addressed a complaint to the Spanish prime minster, savaging Weyler's conduct. It was no doubt with delight that the prime minister made an exhaustive rebuttal of the charges. Along with his protest, he forwarded a letter from the Duke of Tetuán demonstrating detailed knowledge of Senator Sherman's brother, General William Tecumseh Sherman. The duke pointed out that General Sherman would surely have understood and appreciated these tactics, as they were the very ones used during the Civil War to put down the treason of the Confederacy.[47]

The Spanish loyalist press likewise depicted America's former affection for burning and pillage and harassment of noncombatants in Dixie, praising what it saw as Washington's very reasonable attempts to preserve the nation during rebellion.[48]

Clever rebuttals from Spain were no match for dead innocents. Journalists who had begun their coverage in Cuba with the stirring military drama of the rebels began writing about the women, children, and elderly dying in the streets of Havana. Weyler was making progress toward winning the war on a day-to-day basis, but his tactics provoked unease in Madrid and a rising inclination in America to intervene.

That August, Spanish prime minister Antonio Cánovas del Castillo was assassinated at a spa by an Italian anarchist. With the death of the conservative Cánovas and the formation of a more liberal government, it was understood that Weyler's command was in jeopardy.

Two days before the incoming government took power, rumors circulated in London and Madrid that Weyler had been recalled.[49] Caught short by the accounts, Weyler asked the Spanish government to confirm its confidence in him or relieve him of his position.

Despite a ban on public demonstrations in Cuba, loyalist citizens decorated the main thoroughfares to show support for Weyler. The stock exchange was shuttered for the day. Cigar shops closed. A crowd formed in the heart of Havana, the most loyal of Cuban cities. Assembling at Central Park, various groups marched over a half mile to the governor's residence, parading through the streets for more than two hours. According to the official account, twenty thousand people shoehorned themselves into the Plaza de Armas before the long façade of the governor's palace to cheer on Weyler's tactics. Stepping once more onto the balcony high above the throng, he received their good wishes.

Back inside the palace, Weyler met with representatives of groups that hoped he would keep his post. His words, however, were aimed not at his supporters but his critics. Those who opposed his tactics, he claimed, had no basis for condemnation. He had announced from the beginning his intention to avoid treaties and concessions and to "finish war with war." Weyler further pointed out that during General Sherman's March to the Sea and to victory during the Civil War, the American general had destroyed everything in his path.[50]

The wealthy citizens of Havana remained attached to Weyler, but Madrid was more fickle with its affection. Within days, an opponent of *reconcentración* was assigned to take over Spain's colonial affairs, making Weyler's fall official. Three weeks after his request for a vote of confidence, and a year and a half after his arrival in Cuba, the new liberal government recalled Weyler to Spain.

His replacement, Captain General Ramón Blanco, arrived weeks later aboard the same cruiser that had delivered Weyler the year before. Weyler met him aboard ship, then sailed for Spain the same day. He had been given a free hand to impose his will on Cuba for a time, but, as predicted in the pages of newspapers and dispatches and diplomatic cables, the dead had risen to fight Weyler, and had won.

7. Within days of his arrival, Blanco promised the expansion of agricultural zones, the provision of food, and the resumption of plantation work. *Reconcentrados* were encouraged to return to the fields. Madrid authorized the allocation of $100,000 to address immediate suffering, but the funding was minuscule in the face of the humanitarian crisis at hand.[51]

Relief efforts on paper often did not translate to the real world in the middle of a war. Pardons could be requested, and some detainees were allowed to return to cultivating crops, but only if they had identity papers with them and worked on a guarded plantation, which they could not leave. Such half measures would not reverse the fortunes of hundreds of thousands displaced by earlier orders or arrest the suffering that had been set in motion.

Reconcentrados died in swarms. A representative of the US Department of Justice spent two weeks traveling the island, describing burned fields, train platforms clogged with emaciated, begging skeletons, a dozen families squatting in a derelict sugar warehouse, omnipresent beriberi and malaria, and few signs of relief. "Many are too far gone," he noted, "to be saved by the best care and treatment."[52] The situation was not helped by insurgents, who sometimes shot at *reconcentrados* leaving garrison towns and continued to torch any attempt at cultivation.

Spain had no desire for war with America, but had long feared the desire among some American politicians to acquire Cuba through purchase or battle. Faced with a rising death toll, Madrid agreed to suspend duties on all incoming goods arriving as relief, and American railroads offered to carry supplies without cost to the coast.[53] Nationwide, US citizens spent week after week gathering millions of pounds of clothing, quinine, crackers, cornmeal, potatoes, condensed milk, rice, beans, peas, and lard to send to the starving. Spain also responded to the call of the American Red Cross, headed up by iconic battlefield nurse Clara Barton. Military authorities permitted the formation of a Central Cuban Relief Committee to import and distribute aid from the United States. Barton sailed for Cuba in February to open an asylum for *reconcentrados* in Havana.[54]

Wider access to the starving through relief programs and journalists' reportage revealed more graphic details of peasant suffering. "Lying all about were what at first glance looked like heaps of rags; they were Reconcentrados who were able to crawl out into the sun," Fannie Ward reported from the Cuban capital in March. "I have seen misery in many lands, but never anything like this."[55] The situation was by then so dire that even those who lived long enough for help to arrive sometimes did not survive the assistance they received. Great care had to be taken in providing food to the *recon-*

centrados, as they had gone so long on so little that a simple meal could kill them.

Amid the diplomatic clashes and still-unfolding consequences of *reconcentración,* Weyler continued as the avatar of the war long after his departure. For Americans, he remained a quintessential villain—the architect of the machinery of death that carried on in his absence. For Spanish loyalists he remained a hero, a general who could have defeated the rebels if not for the querulous government that had recalled him.

After riots by officers sympathetic to Weyler destroyed the printing press of the newspaper *El Reconcentrado* in Cuba, the United States realized that its own citizens and consuls on the island might be in danger. The administration decided to send the USS *Maine* to Cuba as insurance in the event of anti-American violence.

A US warship could hardly dock in Havana at that moment without complications, but to the surprise of many, the city did not riot. In an attempt to defuse tensions, the captain of the *Maine* offered multiple olive branches to Spanish officials. Townspeople came aboard on guided tours. Mutual toasts to the health of both nations—and Cuba—were drunk. And on the evening of February 12, the captain hosted the secretary general of Cuba and other Spanish notables aboard the ship, voicing his approval that "friendly relations had existed, now exist, and will exist" between the two nations.[56]

8. Three days later, the *Maine* exploded in Havana harbor, sinking the ship and killing 260 men. Americans strongly suspected a Spanish mine had detonated the thousands of pounds of powder charges stored aboard for the ship's guns, but no clear-cut evidence was found. President William McKinley appointed a naval board of inquiry to investigate the cause of the blast.

On the day of the funeral for the sailors who had been lost, more than fifty thousand people lined the parade route in Havana, with a delegation of *reconcentrados* requesting permission of US consul-general Fitzhugh Lee to carry the coffins of the dead American soldiers to their graves. They were refused, and the nineteen bodies buried that day made their way from the governor's palace to Cristóbal Colón Cemetery in horse-drawn carriages draped in American flags and flanked by surviving sailors. More than four hundred *reconcentrados* walked behind the dead in the procession.[57]

While the inquest was still under way, the cry "Remember the *Maine*, to hell with Spain!" became the unofficial American call to war. The *New York Journal* ran a melodramatic piece under the headline "The War Ship *Maine* Was Split in Two by an Enemy's Secret Infernal Machine." The *New York World* remained open to more possibilities, opting for "Maine Explosion Caused by Bomb or Torpedo?"

The *Maine* disaster produced unlimited public outrage; but it was the public's long exposure to Cuban concentration camps that supplied the moral authority to threaten Spain. President McKinley asked for full reports from each consular post in Cuba. The United States condemned conditions in the camps, with Assistant Secretary of the Navy Theodore Roosevelt declaring, "The blood of the Cubans, the blood of women and children who have perished by the hundred thousand in hideous misery, lies at our door."[58] Weyler, safely in Spain but still smarting from his rough treatment by American journalists, was quoted as saying that the *Maine* blew up as a result of the "indolence" of its crew.[59]

As Spain fumbled its efforts to address the results of *reconcentración*, the United States increased its demands. The consular reports came back, and if there had been little doubt what they would find, the stories were nonetheless staggering indictments of the Spanish government and its conduct of the war, centered almost entirely on the *reconcentrados*. General Máximo Gómez, still leader of the insurgency, managed to get a letter delivered to McKinley declaring Spain's monstrosity in conceiving "the concentration scheme, the most horrible of all means to martyrize and then to annihilate an entire people."[60]

A minority of US politicians had long been anxious to acquire Cuba for military reasons. The business community likewise saw the advantages of an American-dominated island. With the policy of *reconcentración* providing more than enough moral legitimacy for intervention, few sectors were still calling for peace. Leaders in Congress advocated for action on humanitarian grounds, without waiting for the results of the *Maine* inquiry.[61] From his perch in the navy, Roosevelt enthusiastically prepared the American fleet for battle.

The investigators' report appeared on March 28, alleging that the *Maine*'s destruction was due to "the explosion of a submarine mine which caused a partial explosion of two or more of the forward magazines." On April 11, two months after the sinking of the *Maine*, McKinley highlighted the horrors of concentration camps in a statement to Congress calling for war.

> The unfortunates, being for the most part women and children with aged and helpless men, enfeebled by disease and hunger, could not have tilled the soil without tools, seed, or shelter for their own support or for the supply of the citizens. Reconcentration, adopted avowedly as a war measure in order to cut off the resources of the insurgents, worked its predestined result. As I said in my message of last December, it was not civilized warfare. It was extermination. The only peace it could beget was that of the wilderness and the grave.[62]

And in truth, the numbers of the dead did continue to swell, passing tens of thousands, a hundred thousand, with some estimates at the time reporting half a million civilian lives lost in the camps. Hasty offers by Spain to allocate limited relief funds for *reconcentrados*, to undo *reconcentración* completely, and to allow an autonomous parliament in Cuba to negotiate with the rebels made little difference. Nothing stemmed the tide. On April 25, 1899, the United States declared war on Spain.

US citizens responded with wild enthusiasm. Volunteers clogged train platforms across America, swarming to sign up. A special center for enlistees, itself dubbed a "concentration camp," was set up in Falls Church, Virginia, to process recruits and ship them off to boot camps.[63] Ancient officers from both sides of the Civil War were given commands. Suddenly, the country found itself misty-eyed over sending former enemies off to fight together, to save the starving *reconcentrados* and expel Spain from Cuba.

On June 10, the US Marines landed at Fisherman's Point, on the windward side of the entrance to Guantánamo Bay, taking a nearby hill. Spanish soldiers, themselves half starved from the island's general desolation, waited until the Marines had unpacked their food before launching an assault, in the hope that they might raid the stores.[64] When the Spanish finally did attack, Marines were pinned down under fire for a brutal week of fighting but held their position, winning the battle and setting up camp at the place they named McCalla Hill.

9. A legend born in the run-up to war with Spain held that at the age of twenty-five, Captain General Valeriano Weyler had been a military attaché in Washington, DC, meeting General Sherman himself and riding into battle with General Sheridan during the torching of Virginia's Shenandoah Valley in 1864. The story, read into the *Congressional Record* in 1898, persisted into the twentieth century, then into the twenty-first.[65] And no wonder: there is something resonant about imagining the unformed Weyler tutored by the US commanders laying waste to the South, patrolling the valley, and learning to wage total war in preparation for Cuban *reconcentración*.

The legend, however, appears to be only a legend. No record exists of Weyler visiting America during this period. But firsthand instruction on total war was hardly necessary. Cuban rebels, too, had been willing to burn homes and force civilians to flee as battlefield strategy. It was the charismatic rebel Lieutenant General Antonio Maceo whose scorched-earth trail first elicited public comparisons to Sherman's March to the Sea.[66] By the time Weyler imposed *reconcentración,* both sides in Cuba had absorbed the lessons of the US Civil War.

Yet over the course of his command in Cuba, Weyler had some 300,000 regular or irregular troops who would carry it out, in contrast to one-tenth that number fielded by the rebels.[67] And Spain did not recall him until the government collapsed—long after the effects of the policy were obvious. Both sides had adopted Sherman's tactics, but only one had the weight of empire behind it to institutionalize starvation and disease for the people.

During a year and a half of *reconcentración,* well over 100,000 civilians died, though with the war that raged simultaneously and incomplete data, no one knows exactly where to peg the figure between that number and the half million that would routinely be cited for the next hundred years. Current estimates hover around 150,000 deaths—approximately 10 percent of the prewar population.[68] The figure is more than enough to say, as historian John Lawrence Tone framed it, that by the time he was recalled, "Weyler had almost destroyed the Cuban independence movement, along with a great part of the Cuban population."[69]

Despite the more indelible memory of the *Maine*'s explosion over time, George Kennan believed that "it was Weyler's reconcentration that finally filled full the cup of Spanish iniquity, and it was the suffering of the reconcentrados, more, perhaps, than any other one thing that brought about the intervention of the United States."[70]

In 1899, a year after the United States went to war with Spain, representatives of developed nations prepared to meet at The Hague in the Netherlands for the first convention on international laws of war and war crimes. There was, perhaps, a moment when the world's impression of concentration camps was negative enough that they might have been outlawed at their birth. But attendees at The Hague refused to take up the issue, and within months, other nations began building their own camps.

10. Events in Cuba had sparked the war with Spain, but the war stretched far beyond the tiny island. Weeks before battle began at Fisherman's Point, American warships sailed halfway around the world to attack Spanish forces in the Philippines. Spain's Pacific fleet offered only brief resistance, surrendering to Admiral George Dewey after seven hours of battle.

Four months of combat in Cuba were followed by four months of peace negotiations and a payment to Spain of $20 million. With the signing of the Treaty of Paris, the United States inherited Cuba, Guam, Puerto Rico, and the Philippines. In less than a year, the United States had gone from a former colony to a global empire.

Filipino rebels, who had been fighting for independence themselves, initially welcomed American forces and weapons, delighted with the general enthusiasm for Cuban independence and a newfound ally against Spain. But American support for independence across the board would prove less dependable. As war raged in Cuba, the United States wavered for weeks over its long-term strategy in the Philippines beyond the initial goal of defeating Spain. The general sent to command the Pacific expedition could not get his superiors to tell him whether he was to assume authority over Manila harbor, take possession of the city itself, or to hold all Spanish-controlled areas of the islands.[71]

Victory over Spain by summer's end clarified little and immediately led to tensions with rebel forces, which wanted outright independence or at least autonomy, citing prewar verbal assurances. Back in Spain, General Weyler, soon to be appointed minister of war, noted with accuracy that America hadn't wanted the Philippines until it realized it could have them. A joke at the time suggested that President McKinley didn't even know where they were. The United States, so focused on Cuba, seemed not to know what to do with faraway Pacific possessions that did not fit into its self-image as a defender of the Western Hemisphere and a champion of freedom-loving revolutionaries.

If McKinley's geographical shortcomings were a joke, his distress over the islands was not. Narrating his anguish to a visiting committee of Methodist missionaries, McKinley described how he initially had no interest in the islands at all, but when they fell into American hands, he had paced the floor of the White House and spent more than one night kneeling in prayer over the matter.[72] He agonized over four options: giving the Philippines back to Spain, leaving them vulnerable to another foreign power, giving them independence, or turning them into a colony. The idea of independence was dismissed almost out of hand, due to the belief that the natives were too backward to govern themselves. In the end, McKinley opted to establish an American colony, civilize the natives, and put them on the path to "benevolent assimilation." He seemed not to expect resistance, as if rebels would automatically sense that occupation by America would be distinct from and preferable to rule by Spain. American soldiers who had signed on as volunteers in order to liberate Cuba ended up thousands of miles away, furious to discover that the defeat of Spain did not mean they could return home.[73]

As the future of America in the Philippines hung fire, troops kept themselves busy by drinking, whoring, and fighting. When negotiations with Philippine forces broke down in January 1899, US forces found that they had not only won Spain's colony, they had inherited a colonial rebellion.

The army's mission was fraught from the beginning. The first general who ruled as a military governor refused the offer to negotiate peace terms, but thought he could win the rebels' support through humanitarian aid and goodwill. The second began punishing those who resisted benevolent assimilation. By the time Major

General Adna Chaffee arrived, the regular war had become a guerrilla conflict. The War Department agreed that with insurgents carrying out ambushes and assassinations, sterner measures were required.

Weyler had praised US conduct during the American Civil War from afar, but Chaffee had lived it firsthand. Serving as a cavalry officer at the age of twenty-two, he rode with Sheridan through the Shenandoah Valley, where troops were told to lay waste to homes, crops, property—everything the eye could see—so that even a crow flying through would have to bring provisions to survive.

Chaffee had similar ideas for how to win his war. By the third year of the conflict, the United States did not altogether forget the promise of benign assimilation, building schools and hospitals, but for every carrot there was a very sharp stick. *Insurrectos* fighting one day, then returning to civilian life the next—much as Cuban rebels had against the Spanish—made it all but impossible to round up combatants or permanently quash the rebellion. The belief that loyalty oaths demanded of and received from locals counted for anything was long gone.

Perhaps the shift to guerrilla warfare alone doomed civilians to become enmeshed in both sides' war strategy. But any half measures were obliterated on September 28, 1901, after a Filipino police chief killed a sentry, triggering an orchestrated massacre of American troops at Balangiga. Guns smuggled past checkpoints in children's coffins were used to kill forty-eight US soldiers in the most lethal incident of the war. The disaster was shocking on many levels—supposed allies had been part of the elaborate plot, and the bodies of the dead were mutilated horribly.

Mass retribution, including the execution of ten unarmed Filipinos and the burning of a town the next day, did not quiet the nerves that had been rattled, including those of Governor General Chaffee, who became convinced that even harsher measures were required to subdue the remaining insurgents. And so in the autumn of 1901,

Chaffee unleashed two generals who would alter the course of the conflict and make history.

11. Brigadier General Jacob H. Smith, like Chaffee, had served in the US Civil War. Shot in the hip at Shiloh in 1862, he had taken a bullet in the chest in Cuba in 1898, and had managed to be an obstacle to his own success and the peace of mind of his fellow citizens for the thirty-six years between. Smith had speculated with money owed as signing bonuses to African American army recruits. He was cited for insubordination, defaulted on creditors, reneged on gambling debts, was court-martialed and nearly cashiered. A short man with broad hips and narrow shoulders, he was fierce in battle and not entirely safe outside it.

Assigned to command in Catbalogan, on the western coast of the island of Samar early in October, Smith marched into the campaign with a will. Newspapers reported his vow to turn the place into a wasteland "where not even a bird could live."[74] Rebels in Samar operated easily from the interior of the roadless jungles, with American troops based in coastal towns like Balangiga, the site of the massacre.

Smith aimed to exact revenge. On arrival, he announced his own policy of reconcentration, ordering civilians into towns, making clear (as Weyler had) that anyone found outside designated camps would not have the luxury of interrogation but would be shot on sight. Those suspected of anti-American activities—including Spanish and "half-breed" locals—were put directly into stockades.[75] Just days into the new policy, a pro-Washington newspaper in Manila was already trumpeting Smith's success: "His policy of reconcentration is said to be the most effective thing of its kind ever seen in these islands under any flag."[76]

That December, Smith explained to the soldiers under his command that even civilized war could not be waged on a humanitarian basis. Later, subordinates would testify that he encouraged savagery, telling one officer "to kill and burn; the more you kill and burn the more it will please me." He instructed the 6th Separate Brigade to turn the island into a "howling wilderness" and to shoot Filipino boys down to the age of ten.[77] The region became an inferno.

While reconcentration was new to the islands, Smith also made use of techniques that had been around longer, adopting tactics employed by the Spanish and the insurgents before them. Possessing little familiarity with the terrain, even less knowledge of Philippine languages, and at times finding translators in short supply, soldiers employed other means to get information. Using civilians as hostages, executing suspects, and burning homes and crops were all considered fair game under the right circumstances.

Torture, that handmaiden to detention, took on many forms in the Philippines. The "rope cure" involved partial lynching to elicit confessions or extract intelligence. Soldiers or allies also made use of the water cure. Salty or dirty water was forced into a prostrate prisoner's mouth or nose until his stomach could hold no more, at which point he vomited—or was punched or kicked until he vomited—and the process was repeated. Smith later summed up his operating policy toward the native population, explaining that Filipinos "must be brought into subjugation, and kept so until they learn that the purpose is to give them freedom."[78]

While Smith's forces introduced concentration camps to Samar, Brigadier General J. Franklin Bell carried out his own plan for subduing Batangas Province on the island of Luzon. Like Smith, Bell had fought in the Indian Wars and the US Civil War. He, too, was known for bravery, having charged seven Philippine insurgents on the battlefield and captured three of them single-handed. (In the more colorful accounts given by his subordinates, he had managed to accomplish this on horseback while naked.)[79]

Unlike Smith, Bell was not an amoral schemer or loose cannon. A square-shouldered man with a bull neck and pale hair parted down the middle, he was beloved by his men and admired by War Department brass and politicians alike.

On arrival in Batangas, the capital of the province, Bell met with his officers in a group to lay out his vision. He provided chairs for his guests' comfort during his lengthy monologue—and perhaps realizing that history would be mindful of his campaign, asked two stenographers to record it. Where Smith refused to temper his rhetoric, Bell laid out his plans in language carefully bounded by approved US military tactics. He expressed complete support for a thorough-going policy of benevolence, he assured his officers, but he feared that the native population had taken it for weakness. Dealing with an enemy that was "cunning, unscrupulous, and conscienceless" required drastic, disagreeable measures. Henceforth, he announced, the policy in Batangas would rely on General Order 100, the Lieber Code set forth during the US Civil War, permitting retaliation and executions—though he did not want summary executions undertaken without his approval.[80]

If Bell was playing both sides of the fence, demanding that officers implement more drastic tactics while paying lip service to restraint, he understood perfectly the risks of not qualifying his orders. The year before, when a colonel filed reports that could be construed as endorsing torture and arson, Bell had written a letter urging him to be more cautious. Bell explained that he was sympathetic to the need to torch a suspect's home or to string him up by the neck to get him to talk, but should these kinds of tactics become a matter of public knowledge, he would not be able to protect any officer involved.[81]

Talk was one thing, but the slate of tactics that Bell chose to address the intractable insurgency did not differ much from Smith's. A week after his meeting with officers, he issued Telegraphic Order No. 2, instructing his officers to establish reconcentration on the outskirts of towns, with garrisons built to support them. Framing them as "zones of protection," Bell explained the sectors as havens for "peaceably inclined" citizens, places to keep them from being preyed on by insurgents. His next order came the following day, laying out the goal of making the populace miserable enough that they

would yearn for peace. "It is an inevitable and deplorable conse-
quence of war," he wrote, "that the innocent must generally suffer
with the guilty."[82]

Bell would continue to argue that by adopting reconcentration—
which he later insisted did not exacerbate hunger among civilians or
increase mortality in the region—US forces were protecting pacific
civilians from insurgents. But it is clear from his orders that, like
Weyler, he believed that all civilians should be treated as prisoners
in the absence of actions that publicly, positively bound them to US
interests.

There was no room for neutrality. In Batangas, as in Cuba, concentration camps were a battlefield strategy to deny food and shelter
to insurgents, as well as a collective punishment to make civilians
suffer along with enemy forces. Herding hundreds of thousands of
natives into reconcentration zones similar to the Cuban model, Bell
was not ignorant of the risks. Shoehorning people short on food and
sanitation into close proximity in a jungle climate held dangers for
civilians and soldiers alike. He brought in smallpox vaccination
teams to sweep through the camps, pricking and inoculating almost
three hundred thousand *reconcentrados*—sometimes by force—in
less than two months.[83]

What is presented in official reports as orderly application of
measured tactics looked very different on the ground. In a private
letter written to a sitting senator, a US Army officer described a
soldier's-eye view of reconcentration, Philippines style:

> Eight miles up a slimy, winding bayou of a river until at 4
> a.m. we struck a piece of spongy ground about twenty feet
> above the sea-level. Now you have us located. It rains
> continually in a way that would have made Noah marvel.
> And trails, if you can find one, make the "Slough of Despond"
> seem like an asphalt pavement. Now this little spot of black
> sogginess is a reconcentrado pen, with a dead-line outside,
> beyond which everything living is shot.

This corpse-carcass stench wafted in and combined with some lovely municipal odors besides makes it slightly unpleasant here.

Upon arrival I found thirty cases of small-pox and average fresh ones of five a day, which practically have to be turned out to die. At nightfall clouds of huge vampire bats softly swirl out on their orgies over the dead.

Mosquitoes work in relays, and keep up their pestering day and night. There is a pleasing uncertainty as to your being boloed before morning or being cut down in the long grass or sniped at. It seems way out of the world without a sight of the sea, — in fact, more like some suburb of hell.[84]

12. In the beginning, the American ideal in the Philippines was "benevolent assimilation," and real overtures were made to build schools, clinics, and roads. The process started with the kind of assumed nobility that led Rudyard Kipling in the first month of hostilities to name the effort of civilizing Filipino natives "the white man's burden," but it descended into bloody savagery in contested areas during the war's final stages.

The irony of supporting a Cuban people dreaming of freedom then suppressing another group of revolutionaries on other islands halfway around the world was not lost on American citizens. Though press stories going out by wire were censored, mail was not, and many accounts made their way back home. Some soldiers wrote letters to their families reporting frankly on torture and shooting, often approvingly. Others, disgusted by apparent atrocities, sent accounts of incidents to newspapers or legislators in the hopes of sparking change. The American public, still euphoric from its morally uplifting, rapid defenestration of the Spanish Empire, was horrified to find itself mired in a ghastly swamp of a war that could not be romanticized, applying the same tactics that Weyler had adopted in Cuba.

The *Buffalo Courier* wrote, "The American people are surely not ready to accept responsibility for concentration camp horrors."[85] The *Baltimore American* observed, "We have actually come to do the thing we went to war to banish."[86] Weyler remained a popular subject of the moral drama, with the *Detroit Free Press* declaring that "Weylerism is Weylerism, whether it manifests itself in Cuba or the Philippines."[87] Days later, the *Columbus Evening Press* chimed in: "Our honor will be clouded with shame if we allow our colonial armies to be officered by a man who adopts Butcher Weyler's barbarous policy of reconcentration."[88] Political cartoonists had a field day with the many levels of hypocrisy involved, including a gleeful caricature of President Teddy Roosevelt carrying a bucket of water labeled "civilization" and preparing to force it down the gullet of a resisting Filipino prisoner's throat.

So many disturbing reports were made that they could not be ignored, even by those firmly in support of the war. Reports of concentration camps drew the ire of some members of Congress, which had not been kept informed, and the Senate Committee on the Philippines launched an investigation in January 1902. The day before testifying, then governor general of the Philippines (and future US president) William Howard Taft assured the public with hairsplitting precision that as far as he knew, "there has never been any thought of establishing 'concentration camps' in the ordinary acceptation of the term."[89]

As the investigation unfolded between January and June, a litany of atrocities, barbaric orders, and reconcentration policies came to light. Politicians pleased with American expansion abroad collided with anti-imperialists who never wanted the United States to take on Spain's colonies to begin with. Some southern legislators were sympathetic to the insurgents in both Cuba and the Philippines, recognizing and disliking the kind of tactics employed by Sherman against the Confederacy even when applied far away. Others were white supremacists who disapproved heartily of the idea of racial mixing and felt it best for the United States to leave the Philippines alone in order to avoid close association with "lesser" races.

Bizarre intersections of policy and history at one point led a northern senator to argue the merits of torturing Filipinos to a southern Senator, who noted that white southerners were not allowed to lynch but the practice was apparently condoned overseas. Senator John Coit Spooner of Wisconsin observed that the US Supreme Court had weighed in on the question, determining that legal protections available to Americans did not apply in the Philippines.[90]

Beyond the politics of imperialism or isolation, the American public was shocked by the conduct of the war. Taft's comments acknowledging the brutality of US methods came to light. It was apparent that Secretary of War Elihu Root had tacitly endorsed this harsher approach. During a filibuster over the issue, Senator George Turner of Washington called General Jacob H. Smith a "monster in human form."[91]

Along with Senate debates, there were trials. During the court-martial of the US Army's Major Edwin F. Glenn over the use of the water cure, his defense claimed that the technique was commonly adopted by the Spanish, by insurgents, and even by policemen in American cities. It did not, his lawyer argued, actually cause pain, just discomfort.[92] Explaining his conduct, Glenn narrated the horrors of the massacre of American troops at Balangiga in detail, until he was interrupted by the judge advocate, who clarified that *he* was on trial in the courtroom, not the insurgents. Glenn suggested that the two could not be separated. "War is a series of retaliations, and the more it is prolonged, the more outrageous some of the acts are, and the retaliation becomes more and more severe. It is nothing but a series of retaliations; that is all that war is."[93]

Glenn had a point, though perhaps not the one he believed he was making. Tempting as it may be to focus on the most egregious examples of misconduct, they could not have occurred so widely without the acquiescence of generals leading the counterinsurgency efforts. The embrace of more brutal tactics after the failure to bring a quick end to the resistance ensured that soldiers would sometimes take matters into their own hands.

A parallel phenomenon had happened at the highest ranks. The first generals who implemented concentration camps had not invented them wholesale. Butcher Weyler had inherited the idea from his predecessor and taken it up with the approval of the Spanish government. The implementation of reconcentration in the Philippines by Generals Bell and Smith was known to their superiors, who permitted the strategy to continue. Though governments wanted to dissociate themselves from the harshest tactics of their generals, the generals had been tacitly encouraged by civilian officials.

In the end, Glenn was handed a one-month suspension and a $50 fine for cruelty in administering the water cure. General Smith, tried for giving orders about making a howling wilderness of Samar and for ordering executions of boys down to the age of ten, was convicted of conduct unbecoming an officer but never reprimanded for establishing concentration camps. He did not receive any prison time.

Even his infamy was short-lived. After his court-martial, Brigadier General Jacob Smith was forcibly retired by President Roosevelt upon arrival in the United States. He headed home to a hero's welcome in Ohio, where he had a "complete nervous collapse."[94]

The other architect of American reconcentration in the Philippines, the one whose master plan was more organized, who was beloved by his men, and who did not have Smith's checkered past, fared better. Bell was spattered by the mud of the Senate investigation that ran during the first half of 1902, but his clearer lines of command and more subtle directions to his subordinates insulated him from the denunciations earned by Smith's freewheeling incitement to violence. Bell's commanding officers also came forward to say that they endorsed his policy of reconcentration, that it followed the code of conduct established in the Civil War, and that it was humanely applied as a last measure against "semi-civilized" brigands.[95] Leaving the most brutal acts to his subordinates, and maintaining a structured framework in which to couch the ferocious actions of his troops, Bell never faced official rebuke.

He rose, instead, to become chief of staff of the US Army. By the time the Senate was considering his nomination in 1906, politicians who had opposed concentration camps as savage and publicly denounced Bell's tactics felt less attachment to principle. "I abominate the things he did, but I have always been compelled to admire the way he did them," said one senator who had previously denounced Bell. "It put an end to insurrection, of course. It would put an end to anything."[96]

13. Estimating concentration camp deaths is complicated, especially during wartime. As they had in Cuba, hunger and disease ravaged Filipino civilians while the army focused on eliminating insurgents and suspects. Along with smallpox, *reconcentrados* had to face beriberi, malaria, dysentery, and typhus. The war in the Philippines as a whole generated estimates of civilian deaths well into six figures, with reconcentration directly responsible for somewhere above eleven thousand fatalities during the four-month existence of the camps.

Everyone indicted or publicly investigated benefitted tremendously from the surrender of most Philippine insurgents and the unofficial conclusion of war in April. Commander of the Army Nelson Miles was sent to the Philippines to investigate and reported disturbing incidents of torture by US troops in the field. But the government had already announced the end of courts-martial related to the conflict. President Roosevelt shelved Miles's investigation. Brutal tactics applied in a prolonged campaign appear different when methods are examined just after a war is won.

In a fit of retroactive justification, the United States would even officially minimize the savagery of Weyler's *reconcentración*. According to the stipulations of the peace agreement with Spain in 1898 at the close of the war, financial claims by US citizens against Spain for its policy of *reconcentración* had to be adjudicated and paid out by the US government. But by the time those claims had worked their way through the system in 1902, the United States had already instituted a parallel system of reconcentration in its own colony overseas. In addition to noting this concenration camp parallel, the adjudicating commission cited US Civil War orders from a half century before authorizing the detention of civilians in enemy territory as prisoners of war without due process. It also mentioned the previously established legality of starving out belligerents, armed or unarmed. Commissioners further noted that given the opportunity to consider the legitimacy of Spanish *reconcentración* in Cuba, the Hague Convention on war crimes in 1899 had not forbidden it.

In a ruling that would save the United States from the financial claims of *reconcentrados* in both Cuba and the Philippines, the commission affirmed that "it is undoubtedly the general rule of international law that concentration and devastation are legitimate war measures."[97] Members embarrassedly acknowledged President McKinley's earlier public denunciations of Spanish concentration camps as violating the laws of war. Those arguments, the commissioners suggested, revealed laudable humanitarian sentiments, but were not legally binding.

By combining Spanish-style *reconcentración* with total war in the Philippines, Bell and Smith institutionalized the legacy of the Civil War and broadened it for future use. Generals Sherman and Sheridan's campaigns of deliberate destruction in the American South were embraced as acceptable war policy and made more lethal. Historian Glenn May has pointed out that by the time Bell made use of reconcentration, the risk to civilians was well known from the Cuban conflict yet went unacknowledged. "An American commander," Glenn wrote, "did not have to issue orders specifically calling for the death of civilians in order to produce many civilian deaths."[98]

In time, Brigadier General Franklin Bell would come to be embraced as the genius of the most successful counterinsurgency operation ever executed by the US military, then or since. When it briefly appeared as if the United States would go to war in Cuba again in 1906, government officials leaked that they intended to introduce a concentration camp system immediately upon occupation.[99] In the end, however, no camps were established: Roosevelt sent in the Marines as an occupying force for two years while the electoral system was improved and a professional Cuban army established.[100]

14. Even General Weyler, "the Butcher," who had faced so much condemnation, was rehabilitated. After returning to Spain, he had four separate stints as minister of war. In more than three thousand pages of memoir covering just his campaign in Cuba, he made a point of noting with pride all the places where concentration camps had been used since he had inaugurated the concept.[101] Upon his death decades later, the Spanish embassy in Washington put out a statement saying he had achieved "lasting glory" after being "accused without proof of excessive severity and of having caused misery in gathering Cubans in insurgent areas into reconcentration camps."[102]

In both Cuba and the Philippines, a succession of generals had appeared in sequence, each one willing to increase the severity of measures taken against civilians. That the methods were devastating to the poor, that they blurred and sometimes erased distinctions between civilians and soldiers, punishing entire populations, did not seem to matter when the places involved were distant and news did not come too often.

Observers and participants alike realized that the collapse of the Spanish Empire and the birth of American colonialism marked a shift in global power. Some newspapers also noted a change in battle tactics arising from these conflicts, declaring barbed wire the most important addition to military strategy to emerge from the Spanish-American conflict.[103]

Less understood at the time was that the nineteenth-century legacy of total war and the generals' systemically applied brutality had already birthed the defining atrocity of the next century. Meanwhile, other generals in far-off colonies had already taken the idea of concentration camps and instituted them on a new continent—Africa.

CHAPTER TWO

Death and Genocide in Southern Africa

1. ON THE SOUTH AFRICAN veld, farmhouses burned easily. With paraffin oil poured over curtains and set ablaze, or dynamite charges nestled in the floor, sturdy structures exploded into debris or blossomed into flame, sending plumes of smoke skyward. It took little time to annihilate a home.

Beginning in 1900, the British Empire's soldiers became experts in these wartime demolitions. Carrying out a scorched-earth policy against Boer families in the Orange Free State and Transvaal, they leveled more than thirty thousand houses and obliterated dozens of towns.[1] Soldiers became proficient at other tasks as well—smashing mirrors to prevent signaling; wetting stored grain or dumping it into the fire; stripping stinkwood window and door frames for fuel; stealing jewelry, candlesticks, and money; burning orchards; and shooting thousands of horses and cattle in a single day. In theory, houses were torched only when an arms cache was discovered or as direct retaliation for sabotage. In practice, procedures were murky as soldiers ransacked homesteads, stealing an oven from one family while taking all the valuables from another, or asking for a cup of milk before slaughtering pigs singly or burning a herd of sheep alive.[2]

The British had already faced a challenge from Boer fighters twenty years before, when the descendants of Dutch settlers had insisted on independence in the Transvaal. After humiliating the British in three months of fighting, Boers there won the right to self-rule in 1881, joining the Orange Free State as an independent Boer republic.

Though granting self-rule, Britain continued to insist that both republics were officially part of the British Empire. And after the discovery of mineral deposits in Boer territory sparked a gold rush that led to British immigration, London began to assert control. Faced with British troop deployments, the Boers demanded the removal of soldiers from the republics' borders. The British refused, and on October 11, 1899, the Boers declared war.

As in the Philippines, the war had begun with more or less conventional battles, but traditional combat had not proven an effective strategy for a small force fighting an empire. Once the British set their sights on securing control of the republics' major cities, Boer leaders switched battle plans. With their horsemanship, knowledge of the country, and skilled marksmanship, they turned to guerrilla tactics, organizing commando raids to harass British forces and supply lines. In response, the British implemented a plan similar to that used in Cuba against the rebels. Long stretches of barbed-wire fence connected manned blockhouses, dividing the countryside into zones and hampering Boer mobility.

Yet the Boers proved effective guerrilla fighters. Just three months into the conflict, Britain felt compelled to deploy nearly two hundred thousand men to southern Africa. By the time British soldiers began appearing on their doorsteps, Boer men of fighting age were rarely found at home. Unable to pin down the commando groups and strike the fighters directly, invading soldiers generally had to settle for punishing women and children. After giving families only a short time to gather what they could carry, British soldiers sometimes watched the women they had ordered out of their homes run back into burning farmhouses to retrieve necessities. Those given the mercy of more time packed possessions in wagons, which some pulled themselves after their animals had been shot. The families were instantly homeless.

2. In the first months of the Boer War, Parliament had been inclined to accept the military's need to act without interference. But as rumors of farm burning appeared again and again, members began to question the War Office, only to have the allegations flatly denied.

After reported pieces appeared in established newspapers, the accusations were harder to dismiss. In a May 1900 debate in the House of Commons, member of Parliament John Bryn Roberts pointed to well-known reporters at respectable newspapers who were now attributing accounts directly to officers they had interviewed—officers who had themselves ordered or carried out the devastation. He read aloud from the *Morning Leader:* "The column commanded by General French, with General Pole-Carew at the head of the Guards and 18th Brigade, is marching in, burning practically everything on the road. It is followed by about 3,500 head of loot cattle and sheep. Hundreds of tons of corn and forage have been destroyed."[3]

Roberts noted that it was one thing to burn homes in retreat, quite another to do so as an invading force, driving civilians before you. Estimating that the tiny Boer force fighting the British Empire was equivalent to the British Empire "fighting eight worlds at once," he wondered whether moderation might be in order.[4]

Accounts of Boer suffering found a sympathetic audience among British pacifists. Emily Hobhouse, a welfare activist recently returned from work with miners in America, was moved by the stories of civilians driven from their homes for the sake of a war many ascribed to simple greed. She had joined the South African Conciliation Committee earlier that year, and after reading soldiers' letters in the papers, organized a women's protest the first summer of the war.

The work was not without its risks, as British soldiers were dying in battle, and many Englishmen saw compassion for Boer families as treason. At a meeting organized by Quakers that July, a hostile audience shouted down Hobhouse and other speakers, throwing chairs at them before storming the stage.[5]

Thirty-nine years old at the start of the war, Hobhouse had already lost her parents to disease and most of her inheritance to failed investment. A round-shouldered woman with a delicate mouth and unruly hair, she had lived in Minnesota and Mexico before moving back to London and settling in a Chelsea apartment. Her influential aunt and uncle, Lord Arthur and Lady Mary Hobhouse, encouraged her liberal activism.

Encountering Boers who had come to England to plead their case, Hobhouse conceived of the idea of a setting up a distress fund for South African women and children. Visiting prominent figures during the fall of 1900 in search of support, she met with cool receptions and fears of ostracism. After managing to raise £300, she revealed to her family that she herself planned to travel to South Africa to distribute the money. Her brother worried that she might catch a disease from the suffering Boers or be slandered in England, to which she replied, "Life has no attractions, Death a good many; so the argument has no weight."

Lord and Lady Hobhouse said they would not try to stop her from going but didn't have enough faith in her plan to fund the trip. She explained that she did not want or expect money from them. In short order, Hobhouse rented out her apartment, bought a second-class ticket, and set sail that December for the Cape of Good Hope.[6]

3. Early complaints by activists and even liberal members of Parliament failed to disrupt the army's scorched-earth policy. Secretary of

State for the Colonies Joseph Chamberlain insisted that no British soldier had been justly accused of wrongdoing, and that the burning of farms had been greatly exaggerated. Where it had occurred, he claimed, it was done only in cases of clear civilian complicity in the rebellion, and regardless, the government could not tie the hands of the military in the conduct of the war.[7]

In July 1900, antiwar MP David Lloyd George noted that Britain was in the process of repeating Spanish atrocities in Cuba. "This war," he predicted, "will brutalise the people, and the savagery which must necessarily follow will stain the name of this country."[8] Months later, MP Samuel Smith declared that by burning homes, the empire was careening toward a catastrophe on the scale of Weyler in Cuba, "storing up for ourselves a heritage of hatred [to] last for generations. Future historians would look upon our present action as one of the most deplorable blunders that this country had ever made."[9]

Newspapers also noted the echoes of the Spanish approach in Cuba, and some of them enthusiastically called on the government to embrace a policy of reconcentration. The *Pall Mall Gazette* advocated the use of camps and recommended adopting Weyler's model but stopping just short of starving Boer civilians.[10] The *St. James Gazette* likewise recommended "copying" Weyler, but in more extreme form: it encouraged the government to relocate the entire population of Dutch descendants to St. Helena, a desolate island two thousand miles away in the middle of the Atlantic Ocean. Or, they suggested broad-mindedly, *reconcentrados* could be sent to Ceylon, even farther from South Africa.[11]

The government tried to gin up popular support, creating propaganda squads of celebrity writers such as Arthur Conan Doyle and Rudyard Kipling to help promote the war. Yet even everyday citizens recognized the path the conflict was taking, writing letters to the editor predicting that if reconcentration were done along Cuban lines, the same starvation and epidemics could easily result.[12] Among those who remembered recent history, it was apparent what would happen next.

4. Emily Hobhouse sailed into port on December 26, 1900, arriving in time to watch the sun rise over Table Mountain and Devil's Peak. Passengers had to wait to disembark, as Cape Town boomed with the business of war: ships clogged the coastline, supplies choked the docks, military trucks filled the streets, and soldiers in uniform seemed to be everywhere.

Her luggage was lost in the melee but later made its way to her, while she spent her first days meeting with local families. Four days into her trip, she wrote her aunt about a soldier who claimed to have taken part in burning six hundred farms himself, and of boys down to the age of eight held as captured soldiers. Rumors had come out of Johannesburg, too, describing "4,000 women and children in some sort of camp prisons there."[13]

She soon made her way to the office of Sir Alfred Milner, governor of the Cape Colony. By then she had heard stories of several large refugee camps, but details about them remained a mystery. Offering her letter of introduction from Lady Hobhouse, she made an appointment with Milner to discuss the condition of Boer women and children. Fear that she was not up to the task she had taken on consumed her.

When Hobhouse finally sat with the governor in his drawing room, she spent more than an hour telling him everything she had learned. For someone with no political portfolio, she was audacious in her requests, pleading for Milner to offer good terms to the Boers in a peace settlement. Current policies, she warned, were creating "thousands of Joans of Arc."[14] She had been told of at least eleven camps and felt certain more existed.

Milner did not try to convince her of the legitimacy of burning homesteads and acknowledged that he himself had been uneasy at the sight of women and children transported in cargo trucks. He offered to do what he could to support her. She got as far as demanding two vehicles—one for clothing and one for food—before he clarified that permission to go to any camp would depend on the approval of Lord Herbert Kitchener, who had taken charge of the war.[15]

Hobhouse first visited a prisoner-of-war camp for wounded Boers, learning the arcane details of military passes required to travel any distance from town. She also found that her plan to distribute funds only with the approval of British civil and military authorities was already alienating radical supporters at home, who, she noted, did not have to live on the verge of martial law, surrounded by soldiers carrying Maxim guns.[16]

Two weeks later, she got approval from Kitchener to go inland. Kitchener allotted her one truck and permission to journey as far as Bloemfontein, six hundred miles northwest of Cape Town. She would be allowed no farther into contested territory. He denied her request for a Boer traveling companion—despite her poor Dutch, she would have to travel alone.

After a day spent directing the packing of a military supply truck with more than ten tons of food and clothing, she was still unsure of exactly what to take. Perhaps the military could be pressured into providing better provisions for those it had rendered homeless, but she feared that necessities would be in short supply. After seeing the truck off, she caught the train to Bloemfontein, winding through the Karoo desert, full of storms and red sand. The dust made its way everywhere, even inside her compartment, covering her skin and hair. The view from the carriage was littered with decomposing bodies of slaughtered cattle and horses, unidentifiable bones, and the occasional razed farm.

On arrival, Hobhouse found herself immersed in a military milieu, the only woman in the station at Bloemfontein. Faced with problems getting a hotel room, she pushed for approval to stay with the widow of a Boer general, which did not make a good first impression with George Pretyman, the British general in charge. After

talking to the captain who had recently served as the camp commandant, it was apparent that soldiers had no more idea "than the
man in the moon" how to handle the civilian crisis that had been
dumped in their laps.[17]

Hobhouse headed off to see her first concentration camp two
miles outside town. On the blazing open veld, uneven rows of
round bell tents splayed along the side of a low hill, with a mortu-
ary tent and tin-roofed hospital buildings at one end. She soon
learned that each family was allotted one tent built out of canvas
hung from a central pole and supported by ropes cinched to stakes
in the ground. In time, there would not be enough of the shelters
to go around, leaving new arrivals to sleep in wagons or railway
carriages.[18]

Making her way down a row of tents in the broiling heat, she
tracked down the sister of a woman she had met in Cape Town.
With no chairs available, they used rolled-up blankets for stools.
Flies buzzed inside and out, forming black carpets over every surface. While Hobhouse asked the woman about life in the camp, a
deadly puff adder slid through the tent. She struck at it with her
parasol until someone brought a mallet to finish it off.

Other camp residents came to visit, too. Hobhouse met a wife
who had been separated from her five children and unable to visit
her husband, who was held prisoner somewhere in Bloemfontein.
Sleeping on the ground at night, she was in the last weeks of pregnancy with a sixth child. "This is but one case," Hobhouse wrote to
her aunt, "quite ordinary, amongst hundreds and hundreds."[19]

There was not enough water; there was no soap; measles were
spreading. Dead bodies sometimes remained in tents long enough
to begin rotting. In a concentration camp of two thousand, almost
half the prisoners were children. On her first visit, she heard of shelters that leaked in storms, children with typhoid, and husbands
punitively shipped thousands of miles away to prisoner-of-war camps
on the island of Ceylon.

Hobhouse acknowledged that the head of the camp wanted to

make life as livable as he could for detainees, but she instantly felt that the creation of the camps had been a colossal mistake. "Do what you will," she wrote, "you can't undo the thing itself which is odious." She was overwhelmed but aimed to show the public that "to keep these camps going is *murder to the children.*"[20]

Within a week after her arrival, she had put out a call for trained nurses and come up with a universal plan to boil river water to stop a burgeoning typhoid epidemic. Some officials offered support, but on the ground she discovered that she was viewed as a fool or a traitor. After thousands of British deaths at the hands of Boer guerrillas, many soldiers seemed to feel that extreme measures were justified to bring an end to the war. Now that these measures had been taken, they were resentful at being saddled with thousands of refugees and a conflict that continued to rage.

The constant disapproval of the soldiers felt like banishment to Hobhouse. When a new commandant arrived, he was less than enthusiastic at discovering her already in his camp. She was no more enthusiastic about him. She made a scene over surveillance of her work, refusing to accept any interference that did not come directly from Milner in Cape Town.

The suspicious captain who monitored her during her visits seemed impervious to her badgering as she tried to make him provide milk for the malnourished or pay attention to the children dying around him. In her frustration, she wanted to hit him.[21]

The censor refused to approve the letter she wrote describing conditions in the camp, so she waited for someone she could trust to carry her letters back and mail them from the coast. Meanwhile, her running tally of camps was nearing forty, and she wanted to see them all herself. She braced herself to leave Bloemfontein.

Feeling cowardly and overwhelmed, she dreaded facing the unknown alone, with her poor Dutch and limited supplies. She knew well what impression she made, "a mere woman, middle-aged, and somewhat dowdy at that."[22] On the train, she found it difficult to push in among the soldiers to get food at each station, so she packed her kettle and a tin of apricot jam and wondered what the next stop would bring.

5. As she made her way over a hundred miles to camps at Norvals Pont and Aliwal North, Hobhouse disappeared into a whirlwind of permits, passes, and cool lakes that existed only as mirages spun by the fierce heat. She traveled mostly in the guard's car on the cargo train, spending one night upright in her seat and another sleeping on the floor of a borrowed room at a roadside hotel inside a circle of bug repellent. Women's bathrooms were generally locked or had been commandeered for use by the military. She lived for days at a time on jam and cocoa.

To her surprise, conditions at Norvals Pont and Aliwal North, two of the more rural camps, were better than those at Bloemfontein. Norvals Pont housed 1,500 detainees, with much less overcrowding. British loyalist refugees fleeing the war got large marquee tents, which stood apart from the standard bell tents of Boer women and children. Camp residents did not have to resort to using river water to drink and cook with, as at Bloemfontein, because the captain in charge of the camp had pipes laid to carry spring water from a nearby farm. The tents had one bed and a table, as well as eating utensils.

Though he had been rebuked for doing so, the commandant had bought clothing for those who needed it, and had some men in the camp build a tennis court where anyone could play.[23] Still, many who had fallen sick at Norvals Pont died due to a lack of trained nurses. And the daytime heat was blistering, with the attending physician unable to test for fever as temperatures inside the tents hovered around 110 degrees Fahrenheit, rendering thermometers useless.

At Aliwal North, she found that the small town of eight hundred had created a committee to prepare for more than two thousand detainees they had been told would be sent by the military. A sympathetic commandant had tried to demilitarize the camp: no sentries were posted, and camp and town residents could mix at will. Rations were more generous, and large families were given a second tent or canvas and wood to expand their accommodations as needed.[24]

It was a relief to find some solutions that could be brought back to Bloemfontein, but even at Aliwal North, clothing was running short. Hobhouse wondered at those who accused the Boers of being filthy when none of the camps provided the basics for hygiene. She went to town and bought soap and material with which to sew clothes, and had them delivered to the camp.

Returning to the misery of Bloemfontein, she aggressively pushed for changes. Despite her empathy, class sometimes loomed as a blind spot for Hobhouse. At Norvals Pont, she referred to the British civilians who had taken refuge in the camp as "generally a very inferior type of underbred English." Others she held in contempt were referred to as "low class." It was necessary, she felt, for teachers of Boer children to have not just manners and morals but good "breeding" as well.[25] Yet without the power that class gave her, how much harder it would have been for a woman of the era to cross the globe to assail the empire's wartime conduct, demanding to speak only with governors and generals. She thought little of any damage to her reputation, using society connections in London to demand attention from the government and accountability on the ground.

Race, too, played a role in Hobhouse's camp relief work. She noted the presence of "little Kaffir servant" girls even in the Boer camps—black Africans who had been taken with their mistresses and herded from burned homesteads into detention. Her first letter back to England after arriving at her own camp had mentioned a camp of about five hundred "Natives (Kaffirs)" on the outskirts of Bloemfontein. She was concerned about the suffering there, addressing the local Loyal Ladies League just a month after her arrival and suggesting they take up the cause of the native camps, where she had been told "there is much sickness and destitution."[26]

She was willing to go hundreds of miles by train to visit other Boer camps, but never set foot in the Native camp close at hand near Bloemfontein. She did, however, continue to call for someone to investigate, asking her aunt in March 1901 whether the British even realized the "Native (coloured)" camps existed. Tremendous sickness reigned in them, she had heard, and the death rate was apparently very high. She recommended that the Quakers send someone. Or perhaps a representative from the Aborigines' Protection Society could visit. But as she wrote to Lady Hobhouse, "I cannot possibly pay any attention to them myself."[27]

6. Emily Hobhouse was hardly alone in choosing not to visit the black African camps. They went unnoted by many of the newspapers and activists in England who took on the Boer camps as part of an antiwar, humanitarian mission. Improving conditions for black Africans was touted as an ideal by British imperialists who supported the war, but actual concern for the effects of the war on this part of the population failed to take root in the field.

As with the Boer families, some black Africans initially came into camps as refugees fleeing raids and fighting. Later, African families were likewise forced out of the countryside during scorched-earth campaigns. The military rationale for detaining Boer women had been the suspicion that they were passing intelligence and food to men on commando duty. But holding women en masse as prisoners of war would not do for public consumption in England. A justification for not releasing them became that women without husbands at home had to be protected from black savages. Soon enough, it was argued that blacks themselves could not be left free on the veld.[28]

As camps were set up, the British began by housing black Africans alongside Boer families. As refugee numbers grew, they began to establish separate facilities for Boer and black detainees. The early, adjacent camps were run by superintendents of the Boer camps, but the British government later set up a Native Refugee Department to administer black camps.[29]

These camps ranged from formal concentration camps to some without superintendents, and even one self-organized enclave of thousands only nominally under government control. Other black Africans ended up outside the black camps, hiding out on the veld, going on commando missions with the Boers, or ending up servants in Boer camps.

Early on, when black men were cleared off the land, they were turned over to the military and expected to work at assigned duties to support their families, who were consigned to conditions worse than those in the Boer camps. Where Boers received tents in the first months of concentration, those in the black camps had to make do with sail covers, sticks, bits of wood, blankets, metal, mud, and anything that might improvise a shelter. Unlike the Boer camps, black camps did not provide free rations, though some exemptions were made for destitute families without a male head of household. It was assumed by the British that Africans had different nutritional needs, which translated into half the provisions given to whites.[30]

Even those who had reserves of grain were not allowed to bring it to the camps, where it might have kept them from taking on work to earn money. Reports are filled with references to supposed native gratitude for the camps and a chance to earn money, but the missionaries who made their way into the black camps got a starkly different impression. "They are in great poverty and misery," wrote the Reverend W. H. R. Brown. "Many are dying from day to day—what is to become of the survivors I cannot think."[31]

One early report from Heidelberg reported that camp residents had nothing to eat but the corpses of diseased cattle.[32] In another black camp, residents managed to raise pigs and sow a crop only to watch British troops trample the field and seize their animals. The loss completely ruined the holdings of some six hundred Africans in the camp, an official report noted, but "the Natives themselves admitted such losses were incidental in wartime."[33]

Those in the black camps found themselves likewise tormented by Boers on commando duty. Night raids at Potchefstroom and Taaibosch led to the death of one native, as well as the loss of money and clothes along with hundreds of cattle and sheep. In response, the

British armed squads of pickets—blacks from the camps—to stand guard. Despite an incident in which guerrillas shot thirteen picketers, as well as worries that arming natives would only provoke new raids and bloodshed, 850 black Africans served as armed guards in black concentration camps.[34]

Trench latrines and overcrowding led to filth and disease. Dysentery, typhoid, chicken pox, measles, and pneumonia afflicted the refugees. At Victoria Nek, the doctor refused to visit patients in the camp, demanding that invalids see him in town.[35] Many camps had no hospital and no nurses. When typhoid swept through these communities, no effort was made to quarantine the sufferers, despite the highly contagious nature of the disease.

As with Boer mothers, black mothers got the brunt of blame when their children died, with one inspector suggesting that they were eating food meant for their sick offspring. "Natives," he wrote, "do not seem to care for their children until they reach a useful age."[36]

Back in 1897, as the newly appointed high commissioner of South Africa and governor of Cape Colony, Alfred Milner had outlined his two most important goals. First, he wanted to restore good relations between the British and the Boers, and second, he aimed to protect native Africans from oppression. But realizing that the second goal rendered the first nearly impossible, he saw even before the war had begun how it would be resolved: "You have only to sacrifice 'the nigger' absolutely and the game is easy."[37]

After the war's end, Milner would be proved right: the British actively collaborated with the Boers to segregate and disenfranchise black Africans. But that population had already been abandoned during the war. In all, more than 115,700 black Africans had been detained in British camps by the end of the war, with no tin hospital sheds, no drives to provide clothing and mattresses for the naked refugees sleeping on the ground, and no hopes of feeding everyone.[38]

Founded and administered by the military, the black camps

never transitioned to civilian control. Missionaries who managed to visit did what they could to draw attention to the crisis, but they were unsuccessful in alleviating the camps' most lethal aspects.

The staggering numbers of black African deaths in concentration camps did not earn condemnation even from the superintendent in charge of native affairs for the Orange River Colony. Attaching the November 1901 statistics for black mortality, he wrote to London, "The death rate appears high, but under the circumstances, I think it can scarcely be called excessive." Fatalities would surely decline soon, he assured his superiors; he felt the situation on the ground reflected "a very satisfactory state of affairs generally."[39] The following month, mortality in the black camps would reach the highest rates recorded during any month, surpassing even death rates in the Boer camps.

By the time peace was concluded, sixty-six camps holding more than 115,000 black Africans littered the veld. More than 14,000—some 12 percent of those who entered these camps—would not survive. Historian Elizabeth van Heyningen has noted that "it is quite clear that most of the official records were destroyed."[40] Incomplete statistics suggest a much larger number of deaths for which there are no records.[41] The British head of the black camp at Bloemfontein, however, had no doubts about Britain's largesse: "To have to leave their homes seems hard on the surface, but to be fed & sheltered and protected without remuneration amply atones for all."[42]

7. Emily Hobhouse found that dysentery and intestinal disease outran her ability to corral aid even in the Boer camps. The mid-war switch from military to civilian administration meant that the army would no longer provide nurses. And the nurses sent up to Bloemfontein from the Cape, she believed, tended toward drink or petty crime and had no discernible training.[43] Even those who were competent went without adequate facilities or medical supplies.

Over time, Hobhouse gained authority, but with it came the

expectation that she would solve a broad range of issues. After authorizing her to distribute supplies and including her name in the new camp rules, the superintendent for the Boer camps asked her to pay for clothes for residents and to provide funds to establish a children's hospital. She refused, declaring the government unequivocally responsible for providing both things.

The government called the camps of the Boer War refugee camps. Hobhouse argued that inmates were not refugees from war but people deliberately made homeless as part of battle strategy, driven into concentration camps as prisoners of war. Under the rules of the Hague Convention, she believed, the government was accountable for the maintenance of prisoners of war. She empathized with the superintendent, who had few available goods and little money to use in ministering to the needs of thousands of people. But she did not want to shield the government from having to address the consequences of its own poor planning and execution of a war strategy involving civilians.[44]

Hobhouse was often accused by British loyalists of being pro-Boer, and she was prone to praising the resourcefulness of the Boer fighters, who appeared to be outwitting the British during her time at the Cape. Perhaps more dangerous to her reputation was her tendency, in private letters and private company, to savage the British army—not just the hypocrisies of camp policies but what she saw as the laziness of the soldiers and the incompetence of officers.

She particularly resented watching the soldiers' brisk trade in sewing machines, chairs, and jewelry, selling items looted from Boer homes to townspeople or back to camp detainees.[45] Still, she was as quick to sympathize with the plight of individual British soldiers as she was with the fate of detainees in the camps. She commiserated with their hardships under siege, mended their clothes, and surrendered novels and cocoa to them in railway stations across the Cape.

Traveling ninety miles on to Springfontein, Hobhouse found the poorest Boers she had yet seen, camp residents without shoes, socks, or underwear. She emptied the pine crates of clothing she had brought along, and the crates were quickly seized and dismantled to make furniture. In the dark comedy that reigned under bureaucracy in wartime, prisoners had very little coal for fuel, while camp rations were meat, grain, and coffee—all of which required cooking.

Meanwhile at Bloemfontein, "the whole talk was of death—who died yesterday, who lay dying today, who would be dead to-morrow."[46] The corpses, most often the small bodies of children, were taken out of the camp at dawn—not through the town, where everyone would see, but along another road to the cemetery, where they were buried together in a mass grave.

Hobhouse knew she was watched in the camps and regarded with suspicion by many officers. But when the *Bloemfontein Post* reported on a speech she had given to a women's group in February, she found herself publicly skewered. Calling her a "lady missionary," the editors assailed her comments and expressed the hope that she would not "teach the refugees at the Refugee Camp, who have so much to be grateful for, to believe they have grievances—grievances quite unimagined hitherto."[47]

Because she was ostensibly in the camps as an apolitical observer, she paid a price for speaking out. Her mail was censored, and she was spied upon. When Hobhouse returned to the camp at Norvals Pont, she was warned by a resident she had met on a prior visit that the nurse and the new teacher were planning to trick her into pro-Boer statements, then report her to the commandant.

Though surveillance measures against her increased, she noticed in May that restrictions in some Boer camps had eased under civilian administration. During the day, guards left their posts, and camp detainees could go to the river or the valley to gather wood or flowers.

Just as crucial to health, the practice of reducing rations for families with relatives on commando duty was stopped. Still, she complained in her letters—in an observation unlikely to generate much sympathy a century later—that the presence of "armed Natives" was routinely used to intimidate and corral the Boers, which "hurts them almost more than anything."[48]

In many cases, the March 1901 shift to civilian administration further muddled questions of financial burdens and disciplinary responsibilities. At Kimberley, Hobhouse found a commandant who stayed away from his camp for days at a time. The existing buildings stood inside a narrow enclosure of barbed wire eight feet high that had cost £500—a staggering sum. She could not fathom how the fence was necessary or useful when the camp lacked a nurse and a functioning hospital.

Just after her arrival at Kimberley, three children in the camp died only hours apart. Before the burial the next morning, she came across a photographer taking portraits of the bodies to give to their absent fathers after the war. Remembering a stop on her last trip, when there was nothing to bury a dead girl in but a sack, Hobhouse was grateful to see that someone had found enough wood to make coffins.[49]

She met with General Pretyman, who had signed her pass on her first trip into the camps four months earlier, and requested authority to work in Kimberley as well as a return pass to Bloemfontein. He was in a foul mood, and in a rhetorical flourish she would become familiar with, he ascribed the death of the children to the unsanitary habits and folk remedies of their parents. She countered that surely sleeping on the ground while sick with measles and having a doctor ignorant of pediatric medicine played a more significant role. The arguments behind their debate would continue to play out for more than one hundred years, with evidence on both sides. But Hobhouse held the moral high ground, arguing that a government that forces civilians into detention, even in wartime, should bear the brunt of responsibility for camp fatalities.

As punishment for her lecture, or just more of the red tape Hobhouse repeatedly denounced, Pretyman said he could not give her a pass for the hundred-mile trip to Bloemfontein but would supply her with authorization good for the six-hundred-mile journey back to Cape Town, where she could ask for permission to turn around and come back. She agreed, still hoping to eventually make her way even farther north to the camps she had not yet seen.

During April 1901, she got as far as Mafeking concentration camp, where she found decent rations but shortages of clothes, soap, candles, and blankets. On the way back she witnessed the clearing of the town of Warrenton, whose women were herded into open coal trucks and carried away from their homes.

The desolation of the countryside was hardly a new sight, but the image of the stunned Boers newly transformed into refugees stuck in her mind as summing up the mayhem and idiocy of war. "Flocks and herds of frightened animals bellowing and baaing for food and drink, tangled up with wagons and vehicles of all sorts and a dense crowd of human beings," she wrote, "combined to give a picture of war in all its destructiveness, cruelty, stupidity and nakedness."[50]

Returning to Bloemfontein, she discovered that the camp population had doubled to four thousand people since her departure the month before. Meanwhile, Springfontein had grown from five hundred to three thousand detainees, with more on the way. In her travels, she saw hundreds in trucks and on cars at train stations, hearing stories of Boers going days without food and children dying in transit. Back at the camp she got descriptions of rations with meat that was maggoty or missing altogether and water pouring into tents during rainstorms. She met with administrators, who had been told thousands more women and children would be herded in, despite no tents or shelters or additional food available for them. Sir Alfred Milner again denied her request to visit the northern camps.

Four months after she had landed in Africa, Hobhouse realized that her dwindling funds and depleted stores of clothing and food could do next to nothing to address the tidal wave of humanity flooding into the camps. She asked for a pass back to Cape Town—the easiest pass for her to get, the one she had resisted the urge to request so many times while she believed there were still things she might accomplish. Only in England, she now felt, could she improve conditions in the camps in any meaningful way. It was time to go home.

She left on May 1, 1901, heading through Springfontein on her way south, running into the same crowd of homeless Boers she had encountered a week and a half before at the train station. The camp superintendent could do nothing for them, as they were not yet part of any camp. They had been burned off the land. The military was through with them, but they were temporarily living outside the civilian bureaucracy.

Hobhouse sat with a mother in a lean-to while her baby died. A husband and wife near ninety years old had managed to flee together; the wife had no skirt. Hobhouse took off her underskirt and slipped it over the woman's hips before leaving. In time, a report came from Bethulie Camp saying the couple was dead.[51]

Too late to be of use on her journey, money arrived from her aunt and uncle, who finally believed in her project and were ready to lend their support. After a final stop at Norvals Pont Camp, she caught the train to Cape Town. She found a berth on the ship that was carrying Sir Alfred Milner back to England, where he would become Lord Milner, a peer of the realm.

8. The Liberal members of Parliament had meanwhile been busy in London, castigating British war policy. They mounted a low-grade perpetual rebellion against official reports about the camps. Registering their unhappiness with the half answers and misleading information fed to them, they noted that other sources sketched a very different picture of detention conditions there.

Even naming was contentious. For the first several months of their existence, the camps had no fixed description. Those opposed to their existence called them camps of detention and the people in them *reconcentrados,* after the Cuban example. Supporters in and outside the military called them camps for refugees. But Hobhouse, along with David Lloyd George, rebelled at the official term.

In Parliament, Lloyd George declared that despite the government telling Parliament the opposite, he had first-person reports from relatives and prior ministers of the empire that the women and children in the camps—even if they had friends or relatives who would shelter them away from contested territory—were not allowed to leave. "There is no greater delusion in the mind of any man," he said, "than to apply the term 'refugee' to these camps. They are not refugee camps. They are camps of concentration, formed by the military as the result of military operations in the field."[52]

If the military managed to keep the camps open despite the bad publicity, the opposition won the naming war. In March 1901, the term "concentration camp" entered the parliamentary record and the English lexicon in reference to the Boer camps as places of military detention for civilians.

Told that Lord Kitchener was "taking all steps to ensure the humane treatment of refugees" in the Boer camps, Parliament demanded to know whether there were in fact different ration scales based on political status for allotting food to prisoners.[53] Was the government, they asked, aware that only 10 percent of the two thousand children in Bloemfontein Camp were receiving schooling?[54] And that instruction was not in Dutch but in English? If conditions were humane, as reported, why were mortality rates increasing, and why did they exceed the rate for combat fatalities among soldiers? Accounts taken from Emily Hobhouse's letters were quoted to counter government assertions and demand explanations, including the question of what conditions the government might be hiding by not letting her go to the northernmost camps.[55]

Upon her return, Hobhouse was lauded and loathed for her efforts. Her eyewitness summaries were hailed and compared to the first-person accounts by US senator Redfield Proctor of *reconcentración* in Cuba, with sympathetic papers saying she had "turned the light of day upon a hell of suffering deliberately created for expediting a policy of conquest."[56]

She revealed the nasty underbelly of war to the British public, but war fever made sympathy for any Boer, even women and children, hard for many to stomach. Still, within days of her mid-June report on camps of women and children in the Cape and Orange River Colonies, the War Office had vowed to consider her recommendations.

Consternation in England and abroad was reflected in mockery and condemnation of the British government. A Swiss political cartoon paired British secretary of state for the colonies Joseph Chamberlain with Herod as a colleague in baby killing, with Chamberlain dismissing Herod as a bungler for his less-effective approach.[57] Allen Welsh Dulles, the eight-year-old son of a Presbyterian minister in Washington, DC, gained newspaper celebrity for writing a book condemning British concentration camps and atrocities in the war.[58] A British satirist suggested that the current campaign was fought primarily as a war of arson and called for a new military decoration, "The Order of the Torch."[59]

It was barely a joke. "The country is now almost entirely laid waste," wrote one soldier that September. "You can go for miles and miles—in fact you might march for weeks and weeks and see no sign of a living thing or a cultivated patch of land—nothing but burnt farms and desolation."[60]

"When is a war not a war?" asked MP Sir Henry Campbell-Bannerman in a June 14 speech in London, answering his own question. "When it is carried on by methods of barbarism in South Africa." Serious threats were made to bring British conduct in the war before The Hague, whose convention defining war atrocities had been put into effect in 1900.

9. Lord Milner's plan was to create good British subjects once the war was over, and he hoped to use the camps to "civilize" the rural Boer farmers and bring them into the empire. To that end, he prioritized the development of schools, with instruction in English.[61] Yet even in adopting a civilizing mission, the government was working at cross-purposes with itself: Lord Kitchener still embraced using the camps for retribution. Feeling that the wives of men on commando duty had "forfeited their right to considerate treatment," he punished thousands of detainees by authorizing their transfer away from their home areas to new camps being set up along the coast.[62]

The perception around the world was that the British had resorted to atrocities, with camp mortality rates shocking British politicians and subjects alike. In the first linking of concentration camps to a holocaust, the Bishop of Hereford wrote to the *Times* of London in 1901, "Are we reduced to such a depth of impotence that our government can do nothing to stop such a holocaust of child life?"[63]

To a lesser degree, the press also used black camps to shame the government. The *Pilot,* a weekly review, excoriated London over mortality rates there, writing, "This was the war of humanity that was to lift the Boer yoke from the neck of the blacks, yet the blacks are dying faster in our camps than both Boers and British combined in the field." The editors added, "If we are not to be disgraced for ever, the thing must stop."[64]

It was a perception that the military would not countenance. Weeks after Emily Hobhouse's report was published, the War Office appointed a Ladies Committee to visit the camps in an official capacity. The women all had professional or activist qualifications, but many of those chosen were a direct rebuke to Hobhouse. The chair of the committee had been directly critical of her in print and refused to meet with her before sailing.[65] Another member, Dr. Jane Waterson, the daughter of a British general, had previously written to the *Cape Times* in response to the movement to reform the camps, declaring herself "not very favourably impressed by the hysterical whining going on in England.... It would seem as if we might neglect or starve our faithful soldiers...as long as we fed and pampered people who have not even the grace to say thank you for the care bestowed upon them."[66]

Hobhouse repeatedly wrote to ask why she was not permitted to serve on the committee, but Secretary of War St. John Brodrick, who had received reports—true, fabricated, or both—of unpatriotic comments made by Hobhouse, stressed to her that he wanted only apolitical members. She would not get a slot.[67]

If she would not be allowed to return to South Africa with the committee, Hobhouse decided, she would go on her own—not to see the camps again but to work with those who had been deported to coastal towns. She set sail for Cape Town on October 5, 1901. Unlike the Ladies Committee, she had no official portfolio; still, the threat of her reappearance rattled the military. Colonial Secretary Joseph Chamberlain suggested that he "did not think the Empire was threatened by a hysterical spinster of mature age" and believed it "foolish to take any notice of her," but Milner would leave nothing to chance.[68] Milner and Kitchener refused to allow her ashore.

When she was struck by illness and balked at being put on the next ship home, nurses were sent to examine her, though she persuaded the women to leave without doing so. The colony's medical officer had fewer reservations—he ordered her to be wrapped in her shawl, carried off the ship, and deposited at the dock next to a passenger liner departing the next day. She was taken back to England without setting foot in Cape Town.

Hobhouse found herself partially vindicated by the report of the Ladies Committee that December, which returned from an extensive tour of the camps with accusations enough to infuriate everyone. If they had been expected to rubber-stamp government administration of the camps, they disappointed their sponsors by reporting on shocking mortality rates that had only gotten worse after Hobhouse's departure. Noting failing after failing on the part of the government, they declared that "the deaths were *not* simply the result of circumstances beyond the control of the British."[69]

But the committee also indicted the behaviors of Boer mothers, whose folk remedies, lack of sanitation, and refusal to follow modern medical advice, they believed, had directly caused many deaths of children in the camps—unlike the "intelligent and careful" British parents they met on their trip.[70] The tension between the legitimate medical qualifications of the committee and its prejudices make their assessment difficult to analyze a century later. Yet members had come away with strong opinions about the adoption of concentration camps:

It is a huge object-lesson to the world in what not to do! for if the children had not been so massed together, the death rate from those terrible infectious diseases would not have been so great. We brought the women in to stop them from helping their husbands in the War and by so doing we have undoubtedly killed them in thousands as much as if we had shot them on their own doorsteps, and anyone but a British General would have realized this long ago.[71]

By the time of the Boer surrender on the last day of May 1902, British authorities had managed to cut the camp mortality rate significantly. Nevertheless, as historian Peter Warwick noted, more than twenty-seven thousand Boer internees died, a number that "probably amounted to twice the number of men killed in action during the war on both sides" and representing some 10 percent of the population.[72] Nearly 80 percent of them were children.

After hostilities ended, Emily Hobhouse continued campaigning to relieve Boer suffering, making appeals for the government to help feed and provide plow animals for farmers whose homes had been burned. Moving to South Africa in 1905, she set up a spinning and weaving school for Boer women at Philippolis.

She was still working there, living in Pretoria and focused on expanding education for Boer youth, when concentration camps began to appear just over the border in the German colony of South-West Africa. A German chancellor had found a way to surpass Kitchener's brutality, inaugurating a new kind of camp.

10. In January 1904, Herero chief Samuel Maharero led an uprising a hundred miles inland from the western coast of Africa, sabotaging rail lines from the coast in a fury over mistreatment by German traders. The Herero pinned settlers down in a fort at Okahandja, going on to several early victories that stung Berlin. Maharero's rebellion obliterated a messy alliance with German colonial rulers that had endured for a decade.

The governor of the colony, Theodor Leutwein, had lived in South-West Africa for the duration of that alliance, which he had negotiated and then navigated during his tenure. He had learned how to bribe and play tribal factions against each other to limit blood-shed. He felt certain a peace settlement could be reached. But Kaiser Wilhelm II and officers of the German High Command were uninterested in bargaining.

A month after the uprising began, Leutwein was told to extract unconditional surrender from the Herero.[73] He suspected that the order signaled a plan for the complete extermination of the tribe. Reminding his superiors that native labor was vital to the economy, Leutwein cautioned them not to listen to "fanatics who want to see the Herero destroyed altogether."[74] Three months later, he was relieved of his military command.

As with Weyler in Cuba, the man sent to secure the colony was known for his brutal methods, and demanded a free hand without interference from politicians.[75] General Lothar von Trotha had seen action in both Africa and the atrocity-riddled Boxer Rebellion in China, and remained a fan of bloody, blunt force. Despite the fact that the conflict had largely subsided before his arrival in Africa, von Trotha spent his first two months on the continent plotting a decisive offensive—what one soldier referred to as "a mousetrap." His subordinate, a major named Ludwig von Estorff, was prepared to pin down the Herero forces, then press them into negotiations to settle the war. But von Trotha did not intend to use the mousetrap for that purpose.

In August, von Trotha crushed most of the remaining Herero forces at Waterberg, in the north-central part of the colony. Having secured access to water necessary for the survival of the Herero and their cattle, he issued an order unique in the history of colonialism:

> I, the Great General of the German troops, send this letter to the Herero people. The Herero are no longer German subjects. They have murdered and stolen, they have cut off the ears, noses and other body-parts of wounded soldiers, now out of cowardice they no longer wish to fight. I say to the people anyone who delivers a captain will receive 1000 Mark. Whoever delivers Samuel will receive 5000 Mark. The

Herero people must however leave the land. If the populace does not do this I will force them with the Groot Roor [Cannon]. Within the German borders every Herero, with or without a gun, with or without cattle, will be shot. I will no longer accept women and children. I will drive them back to their people or I will let them be shot at.

These are my words to the Herero people.

The great General of the Mighty Kaiser.[76]

He followed up with a clarifying order suggesting that he wanted men shot but did not intend for troops to commit atrocities against women and children—merely to shoot over their heads to frighten them away. But writing later in a letter explaining his bloody tactics, von Trotha declared that tribes "yield only to force. It was and remains my policy to apply this force by unmitigated terrorism and even cruelty."[77] Herero men were hanged in front of women, who were sent with the proclamation back to their people to say what they had seen. What had been a barbaric standard of engagement before the extermination order became open season on the Herero.

Only 1 percent of South-West Africa consisted of arable land. Most of its territory lay in desert and semiarid regions. Major Estorff, who had hoped to end the war with negotiations followed von Trotha's orders. The Herero had been flushed eastward, toward open desert. If they were seen, they would be shot. But fleeing without provisions, cattle, or access to guarded watering holes, they had no chance for survival. Many died of exposure in the sands of the Omaheke Desert. Countless additional Herero caught in the field were executed on the spot after summary court-martial. Feeling that "crushing people like this was in equal measure cruel and insane," Estorff had told von Trotha that the people had been punished enough, but von Trotha kept to his strategy.[78]

Mass executions, however, did not sit well with the Reichstag. Two months after the extermination order was issued, German chancellor Bernhard von Bülow responded to pressure from the left and persuaded the Kaiser to rescind it. But the Herero had little reason to rejoice—new orders from Berlin mandated limited executions and forced labor for those spared from death. Still, some desperate Herero survivors who had nowhere to go got word of the changes and made their way back to German settlements to turn themselves in. Von Trotha had the prisoners put in arm and leg and neck irons, until Chancellor von Bülow stopped that as well, worrying that it would keep the remaining natives from surrendering.

Meanwhile, von Bülow had threaded the needle of how to remove the Herero as a military threat while keeping them as a labor source. "I am of the opinion," he wrote to von Trotha, "that the surrendering Herero should be placed in *Konzentrationslager,* concentration camps, in various locations of the territory, there to be put under guard and required to work."[79] The strategy was not alien to von Trotha: the general had an almost mystical faith in Lord Kitchener, the strategist for the South African war and its policy of concentration camps, seeing him as a guiding star as he navigated his own country's conflict.[80]

11. The first German concentration camps in South-West Africa were built at military posts. Where the British Empire had insisted the Boer families in their care were refugees, Germany embraced the notion that every Herero—man, woman, or child—was a prisoner of war. All wore stamped, numbered metal tags. All were swept into cramped shelters, many of them skin-and-rag huts like those in the black camps set up by the British in South Africa. Some children were taken as personal slaves for German officers. More of them, male and female, were forced into hard labor on projects run by the military. Other Herero were provided as workers to private companies.

On the hillside at one of two camps at Windhoek, thick thorn-bush perimeter fencing hemmed in row after row of *pontoks*—patchwork round huts—nested together in lethal proximity. Other prisoners slept hundreds together with no shelter beyond a sailcloth canopy for a roof. The colonial capital had a population of 2,500 inhabitants at the time, but at its peak, the concentration camps at Windhoek held nearly three times as many people.

After months in the desert, many of the prisoners were half dead on arrival: "Dressed in rags or totally naked, starved to the bone," a missionary at Windhoek wrote upon seeing the Herero come in.[81] Another missionary at Kharibib Camp wrote of the newcomers, "Some of them had been starved to skeletons with hollow eyes, powerless and hopeless, afflicted by serious diseases, particularly with dysentery. In the settlements, they were placed in big *kraals* [corrals], and there they lay, without blankets and some without clothing, in the tropical rain on the marshlike ground. Here death reaped a harvest!"[82]

Missionaries initially betrayed the Herero, helping to lure them out of the bush even after it was clear that they would face disease and atrocities in the camps.[83] And territorial disputes between Catholic and Lutheran missionaries for access to native converts occupied perhaps more of their time than was decent, given hardships faced by prisoners. But missionaries also attempted to alleviate suffering in the camps, running a sick bay at Windhoek, supplying clothing and bedding to prisoners, and advocating for cooking implements and better food. They also provided eyewitness accounts of the camps. Treating the prisoners, they noted firsthand the results of the thick rawhide whips used by guards, the endemic starvation, and the relentless severity of life in the camps. "Finally the mission could no longer merely look on," wrote a missionary named Meier, when "on certain days often 10 or more corpses were carried out."[84]

In addition to the inhospitable climate and disease, and the terrors of life in the camps, brutal labor conditions on work details took their toll as well. Prisoners were forced to carry goods, with one South African newspaper reporting, "The loads...are out of all proportion to their strength. I have often seen women and children dropping down, especially when engaged on this work, and also when carrying very heavy bags of grain, weighing a hundred or more pounds."[85] Women in the camps were further subject to rape and forced prostitution. As a result, sexually transmitted diseases, including venereal typhoid, raged alongside more typical camp diseases, likewise afflicting whites in nearby towns.[86] Souvenir postcards were made of native girl and women prisoners, their blouses torn open and hanging in tatters so they could be photographed half naked.

War with the Herero was followed in 1905 by an uprising of the Nama people in the south. Major Estorff, the acting military commander at the time, negotiated a surrender that would permit the tribe to return to its hometown. With the arrival of a new governor, however, the promise was broken.[87] Nama prisoners joined Hereros in detention and forced labor. Bordering stretches of desert and along the chilly coast, a half-dozen camps around the colony held more than seventeen thousand prisoners.

Despite the adoption of some humane measures—detainees were paid a minuscule amount in wages, and families were no longer broken up—fatalities continued.[88] Women outnumbered children, and children outnumbered men, presumably because so many men had been shot. Prisoners' rations included flour, rice, and salt—but not enough to survive. The rice often proved useless; it was an unfamiliar food to the Herero, who lived off meat and milk from their cattle. Moreover, they lacked utensils with which to cook it. Medical reports assured the government that fruit was also provided, but rampant scurvy in the camps points to its absence.[89]

12. One camp became legendary for its horrors. *Haifischinsel*, or Shark Island, a tiny slip of land just off the coast, stretched 1,300 yards long by a little more than 300 yards wide, an unforgiving granite outpost connected to the continent by a narrow causeway. The camp huddled beneath a lighthouse on the most exposed portion of the island, with the surrounding rocks beaten by the harsh winds and tides of the Atlantic. Open to the ocean on one side, detainees'

tents were hemmed in by barbed wire and guards on the other. Among German troops, it would come to be known as Death Island.

Edward Fredericks, a Nama tribesman, described his experience of surrendering and being exiled to Shark Island in 1906: "We were beaten daily by the Germans, who used sjamboks [whips]. We lived in tents on the island. They were most cruel to us. Food, blankets, and lashes were given to us in plenty, and at night the young girls were violated by the guards....Lots of my people died on Shark Island. I put in a list of those who died, but it is not complete. I gave up compiling it, as I was afraid we were all going to die."[90] In time, even the chiefs among the prison population began to despair, with Nama leader Samuel Isaak telling one missionary, "These people are doomed."[91]

The medical tent at the camp was avoided by detainees; missionaries reported that sick natives did not survive treatment there. The doctor's tendency to autopsy the dead cannot have helped his reputation among the living. Other medical experiments were conducted offsite, with the severed heads of deceased Shark Island detainees used by German doctors developing race theories about the evolutionary proximity of black Africans to apes. Detainees in the camp at Swakopmund were assigned to work scraping down the skulls of the dead before specimens were shipped back to Germany.[92]

Missionaries began sounding alarm bells about the number of deaths in the Shark Island camp, making arrangements to visit. Prisoners in other camps began to get word as well. Protestant evangelist Heinrich Vedder passed along an account of one Herero man who committed suicide by tearing open his neck with his bare hands in order to avoid being sent to Shark Island.[93] The camp's apocalyptic reputation was such that it was forbidden for anyone to tell detainees where they were being sent, for fear they would revolt or escape.

When missionaries trying to save hundreds of detainees got military approval to move them from Shark Island to another camp, the governor denied the transfer specifically because the captives had been so mistreated. "Those prisoners transferred to Shark Island through trickery will not likely forget their time of imprisonment on the island any time soon," he wrote. "[If] they are let loose they will spread their stories of hate and mistrust against us."[94]

13. As belated word of von Trotha's extermination order made its way around Europe and the United States, stories appeared describing hundreds upon hundreds of skeletons found littering the desert. The German press reported demands for von Trotha's recall.[95] Meanwhile, the acting governor argued that punishment in the concentration camps was still necessary in order to ensure that the Herero "will not revolt again for generations."[96]

With the appointment of Ludwig von Estorff as the commander of the colonial army, however, Shark Island's use as a camp would soon end. Estorff had opposed General von Trotha's plan from the beginning, as well as the brutality that followed in its wake. Visiting the island to investigate, he was horrified at conditions in the camp. Yet his efforts to transfer detainees out were blocked by the colonial government. "Plans at headquarters to take women and children to the north where the climate is more wholesome have been opposed by the Administration," Estorff wrote. Not only did the government refuse his request, it made an odd attempt to justify the decision, reminding him that "Britain has allowed 10,000 women and children to die in camps in South Africa."[97]

In the end Estorff prevailed, but it was not until March 31, 1907, that the war ended and camps still holding detainees were shut down. Between the deliberate genocide in the desert and the informal one in the camps, more than sixty thousand Herero and ten thousand Nama died during the conflict in South-West Africa, reducing the Nama population by half and nearly exterminating the Herero.[98]

The legacy of concentration camps in both African colonies did not end when the barbed wire and tents disappeared. Selective memorialization of the dead reverberated in tragic ways. In ledgers compiled at the end of hostilities to account for the lives lost in the camps during the Boer War, the Dutch Reformed Church—which had both black and white members—did not even bother to include fatalities in camps for black Africans.[99]

Weeks after Emily Hobhouse's return to London in 1901, with war raging, her ally (and future prime minister) David Lloyd George spoke before Parliament, saying,

> Who would have thought when General Weyler had his concentration camps in Cuba that similar measures would be adopted within the bounds of the British Empire?...I would venture to say, looking at these 40,000 children in the camps, that we are only sowing the seeds of discontent, and that we may reap a terrible harvest some day—not perhaps this year or next year, but in time coming a nation will grow up which will remember all these iniquities.[100]

As if answering Lloyd George's question months later, with the war still under way, Milner wrote to Chamberlain, "It dawned on me personally...that the enormous mortality was not incidental to the first formation of the camps and the sudden inrush of people already starving, but was going to continue. The fact that it continues is no doubt a condemnation of the camp system. The whole thing, I now think, has been a mistake."[101]

Lloyd George proved all too correct in his assessment that the repercussions of concentration camps would be long-lived and profound. When surrender was negotiated, the British conceded on race laws in order to reconcile with defeated Boers, abandoning the rights that existed at least on paper in other colonies and fostering a hierarchy of legal distinctions that evolved into the institutionalized racism of apartheid.

At the 1913 dedication of a memorial to the dead of the camps in South Africa, Emily Hobhouse addressed race directly, asking, "Does not justice bid to remember today how many thousands of the dark race perished also in the concentration camps in a quarrel which was not theirs?" But in 1963, when the Afrikaner government published the text of her speech, Hobhouse's eulogy for the black Africans who lost their lives in the camps had been removed.[102]

The dead of the black concentration camps were erased, while the memory of Boer families who had died became a rallying call for white Afrikaner nationalism. The ritualized martyrdom of "all these iniquities"—especially the very real tragedy of wives and children lost in the camps—fed the flames of state-sanctioned race terror in South Africa until 1991.

In neighboring South-West Africa, for a brief window during the First World War, details of the Nama and Herero genocide would be mercilessly recorded by the British in an attempt to show the brutality of the Germans who were now their enemy. After shocking the world's conscience and serving its purpose in postwar territorial negotiations, however, the British blue book documenting atrocities against the Nama and Herero would be as forgotten as the black Africans who died during the Boer War.

Yet the strategy of using civilian camps in wartime would not be similarly forgotten. During the first decade of concentration camps, four empires had carried a lethal concept to three continents. Seeds of much that would unfold in the coming century had already sprouted—not just the physical manifestations of barbed wire, rotting food, and watchtowers, but the arguments supporting wholesale detention for purposes of protection, reeducation, or extermination. The bureaucracy and the brutality of the camps would soon blossom on a scale that could hardly be imagined. First, however, the world would find a way to forget just how lethal the first concentration camps had been.

CHAPTER THREE

The First World War and the War on Civilians

1. WHEN AUSTRIAN ARCHDUKE FRANZ Ferdinand was shot point-blank in the neck on June 28, 1914, news of his assassination rico-cheted from Sarajevo across Europe before nightfall. In the ballroom of a Parisian amusement park that evening, painter Paul Cohen-Portheim asked an influential count what he thought was going to happen next. "Why should anything happen?" replied the count, looking surprised. Cohen-Portheim felt relief. The man was known to be close to Emperor Franz Joseph. If nothing came of the assassi-nation, he could still take his annual vacation to England.[1]

It was possible to believe on June 28 that the archduke's death would have few repercussions, but by the end of July that illusion had disintegrated. After several weeks painting the cliffs of Devon-shire and avoiding newspapers, Cohen-Portheim traveled to Lon-don, where he discovered that Serbia and his native Austria were at war. He considered withdrawing the money he had deposited at the local branch of his German bank, but tellers there assured him that talk of broader war was foolishness. After a few days spent with friends on the outskirts of the city, he returned to find that his bank could no longer make payments in England. His funds had effectively vanished.[2]

After Germany entered the fray, declaring war on Russia on August 1, Cohen-Portheim joined a crowd trying to enter the German consulate, hoping for safe passage home. A diplomat stepped from the doorway to say that two ships had been chartered but would carry only military reservists—everyone else was out of luck. Cohen-Portheim was stranded in London with only £10 on which to live.

On August 4, just over a month after the assassination, Britain declared war on Germany. Parliament passed the Aliens Restriction Act the next day, requiring every foreigner born in Germany and Austria-Hungary to register with the police. Overnight, Cohen-Portheim had become an enemy alien. He visited one local police station, only to be sent on to another, where they were not yet sure what to do with him. Making a trip to the still-neutral American embassy, which was handling communications with Germany, he found that it, too, could do nothing to help.

After avoiding news for weeks, Cohen-Portheim suddenly could not get enough of it, reading newspaper after newspaper. It became apparent that the police station he had visited had failed to give him a registration card, which would have more fully informed him about his new, restricted life. He learned that he was not allowed to send letters to his family. He could not travel without permission more than five miles from his registration site. He could not own a camera, a car, an airplane, a motorcycle, or a carrier pigeon.[3] He was further forbidden naval and military maps, clandestine signaling devices, guns, and ammunition, along with other items he learned about well after he had unintentionally violated several of the new rules.

Though vague on the behavior expected of enemy aliens, he felt his new pariah status acutely. "Everybody felt something extraordinary was expected from him," he wrote in his memoir. "But no one—except the soldiers—quite knew what to do in order to show his devoted patriotism."[4] Cohen-Portheim was haunted by the story of a waiter who committed suicide after discovering that he had been born in Germany.

For years, British papers had sounded the alarm about nefarious Germans, and in the eyes of many, registration of enemy aliens did little to settle the issue. "Does signing his name take the malice out of a man?" cried the *Daily Mail*.[5] As early as 1909, the press had reported (entirely imaginary) zeppelin sightings on the British coast and warned of the threat posed by an expanding German navy. Newspaper magnate Lord Northcliffe, owner of both the *Daily Mail* and the *Times* of London, further stoked the fear of invasion, warning that German waiters and barbers lurked at the heart of a hidden spy network.[6]

During the first month of the conflict, reports of German atrocities in Belgium and France exploded into headlines, with stories of prisoners of war lined up before firing squads, children bayoneted, and 850 civilians executed in reprisals at Liège.[7] While some members of Parliament expressed outrage that so few aliens had been rounded up on the home front, government ministers urged restraint. "To arrest all aliens wholesale irrespective of their guilt or innocence," declared Lord Chancellor Viscount Haldane, "was a policy as inhuman as it was inefficacious."[8]

Even though he was at liberty, Cohen-Portheim found himself in an untenable position. Widespread animosity toward Germans strained his London connections. Invited to join two friends in the countryside at Surrey, he managed to get permission to travel only as a result of the influence of their father. He stood by as one companion—a delicate art enthusiast—enlisted in the military. Months later the young man became an officer, only to die in battle at Flanders that fall. When the second friend was killed in action weeks later, Cohen-Portheim knew he had to leave Surrey.

Asking for a loan for living expenses from an acquaintance, he returned to London. Hotels were too costly as a long-term solution, but he had no idea where he would be allowed to stay. He wondered whether the war could last as long as Christmas, and if so, how he would manage to get by. He looked into sailing to America but was denied permission to leave. Police interrogations about his finances, his employment, and his intentions became more and more humiliating. Most of his friends were in the army or already dead. After zeppelins began to fly over London, reprisals against German people and shops began. With nowhere to go and no one to talk to, he had a mental breakdown.[9]

2. Recovering in a nursing home, Cohen-Portheim was offered paid work by a Russian acquaintance, and his outlook improved. But on May 7 of the following year, the German submarine *U-20* torpedoed the British ocean liner *Lusitania,* sinking it in eighteen minutes. Because there was time to launch only a handful of lifeboats, more than a thousand civilians died.

Anti-German riots flared up across the British Empire, from Johannesburg to Melbourne, erupting in three dozen neighborhoods in London alone. Looters ransacked German pubs and bakeries, stomping the daily bread and causing shortages the next day; children carted away stolen goods in wheelbarrows; windows were broken, dishes handed over to onlookers, pianos and harmoniums burned. In Liverpool, police took Germans into protective custody. The riots gave hard-liners the chance to declare that mass internment was in the interest of enemy aliens themselves.

Yet the question of foreign civilians in wartime was not a new problem. Jurist William Blackstone had defined the term "alien enemy" in his landmark *Commentaries on the Law of England* in 1766. Summing up centuries of British common law, he wrote, "When I mention these rights of an alien, I must be understood of alien friends only, or such whose countries are in peace with ours; for alien enemies have no rights, no privileges...during the time of war."[10]

As part of a controversial set of Alien and Sedition Acts, the United States had created its own Alien Enemies Act in 1798, authorizing the apprehension, arrest, or removal of male enemy aliens over the age of fourteen. Seen as a political cudgel used against immigrants, three of the four acts expired or saw portions repealed during Thomas Jefferson's presidency. But the Alien Enemies Act remained on the books.

By 1914 anti-alien groups in Europe and America had spent decades promoting peacetime legislation aimed at curtailing foreigners' rights. In the wake of organized attempts to connect immigrants with crime, the passage of the Alien Act of 1905 in England had allowed the government to refuse entry to immigrants deemed undesirable, from the destitute to anyone perceived as a threat to the public good.[11]

Tottenham, in North London, witnessed an armed robbery by Bolsheviks in 1909. After the city's East End became the scene of a shootout in 1911 during an attempted jewel heist by Latvian revolutionaries, immigrants were indelibly linked in the public mind to political violence, which occasionally led to anti-alien hysteria.[12]

The British popular press had likewise made use of language of degeneracy, dishonor, and disease to frame the risk posed by immigrants, often Jewish ones. Reporting on "anti-Jewish riots" in South Wales in 1911, Hilaire Belloc wrote, "It is an unfortunate but unquestionable fact that everywhere a sort of Jew presents himself to the public view, not only as an oppressor of the poor, but what is more intolerable, an alien oppressor."[13]

Once war was under way, anti-alien rhetoric escalated. *The Scottish Field* asked, "Do Germans have souls?" Whatever the correct answer, the paper suggested, "Our children's children will still look upon Germans as belonging to an accursed race, a race that stinks in the nostrils of every human being who understands the meaning of honour."[14]

Physically isolating aliens as a solution to political crisis played into other leading ideas of the day. Public health and eugenics, two young fields—one legitimate, one pernicious—preoccupied themselves with hygiene and degeneracy. The fear of moral or physical corruption spread by foreigners leading to national decline folded into nationalist sentiment, sealing the fate of enemy aliens.

From the beginning of the First World War, warring nations had paired their own statutes or customary law with the Hague Conventions to arrest individual enemy aliens suspected of spying. But virulent propaganda on both sides exacerbated existing anti-alien sentiment, resulting in calls for vast, unprecedented internment.

Pressured by Parliament to detain all enemy aliens, British home secretary Reginald McKenna initially resisted, saying he would proceed under the Hague articles, in which the military was responsible for deciding whom to arrest. Internment, he noted, was traditionally reserved for enemy aliens who were military personnel or a danger to the nation, not the mass of foreigners from whom "there is less risk than there is from the ordinary bad Englishman."[15]

After the *Lusitania*'s sinking however, the political will to insist that not all enemy aliens were suspect vanished. The existing law, meant to address spies and soldiers who happened to be in a country when war broke out, would soon be wielded against civilians.

3. Less than a week after the *Lusitania*'s destruction, the government announced that all male enemy aliens of military age would be rounded up, with plans to intern them in a camp on the Isle of Man. Cohen-Portheim had heard that Afrikaner women and children had been detained in harsh conditions by the British during the Boer War and that these concentration camps had been seen "as a cruel expedient." Hoping that the new camps would not resemble their forerunners too closely, he assured himself that "at present no doubt internment meant something quite different."[16]

At that point, no one seemed to have any idea what mass internment would involve—when it would start, how it would work, or how long it might last. Cohen-Portheim returned to his local police station to ask about the new policy and was told that for the time being, no one was planning to arrest him.

On May 24, a detective visited and told the painter to turn himself in at the police station at 10 a.m. the following day. Asked what prisoners should bring, the officer said, "I would pack as if you were going for a holiday."[17] Cohen-Portheim filled two trunks in the hope that he would be gone a few days at most. In the morning, his last friend in London accompanied him as far as the courtyard of the police station, then said goodbye.

Inside, he learned he would be sent to Stratford, which he assumed to be Stratford-upon-Avon. He received permission to ride there in a taxi with three other detainees and discovered that the government had a different Stratford in mind: a district in the eastern suburbs of London. He arrived in the East End to see a thousand German and Austrian men of fighting age squatting together in an open hall under a bombed-out glass roof. Given a metal disc bearing his prisoner number, Cohen-Portheim was relieved to learn he would have to stay there only one night.

Straw mattresses covered cot frames, and there was nowhere safe to put belongings. Those who wanted to go to the bathroom had to raise their hands like children. A guard rifled through his sketchbook and kept it. Soon it was evening and the lights were extinguished. He lay in the dark, feeling queasy and watching the shadows move.[18]

At 6 a.m., armed guards marched the new prisoners through the streets of London to the train station. Crowds lined their path, spitting, hurling objects, and shouting about "Huns" and "baby killers." At the station, the prisoners' nightmare suddenly reversed. They boarded a comfortable train to the coast that provided a good meal served by friendly civilian waiters. On arrival, soldiers took over again, ordering them onto a steamer, where they were locked into the hold standing upright while they sailed across the Irish Sea to Knockaloe Internment Camp on the Isle of Man, which would eventually hold more than twenty-three thousand enemy aliens.

Approaching Knockaloe in darkness, Cohen-Portheim saw a bright chain of arc lights on a hill, illuminating barbed-wire fences that reached as high as eighteen feet. Thousands of inmates crowded inside the wire out of boredom, hazing new arrivals by imitating their British tormenters: *Huns! Baby killers!* Stepping through the outer gate, he saw expanses of open space on his left, with groups of wooden barracks on his right. Each block of barracks held one thousand men surrounded in its own barbed-wire perimeter, with five blocks to a camp and five camps in all. As he entered Camp Two, Cohen-Portheim's feet sank into muddy clay. He surrendered the metal disc with his prisoner number and hoped for an end to the war.

4. The internment of enemy aliens during the First World War launched a vast social experiment. On foot, by boat, and by train, foreigners were herded first into defunct jails, abandoned amusement parks, or children's holiday camps never intended for use in winter. They slept in cabins, hastily built barracks, and bell tents in the middle of nowhere. Newly constructed camps were filled before they were finished. Existing buildings had barbed-wire emplacements mounted atop perimeter walls. Armed guards manned watchtowers. People not suspected of criminal behavior found themselves suddenly subject to military measures and discipline.

The experience of mass internment during the First World War detailed by Cohen-Portheim was multiplied hundreds of thousands of times around the globe. In November 1914, Germany moved to arrest all British, French, and Russian men between the ages of seventeen and fifty-five, and by war's end was holding more than 111,000 enemy aliens.[19] During the same period, France interned 60,000 German and Austro-Hungarian civilians; Bulgaria rounded up more than 14,000 Serb and Croatian noncombatants; and Romania held 6,000 civilians, mostly Germans and Austro-Hungarians.[20]

The British decision to intern enemy aliens throughout the empire triggered global reciprocity. Camps sprang up everywhere. In October 1914, enemy aliens in South Africa were divided by gender, the men housed in military camps with prisoners of war and women and children billeted as refugees. The same year, Slavic miners were sent to live in tents in Rottnest Island, off the coast of Australia, and forced to cook their food over open fires. Turks making a pilgrimage to Mecca in 1915 faced arrest on arrival, followed by internment in British camps in Egypt. French and British civilians in Jerusalem that year were interned in hotels and designated as hostages to be executed, three for every Ottoman subject killed by bombing. Fortunately, the threat was never carried out.[21]

After joining the war in April 1917, the United States would proceed with some restraint in the matter of mass detention, its ambassadors to London and Berlin having already witnessed the dangers of hasty internment. The Alien Enemies Act of 1798 still gave President Woodrow Wilson authorization to decide the fate of foreigners in wartime, and the by now familiar restrictions on items such as weapons, cameras, and radios were imposed. Draconian measures were implemented to sharply curtail civil liberties in other arenas—a new Sedition Act was passed, and an Espionage Act accompanied it, authorizing repression of all political dissent as well as surveillance of any individual suspected of being disloyal.

Despite a German-speaking population of more than two million people at the start of the war, only 10,000 initial arrests were made, leading to individual interviews and the detention of slightly more than 2,300 enemy aliens, nearly all Germans.[22] Twenty-two-year-old future FBI director J. Edgar Hoover, just months out of law school, honed his skills detaining civilians at the helm of an Enemy Alien Registration unit.[23]

5. In 1899 and again in 1907, diplomats at the Hague Conventions had attempted to agree on rules of civilized warfare, from the launching of explosives out of balloons to the use of poison gas. The Geneva Conventions held in 1864 and 1906 focused on improving conditions for wounded soldiers, sailors, and the personnel treating them. Ironically, those early attempts to think through humanitarian standards for combatants ended up doubling as the benchmark for a class of prisoners the agreements had failed to envision in any substantive way: civilians.

As diplomats negotiated improvements to the conditions of

detention, Red Cross representatives worked alongside neutral countries as go-betweens for belligerents, forwarding millions of parcels, tens of millions of letters, and trying to broker prisoner exchanges. Across the next century, the Red Cross would find itself perpetually trying to address harsh conditions in both civilian and POW camps without endangering their future access to prisoners. During the First World War, Red Cross officials visited more than five hundred camps in thirty-eight countries.[24] Wartime reports by individuals and member organizations archived at International Red Cross headquarters in Geneva sometimes provide specific names and prisoners to search for; more often they relate generally bad conditions or reports of stories of mistreatment by guards.[25]

During the first months of the conflict, German soldiers executed thousands of civilians in Belgium and France, but they soon turned to more conventional warfare as the two sides dug in. "By and large, civilian massacres did not make their way into the enemy alien camps of the First World War. Which is not to say that there were no incidents of overt violence against civilian detainees—five unarmed prisoners had been shot dead in the mess hall at Douglas Alien Detention Camp on the Isle of Man early in the war, leading to a government inquiry.[26] But in most enemy alien camps of the First World War, detainees were at greater risk of mental illness or malnutrition than they were of execution at the hands of the detaining power.

6. The morning after his arrival at Knockaloe Internment Camp in May 1915, Cohen-Portheim listened to the camp commandant's assurances that prisoners would be treated with kindness and consideration—which made his heart rise briefly. But if they tried to escape, the commandant added, they would be shot. Prisoners then learned that latrines had not been built yet, but it was hoped they would be finished soon.[27]

Knockaloe would not see the kind of disease that had plagued the first generation of concentration camps, due in part to the public health improvements made in the planning phases by Lieutenant Colonel H. W. Madoc, chief constable of the Isle of Man. Madoc, who had served in the Boer War and witnessed the tragedy of its camps firsthand, made a deliberate attempt to avoid the unsanitary and lethal conditions that had developed in Southern Africa after poor campsite selection and construction.

During the winter, temperatures at Knockaloe would become unforgiving, but that summer, prisoners could lie on a grassy hill and stare at the sky. In a camp with no adults over fifty or under eighteen, and no women at all, detainees had to appear only for morning and evening roll call. Cohen-Portheim was prepared to make the best of circumstances for the week or two he thought might reasonably pass before his release.

As prisoners settled in and their belongings arrived, he found that the first of two trunks he had packed had disappeared. He managed to retrieve the second one, but it contained only the holiday gear he had optimistically packed: bathing attire, evening wear, and white flannel suits. He began to wear the white suits regularly, to the amusement of fellow internees.

The lack of individual identity as a prisoner felt far worse to him than the loss of freedom; he would maintain a sense of himself however he could. He used his little remaining money to acquire two nails to hang his clothes on and two boards for a headrest.

Cohen-Portheim's lot improved further when he discovered that he could receive not just letters from home, but small sums of money. An economic hierarchy developed overnight, with some detainees hiring themselves out as servants to others. Class division reared its head again when those with funds were allowed to request transfer to a "gentlemen's camp," at Wakefield, in West Yorkshire. Hearing of better conditions there, Cohen-Portheim signed on.

After another march of some miles, a train ride, and a steamer to Liverpool, the "gentlemen" were loaded into Black Maria police vans. A fellow detainee who seemed to have prior experience riding in a Maria began to compare notes with him as Cohen-Portheim tried to elude conversation. Climbing out of the vans, they were met again by an angry crowd in the street before being loaded onto another train. Prisoners discussed how Lofthouse Park, the estate at Wakefield, would provide individual rooms for them. Someone had read in a newspaper that it had a golf course.

Disembarking from the train, they were walked through the streets, this time with no hazing. They climbed a hill and found more barbed wire and a gate—the very recognizable symbols of a concentration camp. Then they caught sight of the Lofthouse Park mansion, which was just as advertised but tucked away on the other side of the fence.

Cohen-Portheim had taken a chance and switched camps, only to wind up with the same dirty, cramped quarters, the same boredom, the same omnipresent barbed wire—and rations that were cut and cut again as the war dragged on. But at Wakefield, the gentlemen's camp where he would spend almost three years, he was expected "to pay ten shillings a week for the privilege" of being a prisoner.[28]

7. For every four Paul Cohen-Portheims navigating internment in England, one Englishman was undergoing a parallel experience in Germany.[29] Israel Cohen, a British-born stringer covering Berlin for the *Times* of London and the *Manchester Guardian,* likewise failed to foresee how the archduke's assassination would rope nation after nation into a larger conflict. He, too, went on a rural holiday assuming the matter would soon be resolved, only to find himself stranded when war broke out.[30]

If the British were obsessed with German espionage, Cohen found that German paranoia was focused instead on Russian spies, which he discovered when he was mistaken for one and arrested. After proving his nationality he was released, but when he tried to register as an enemy alien at his local precinct, he was handed a set of prison clothes and put in detention with other stunned civilians. They passed the days writing influential Berlin acquaintances to ask for help and speculating how long the war would last. Six months, Cohen hazarded, but his cellmates could not imagine surviving that long.

Released a second time through the intervention of a representative of the War Office, Cohen was told to report to his police station every third day. He sensed, however, that his freedom would not last long. After Britain rounded up several thousand Germans in its colonies and rumors of British abuses began to circulate, Germany followed suit in November, issuing a general order for the detention of all British subjects between the ages of seventeen and fifty-five. As with the development of concentration camps in Southern Africa near the turn of the century, the British again led the way, with Germany once more following suit—this time not out of inspiration, but in retaliation.

An officer appeared at Cohen's door the next day and placed him under arrest. He handed the officer a cigar and took his time packing and eating breakfast, leaving the newcomer to reassure the distraught landlady that her lodger might be held only a few days. Cohen, however, suspecting that fate would not be so kind a third time, packed books and writing materials along with his belongings. As they walked to the police station, the detective reminded him, "You have only your own Government to thank for this."[31]

Like his double in England, Cohen had to share the cost of a group taxi ride from the police station to deliver himself to his own internment. After a brief stop at Stadtvogtei Prison, where he had been held before, he was brought out with his possessions, lined up with other detainees in rows of four, and marched through the streets of the city under armed guard, with soldiers beating stragglers to keep the lines moving.[32] They made their way to a train at the Alexanderplatz station, which deposited them a short march away from a former racetrack outside Berlin. They had arrived at Ruhleben concentration camp.

Lined up inside a walled compound next to redbrick stables, the detainees were lectured by their commandant. He hit on the familiar refrain blaming the British government for being the first to turn to mass detention of aliens, but he also reminded guards that the men before them were not criminals. Prisoners were assigned to rooms on the ground floor, box stalls in the stables or cramped quarters on straw in the hayloft. Cohen found himself bunking in a stall with three other men.

Several times a day, detainees had to line up for roll call or announcements. Postcards in pencil were permitted, and prisoners who felt they were held in error were invited to submit petitions for their release—which were universally rejected. Alcohol, cards, and smoking in the barracks were forbidden. Sharing one spoon among four bunkmates, the detainees ate their soup, drank their thin cocoa, and used any money they had to buy additional food at the camp canteen. Prisoners kept flooding in, from Munich, from Hamburg, all with stories of their arrests and rude or kind treatment from soldiers.

A week into internment, the commandant summoned detainees and asked Jews to step forward. Cohen did, though many whom he knew to be Jews did not. The assembled Jewish contingent was asked who among them would like kosher meals, because the head of a kosher soup kitchen wanted to feed those who wished to remain observant. Some seventy Jews took up the offer and found themselves segregated from the main prisoner population and taken back to the railway station. Several men who had not declared themselves Jewish were involuntarily exiled by other detainees. When the sleeping quarters at the railway station proved insufficient and the poorly stored food gave the detainees diarrhea, they were taken back to Ruhleben, where they were exiled to the hayloft of a separate barracks with even more crowded quarters and worse conditions.

Israel Cohen was dismayed by life at Ruhleben, yet he was in some ways fortunate. Enemy aliens from the East, mostly Russian-Polish seasonal workers exempt from alien camps, were instead assigned to forced labor.[33] Thousands of Ukrainians in Canada were similarly detained and required to work on infrastructure in Alberta. Equally unlucky were tens of thousands of industrial workers in France, women deported far from their homes to agricultural labor and forced to undergo regular gynecological examinations as suspected prostitutes.[34]

Still, a concentration camp at a racetrack in Berlin was bad enough. "Tragedies are being slowly and secretly enacted behind the brick walls and barbed wire fence of Ruhleben," Cohen wrote, "tragedies that will never be known beyond the immediate circle of those whom they concern—of men torn from their families, reft of their livelihood, and tormented daily by gnawing anxiety about the future struggle for which physical privation and mental depression are rendering them more and more unfit."[35]

The still-neutral American ambassador to Germany, who had been functioning as a go-between for London and Berlin, pressed for access to the camp at Ruhleben. Permitted entry, he outraged his German hosts by denouncing the "inhuman conditions under which the prisoners were compelled to live."[36] He arranged for a doctor to visit, who analyzed the caloric intake of the detainees and declared it a "starvation diet." A German doctor concurred with some of the findings, pressuring the government to improve conditions.

Israel Cohen was released in June 1916 as part of a midwar prisoner exchange. But his fellow Cohen, Paul Cohen-Portheim, whose experiences had at many points mirrored his own, remained stuck at Wakefield in England. He spent two more years in the gentlemen's camp as the war wore on.

8. There and elsewhere, a strange balance of mediated negotiations over enemy alien detention began to evolve, in which each country wanted to preserve the right to denounce others for atrocities and mistreatment of prisoners. In this way, an accepted global repetoire of detention policies emerged for how to humanely lock up innocent civilians.

Under international law, a bureaucracy of detention flourished to administer the camps. Hague Convention Article Five authorized internment of prisoners in a town, fortress, camp, or other location, but stated that they could "only be confined as an indispensible measure of safety." Article Fourteen required prisoner of war information bureaus to identify and track all prisoners, which was taken to include internees. At the heart of internment conditions sat a portion of Article Seven, which required prisoners of war to "be treated as regards board, lodging, and clothing on the same footing as the troops of the Government which has captured them."

In the first decade of concentration camps, civilian detention had been used within a single country at a time, sometimes in just one or two contested regions. During the First World War, the idea of reconcentration was unhitched from battlefield strategy and spread across the world. Individual countries still had camps, but imperial powers developed networks of detention managed globally, based on fears of spies and conspirators and fifth columnists.

Most camps were established away from front lines—many of them thousands of miles from combat zones. The establishment of camps predominantly outside contested territory resulted in reduced disease, few deaths, and no mass fatalities.

European powers had resurrected and reinvented concentration camps. They no longer had to rise out of the local chaos of warfare, but instead represented a deliberate choice to inject the framework of war into society itself. Previous conflicts had not been entirely without civilian prisoners, but away from the front, even enemy soldiers had often been released on parole or deported after vowing not to engage in war-related activity. But in an era of total war and widespread conscription, it was understood that any male of fighting age was a potential soldier. Generals worried that able-bodied foreigners deported to their home country one day might show up on the battlefield the next.

Yet even when correctly implemented, anti-alien statutes sometimes worked against their stated goals. Pro-internment newspapers in England noted the arrests of Prussian Poles along with German and Austrian subjects. Prussian Poles were technically enemy aliens who fit the provisions of the law; however, they belonged to a region rebelling against the German Empire and were allied with the British war effort. The British press began using the phrase "technical enemy aliens," clarifying that the internment they had called for was not supposed to include people who had taken a stand against Germany. To address the problem created by wartime alien laws in the United States, a special "Slavic Legion" regiment was formed for immigrants from areas like Yugoslavia and Czechoslovakia, which had resisted enemy rule.[37]

Frontline belligerents such as France and Germany faced additional challenges. As the same territory was lost and regained again and again during the war, questions arose about where the sympathies of a given town or village lay, and to what degree residents were inclined to sabotage the current occupying force. Rumors of franc-tireurs, Belgian and French irregular saboteurs and snipers, haunted invading German forces. Noncombatants near the front lines were badly treated by both sides, facing some of the worst conditions of the war.

On the whole, internees knew that a concentration camp offered relative safety compared to life in the trenches. But internment had its price. Even in places where they had spent decades as part of the community, foreigners' businesses were ransacked or shuttered, their assets seized by governments. Internees slept in floating prison ships, tents, huts, converted factory floors, barracks, horse stalls, jail cells, and hotels, often in overcrowded conditions. Not all these locations featured barbed wire, but it remained the defining symbol of the camp experience. Also now standard were at least two roll calls a day, which in the larger camps sometimes went on endlessly until everyone was accounted for. Internees were not soldiers but a new kind of low-grade hostage. Not expected to fight or die, they only endured.

9. Enemy alien internment marked the next step in the evolution of concentration camps, but enemy aliens were not the only civilian detainees during the First World War. The fog of war and martial

law accompanying it gave cover to other innovations in detention. Britain launched a parallel detention system for suspected Irish terrorists, and the Ottoman Empire used camps as part of organized genocide against its Armenian citizens. In both radically different cases, wartime powers provided legal justification for disturbing domestic policies.

In the midst of war in Europe—one that was not going particularly well for Britain in 1916—the Irish Republican Brotherhood took up arms in the Easter Rising and declared independence from the United Kingdom. After six days of fighting and nearly 500 deaths, the rising was put down. With chaos in Dublin, plans to arrest 50 to 100 people were scuttled, and police and army conducted broad sweeps instead. Mass arrests followed, netting some 3,500 suspects, half of whom were sent to internment in England.[38]

Under the Defence of the Realm Act, Irish detainees were sent to Frongoch internment camp. For lack of a better way to hold suspects not slated for trial, the men were detained on the same basis as enemy aliens, guarded in concentration camps run by the army but under the control of the British Home Office.[39] A significant number of these detainees had had nothing to do with the Easter Rising.

Held together without trial for eight months, the leadership organized a cadre of future republicans among their fellow inmates, earning Frongoch a nickname as the "University of Revolution." In addition to political indoctrination of those who were willing, prisoners conducted "lectures, lessons in Irish, dancing, chemistry, architecture and other scientific subjects."[40]

In the wake of World War I, as the Irish again declared independence, the British would use Ballykinlar internment camp in Ireland to hold thousands of prisoners suspected of affiliation with the Irish Republican Army. Brutal auxiliary police tactics paired with extended internment became fixtures of the response to bombs and rumors alike, while Irish detainees fought their captors using hunger strikes and writs of habeas corpus challenging their detentions as illegal. As early as 1921, members of Parliament began to argue over whether camps for the Irish were resurrecting the ghosts of the Boer War by imprisoning women and children.[41] British internment of Irish republicans would nonetheless persist for most of the century, and would be cited decades later as providing a model for other countries turning toward extrajudicial detention for domestic radicals.[42]

Although the vast majority of civilian detention between 1914 and 1919 occurred without the mass mortality that resulted from the early camps, concentration camps had not left behind their brutal roots. They were still more than capable of adopting harsher measures. During the First World War, the Ottoman Empire debuted a strategy that would turn out to be shorter-lived than British tactics in Ireland but far more lethal, using camps to hasten the extermination of its Armenian population.

By the time the Great War had begun, the Ottoman Empire had hemorrhaged much of its territory, with Romania, Serbia, Bulgaria, and Montenegro all gaining independence. Millions of Muslims fleeing lost territories swamped the remaining empire and presented an ongoing and intractable refugee crisis.

The roots of this crisis, however, went further back than the influx of refugees. A minority Armenian population had long been part of the Ottoman Empire, living in eastern Anatolia and in Constantinople amid Muslims, Greeks, and Jews. Each non-Muslim group, including Armenians, possessed second-class citizenship. Assigned by law to wear specific colors of clothing, they had to give way on the street to Muslims. They were subject to a mix of secular and sharia law, and their homes could not be taller than those of their Muslim neighbors.[43] Still, a subset of Armenians had managed to thrive financially and culturally, becoming a visible target on which opponents could focus the envy of those less fortunate.

This local resentment and government-stoked racism fused in the late nineteenth century and, in response to an Armenian tax revolt, exploded in a series of massacres. Accounts of people burned alive, raped, and murdered—some eight thousand people in a forty-eight-hour period—set the stage for three years of massacres, some eighty thousand dead, and greater bloodshed to come. Sporadic mass killings led to an agreement in early 1914 in which two non-Turkish inspectors general were sent to observe conditions in eastern Anatolia, where the majority of Armenians lived. Once the Great War began, however, the Armenian Reform Agreement was voided.

In April 1915, thousands of politicians, teachers, writers, doctors, bankers—the leading voices of the Armenian community around the country—were rounded up and taken to prison without warning. Afterward, exile and executions began again in earnest, and expanded exponentially. Civilians at Musa Dagh on the Mediterranean Sea managed to hide outside town for more than a month until they could be rescued by a French ship, but a majority of residents elsewhere were exterminated or sent southward. A month into the killings, the French, British, and Russian governments issued a joint declaration, listing sites of massacres—including one hundred villages near the town of Van—and stating that they would hold Turkey directly responsible for crimes "against humanity and civilization."[44]

Blaming Armenian conscripts for a brutal early defeat in battle against Russia, the government had invented an imaginary "military necessity" for ethnic cleansing of the region. As the slaughter continued, women, children, and the elderly were driven out of their homes and off their land, pressed into forced marches toward the Syrian desert. There, military escorts herded them into holding camps away from sustenance or salvation and held them until death.

En route to these "relocations," as the government called the process, Armenians were at the mercy of soldiers and civilians alike, robbed of their possessions and even their clothing. In the camps, they suffered additional torture, rape, and murder. The majority of the relocated who did not die through other means were exterminated in 1916.

Four months after being forced from her home, Elise Habogian

Taft arrived at the camp of Katma with her family, where she found death omnipresent:

> After the rains finally stopped, father and I left our tent in search of drinking water. The sight before me was horrible beyond description. Hundreds and hundreds of swollen bodies lay in the mud and puddles of rain water, some half-buried, others floating in rancid pools, together with rotted bodies and heaps of human refuse accumulated during the week-long rain. Some victims — only the upper torso emerging from the mud and puddles — were breathing their last. The stench rose to the heavens. It was nauseating beyond belief. The scene was like a huge cesspool laid bare and made to stink even more under a hot sun. Just being there made me sick, and I asked father to take me back to our tent. There was no chance of finding safe drinking water.[45]

Armin Wegner, a German soldier and medic stationed along the Baghdad railway during the war, witnessed the human exodus and the spectacle of death. He took photographs of the devastation near Der-el-Zor, in a landscape of sun-blistered earth and blankets propped by sticks masquerading as tents. In them, families with nothing at all doze on the open ground, their clothes already worn ragged. A man searches a child's head for lice. Skeletal children lie down to die in the dirt. Small corpses are scattered along a gutter outside a town wall. A toddler squats next to the naked remains of a murdered man. Horrified by what he was seeing, Wegner took hundreds of photos of camps and convoys, smuggling supporting documents and images to the outside world until his own arrest and detention by German forces at the request of the Turkish command.

Two dozen concentration camps in what is today Syria and Iraq served as holding pens for the dying and the dead as they were marched deeper into the desert.[46] Though the Turkish government claimed that the deaths were an unfortunate result of the war, historical evidence shows that the root cause of the tragedy lay in ethnic cleansing and a desire to expropriate the wealth of a community seen as benefitting at the expense of Turks. After the genocide, Minister of the Interior Talaat Pasha asked US ambassador Henry Morgenthau for a list of Armenians who had taken out life insurance policies with American companies. "They are all practically dead now and have left no heirs to collect the money," Talaat said. "The government is the beneficiary now." In his account of the meeting, Morgenthau wrote that he grew infuriated with Talaat, refused the request, and left the room.[47]

As former United Nations war crimes judge Geoffrey Robertson has noted of the deaths of Armenians, "There was, until the Nuremberg Charter in 1945, no international criminal law to punish the political and military leaders of sovereign states for the mass murder of their own citizens."[48] No legal mechanism existed for the victorious Allied forces to punish the Turkish government.

After the First World War, the new Turkish government tried the trio of pashas and their subordinates who had authorized violence, sentencing them to death in absentia. Three lesser officials were hanged. By the time some of the responsible parties were shipped back to Turkey to face justice, however, a new government was in place, and architects of genocide were welcomed back into positions of responsibility in a new Turkish nationalist movement. The Turkish government would undergo a miraculous transformation into a secular modern state that would last, with some tribulations, for a century, but it would also spend those years refusing to acknowledge the deaths of more than a million Armenian civilians as due to anything other than standard military measures taken during the Great War.

10. The Armenian experience was the exception in the use of concentration camps during World War I; detainees in even the worst enemy alien camps around the world did not face genocide. But for

many, the experience led to lesser but very real afflictions. By February 1918, Paul Cohen-Portheim neared the end of his third year in a British concentration camp. He had abandoned painting for writing, the extroversion of bohemian experience for the introversion of mysticism, séances, and a newfound spirituality that—despite his romantic view of his explorations in his telling—reads like a struggle to keep sane. Reading voraciously and developing an interior life, he resisted the helplessness he felt.

Others did not fare as well. In 1919 the diagnosis of "barbed-wire disease" was first offered by Swiss doctor and Red Cross observer Adolf Lukas Vischer to describe the effects of ongoing internment on civilians and combatants alike.[49] Amnesia, disorientation, and chronic anger plagued prisoners. "Try to imagine," Cohen-Portheim wrote, "though it is impossible really to understand without having experienced it—what it means, *never* to be *alone* and *never* to know *quiet*, not for a minute, and to continue thus for years, and you will begin to wonder that there was no general outbreak of insanity."[50] Despite the absence of overt abuse in most camps, the combination of monotony, unknown release date, diminishing rations, lack of privacy, sexual deprivation, and prisoners' helplessness to change their situation fostered profound mental illness among detainees. "I realized that I was no longer I, an entity," he recalled, "but a small particle of a whole, of an undesired community, called The Camp."[51]

Paul Cohen-Portheim could not later recall a single prisoner at Wakefield entirely free of mental illness, though in some cases the consequences of detention played out long after the war's end.[52] Prisoners, he wrote, "had survived the adaptation to camp life but they had not enough strength left for the second and quite as difficult adaptation to normal existence."

Distressing as internment was, people like Paul Cohen-Portheim actually were enemy aliens, the intended target of emergency legislation. And some, like "Dr. A," a Bolshevik revolutionary born in Berlin, were surely just the sort of detainee the authorities had hoped to capture. Yet others at Knockaloe had been swept up in bungled operations. "Yankee," a bunkmate without a word of German, was so obviously American his fellow prisoners were baffled at his detention. The presence of "Schulz," a Native American who knew only Spanish and had been born in Mexico, remained even more inexplicable. And an Australian nicknamed "Billie" had been waiting ten months for identity papers from home, to no avail.[53]

While some civilian prisoners were forced to work or could volunteer for paid work, many found themselves at a loss to fill their days. Internees sought to alleviate boredom in as many ways as they could imagine, and they had time to imagine almost anything. At Wakefield, Cohen-Portheim reported prisoners forming standing committees and taking up leadership positions within the camp, administering daily life "though there was very little to administer."[54]

Detainees worked to improve the barracks and space available to them with whatever resources they could find. They set up lecture series led by educated prisoners. They performed plays, with men taking the female roles. They painted pictures; they read books. They rehearsed extravagant cabaret performances for other compounds in the same camp. Heterosexual men became intimate friends and even public companions, relationships that were accepted without comment.

As regular channels of communication with the outside were established, books were donated. Camp libraries grew to thousands of volumes; technical courses meeting guidelines were approved as trade certifications. German prisoners were promised that educational courses they took would be recognized as university-level instruction by the government in Berlin. British prisoners could work toward qualification for Oxford or Cambridge upon release (and return home), and could even earn university degrees, though it is not clear how often this happened.[55] All these activities helped to pass the time, and in some cases prepared internees for the future.

Allotted a personal space of six by four feet ("a coffin is six feet by two," Cohen-Portheim noted), prisoners had no choice but to begin to build their own camp culture.[56] For those forced to live life in public, the cavalcade of activities at least served as a dressing on the open wound of endless imprisonment.

Early in the war, politicians had tried to carve distinctions between the "friendly alien" and "enemy alien," but the project of assigning loyalties to people en masse was useless. For all the businesses closed, livelihoods wrecked, families sundered, and funds dispensed to build and guard camps, mass arrests of enemy aliens in Britain provided no discernible benefit. Heading into the Great War, Germany's spy network was already crippled, with Britain quickly rounding up known agents in the first days of the conflict. Due to early arrests and trials, not one German national living in England at the start of the war was linked to wartime espionage.[57]

Of course, not every enemy alien ended up in detention during the First World War. Some among the aristocracy in Europe were spared the humiliation of concentration camps through family connections. In the United States, many enemy aliens were exempted from both detention and conscription, prompting demands that a heavy tax be assessed on those left at liberty.

Nonetheless, internment altered the lives of hundreds of thousands of foreigners around the world. In 1915, just as James Joyce began writing his masterwork *Ulysses*, his brother Stanislaus—and nearly Joyce himself—was held in Austria as a subversive for the duration of the war. In the novel, which is set in 1904, Joyce denounces the Boer War, with its "bloodboltered shambles" and its "forecast of the concentration camp."[58]

Irish nationalists loathed the British imperial project in South Africa and had written extensively against it, but it is hardly a wonder that Joyce also pointed to future camps in the novel. While he worked on that chapter of *Ulysses*, nationalists had already been remanded to detention in concentration camps after the Easter Rising.

Camps were filled with the famous and the infamous. Russian revolutionary Leon Trotsky was intercepted as he sailed from New York City on his way to Russia to greet the Bolshevik Revolution in 1917. Detained for several weeks as a political prisoner in a concentration camp in Nova Scotia, he used the time to proselytize fellow prisoners. Boston Symphony Orchestra conductor Karl Muck, a Swiss national born in Germany, found himself in Georgia directing the internment camp orchestra at Fort Oglethorpe in 1918 after accusations that he had refused to perform the American national anthem. James Chadwick, who would later win a Nobel Prize for discovering the neutron, spent years as a prisoner with Israel Cohen at the Ruhleben Camp outside Berlin. In one attempt to bridge the enmity that divided countries during wartime, Chadwick and a friend continued their research, using equipment donated by Austrian physicist Lise Meitner and German Max Planck.[59]

So it happened that individuals worldwide submitted more or less docilely to the experience of concentration camps in order to ride out their term as a socially undesirable element in a time of crisis. Widespread propaganda in use on all sides drove the message home, advancing the idea of war as the obligation of every citizen to enmity—enmity that carried over to civilians, even women and children.

Meanwhile, the specter of mass relocation and detention of native populations that had set the stage for concentration camps in the nineteenth century had not vanished. Detention and limited rights continued to haunt the periphery of laws dealing with indigenous peoples. Even before the First World War had begun, Australian states updated colonial-era laws dealing with Aborigines, allowing greater control by governing boards of nonindigenous administrators.

With many Aborigines living on reserves, at stations or in camps, these boards were given authority to set racial restrictions on marriage, assert legal custody over children, and place minors in indentured servitude.[60] Over time the boards would attempt to push indigenous populations out of towns, forcibly relocating them from one reserve to another and eventually gaining the power to detain indigenous people at will.

In 1910 at the Brungle Aboriginal Station, indigenous men who refused orders to leave were charged with trespassing. At Darlington

Point, also in New South Wales, families were threatened with loss of their children if they did not stay where they were told.[61]

In the United States, widespread eugenics movements soon provided for state-level detention of the chronically poor, the blind, the deaf, and "imbeciles." In the aftermath of the war, states began using civilian detention for social hygiene. World War I had created a template for quasi-benign internment of whole classes of people.

But the root of internment, the wartime xenophobia that sparked these innovations in detention, should not be forgotten. The Canadian town of Berlin was renamed amid rioting. German curriculum was eliminated from schools. Sauerkraut became "liberty cabbage." In the United States, paranoia led to the 1918 lynching of Robert Prager, a German immigrant. The phenomenon was so senseless and extreme that sociologist Robert Bartholomew has labeled it an incidence of mass hysteria.[62]

11. Cohen-Portheim was released in February 1918, as part of a prisoner exchange brokered by neutral Holland. While en route, he found that the arrangements for his return home had fallen through, with Germany suspecting its own people of being spies for the British.

The Dutch intended to intern the new arrivals for the time being, but by then freedom was too dear to the prisoners, who staged a nonviolent revolt and insisted on liberty within the city boundaries of Rotterdam.

Returning to Germany later that year, Cohen-Portheim found food scarce, the economy in ruins, and the country stumbling into a civil war. Given how often circumstances demonstrated his optimism to be unfounded, he proved surprisingly fair when writing about his years in British camps. His memoir *Time Stood Still* was published in 1931 to widespread acclaim, with the *New York Times* describing it as a civilian *All Quiet on the Western Front.*

An Austrian Jew, Cohen-Portheim died in 1932, a year before Hitler came to power. Of his days boarded among strangers, with no vocation, no privacy, and little hope for release, he wrote that he had somehow managed to avoid irreversible harm to himself.

But in evaluating the moral nature of the camps, he was less accommodating. If the concentration camps of the Great War had not done him permanent damage, he saw himself as the atypical patient who comes out of an epidemic healthier than before. His own good fortune, he wrote, "must not prevent me from considering a disease a disease nor induce my readers to think that I call good what in itself is evil."[63]

In the rubble of devastated Europe, however, there was little time for extended reflection on internment. The best parts of the camps—the Red Cross packages, the classes, the libraries, the orchestral performances—had normalized life in detention and made it appear harmless. A few prisoners had rioted or been shot; some had escaped. Forced labor had taken place in Canada and been widespread on the Eastern Front, but at least in sheer numbers, World War I's concentration camps could not compare to the unprecedented tragedy of the war itself, which saw millions maimed, gassed, or killed. In the wake of this vast carnage, it is perhaps no wonder that the first mass internment of enemy aliens has largely been forgotten.

In all, records from the First World War document more than 800,000 civilian internees, with hundreds of thousands more forced into brutal rural exile. Concentration camps in Britain had housed more than 32,000 enemy aliens. Canada interned more than 5,000 Ukrainian and Austro-Hungarian aliens. In Russia, foreigners from Germany, Austro-Hungary, and Turkey were exiled to villages in the far reaches of the tsar's empire, with roughly 300,000 enemy aliens deported or interned before the Bolshevik Revolution led to a separate peace early in 1918.[64]

The praiseworthy attempt to standardize and humanize internment conditions had rehabilitated the idea of concentration camps, rescuing them from their heinous colonial roots. Yet once the public had adjusted to the idea of preemptively imprisoning innocent foreigners, all that had to be done was to transfer that "foreign" danger—with the underlying fear of crime, degeneracy, and disease—and assign it to another target group. The identification of a pariah class, the registration and rules limiting conduct, followed by arrests and civilian detentions; the roll calls and prisoner numbers, the barracks, the watchtowers, the armed guards—by the end of the war, civilians everywhere had experienced it all as a seemingly necessary inconvenience in the service of a national cause.

The concept of concentration camps had been standardized, bureaucratized, and globalized. The prewar establishment of the idea that immigrants posed a danger that necessitated government control gave way to the concept of aliens as an undifferentiated group, which made it possible to see civilians everywhere as a collective threat during wartime. The idea of locking up noncombatants en masse—a concept that had been shocking twenty years before, when applied to peasants in rebellious regions of Cuba or the Philippines—became the standard approach to foreign grocers and journalists on the streets of London or Berlin. Yet none of the nations establishing the new, more humane model of concentration camp in the heart of Europe appear to have realized how flexibly detention could be applied, how dangerous modern innovation could make it, or how easily it could be weaponized.

CHAPTER FOUR

Gulag Rising

1. CANADIAN AUTHORITIES RELEASED RUSSIAN revolutionary Leon Trotsky from Amherst Internment Camp in Nova Scotia on April 29, 1917. Like other internees, Trotsky had not been charged with any crime. Unlike them, he was not even an enemy alien; he was a political prisoner. While interned—apparently at the request of the British government, which did not favor radicals—he had made life as bitter as possible for the camp commandant, a veteran of the African campaigns who routinely expressed the wish to get him alone and do him harm.

As hypnotic and incendiary in detention as he was in front of a crowd, Trotsky had spent a significant amount of his time seeing to the political indoctrination of the Germans who made up the bulk of the inmates. When public awareness of his detention in both Russia and the West ratcheted up international pressure to release him, camp administrators were furious over surrendering their prize pig. In his memoirs he would recall with delight how German sailors and workers gathered to cheer him upon his departure, while an impromptu detainee band saw him off with a revolutionary march.

It took Trotsky less than a week to cross the Atlantic and drop like a Molotov cocktail into the middle of the Russian Revolution.

The Romanov dynasty had ended in his absence, but he had no intention of letting history move forward on its own. Arriving two months after the abdication of Tsar Nicholas II, he stepped off a train in Petrograd to find a city in wobbly pandemonium and a vast crowd waiting. The bespectacled, goateed visionary was lifted up and carried through the throng.

The empire had collapsed. Fellow revolutionary Vladimir Lenin had returned from abroad, too, given special passage through Germany, where he could have been interned as an enemy alien had Berlin not been so taken with the prospect of unleashing him on Russia. At that moment, every political future was imaginable.

Sticking a thumb in the eye of the coalition government, Trotsky backed armed street demonstrations that July, which led to his arrest and detention. Months later, the Bolsheviks had better luck, pulling off a nearly bloodless coup and sending the last prime minister of the Russian Provisional Government fleeing Petrograd in a borrowed Renault.[1] Revolutionaries had seized the helm.

Amid waves of intimidation and arrests by the Bolsheviks, elections were allowed to go forward. Tallying results from across the country took weeks, and in the end, the Bolsheviks ended up with less than a quarter of the vote.[2]

By the time of the first meeting of elected representatives of the Constituent Assembly in January 1918, the Socialist Revolutionary Party, which earned the most votes in the election, had split on whether to support Bolshevik leadership. In response to political resistance by some delegates during the first sessions, Bolshevik guards locked the front doors to the assembly hall during a break, later refusing to let delegates reconvene. As the Constituent Assembly was dissolved, Russia's brief experiment in democracy ended quietly. Trotsky began to build a Red Army. Within weeks the country descended into civil war.

Trotsky's fury over his stay in a camp had not faded after his return home: he recorded all the details in *A Prisoner of the English*, a pamphlet about his time in Canada. In the heat of the Russian Civil War, as head of the army, he took the time to have the text mass-produced for the traveling libraries that went to the front with troops. His story of being put in a concentration camp with no charges and no judicial process was listed as one of the crucial documents to be made available to soldiers, along with Lenin's *Imperialism, The Highest Stage of Capitalism* and *The Communist Manifesto*.[3]

Yet his fury seemed to focus on his own detention rather than on opposition to camps themselves. In June 1918, just a year after his release from internment in Canada, Trotsky wrote a memo proposing concentration camps for a group of Czech prisoners of war who refused to disarm. The same month, he recommended establishing concentration camps in which the bourgeoisie would be "organized into rear-service battalions to do menial work (cleaning barracks, camps, streets, digging trenches, etc.)."[4] These were just the kinds of chores Trotsky had been required to perform in the camp at Amherst.

Meanwhile, the tsar's notorious Okhrana secret police force had vanished, giving way to the Cheka, which soon applied even more aggressive tactics. The month Trotsky first proposed the use of concentration camps in Russia, a three-person Cheka tribunal was appointed with the power to sentence individuals to summary detention, execution, or exile. Assassination lists were created. Swaths of the aristocracy were eliminated. The liquidation of the bourgeoisie was mandated.

Workers were the heroes of Communist ideology, but not all workers were in favor of Bolshevik rule. To address this challenge, Felix Dzerzhinsky, head of the Cheka, recategorized workers who were unhappy with the system as no longer truly workers. The solution lay, he suggested, in using concentration camps as "a school of labor" for these misfits.[5] Lenin, too, embraced the use of camps that summer against rebels south of Moscow, ordering officials to lock up "unreliable" elements "in a concentration camp outside town."[6]

After Lenin was nearly killed in an assassination attempt that fall, terror was strategically imposed. On September 5, 1918, a "Resolution on Red Terror" was issued, ordering the "safeguarding of the Soviet Republic from class enemies by way of isolating them in concentration camps."[7]

The legacy of the concentration camps of the First World War—a war that had not yet ended—was taken up and transformed. Despite their withdrawal from the conflict, the Bolsheviks were slow to release many enemy aliens interned under the tsar. The detainees provided valuable labor; some would never be permitted to return home.

As others were released, however, Russia's detention sites began to empty just as its new revolutionary leadership started to fill them with domestic enemies instead. Because the Bolsheviks immediately took a stance in favor of concentration camps, one form of civilian detention flowed into the other with no gap between them. While still detaining foreigners from the global conflict, state terror was launched to kill or imprison Soviet citizens.

Concentration camps expanded in terms of both population and numbers of sites during the Russian Civil War. Ad hoc locations such as churches and cloisters were transformed into regional camps with formal regulations. Prisoners, including the ill and hungry, were often expected to help pay their own way via labor. Civilians in communities were press-ganged on the spot into ditchdigging and road building. Alongside a traditional justice system for ordinary crimes, an alternate concentration camp system run by the secret police began to grow.

Through it all, reactionaries and radicals continued to resist. The reactionaries were killed or exiled; the radicals—anarchists and revolutionaries of various stripes—were harder to get rid of. They possessed decades of experience fighting the tsars, an experience that for many included previous stints in labor camps as they had fought to overthrow the government. The threat of camps did not cow them.

Some were icons who needed to be kept far from the world stage, where they were revered by leftists. With this in mind, officials opened camps for political prisoners in the far north, on the coast of the White Sea at Archangel. Detainees were tortured, exiled, put on trial, shot by the hundreds, and even occasionally indulged with special camp privileges in an attempt to silence international opprobrium. Yet even after their defeat in the civil war, the Russian revolutionaries who were left in camps remained a thorn in the side of the new Soviet leadership.

The Union of Soviet Socialist Republics was officially founded in December 1922. With the Cheka's dissolution the same year, there was a moment when the fledgling camp system and its extrajudicial abuses might have tapered off or ended for good. Moved to another department and effectively demoted, the former head of the Cheka was slated to run just two prisons. But the die was cast when he also managed to keep control of the special camps.[8]

In November 1923, a stroke-hobbled Vladimir Lenin signed off with Trotsky, Dzerzhinsky, and Joseph Stalin on establishing the Solovetsky Special Purpose Camp as the cornerstone of this system. Although Lenin would be dead two months later, his creation of a camp at the former monastery grounds on the Solovetsky Islands in the subarctic waters of the White Sea represented one of the most consequential edicts of his rule. Prisoners at Solovki were placed under the control of the secret police, who were assigned to develop agriculture, fisheries, and lumber harvesting industries while reeducating and rehabilitating the dissidents through work.[9]

With that decree, camps passed from being a part of the civil war to gaining a permanent foothold in Soviet society. Concentration camps were grafted onto the centuries-old tsarist tradition of penal labor and exile, nurturing a detention system unlike any the world had seen. For the first time, a new government had from its inception integrated a camp system into its institutions.

2. In the years that followed, Petrograd, formerly St. Petersburg, was renamed Leningrad. The department names for the secret police were even more frequently replaced, generating new acronyms over time—NKVD, GPU, OGPU, MVD, and KGB. It was understood by the public that both the city and the police remained essentially the same. The policemen would continue to be known as Chekists for decades to come.

Early in the morning on February 8, 1928, a Cheka agent came without warning to the Leningrad home of Dmitri Likhachev.[10] Twenty-one years old, Likhachev belonged to an esoteric association of friends called the Cosmic Academy of Sciences. After an invitation from an old classmate to join the group, he had contributed a satirical paper denouncing Bolshevik changes in Russian spelling and was awarded the academy's Chair of Melancholy Philology. When the head of the group later received a (fake) telegram from the "Pope of Rome," the secret police took notice.[11]

It was a dangerous moment to embrace an idiosyncratic group. Four years after Lenin's death, Joseph Stalin had won the struggle for succession, kicking Trotsky out of the Communist Party and exiling him to Kazakhstan. Soviet intelligence expanded domestically and abroad, and the Communist Party voted Trotsky's opposition views incompatible with membership. "Trotskyite" quickly became a hazardous label. Even apolitical associations drew suspicion.

Still, some pretense of evidence was generally required for detention. In Likhachev's case, the uniformed officer consulted his notes, walked over to a bookshelf in the study, and pulled out a volume of *The International Jew*. Automaker Henry Ford's anti-Semitic, anti-Communist opus had found an enthusiastic audience in Russia among those opposing the Red Army during the civil war, but anti-Soviet texts were no longer permitted in Stalin's Russia. Likhachev belatedly recalled a surprise visit the week before from a university acquaintance who had pored over his library.

Owning one forbidden book was pretext enough. The investigator took Likhachev away in a black Ford. Arriving at the Shpalernaya Street prison, he surrendered his watch, money, and a cross necklace, and was taken to cell 273. Over time his cellmates would include a descendant of the man who had established the tsarist prison system, a child suspected of spying, a Chinese boy, and a thief. After two days spent cleaning the cell of fungus, Likhachev was taken for questioning. The thief told him to wear his coat and pretend to be sick, a strategy that seemed to preserve him from the worst parts of the ordeal.

He spent six months in detention while agents conducted their investigation. After a single interrogation and no trial, Likhachev was one of a group of men called before the head of the prison. Sentences for detainees were read out in a solemn tone, with Likhachev receiving five years. Decades later he would remember with awe the fearlessness of a cellmate who responded with apparent impunity, asking, "Is that all? May we go?"

Likhachev's family came to the station to see him off but they were kept away by guards wielding bayonets as he was loaded into a prison car. Once inside, he was handed the things his family had delivered, as well as flowers and a cake from his university. The train headed hundreds of miles north to the port at Kem, across the White Sea from Archangelsk, where the first special camps had been. Descending from the car, Likhachev took a boot to the head as guards shouted, "Here the power isn't Soviet, it is Solovki power."[12] Detainees spent the night standing upright in a locked shed, and the next morning were loaded into the hold of a wooden steamer without adequate breathing room. Passengers who survived the forty-mile voyage stepped from the ship onto the jetty. The living were counted; the dead were carried out. They had arrived at the Solovetsky Special Purpose Camp.

At Solovki, terror had gained an address in one of the most strange and beautiful places on earth. The onion-domed kremlins of the five-hundred-year-old monastery built by Russian Orthodox monks rose high above the stone walls surrounding the complex. Ice locked in residents of the six main islands for months each winter. Forests of fir trees stood against the snow. In spring and summer, cabbages and fruit trees grew, and seals hunted fish off the omnipresent coastal rocks.

Located offshore in the northwest corner of Russia, just over a hundred miles from the Finnish border, the monastery was also a strategic asset. After dislodging Allied forces that had supported the White Army in the civil war, Soviet authorities had taken over the monastery in 1920. They sent historians to study the site and find whatever remaining treasures had not already been stolen or requisitioned during the conflict. The hunt for hidden jewels and icons would continue for years, eventually contributing to the on-site establishment of an "antireligious" museum.

The first boat carrying political prisoners arrived from the mainland in the summer of 1923. These prisoners initially received more food than other detainees and got reading material through the political Red Cross, which had long advocated for revolutionaries under the tsars. In addition, the majority of prisoners had to perform hard labor, from which the politicals were exempt.

At first, Solovki stood as a point of pride for the Soviets, public proof that they would take every opportunity to rehabilitate recalcitrant citizens into Soviet workers. But the outside world was sometimes reluctant to praise their self-proclaimed largesse. After stories circulated of hunger, disease, and the execution of six political prisoners during a protest on December 19, 1923, Solovki descended into notoriety, gaining a reputation as "the most dreaded prison in Soviet Russia."[13] A Committee for the Defense of Revolutionists Imprisoned in Russia sprang up, publishing lists of those held on Solovki to contest Soviet statements that the islands were populated only by criminals and profiteers.[14]

True believers in the Revolution found themselves excusing the new camps as a necessary evil in the march toward a better future. But even skeptics acknowledged that the horrors of life on Solovki did not look so singular in the context of Devil's Island, the penal site run by France, and the five thousand Boer prisoners of war who had been deported to Ceylon by the British. Brutal offshore detention had a long tradition. Observers did not yet realize they were looking at something very old, but also something new.

3. In Bathhouse No. 2, Likhachev and the other arrivals stripped in the cold and showered, waiting hours for their clothes to be deloused and returned. As they walked through the small stone arch of the Nikolski Gates onto the monastery grounds, the religious Likhachev

removed his hat, overcome by the solemnity of the moment. Prisoners were searched and taken to their quarters. Likhachev, who in his student cap appeared more privileged than the others, was asked to produce a ruble. He did, and suddenly space was cleared on the middle level of the bunks. Sick prisoners had rights to the top beds. On the floor underneath the bottom level lurked naked street children who stuck their hands out, pleading for bread from newcomers. Sent to Solovki for vagrancy and abandoned to their fate, they did not work, nor did they receive rations. The authorities ignored them, and each begged as long as he could before starving to death.[15]

Years into Soviet rule, concentration camps were common enough that families knew how to prepare their loved ones for extended detention. As in several earlier and later systems, prisoners were allowed to bring certain possessions along, in the perennial attempt to reduce the cost of running the camps and to prove that they were not inhumane. A bag stuffed with human hair made a good mattress for the hips if prisoners had to sleep on concrete or wood. A mug was invaluable, holding water or soup at camps where no utensils were provided. Russian camps were rarely located in temperate regions — and so Likhachev's parents had given him a child's small, soft blanket, which he spread diagonally to cover as much of his body as possible.

He was better equipped than many who arrived on Solovki, but unlike the politicals and the criminals, he had no prison experience to fall back on. A thief warned him to sleep with his boots under his head and his feet through the sleeves of his coat so no one could steal them at night.

Every batch of new arrivals spent months in quarantine company No. 13 — most of them doing brutal logging work — before some got moved to other assignments. Likhachev's prior medical evaluation earned him lighter labor duties, which were harsh enough: splitting wood, dock work, repairing machinery, carting pig manure, and pulling a loaded sled while hitched into a harness.

Joining the main camp population after quarantine, Likhachev developed a high fever and came down with typhus. He ended up fevered and delirious in a segregated sick bay, where he was robbed. After his recovery, a work pass that permitted him to exit and enter the Nikolski Gates on errands revealed Solovki's layout. He learned that the political prisoners—the self-identified anti-Soviet revolutionaries—were held behind watchtowers and barbed wire near two separate hermitages. The remaining prisoners were segregated into different sleeping quarters by company, based on their duties. He visited the refectory, the roll call grounds, the cemetery, the museum, the theater, and "the tiny room under the bell tower where executions were carried out one at a time" with a bullet in the back of the head.[16]

Despite its isolated location, Solovki contained a whole universe. It had dams and locks, a power plant, and a hospital. Some of the monks who had stayed behind trained prisoners in the still-operating creamery and bakery. As a bastion of progressive Soviet thinking, the camp was permitted a scholarly journal, internal publications, and even a newspaper sent to the outside world that garnered subscriptions across the Soviet Union.

The Soviets, eager to remove high-profile political dissidents and cultural and religious leaders who might oppose them, funneled these detainees into a small number of places, creating intellectual and political hothouses. Across the 1920s, this impulse built an unofficial university at Solovki, where Likhachev found an intellectual haven. In effect if not always intention, the establishment of the first permanent Soviet concentration camps aided prisoners in continuing a life of the mind in defiance of—or even by virtue of—their banishment from society. It was a museum of the intelligentsia.

Artistic endeavors were tolerated and even encouraged for publicity purposes, though they developed a life of their own. An internal theater allowed the production of Gorky and Chekhov plays—even *The Flea,* an adaptation by Yevgeny Zamyatin, whose dystopian novel *We* had been banned by the Soviets five years earlier. The antireligious museum logged treasures from the monastery and did substantial original research. Intellectuals on Solovki attempted to "emphasize in every way the absurd, the idiotic, the stupid, deceptive slapstick quality of everything that went on there—the foolishness of the organization and its orders, the fantastic and dreamlike nature of all the island life (a world of strange dreams, nightmares, devoid of meaning and consistency)."[17]

Yet by the time Likhachev arrived in the far north, Solovki and its subcamps had also become famous in Russia for sadistic punishment. Work in swamps and peat bogs or endless logging exhausted the starved prisoners. Those who could survive the hard labor faced arbitrary, surreal discipline. Word leaked out of torture in which naked prisoners would be tied or left on rocks to be bitten to death by swarms of mosquitoes.[18]

The punishment cells in the Sekirka Chapel, which sat atop a hill above a high and winding path of hundreds of stairs gained particular notoriety, with stories of people forced to eat their own feces, to sleep naked in the highest towers in the dead of winter, or to sit atop poles with their legs hanging down and stones tied to their ankles hour after hour.[19] Reports emerged of the near dead being doused in cold water or thrown down the long stairway to finish them off without wasting a bullet. Tales of Solovki misery were so varied and perverse that accusers faced allegations of exaggeration; however, it was widely understood that life at Sekirka often meant death.

4. On release from the sick bay, Likhachev was excused from hard labor and assigned to Krimkab, the criminology office that studied prisoner life. His fellow company members asked the commander to make him sleep in the hallway for a week, to be sure he was no longer contagious. Eventually they settled on letting him in but keeping his belongings—which had apparently already infected his doctor with typhus—in the hall.[20]

Detainees in the main cathedral slept in bunks stacked three or four high, but Krimkab company occupied smaller quarters. With five other prisoners, Likhachev shared a cell containing beds, a table, and a wooden monk's bench. A lamp lit the room until ten each night, when power was cut. At the end of the workday, smoke from prisoners' cheap *mahorka* tobacco choked the room, but at sub-arctic Solovki, keeping the windows shut against the cold took precedence over easy breathing.

Likhachev's parents requested permission from the Cheka to see him, asking for help from the Political Red Cross when they received no response.[21] Eventually they were allowed two visits a year. He passed the days writing about gambling etiquette among prisoners. He took walks with a professor of climatology who wrote down weather data on Solovki perimeter fences as they checked the grounds, without ever finding out if or how the professor relayed the information to the mainland. His former schoolmaster, also in the Krimkab, defined a psychological illness he had observed in which detainees obsessed over improving their situation, trying to gain even minute advantages over other prisoners.

They could not know it at the time, but they were witnessing a phenomenon in its infancy. In such behavior, the demeaning character of the future Gulag could be glimpsed. As Alexander Solzhenitsyn would later describe it, "A struggle for the soft cushy spots through bootlicking and betrayal was already going on."[22]

In the outside world, even before Likhachev's arrest, former prisoners had begun to point out the hypocrisy of the benign image of Solovki presented by Moscow. Boris Cederholm, a Finnish businessman arrested by the Cheka, was finally extricated by his government in 1926 after two years in detention and several weeks on Solovki.[23] His memoir *In the Clutches of the Tcheka* appeared in English in the West, describing prisoners at hard labor in freezing temperatures without clothes or utensils, starved or shot without the slightest compunction on the part of camp administrators. The US Congress began to consider a ban on imports known to be made using "convict labor," with a particular eye on Soviet lumber and matches.[24]

To counteract the denunciations, Soviet authorities sent a crew to the islands to film a documentary. Highlighting the beauty of the landscape and the elegance of the monastery, cameras featured the museum, theater, and catacombs. They visited cages filled with playful foxes, fishermen at sea, women packing herring, men tanning hides, and lumberjacks at work. Prisoners looked merry at roll call, meals were rollicking, food plentiful. The camp store had luxury items, piles of packages at the mail center reached almost to the ceiling, and there was even a Solovetsky airplane. Soldiers and Chekists played themselves, as well as "the roles of well-fed, compliant prisoners."[25] Snow and ice made the briefest of cameos. There was no violence or even a stern face. When workers' collectives on the mainland were shown the film in 1928, one viewer asked how a country could go so wrong, pampering criminals on Solovki when there were starving and unemployed citizens everywhere.[26] They had made Solovki look like a wonderland.

Still sensitive to criticism, the Soviets were often reluctant to allow unscripted outsiders in, despite the policy authorizing visits. As international denunciations of Solovki continued, they took additional steps to preempt it. In 1929 Maxim Gorky, perhaps the most celebrated Soviet writer of the day, was lured from his apartment in Italy back to Russia. Cosseted by the Communist Party, he agreed to review the great achievements of the state. Without warning, his trip to see industrial sites was derailed. Instead, he ended up on a ferry named after a Cheka leader, sailing to Solovki.[27]

Prisoners heard from the radio station that Gorky was coming. Detainees could hardly wait for him to tell the world what was happening on Solovki: "Gorki will spot everything, find out everything. He's been around, you can't fool him. About the logging and the torture on the tree stumps, the *sekirka,* the hunger, the disease, the three-tier bunks, those without clothes, the sentences without conviction...The whole lot!"[28]

Before Gorky's whirlwind visit, contingents of prisoners were hidden in the forest to lessen evidence of overcrowding. Sick patients were given new gowns to wear, and fir trees were cut down, transported, and stuck upright into the ground to make a welcome corridor along the road through the labor colony. Gorky visited the sick bay, a labor camp, and stopped in at the children's colony that had been formed since Likhachev first encountered the urchins hiding under his bunk.

Gorky asked to speak to one boy privately and stayed with him a long time. Standing outside with the rest of the crowd, Likhachev counted forty minutes on the watch his father had given him. He recounts that Gorky emerged weeping and climbed the stairway to the punishment cell at Sekirka.

Yet when Gorky's anxiously awaited piece on the trip came out, the section about Solovki was relegated to Part Five of the report, with the devastating conclusion that "camps such as 'Solovki' were absolutely necessary.... Only by this road would the State achieve in the fastest possible time one of its aims: to get rid of prisons."[29]

Through some willful or unintentional blindness on the part of one of the few people who might have protected them—it is as difficult now as it was then to see how Gorky could not have understood at least some of what he witnessed—the prisoners came to realize that no one would save them from Solovki.

Meanwhile, three sailors who had managed to escape described in detail the abuses taking place in Soviet camps. Cheka director Genrikh Yagoda sent a commission to investigate the escapes. As agents swept through the camp, a series of arrests were made. Prisoners as well as guards suspected of a variety of infractions—including "cruelty to prisoners"—were executed immediately next to an open pit outside the monastery gates, at the Sekirka, and on outlying islands.

Likhachev's parents were on the island at the time, having come for a second visit. He was sleeping with them in the room they had "rented" from a guard they paid on the ferry from Kem. Someone from Likhachev's company came to relay the news that officials had been at his cell hunting for him. He left his parents and hid in a lumberyard all night, watching the stars wheel overhead and listening to the sound of executions in the distance.[30]

The killings were a haphazard effort that fulfilled the bureaucratic impulse to be able to report to superiors that something had been done. Guards said to have abused detainees had been shot. Others who had displeased administrators were also killed. But no one came looking for Likhachev again.

5. Accusations, abuse, and execution could be the fate of any prisoner, but those on hard-labor details faced additional threats. Likhachev recalled seeing prisoners sleeping at night in open trenches that they had dug as improvised shelters. In the logging camp, one Chekist overseer bragged that prisoners were driven so hard they would sometimes resort to amputating their own hands or feet to get removed from the work detail.[31]

Likhachev laid the lethal pace of the logging work at the feet of Naftaly Frenkel, the man in charge of timber exports.[32] Arrested and sentenced to ten years of hard labor, Frenkel had arrived at Solovki in 1924 and had so pleased his superiors that he was quickly appointed a guard. He soon emerged as a driving force in the islands' transformation from an isolated concentration camp to an economic network of detention and labor, receiving early release from his prisoner status as a reward for his contributions. He aspired to making the camps profitable for the Cheka, and was notorious among detainees for a statement that Alexander Solzhenitsyn would later declare the supreme law of the Russian camps: "We have to squeeze everything out of a prisoner in the first three months—after that we don't need him anymore."[33]

Solovki's lumber production grew due to radical changes spurred by Frenkel's administrative schemes. A ferret-faced man loathed by inmates, Frenkel came to represent the mercilessness of Solovki's labor system. He is credited with the shift to a tiered ration system for food and labor, requiring prisoners to meet quotas and feeding them in proportion to the kind of work they did. During Likhachev's time on Solovki, one plan for prisoners doing heavy labor allocated a little less than two pounds of bread and three ounces of meat per day. Sick prisoners often did not get enough food to survive.

The focus on linking food rations to a prisoner's output fundamentally transformed Soviet concentration camps. The premise of using labor to reeducate problematic citizens to be part of a bright Soviet future gave way to the idea that detainees themselves represented raw materials to be consumed in building that future.

In reality, Frenkel did not invent the tiered ration system from scratch. Likewise, the shift from idealized rehabilitation to a more permanent system maximizing forced labor may have been inevitable. Stalin appeared impressed with the possibilities of detainee labor and believed in the profitability of the Solovki endeavor (despite the fact, as Anne Applebaum has noted, that Solovki required a subsidy of 1.6 million rubles in 1929—perhaps due to graft).[34]

The Communist Party, too, was convinced. The first Five-Year Plan was implemented in 1928 in the hope of accelerating Soviet industrialization and development. Prisoners would become an indispensable part of that plan, and the Solovki model for forced labor, quotas, and a sliding food ration scale would become standard everywhere.

Sealing the prisoners' fate, the Cheka met late in 1929 and proposed creation of the *Glavnoe Upravlenie Lagerei,* what would eventually be known as the Gulag. Transferring control of all the camps and their labor output to the OGPU—the current secret police—the massive new camps administration was officially inaugurated on April 25, 1930, while Likhachev was still at Solovki.

An initial work project was plotted: a 141-mile canal from the White Sea near Solovki southwest to the Baltic Sea. Despite routing the dig through two existing lakes to ease the work of excavating an eighteen-foot-wide channel, it was a staggering undertaking and was slated to be completed in just two years.

With the first Five-Year Plan under way, even larger projects loomed. In 1929, a new part of the plan was added, and individual farms were swallowed by agricultural collectivization. Russian peas-

ants and farmers suffered wrenching changes. Grain was requisitioned; shortfalls occurred. Those wealthier farmers, deemed *kulaks*,
who in imagination or reality were resistant to the plan, were forced
with everyone else into collectives. Peasants formerly allowed to sell
their surplus on open markets found they were limited to selling to
the government at fixed prices. Grotesque propaganda showing ape-
like peasants stealing from the people did not reconcile farmers to
Soviet rule.[35] Across the country they slaughtered their cows and
sheep in defiance of demands that the animals be turned over to the
state. Livestock populations fell; farm production dropped even
more drastically. Subsequent famines led to the deaths of millions.

Enforcement of collectivization would have profound effects on
the Soviet people. Under the auspices of the greater Gulag system,
nearly two million peasant families were punished with exile to new
settlement villages in Siberia; others were sent to Kazakhstan.[36]
Many were executed; some one hundred thousand individuals ended
up in the more traditional labor camps of the Gulag.[37]

Article 58 of the penal code, enacted in 1927, likewise added to
the number of those eligible for detention in the Gulag. The expanded
statute broadly defined who could be detained as a counterrevolutionary. Those who committed violence against the state were still suscep-
tible to arrest, but under the revised law, those who created anti-Soviet
propaganda, those who carried out their duties carelessly, and those
who simply failed to report counterrevolutionary activity committed
by others were considered just as culpable. The counterrevolutionary
offenses included in Article 58 suddenly meant that deeds that would
have been minor crimes, or not crimes at all, could bring years of
detention. "In all truth," wrote Solzhenitsyn, "there is no step, thought,
action, or lack of action under the heavens which could not be punished by the heavy hand of Article 58."[38]

Under the tsars in previous centuries, Polish insurgents resisting
Russian rule or political prisoners convicted for offenses against the
tsar were shipped off to remote Siberian *katorga*, working in mining
or logging. Their penal labor had often been brutal and unfair, but it

had come after conviction in an actual trial. Compared to penal labor under the tsars, Gulag workdays were longer and the rations shorter. A daily quota for earth mined by a single Decembrist prisoner at Nerchinsk under Tsar Nicholas I was 118 pounds; in the Soviet era, the same lone prisoner might be expected to excavate 28,800 pounds.[39] And while tsarist courts had long sentenced political prisoners to labor camps, the Gulag was orders of magnitude larger from its very beginning. The Soviet Union had grafted the worst of Russian penal history onto the extrajudicial detention of internment, creating a vast malignant enterprise. And it would continue to grow.

6. By the time Likhachev was called from Solovki to work on the Baltic–White Sea Canal, many of his fellow detainees at Solovki had already been shipped out. Eventually, a friend who had been sent to the project as an administrator requested Likhachev's transfer to help keep books for the project. Knowing that he could be called at any time for immediate departure, Likhachev kept his belongings packed in the plywood suitcase he had brought from Leningrad.

After he received his summons in the summer of 1931, he reported for departure, along with a trumpeter from the music company who had been assigned for transfer as well. They sat through hours of delousing and a serenade from the musicians, only to be sent back to their cells for two more weeks. A second call came; they were serenaded again, and again returned to their cells. On the third try, enthusiasm for any musical send-off had evaporated, but Likhachev finally escaped Solovki for good.[40]

The theater closed the same year, and along with it went the camp's baroque mix of cinematic offerings, adventurous publications, mass killing, reflections on Russian religious thought, hobnobbing aristocrats, socialist revolutionaries still dreaming of overthrowing the Bolsheviks, and the execution stairs of Sekirka Chapel Hill. Solovki would evolve into the new kind of labor camp it had helped spawn: random, baroque punishments declined; prisoners were worked to death rather than shot; and any artistic endeavors became preprogrammed activities aimed at supporting Soviet ideals.

Never again would such a rich collection of pre-Revolutionary culture be allowed to flourish in public, let alone in a concentration camp. By then, Russia had killed most of its intellectuals or driven them into exile. Solovki had gone a long way toward purging whole classes of people from the Russian firmament. The best aspects of Solovki died or were dispersed, while the hard-labor facet of the island experiment, which failed to make good on its economic promise, was set in place as Solovki's legacy to the Gulag.

Arriving at the worksite for his new job, Likhachev was again spared hard labor. As promised, he was pulled from the group of prisoners and escorted to his quarters, then trained to run the main prisoner card index for the canal project.

The first massive Soviet production descended quickly into tragedy. In all, more than 175,000 prisoners would be shipped in to provide labor on the canal. Touted as a way to expand Soviet trade and establish a stake in modern shipping, the waterway was excavated by prisoners working in medieval conditions. Most were forced to dig with shovels and hand tools, using wooden trucks with wooden wheels nicknamed "Fords" to haul stone away.[41] Along with widespread injury and illness, official counts record some 12,000 deaths, but later scholars estimate that total deaths exceeded 25,000, or one in seven of the prisoners sent to build it.[42]

At times it seemed as if nearly as much energy was expended on glorifying the effort as on actually digging the canal. Daily contests were held between brigades to see who could excavate the most. There were artistic contests, too, with financial rewards for the best artistic production about the project. The winning play recounted the tale of an English journalist who comes to the worksite expecting to see horrific conditions, but instead is so inspired by what he finds that he decides to stay. It is perhaps a sign of the coded methods prisoners found to insert their own commentary that the protagonist's name, which appears in English transliteration rather than Russian, is "Mr. Stupid."[43]

For Likhachev, an office job meant more than not having to dig; it meant survival. He slept on a top bunk next to a searing chimney pipe, and washed himself in a water pump on the street outside the barracks. His supervisor friend, who was also a prisoner, lived in a separate building nearby where they went to eat lunches cooked on a small stove, sharing the same pot.

He could feel freedom approaching. He was moved south to new sites as the canal progressed, tracking shipments as a dispatcher at the train station. Away from the camps, he rented space in the dining room of a private home, where he slept on not a layer of boards but a real mattress. Taking advantage of the liberties he could access due to his position, he sneaked off twice to Leningrad, even attending the ballet. He was caught by a patrol there once, but was saved by whoever answered the phone when soldiers called to verify that he had permission to travel.[44]

Suddenly, word came down that in recognition of his service as a "shock construction worker" on the canal project, he would be released six months early. In addition, he would not, after all, be restricted from living in any particular region of the country. In August 1933, he left for home, to try to face the challenge of continuing life as a former concentration camp prisoner.

The early releases of Likhachev and his codefendants in the case against the members of the eccentric Cosmic Academy of Sciences coincided with the early completion of White Sea Canal. Thousands of others were likewise granted suspended sentences, and the channel was celebrated as a beacon of Soviet achievement and the success of corrective labor. "Soviet power can be merciful as well as merciless," crowed *New York Times* reporter Walter Duranty, who soon won a Pulitzer for his fawning coverage of Stalin's first Five-Year Plan.[45]

As infrastructure, the canal was a failure. In order to meet the deadline, plans had been changed at the beginning of the project to have prisoners dig only ten to twelve feet deep instead of the eigh-teen feet originally envisioned. As a result, only barges and pleasure boats could move through, which made the new route useless for most industrial needs. On May 28, 1933, the first ship to sail through was *The Chekist*.[46]

Nevertheless, as the first massive works project involving concen-tration camp labor, the effort was a propaganda and engineering success. Even with little in the way of tools, workmen had stayed on schedule. They had even developed an innovative system of wooden locks. The true legacy of the canal, however, lay elsewhere. The vast scale of the White Sea Canal project and the labor force needed to construct it represented a new era in the evolution of concentration camps. They could be used to build a country.

7. Penal colonies had existed long before the Russian Revolution. But the establishment of a centralized Gulag authority running industrial sites ensured that far larger enterprises built on forced labor would become a defining feature of the Soviet state.

During the construction of the White Sea Canal, an even more ambitious effort had begun. Soviet state security founded the Dal-stroy Corporation to take advantage of ore deposits in the inaccessi-ble northeastern regions of the country along the Kolyma River basin. Announced as one of the largest gold deposits ever discov-ered, Kolyma became the destination for concentration camp inmates assigned to work in the bitter Siberian climate. The major project in the 1930s was clearing what would come to be known as the "Road of Bones" for a highway connecting the mountainous Siberian interior to Kolyma and Magadan on the eastern coast.

First, inmates had to be shipped north from the endpoint of the Trans-Siberian Railway on the eastern coast of Russia across the Sea of Okhotsk. Tight quarters and deadly conditions in transport ships could be as lethal as the hard labor that awaited the prisoners. Those who survived the journey were forced to build the town of

Magadan and then clear a road inland. Snowstorms limiting visibility lasted days at a time, and away from the coast, temperatures dropped to an average low of minus 36 degrees Fahrenheit. As on the White Sea Canal project, primitive shovels and wheelbarrows were common tools.

In 1936, the *New York Times* devoted a two-and-a-half-page spread to development in northern Russia under the title "Taming the Arctic: Russia's New Empire," with only a handful of lines acknowledging the "convicted felons" responsible for the railroad and mining work on the new frontier.[47] Years later, US vice president Henry Wallace would fly to Kolyma, where he was given a tour by Chekist generals. He was impressed with what he saw as the can-do spirit of the place, comparing the camps to the Tennessee Valley Authority. He described how one of the administrators, Nishikov, "gamboled about, enjoying the wonderful air immensely."[48]

Savaging Wallace's naïve description of Magadan, former Kolyma inmate Elinor Lipper wrote, "It is too bad that Wallace never saw him 'gamboling about' on one of his drunken rages around the prison camps, raining filthy, savage language upon the heads of the exhausted, starving prisoners, having them locked up in solitary confinement for no offense whatsoever, and sending them into gold mines to work fourteen and sixteen hours a day."[49]

"Every night we were listening for knockings at the doors," one Kolyma inmate, or *zek*, said years later in an interview. "When you heard knocking at the door, it meant somebody was being taken."[50] Detainees learned that their labor-dependent rations could make the desire for food lethal: "Those who wanted to get more worked themselves to death."[51]

With a worldwide depression under way, global reaction to events in the Soviet Union was split. Stories of horrific labor conditions and Bolshevik tyranny inspired denunciations from those already distrustful of Communism. Mainstream news outlets estimated that as many as a million Russians might be in detention, but they did not know how to interpret the system as a whole, calling it "equivalent to the 'concentration camps' which the European countries established for enemy aliens during the World War."[52] Yet those who had grown suspicious of capitalism and thought it a failed model looked for economic hope in what appeared to be stunning Russian achievements.

As with many camp systems, accurate numbers in the Gulag are impossible to pin down. Historians estimate, however, that nearly a million prisoners were funneled into Kolyma in all, with perhaps a tenth of them dying there. The dead were not counted or memorialized; many fell into oblivion.

Kolyma opened for business, and the White Sea Canal was finished. With the machinery of the Gulag in place and other projects beginning, new arrivals continued to be fed into the Gulag's vast machinery. Yet Stalin would soon drag Russia into an even darker era, inflicting a whole new Terror on the children of the October Revolution.

8. By the time secret policemen entered Margarete Buber-Neumann's Moscow hotel room carrying her arrest warrant, she had been expecting them for more than a year. Since April 1937, when her husband had been detained, she had kept a bag packed. During that time, she had sold off her belongings—camera, radio, books, clothes—in order to eat. When agents came for her, she had little left in the way of possessions to take along.[53]

Buber-Neumann and her husband, Heinz, had both been born in Germany, eventually becoming members of the Communist Party there. He had held a seat in the Reichstag, traveling to Russia to meet with Stalin and organize violence against the Nazis and the Weimar Republic alike.

After Hitler's rise, however, Heinz had been denounced in Communist circles. The couple fled from city to city, ending up with false papers in Switzerland, where he was arrested. Eventually they were deported via steamship to Leningrad, where they arrived in May 1935. Still in disgrace with the Party, they half expected to be arrested upon disembarking. Yet in that moment, Russia still seemed a better choice than extradition to Nazi Germany.

Instead of being detained on the spot, they were sent on to Moscow and given a room at the Hotel Lux, where top foreign Communists stayed. Soon they were told that a mistake had been made, and they would have to relocate. Heinz refused to go. Eventually the request was dropped, and they braced for their Soviet future.[54]

It was a season of butchery, with the Party in the midst of devouring its own. After the assassination of one of Stalin's lieutenants months before, seventy-one people had been arrested in as many hours, including the head of internal affairs for Leningrad.[55] Two days later, all but five had been condemned to death by military tribunals and shot. By February 1934, summary executions were still on the rise and were publicly acknowledged. Even as Soviet leadership downplayed the chaos, Party newspapers published lists of those shot and their offenses. State-sanctioned terror could not be instilled without actively intimidating its targets, and this included public recognition of the executions.

Confronted with the indignation of leftists around the world, Soviet representatives justified the deaths by citing "terroristic activities" against the government.[56] Asked directly by reporters about the possibility of a new Red Terror campaign, a Soviet State Planning official explained that no new Terror would be necessary "because there is no one left to purge."[57]

That was wishful thinking. Government-led massacres had been part of the Soviet experiment since before the formal establishment of the Soviet state, but in the 1930s Stalin's totalitarianism unleashed official terror that would eclipse historical comparisons. Chaos triggered by massive societal restructuring under the Five-Year Plan had destabilized the country, forcing party leaders to redefine loyalty. The last vestiges of independence were replaced with a cult of personality built around Stalin. Those who had criticized corruption or espoused minor variations in ideology were also rounded up. Dissent became heresy.

Arrests continued in waves as Buber-Neumann arrived in Moscow.

A series of show trials began in which senior party members confessed to sabotage and doctrinal heresies, and begged for forgiveness. Buber-Neumann herself translated the account of the first trial into German for Comintern distribution abroad.[58]

Those outside Russia understood that dramatic changes were afoot, but no clear picture was emerging. Perhaps there really were elaborate plans to wreck the economy and destroy the Soviet government. Why else would people publicly confess to crimes they hadn't committed? This fuzziness arose in part from the stellar propaganda provided by the show trials and thanks to tight party controls over news in the Soviet Union. Additional confusion in the West was due to sympathetic reporting by journalists. America still had Walter Duranty, who openly admired Stalin's modernization efforts, in keeping with his earlier observation that "you can't make an omelette without breaking eggs."[59]

Meanwhile, under pressure from the authorities, Buber-Neumann's husband confessed to doctrinal heresies and begged for forgiveness. To show good faith, he denounced fellow residents at the Lux. His neighbors in turn denounced him. Asked by the Soviets to produce testimony herself—and certain that she would go down with Heinz if she refused—Buber-Neumann criticized ideological "lapses" made by both of them.

In 1937—the year Heinz was arrested—and 1938, when agents came for Buber-Neumann, Soviet authorities shot more than 682,000 people, averaging in excess of nine hundred executions a day.[60] During the same two-year span, as many or more were sentenced to the Gulag.

As with every aspect of Soviet production, lists were created, with quotas for each region detailing how many were to be shot or imprisoned. The reeducation ideals of the early Gulag, manufactured as they often were, had vanished. Politicals had long since lost their special privileges. Prisoners could no longer assume that they might serve their sentences and return home. Camps faced overcrowding; rations were cut.

Executions swept through camps as well, with accusations of "wrecking" and Trotskyism flung at those who held technical positions. Many of the surviving early revolutionaries—those who had fought the tsar but had also defied Soviet rule—were finally killed. Gone as well were iconoclasts like the poet Osip Mandelstam, who mocked Stalin in verse privately and spent the rest of his life in a camp or in exile, finally dying in 1938 en route to serve a new sentence at Kolyma.

In the era of the Great Purge, even camp administrators were at risk. Eduard Berzin, administrator for the Dalstroy Corporation at Kolyma for five years, was executed as a spy in 1938, as was his replacement Stepan Garanin. Such, too, was the fate of the former head of Solovetsky Camp, Fyodor Eichmanns, and Genrikh Yagoda, codirector of the White Sea Canal Project and head of the secret police from 1934 to 1936. After authorizing the arrest, torture, or killing of more than a million people, Yagoda's successor Nikolai Yezhov was himself tortured and executed two years later.

Among the sea of remaining casualties of the purge was Buber-Neumann's husband, Heinz. In November 1937, seven months after his arrest, a tribunal condemned him to death. He was shot the same day, though decades would pass before the Red Cross informed his wife of his fate.

9. Arrested at the Lux early in the morning, Margarete Buber-Neumann found herself far from home, riding in a Ford with two agents on her way to Moscow's notorious Lubyanka Prison.[61] There had been so much time to imagine the moment; Buber-Neumann thought she was ready. Wives always had time to prepare, she realized, because the Cheka came for the husbands first.

After a humiliating cavity search, she spent just three days at the Lubyanka, where she was spared torture and interrogation. Grateful for the reprieve, she assumed that being Heinz Neumann's partner provided evidence enough. A Black Maria carried her away to Butyrka, a tsarist-era prison converted to a remand center.

Shoved into a cell designed for twenty-five but holding more than a hundred prisoners, Buber-Neumann felt she had entered a chamber filled with worms. Half-naked women swarmed in the half-light from opaque windows. Tiers of plank platforms represented an unsuccessful attempt to give everyone room to sleep. As the newcomer, she had to take the space next to the *parasha*—the latrine bucket—with a seizure-prone neighbor next to her in the filth.[62]

While they waited for their investigators to resolve their cases, inmates devised a way for those leaving the prison to signal the length of their sentences. As they went down the stairs, those heading off to camps would flash the number of fingers equal to their sentence behind their backs. Since everyone was reporting five years, veteran prisoners expressed relief. Under the previous commander, they explained, the standard had been ten. Five would be a gift.

During months of detention, Buber-Neumann was interrogated four times and asked to sign a statement admitting counterrevolutionary actions. The process took so long that she began to wonder whether she might be freed. But there were also grimmer portents, including a skeletal, scurvy-ridden cellmate who had just returned from nine years at Kolyma and appeared to be headed back.

Though Buber-Neumann escaped torture, many were not as lucky. Others reported beatings, being forced to stand for days at a time, having to sit on scalding steam pipes, and being throttled. The Soviet interrogation repertoire was also known to feature bright lights, sleep deprivation, beating, and rats, as well as isolation in small spaces.[63] One of Buber-Neumann's Kolyma cellmates disappeared without fanfare one day, only to return completely unrecognizable after forty days spent in darkness and solitary confinement.[64]

The prisoners' fates had already been decided by the time they arrived at Butyrka. It was understood that most were innocent of the charges against them (and that many of the rest were guilty of trivial offenses). Yet the system was invested in maintaining the façade of its legitimacy and the cooperation of the detainees in supporting it.

Not only did the arbitrary rules of the state have to be revealed as appropriate, prisoners were pressured to embrace their guilt to reinforce the harsh measures. Though people often refused to sign false confessions, investigators would spend months trying to elicit material to fit the charges, in order to justify the predetermined sentence. The surveillance, the targeted arrests, the denunciations implicating others, and the tortures all functioned not as separate components but as integral elements in a mockery of a legal process grafted onto a domestic concentration camp system.

After six months in detention, Buber-Neumann received a five-year sentence. She was put again into an overcrowded Black Maria and taken to a holding car at a train platform. Sitting on a ledge near the roof of the car, she learned to roll a cigarette, smoking bitter *mahorka* for the first time.

The journey to the camp, too, was a component of the Gulag, often one of the most harrowing aspects of the experience. Buber-Neumann spent weeks in transit heading east, jammed into a railway car without knowing where she was bound. Those who had already served time discussed possible destinations and work details—mining, roadwork, agriculture—debating which was deadliest. Arriving at a transfer point, they stood for roll call after roll call and slept overnight in a rat-infested cell of the local prison. The women's eating utensils had been taken from them on leaving Moscow, so they scavenged the floor of their rail car until they found a discarded tin, which they used in rotation. Guards watched them at all times, even on the toilet. After too many bathroom requests, a two-minute limit per visit was set, and prisoners were held to a maximum of three visits each twenty-four hours, which were better privileges than those in many other convoys got.

The new *zeks* traveled a thousand miles from Moscow and crossed the Ural Mountains before learning their destination: Karaganda, in the southern Soviet Republic of Kazakhstan. Hustled out of the railcar amid shouting, they were marched stumbling in the cold to the quarantine area, a stand of huts surrounded by barbed wire with a watchtower at each end. They spent hours there for roll call before being assigned quarters in a low clay shelter. Stepping inside, Buber-Neumann found that the floor had been dug out below ground level. There was not much more than a battered stove, some coal, and an axe.

She made two beginner's mistakes. Looking for kindling to start a fire, she began to hack up a stray wooden crate, only to come under attack by the crate's furious owner. Later, after eating a gift of buttered bread and a pickle from another prisoner, she learned that it had been offered in exchange for sex. She extricated herself by playing the confused foreigner.

When her quarantine period ended, Buber-Neumann was assigned to a distant part of the compound, a subcamp that did not even have barbed wire—guards simply shot anyone who wandered too far outside the perimeter. After four nights sleeping in the washroom, she and a friend were given a door on blocks to use as a bed. They took turns sleeping on the side with the metal lock.

In a lucky break, the finance manager sent her for office work despite her weak Russian, assigning her to keep tractor service logs, recording blame for any machines out of commission. To get to work each day, she walked from her hut—where she now had the bed-door to herself—across a dam that backed up a pond. The dam's reservoir provided water to an irrigation system for a whole array of foods that never appeared in detainees' provisions: tomatoes, potatoes, and a host of vegetables.

When the harvest came, she was also expected to volunteer with "shock brigades" doing fieldwork from dawn until midday. At one o'clock, prisoners returned to their regular labor details to work seven hours more. They were paid modest wages at regular intervals, with fieldwork paying immediately. After a learning period, prisoners were paid for their skilled work as well.

One day two ducks were spotted swimming in the pond. In a landscape where vultures reigned, the prisoners were entranced, giving up some of their precious bread to feed the birds. After work, Buber-Neumann headed back to the pond and found the creatures still there. She wondered whether they might stay. Perhaps there would be ducklings.

Later that day, a shot rang out and everyone came running. The commandant was firing at the ducks. The doomed birds did not even try to escape, and before long both had been killed.

Furious, Buber-Neumann impulsively decided to take her fate into her own hands—she would make an appeal to the Supreme Court to reverse her conviction. Her coworkers expressed terror at the prospect and warned that she was asking for trouble. But the following day, still bent on doing something, she went to the office of the camp commandant and made her request. He welcomed her cordially, going so far as to encourage her to fill out an application in her native tongue. Two weeks later, she was moved to the punishment compound.

Her rashness had landed her behind barbed wire again, in even worse conditions than before. Amid piles of human excrement, criminals and politicals targeted for close supervision mixed with recalcitrant camp rule-breakers, all under the eye of the trusty, a prisoner who had been put in charge of their section. Detainees slept on pieces of wood or twigs. Lice were more prevalent, and bedbugs crawled into her nostrils at night.

Buber-Neumann was sent to do full-time fieldwork, with a quota to weed a furrow over a mile and a half long each day in order to receive a pound and a half of bread and a ladle of thin millet soup. She fell hopelessly behind and lost bread as punishment before receiving help from another prisoner.

The politicals looked down on the criminals as thugs; the criminals looked down on the politicals as traitors. Buber-Neumann loathed being surrounded by insults and cursing. She ended up fighting just to protect herself. The criminals mocked her as "the German Fascist."[65] Those who had arrived before her were underweight and missing teeth. She was not sure she would survive. And yet when they called her out for an assignment elsewhere, she was reluctant to go, fearing that the next situation might be even worse.

She moved from site to site within Karaganda, yoking oxen to draw water, sorting rotten potatoes, running a grain-cleaning machine, and at the last, distributing clothing. With state censorship, work quotas, and the threat of punishment, Soviet society outside the barbed wire had itself become a kind of camp; meanwhile, the camps had become the society writ small.

She encountered kindnesses along the way, but affliction was the underlying condition in the Gulag. The cattle gave her brucellosis, a contagious bacterial infection that put her in the hospital for two weeks, where her last remaining possessions were stolen.[66] In despair, a former hatmaker hanged herself from a beam. The women found a spy in their midst who was reporting on them to the camp administration. Buber-Neumann broke a bone in her foot but worked through it so as not to lose her post in the vegetable cellar, where she could steal food for herself and her friends. In a particularly bitter blow, she was called before the commandant and told that she would sleep in the punishment compound until the end of her five-year sentence.

10. September 1939 brought war in Europe, with Germany invading Poland from the west and Russia advancing weeks later from the east as part of the Molotov-Ribbentrop Pact. Along with effectively partitioning Poland, Russia and Germany agreed to divide other Eastern European and Baltic states into spheres of influence.

Word of the "friendship pact" spread through the Gulag. Before the invasion, Russia had drummed home the threat from German Fascists; now the two countries were partners. Some prisoners, however, preferred an antagonistic Berlin. In camp, Buber-Neumann met a blacksmith who told her of a Kazakh resistance movement prepared to fight the Soviets alongside the Nazis if the latter ever came to Karaganda. Reminding him of Hitler's known savagery, she said,

"At the very best it would mean replacing one dictatorship by another."[67] But many in the Gulag could not imagine anything worse than life in concentration camps under Stalin.

In 1939, Poland did not have to choose between dictatorships, but had two imposed on the country at once. Civil society was demolished. The Gulag rapidly shifted to accommodate prisoners arrested during Soviet expansion. Russian forces sent approximately fifteen thousand Polish reserve officers east by truck and train to special Gulag camps in the Soviet Union.[68]

Initially they were treated as political prisoners, with a new police directorate and detention sites set up to deal with them. The officers wrote letters home, underwent interrogations, and were subjected to a steady diet of Soviet propaganda. After trying to recruit several prisoners as spies, NKVD chief Lavrenty Beria sent in special executioners who killed the officers in private one by one, loaded their bodies onto trucks, and buried them in mass graves.[69] When the bodies were discovered three years later, the Soviets blamed the Nazis.

Meanwhile in Poland, a fraudulent election had been conducted a month after the invasion, ostensibly showing support for the annexation of Russian-held territory into existing Soviet republics. New Soviet passports were issued to Poles. Chekists swept in behind the army, arresting more than a hundred thousand citizens who were judged problematic. The usual troika was convened, with the Gulag or a death sentence applied in nearly every case. More than 8,500 civilians were executed outright.[70]

Many Poles were deported to northern camps, including Vorkuta, a mining center carved by prisoners out of ice and snow. At the beginning of 1940, the site had a population of only two thousand prisoners, but by the mid-1950s, hundreds of thousands had entered its gates.[71] The camp's location was so new and obscure that newspapers did not at first know where on the map to place it.[72] In time, the camp complex at Vorkuta would grow into a permanent city, like Magadan in the east.

The Politburo further demanded the deportation of whole groups of Polish policemen and civil servants, along with their families.[73] They were loaded onto cattle cars in February 1940, traveling two thousand miles or more to the same resettlement camps that had received the *kulaks* in the 1930s. Many of them ended up in Kazakhstan, not far from where Margarete Buber-Neumann was imprisoned at Karaganda.

The Molotov-Ribbentrop Pact had repercussions outside Poland as well. At the end of 1939, Buber-Neumann learned that she would be leaving the camp before the end of her sentence. Her friends gathered sixty rubles, along with dried fish and bread, to send off with her.

Saying goodbye was difficult; it was always possible that those left behind would die at Karaganda, or Kolyma, or some unknown camp. Memorized addresses and a letter were given into her care with the universal refrain "Don't forget me."[74]

After a night ride in a Siberian sledge and a train back to the Karaganda reception center, Buber-Neumann was fingerprinted and interviewed. When asked whether her health had suffered from her time in the camp, she feigned shock that anyone would think such a thing. Asked whether she had any complaint regarding her treatment in the camp, she said no. She would not make another unforced error.

Police handlers escorted Buber-Neumann to the railway station. Prisoners were normally let off at loading docks or outside town. This time, however, Buber-Neumann stood with another prisoner in the waiting room alongside free citizens. They got on the 6:00 p.m. passenger train to Moscow with no idea what would happen at their destination. Their escorts gave them bread and canned pork and each enjoyed a real bed. Crossing the steppe and the Ural Mountains, they had time to pick the lice off each other and eat in a restaurant. On arrival in Moscow, their escort—a Chekist—bought them ice cream and stuffed pancakes. Exiting the station, however, they saw the ubiquitous Black Maria, which carried them back to Butyrka Prison, where Buber-Neumann had first been sentenced.

Yet Butyrka had changed. Buber-Neumann found herself in a

cell with other German women. They were given clean sheets and beds, their own ceramic plates and utensils, and normal food, not prison fare. It was still unclear what was happening. Would the Soviet Union turn over fellow Communists to the Nazis? Would they be released in Lithuania or to some other nation? Had they been pardoned by the party? They did not know.

But after two weeks of pampering, in which they read library books and visited a hairdresser, guards removed Buber-Neumann and a German Jewish schoolteacher from their cell and loaded them into the police van a final time. Again they were driven through the streets of Moscow, where Buber-Neumann had lived with her husband in 1933.

From the van, they climbed down into a train yard. This time, they would not be standing on the passenger train platform; a prison railcar sat waiting for them. Looking around, Buber-Neumann saw the White Russian Station in the distance. Everything fell into place. Only trains to Poland and the West ran on these lines. She told the others, "They're sending us to Germany."[75]

Along with Buber-Neumann and the schoolteacher, twenty-eight men climbed into the prison car and rode westward. Most had been serving sentences of ten to fifteen years, and several had come from Solovki. Their escorts still offered them extravagant foods, but as the last of the possibilities for alternate routes slipped away, it became clear that there would be no last-minute salvation. Unable to eat, the detainees refused food they had longed for in the Gulag only weeks before.

At the end of the line, they were taken off the railcar. Buber-Neumann spotted a sign that read "Brest-Litovsk." They had arrived at the border with Nazi-occupied Poland. The women were put in a truck with an injured prisoner and an elderly professor, while the rest of the detainees had to walk. They soon got to the bridge over the Bug River.

A group of *Schutzstaffel*—SS men—crossed over from the other side and saluted their Chekist guards. The Soviet chief began to read a list of names, Margarete Buber-Neumann's among them. A few prisoners started to protest, but the SS took command and marched them over the bridge into German territory.

11. Those Buber-Neumann left behind in the Gulag also began to feel the effects of Poland's dismemberment as new prisoners arrived. More than a hundred thousand Poles were arrested in a two-year period from 1939 to 1941, and more than three hundred thousand individuals and their families were sent eastward into exile.[76]

It was soon evident that Polish prisoners were culturally very different from Soviet detainees. Across two decades, Russia's isolation and devastated economy had led to insularity and grinding poverty. A camp system whose only dissidents—revolutionaries, monarchists, and those inclined toward constitutional democracy—had been liquidated during those decades found much to learn from the new prisoners. Detainees received an education about everything from tailored clothes and modern brassieres to organizing political strikes. With the addition of the new foreign prisoners and harsher internal penalties for labor infractions, the Gulag camp population, including its associated colonies and prisons, grew by almost a million between 1939 and 1941.[77]

That expansion halted when Germany invaded Russia on June 22, 1941. Pushing eastward, the Wehrmacht drove history's largest invading force deep into Russia during the first months of Operation Barbarossa. After initial confusion, the Soviets would manage to stop the advance. Yet by September, German soldiers stood outside Leningrad; by the end of November, they were closing in on Moscow.

On the first day of the invasion, twenty-two-year-old student Alexander Solzhenitsyn was riding a train north to take his second-year exams at the Moscow Institute of Philosophy, Literature, and History.[78] Upon arrival in Moscow he immediately headed to a recruiting office, but officials there insisted he return home to enlist. After several days spent getting back to Rostov, he tried again to sign up, but a childhood disability disqualified him from service.

An aspiring writer, Solzhenitsyn had long seen battlefield experience as the crucible in which great authors were forged. During his honeymoon just the year before, he had written a poem predicting the triumph of Leninist revolution through global war and mayhem. ("We will die!! Upon our dead bodies, the Revolution will ascend!!!"[79]) He longed to go to war.

A second attempt at enlistment was also refused. But after Wehrmacht victories mounted and the Soviets faced rout after rout, all reserve forces were mobilized. Still more soldiers were needed. Russia grew less choosy about physical standards; Solzhenitsyn was called up.

He would spend almost four years at war. From his first days in the army, he carried a briefcase of papers with him, despite the jokes it provoked. Writing began to fill the spare time that war sometimes afforded. Starting out mucking stables, he was ridiculed by Cossacks for his ignorance of horses.[80] By July 1944, however, he was captain of an artillery battery and won the Order of the Red Star for taking out enemy guns.

A profoundly patriotic man, Solzhenitsyn prided himself on his rank and on his unit's discipline. Still, he was not above using his position to further his writing. A forged army pass and military garb sent to his wife, Natalia, made it possible for her to join him for a few weeks at the front. She spent time in the field with him, transcribing his attempts at fiction, though she was less indulgent about his wish for her to stand at attention when he entered the trench.

As Solzhenitsyn rose, the momentum of the war began to shift. When the German invasion aborted the Molotov-Ribbentrop Pact, the Polish government in exile and the Soviet Union had become grudging allies. Through the end of 1941 and into 1942, the sentences of Polish prisoners in the Gulag were commuted, as were those of Czech detainees, with many joining Polish units formed to fight against Germany.

Yet as it moved westward, Soviet power's dark side revealed itself in reprisals, rapes, and plunder. Solzhenitsyn saw an NKVD tribunal set up to sentence and deport locals. He witnessed an execution at Novosil conducted as if it were a party. Invited to stay the night to continue the festivities, he declined.

At Novosil, he had also run into Nikolai, an old friend. While stationed together, they talked about their war experiences, politics, and the future of Russia. Agreeing that the USSR had lost its way, they developed "Resolution No. 1," a call for a new party that might throw off the shackles that trapped the Soviet system in the feudal, exploitative past.

Even after the friends' battalions went their separate ways, they kept in touch. In their letters, Stalin came in for his share of mockery, referred to as "the moustachioed one" and "big shot." Solzhenitsyn delighted in their companionship, though over time Nikolai became less enthusiastic in their exchanges.

Solzhenitsyn's vision of himself as a writer who might transform his country persisted. The army had been just the transformational experience he had sought to send him on his way. He had overcome early ridicule to become a respected—if sometimes self-important—officer. He had served the motherland, tested himself, and seen sights that he planned to use as fodder for any number of novels. As Soviet troops advanced to meet British and American forces in the west, they sensed that victory could not be far away.

Then, three and a half years into his service and nearly eight hundred miles from Moscow, he was called to the office of the brigadier general. He found himself in a meeting with other military personnel. The general asked him for his revolver, wrapping it carefully before putting it into a desk drawer and telling him he could go. As Solzhenitsyn wondered whether he was being sent on a special assignment, two officers stepped from the corner, ripped off his epaulets, and took the star from his cap.

The censors had seen his letters with Nikolai. Placing him under arrest, they escorted him out of headquarters and drove him back through the ravaged landscape, getting lost in enemy territory under mortar attack before surrendering the map to Solzhenitsyn. Foolishly still carrying his briefcase full of notes and writings about his errant country, he led them on days of travel: to the train at Minsk, onto the metro in Moscow, past the Metropole Hotel, until they finally came to the doors of Lubyanka Prison, where so many people had disappeared.[81] From there, he was sent to Butyrka Prison, like Margarete Buber-Neumann before him. And on July 27, 1945, he was convicted without trial as a counterrevolutionary under Article 58, receiving an eight-year sentence.

12. When concentration camps in western Russia came under threat from Nazi forces just after the invasion, wholesale orders for evacuation had been carried out with brutal speed. Sometimes trains were available for nightmare journeys in what one inmate called a "filthy stinking motherfucking cattle car."[82] At other times, prisoners were propelled at gunpoint on forced marches. Those who could not keep up were shot. The NKVD realized that it was easier to release prisoners with brief sentences or who had committed minor crimes than to evacuate them, and ended up extending amnesties to such prisoners in camps across the country.

Between the beginning and the end of the war, the population of the Gulag had been cut in half. Amnesties did not generate the majority of the reduction, however. War conditions triggered widespread starvation and illness, with increasingly lethal effects. Rations fell by a third, while war production needs increased. More than 820,000 Gulag prisoners and settlers died during the war.

After Margarete Buber-Neumann left the camp at Karaganda, its annual mortality rate climbed to almost one in three prisoners.[83] The dramatic death count was noted and discussed, and administrators were threatened with replacement, but Moscow made no special provisions to address the lack of food and the overburdened hospital.

For nearly three decades, concentration camps had played a key role in asserting Soviet authority over a vast territory, serving as a bridge between the Civil War that gave birth to the state and the Second World War that would establish it as a superpower. Yet the Gulag was a vulnerable institution. Neither self-sustaining nor productive in the long run, the system required tremendous resources, and the economic burden of the camps had weighed heavily on the Soviet Union in wartime.

Still, as historian Steven Barnes has pointed out, "The Soviet leadership never entertained the notion of dismantling the system."[84] The USSR had always had a camp system; its tendrils had grown into agriculture and industry, as well as becoming a key facet of government interactions with citizens. The Gulag was intrinsic to the state itself.

Despite military victory in 1945, the Second World War devastated Russia. More than a million Soviet Jews were executed by Einsatzgruppen and Order Police battalions following the German advance—sometimes with the collaboration of the local population. The siege of Leningrad alone added the starvation deaths of another 750,000 names to the book of the dead.[85] And yet the two tragic events together were only a fraction of wartime civilian casualties. In addition to noncombatant deaths, military fatalities alone exceeded eight million.

In the wake of the war, the government encouraged prejudice against returning Soviet troops, suggesting that they had not been taken prisoner but had "given themselves over to the enemy."[86] Fearing that Soviet noncombatants would face similar repression, Allied forces were initially reluctant to return them to Moscow. Both groups were required to be processed through filtration camps, undergoing detention and interrogation while their loyalties were assessed. In the end, however, just one in sixteen people returning from the West ended up in the Gulag, most of them soldiers who had been taken prisoner or those who had joined pro-German auxiliary units.[87]

Yet after its numbers had been reduced during the war, the Gulag population, independent of the colonies, would expand again and peak at two and a half million prisoners by 1950.[88] Meanwhile, in occupied Germany and Poland, the Soviets had converted Nazi sites, including Buchenwald, to special concentration camps under the control of the secret police. Hundreds of thousands were detained in isolation from the world in these "silence camps," from which many were deported eastward.[89]

Though the West quickly shifted to focus on the specter of spreading Communism, those detained in concentration camps were largely invisible once the Iron Curtain divided Europe. Arrested in Dresden in 1945, American citizen John Noble was sent by the Soviets to Buchenwald. Held there until 1950, he was then shipped to Vorkuta with a fifteen-year Gulag sentence.

Spending his first years in the coal mines, he worked with convicts who weighed less than a hundred pounds. Through contact with a barber, he managed to smuggle out a postcard that made its way to Germany and then to his family in the United States. President Dwight Eisenhower negotiated his return, which led to a prisoner exchange.[90]

Back home, Noble wrote a newspaper serial and then a bestselling book, *I Was a Slave in Russia,* about starvation, prisoner deaths, strikes, and even deadlier Gulag camps farther north. He found a welcome reception in the anti-Communist Christian evangelical community, but the prisoners' fates received less fervent attention from US government officials, who were focused on Soviet espionage and military actions. The larger world still did not recognize the enormity of the system.

Unlike Noble, Alexander Solzhenitsyn was spared work in the mines, but he was given his own share of harrowing labor. In order to avoid "general duties" in the Gulag, he managed to get himself appointed shift foreman in a clay pit at New Jerusalem—only to end up with a crew of professional thieves who refused to work. He wound up digging clay himself, unable to meet even half his daily quota. None of the rest of the men could dig quickly enough either, and everyone was kept until nightfall, when they were sent back to barracks to sleep in wet clothes on hard boards in the cold air. Only weeks in, he could not imagine how he would survive eight years.[91]

Yet the arbitrary nature of the Gulag could also deliver gifts. An unexpected transfer removed him from the clay pits of New Jerusalem and sent him to a camp at Kaluga Gate, in Moscow. He avoided general duties by gaining a post as a "norm setter," but this, too, exacted a cost. Quartered with the "trusties," many of them criminals and ambitious types appointed to rule over the rest of the *zeks,* he was groomed as an informant. Signing a pledge to report any prisoners making escape plans was the darkest moment in his Gulag career, though he does not appear to have made himself useful as a stool pigeon.

From his first night, Solzhenitsyn slept in his boots so they would not be stolen. As had millions in the Gulag before him, he mastered the art of angling for a good bunk and suffering when he had no tobacco. After the ignominy of his service to the authorities at Kaluga, he began to develop humility. He knew that when he benefitted, others would likely suffer. As Dmitri Likhachev, that veteran of Solovki, later told Solzhenitsyn: "If I am alive today, that means someone else was on the list for execution in my place that night; if I am alive today, it means that someone else suffocated in the lower hold in my place; if I am alive today, it means that I got those extra seven ounces of bread which the dying man went without."[92]

Filling out an occupational history at Kaluga Gate, Solzhenitsyn optimistically wrote "atomic physicist" on the form and was rewarded with three years in relative luxury at a *sharashka,* a secret scientific research and development institute, working on acoustics and the human voice. But the Gulag was nothing if not capricious. Transferred again, he lost his protection and went to work at a foundry, returning to the hard labor, hunger, strikes, and death that had become the landscape of the camps. While he spent years in the company of strangers, eating and sleeping without privacy day after day, his wife, facing her own hardships for having a counterrevolutionary as a husband, took his advice and filed for divorce.

Yet on February 9, 1953, his sentence had been served, and Solzhenitsyn was released into permanent exile. His last taste of the Gulag was the journey out: a prison car, a train, a night in jail, six miles on foot, and a final truck ride into Kok-Terek, a tiny village in eastern Kazakhstan, where his papers indicated he would be exiled in perpetuity. Still in the army overcoat he had worn all the way from the battlefield on the day of his arrest eight years earlier, he spent his first night wandering outside. He could not return home, and he was forbidden to ever return to Moscow. But he was free.[93]

13. Stalin's death the following month marked the beginning of the end of the Soviet Gulag. But much as it had taken years to build, it would take years to dismantle. In 1956, during a thaw in party control, Nikita Khrushchev made a speech denouncing the purges and the cult of personality Stalin had built, citing "exceedingly serious and grave perversions of party principles, of party democracy, of revolutionary legality."[94] But four more years would pass before the Gulag as an institution formally ended.

The system had been dismantled without revolution. Camps had fallen into public disfavor but had not disappeared entirely; arbitrary detention and torture were still in use. Hard labor sentences would continue within the penal system for decades, though psychiatric hospitalization with forced treatment for a time became a favored way to handle dissidents. The ghosts of the Gulag hovered in the background.

A brief official willingness to indulge in introspection followed, leading to the publication of Alexander Solzhenitsyn's first novel. *One Day in the Life of Ivan Denisovich* offered a snapshot of Gulag life without its most graphic moments, building pathos for an unfortunate *zek* who had kept his decency amid the humiliations and impossible suffering within the system. Its first printing—nearly one hundred thousand copies—sold out almost instantly in the Soviet Union. It was rushed into translation around the world.

The response was astounding. But Solzhenitsyn had something more ambitious in his sights: a chronicle of the entire Gulag, revealing its roots under Lenin and how extrajudicial detention had been part of the corruption of the Soviet state from the beginning. He conducted secret interviews with hundreds of informants, tracking survivors of Solovki and early camps, doing clandestine research in archives. When he was awarded the Nobel Prize in Literature in 1970, rumors began appearing in Western newspapers that he had a bigger project in the works, perhaps to be called "The Archipelago of Gulag." Reporters had no way of knowing that the massive effort was already finished.

But when Russia began clamping down on the writers it had so recently liberated, Solzhenitsyn fell further and further from favor. He was kicked out of the writers' union but continued to work clandestinely. He scribbled in tiny letters on scraps of paper and small notebooks that could be easily hidden.

He had folded an expanding fury into thousands of pages. Couriers ferried Solzhenitsyn's microfilm manuscript to Europe in the hope of ensuring its eventual publication. In the meantime, a friend driving his car was beaten up. His secretary was detained by the police and interrogated for a week, eventually giving up the location of a hidden copy of the manuscript, after which she was said to have committed suicide. Feeling the secret police closing in, Solzhenitsyn sent word to trigger the publication in Paris of the first volume of *The Gulag Archipelago, 1918–56: A Literary Investigation*. Six weeks later he was arrested and deported to Germany.

"It is unthinkable in the twentieth century," Solzhenitsyn wrote, "to fail to distinguish between what constitutes an abominable atrocity that must be prosecuted and what constitutes that 'past' which 'ought not to be stirred up.' "[95] His compendium was the most explosive account of a concentration camp system ever written, triggering diplomatic crises between Moscow and the West, and a concentrated effort on the part of Soviet intelligence to smear Solzhenitsyn as a drunk and question his sanity.

Yet smearing the man would not be enough to erase his accomplishment. The damage was done; Solzhenitsyn had laid out the arbitrary Soviet denial of humanity to millions of its own people stretching back to the Russian Civil War. Showing not only how the state built the camps but how the camps built the state, he made an argument that the two were morally inseparable and equally corrupt. Stalinism had not been some wave of excess but the natural evolution of everything that had come before.

Somehow out of clandestine interviews and secret glimpses into archives in a repressive regime, the former prisoner had managed to write an urgent epic depicting the underground country of concentration camps while living within the police state itself. From Moscow to Solovki, from Vorkuta and Kolyma to Karaganda, he re-created the long journeys into exile, a society warped for four decades or more by the nightmare dream of a workers' paradise, offering the tales of those who came back and an elegy for those who did not. Future scholars would have access to numbers and official records, with conservative estimates suggesting that eighteen million prisoners were sent to the Gulag during its official years of operation, with between one and a half and three million dying there.[96]

It is a peculiar truth that the Soviet Union had shown the world how to transform wartime detention into a peacetime institution, recasting concentration camps as a foundation of society. Even where there was no external war, the state showed that it could invent internal enemies to fight on an ongoing basis, developing a permanent class of camp administrators, secret police, and interrogators—of whom, as Solzhenitsyn wrote, nothing extraordinary was required, "only that they carry out orders exactly and be impervious to suffering."[97]

For the rest of the century the Gulag would serve as a model and a muse for other revolutionary states. Each state would embrace concentration camps briefly on an experimental basis or permanently on a vast scale, and in doing so declare a willingness to inflict suffering on civilians en masse in order to reinvent the world.

CHAPTER FIVE

The Architecture of Auschwitz

1. ONE MONTH AFTER TORCHLIGHT parades swept Germany and millions cheered Adolf Hitler's inaugural speech as chancellor, the first Nazi concentration camp opened in March 1933 near the village of Nohra, in the eastern state of Thuringia. Created in haste, the camp was located on the grounds of a military training school near the debris of a decommissioned airfield. The village itself sat on the western outskirts of Weimar, home at one point to Schiller, Bach, and Goethe. The city also had been the birthplace of the German constitution, which Hitler would destroy less than two months after taking office.

The prisoners, who were political opponents of the Nazis, began arriving on March 3. Detainees at Nohra slept amid filth on piles of straw and blankets. The camp had no watchtowers or barbed wire, no striped uniforms or crematoria—just detention and interrogation under the almost maternal-sounding term "protective custody."

On the second day, Nohra's population swelled to nearly two hundred detainees, who slept on the first floor of one wing of the three-story brick school, guarded by brown-shirted storm troopers. In a token nod to legal niceties, since the prisoners had not yet been convicted of anything, they were taken to the local polling station and allowed to vote in the March 5 elections—which led to a ten-fold spike in Communist ballots for the small community.[1]

After nighttime arson ravaged the national legislature in Berlin on February 27, the government had taken advantage of the crisis to pass an emergency law. The resulting Reichstag Fire Decree suspended civil liberties, including habeas corpus—the right to question the legality of detention. Under the vague new parameters of "protective custody" set out by the decree, authorities detained individuals indefinitely without evidence or charges. By arresting Communist and Social Democratic Party members—on whom the fire was collectively blamed—Nazis and their supporters removed political opponents, intimidated the public, and consolidated power. Hundreds, then thousands, were quickly rounded up and held in Nazi paramilitary barracks or police stations around the country, where they were beaten and questioned. The Reichstag Fire Decree became the legal basis for the existence of the first Nazi concentration camps.

The camp at Nohra lasted just six weeks. Most prisoners eventually signed agreements to forgo additional involvement with the Communist Party and were released. Those who refused were transferred to the protective custody wing of a nearby prison. During the weeks it took to deal with Nohra's detainees, another half-dozen temporary facilities appeared around the country. But the Nazis wanted a more permanent arrangement.

Immediately following Heinrich Himmler's March 9 appointment as the acting police commissioner for Munich, he toured the grounds of the shuttered Powder and Munitions Factory at the town of Dachau. During the First World War, the factory's workforce had grown from twenty-two workers to nearly five thousand. The finished facility had included more than three hundred buildings. As the complex expanded to accommodate the workers, Russian prisoners of war were brought in to do construction work.[2] Forced to close after the war, the site had fallen into disrepair and nearly been turned into a gynecological treatment clinic before the government took an interest in it. Himmler quickly made up his mind.

A crew was sent to the factory grounds the following day to begin restoring electricity and plumbing. A week later, Himmler announced the establishment of a five-thousand-person camp for those held under protective custody. Slated to be Germany's first permanent concentration camp, Dachau would fall under the control of the regional Bavarian police.[3] Prisoners were to stay in the old factory manager's house while barracks were readied for the larger mass of detainees to follow.

On March 22, the inaugural contingent of prisoners arrived in a large black bus driven to the entrance gate in the stone wall surrounding the former factory grounds.

2. In the first weeks under Hitler, arrests, beatings, and interrogations expanded exponentially as the Nazis solidified their rule. By the end of April, more than 35,000 people had been arrested in Prussia and Bavaria.[4] With traditional jails and lockups at full capacity, other temporary camps like Nohra sprang up in large abandoned spaces.

Such an ad hoc beginning might appear improvised, as if Nazi leadership had unwittingly stumbled its way into the *Konzentrationslager* system. Yet the Nazi dream of concentration camps was not new; it had begun as a revenge fantasy during the first year of the party's existence. In September 1920, at a speech at the Münchener-Kindl-Keller brewery in front of 2,000 followers, the future Führer brought up the idea of camps for enemies, justifying the idea by noting that "in South Africa, the British deported 76,000 women and children to concentration camps."[5]

Hitler was fetishizing the martyrdom of a Germanic *volk* in British camps twenty years earlier in Africa, but he was also mindful of more recent detentions. At the end of the First World War, the harsh measures of the armistice had required Germany to immediately release all its prisoners of war, military and civilian. But Britain and France had not responded in kind.[6] Stories of German deaths in British concentration camps—which had circulated for years— continued to appear. Long after hostilities ended in 1918, hundreds of thousands of German prisoners still languished in Allied camps.[7] In French territory, German prisoners were assigned to labor, clearing streets and rebuilding bridges destroyed by their countrymen.[8]

In the wake of Germany's bitter defeat, Social Democrat Kurt Eisner, prime minister of the brief-lived secessionist Bavarian People's Republic, had refrained from demanding the release of fellow Germans who were still prisoners in concentration camps in France and England. Defending the choice, he said that he would instead humbly appeal to the Allies' sense of humanity and justice.[9] Eisner was assassinated by a German nationalist nine days later.

Hitler nursed a grievance over Eisner's position for years afterward and railed at the notion of his countrymen left to rot in concentration camps abroad. In a speech at a Munich circus hall in September 1922, he suggested that Eisner's disregard for the fate of German patriots was shared by all Jews—that Eisner had only said aloud what the rest of German Jews had been thinking. These Jews should learn, Hitler said, "how it feels to live in concentration camps!"[10]

A year earlier Hitler had been even more explicit in an article for a Nazi newspaper. Hitting on the same theme, he called for the hanging of those who had turned their backs on Germany in order to collaborate with Allied forces. The rich should be forced into national work service, he wrote, and "the Jewish undermining of our people should be prevented by, if necessary, keeping their provocateurs secure in concentration camps. In short, our people should be cleansed of all poison from above and below."[11]

The words, uttered two decades before the establishment of death camps, were more than rhetoric. A plan to round up "security risks and useless eaters" and organize them into "collection camps" for labor projects was part of the November 1923 constitution that the National Socialist German Workers' Party, or Nazis, intended to impose if they had succeeded in overthrowthing the Weimar Republic during the failed Beer Hall Putsch. From the earliest years of the party's existence, Hitler had repeatedly signaled not only a commitment to concentration camps but also a clear agenda for how they would be used: the suppression of political opponents, the provision of useful menial labor, and the removal of unwanted social or racial elements—particularly Jews.

In his earliest surviving piece of political writing, dated September 16, 1919, Hitler wrote that the key was to recognize that Jews could not be assimilated, that they would always remain foreigners. Outlining what he claimed was a "rational" form of anti-Semitism, he went to great lengths to try to establish the "alien" nature of Jews. Just months after the Treaty of Versailles, while still a corporal in the military, he wrote that what needed to happen was not random violence against Jews, but the "legal struggle against, and eradication of what privileges the Jews enjoy over other foreigners living among us (Alien Laws)."[12]

Much attention has been given to Hitler's florid anti-Semitic rhetoric from his earliest days. Less known is the degree to which the specific policy he was advocating early on had been previously enacted. The First World War had barely ended when he wrote that he wanted German Jews relegated to the status of foreigners. Key elements of what Hitler initially proposed for Jews were the measures that most belligerents in the war, including Germany, had just used against unwelcome foreigners. Loss of property, removal from participation in society, and detention in concentration camps had been the universal standard for enemy aliens, who had been treated as an undifferentiated group—a pariah class—by many nations during the war.

Hitler's early embrace of concentration camps represented less of a leap than it would later appear. He was aware of the British camps in South Africa, and eagerly employed them for his own rhetorical ends. But the more recent history of concentration camps for radicals and foreigners during the First World War directly exposed a politicized Hitler to their social and military uses. And it was that wartime model that the Nazis would take up and transform into a more brutal incarnation, to eradicate their real and imaginary internal enemies.

3. On the afternoon of April 11, 1933, six SS men in civilian clothes stormed out of a car on the streets of Munich, arresting Communist leader Hans Beimler and another party member. Beimler, who had once dared the Nazis to show their faces in the town of Dachau, had not realized that the Communist resistance would effectively be cut off at the knees. No military confrontation had moved the workers to rise and fight invading storm troopers at Munich or Dachau. Instead, seeing the groundswell of support for the Nazis, Communists fled the country or, like Beimler, found themselves arrested in targeted sweeps.

After searching the men, the SS took them to police headquarters, where a crowd gathered to mock Beimler ("Now it's all over with the world revolution!" and "We'll meet again in Dachau!").[13] Overjoyed to have captured a high-profile Communist who was also an elected member of the national legislature, the Nazis escorted their new prisoners to the political section upstairs, where storm troopers and SS members continued to press into the room for a chance to see Beimler while he was searched for weapons and incriminating papers.

Interrogated briefly about his membership in the party, he wrote a statement affirming it, reminding his examiners that he had also been elected to the Reichstag three times—most recently on March 5. For his pains, he was told that he would be held in precautionary arrest. Handcuffed by one wrist and pulled down a hallway he recognized from previous detentions, he realized they were headed toward the jail. He felt surprised to have gotten off so easily. It was not until they passed the stairs without going down them that he began to realize that this detention would be different.

As Beimler was led through a room that had been converted to sleeping quarters for guards, storm troopers in the hall found out who he was. A fierce whoop went up, and men began to fall in behind, until all but five or six were told to stay back. Those who were allowed to proceed followed as Beimler was taken under a stairwell into a windowless room with a bare lightbulb, a table, and a straw mattress. Ordered to remove most of his clothing and lie facedown on the table, Beimler tried to comply, but the commandant clamped him in a headlock, dragged him farther up the table, and held him down while the other men went to work on him. Blows from their rubber clubs struck his bare back, and at some point after dozens of strikes, Beimler lost consciousness.[14]

When he came to, he was ordered to dress quickly and asked whether he still imagined himself an elected Reichstag official. Enraged by his answer, his captors threw him down on the table and beat his swollen, lacerated body again. When they were finished, he was marched back to the jail, where he spent two weeks in a communal cell before being called out with a dozen or so other prisoners. The assembled group was told that they were headed to Dachau, and anyone who tried to escape would be shot.[15]

Loaded into a vehicle with other detainees, Beimler rode northwest from Munich. Approaching the compound, he pondered the layers of barbed wire that surrounded the camp and marked the end of the line. While prisoners poured out of the vehicle, paramilitary storm troopers (SA) and SS men with long pistols and oxtail whips stood in front of the administration building. Hectored into lining up in rows, the prisoners learned the proper response for roll call, repeating the procedure over and over.

The commander who had wrestled Beimler into a headlock during his beating had come along for the ride and now placed him at the head of one line. Unrolling a placard that read "A hearty welcome!" he hung it around Beimler's neck. A few prisoners were separated from the rest, with Jews told to join Beimler's group. The new arrivals were marched in a double line through the camp, past prisoners pulling rudimentary stone cylinders three feet in diameter to flatten and pave roads. Beimler recognized several detainees as former regional officials.

Brought into an open hall, the new arrivals were told to empty their pockets. Beimler failed to move quickly enough. An SS man named Steinbrenner snatched a small pencil from a side pocket and held it up as evidence that Beimler was attempting to smuggle items into the camp. "Two weeks strict arrest," the major replied, even though writing instruments and paper were soon returned to detainees. Beimler suspected that they needed an excuse to segregate their prize prisoner from the rest. He was taken away, along with a policeman who had been accused of informing on the Nazi Party.

As they waited to be let into the camp bunker, Steinbrenner beat them with his whip. Beimler was put into cell number 3, which he soon realized had formerly been a bathroom for the decommissioned munitions factory. Worried about fumes escaping from the open drainpipes, he looked up and noticed a square window perhaps eighteen inches across. A wooden bed was the only furniture he saw.

He did not have long to get his bearings before three SS men, including Steinbrenner, barreled into the room and began yelling. Steinbrenner struck him on the head and shoulders, instructing him to take off his jacket and drop his trousers. Thrown over the corner of the bed, Beimler was beaten by all three until he quit moving. Forced to stand, he noted strips of skin hanging from Steinbrenner's whip, while he was asked whether he would now confess to betraying the workers. He assumed that another assault was imminent, but the squad left for the next cell, where they could be heard hitting the policeman accused of being an informant.

Soon after, the warden came in and asked whether he had any requests or complaints. Beimler said nothing. The warden handed him a six-foot length of rope and instructed him to hang it from an old valve on the overhead water pipes. Climbing up onto the bed to slip the end of the rope with a loop over the stopcock, Beimler realized he had been handed a noose. As he stepped off the bed, he was told to always stand at attention when prison staff entered the cell.

And if he ever felt overwhelmed, the warden explained, the rope was at his disposal.

Beimler had heard at the police station that his friend and former Communist Party secretary Joseph Götz had been held at Dachau for weeks. Calling out on his first day, Beimler discovered that his friend was in the cell next to him. Götz soon warned him that Dachau was a very bad place. The daytime beating had only been the beginning. He should gather his courage for the night.[16]

4. In the weeks between Himmler's first visit to the abandoned munitions factory and Beimler's arrival, Dachau had quickly expanded from its first hundred prisoners to its first thousand. On April 1, Himmler became head of the political police in Bavaria, and in his capacity as the commander of the SS, he used his new position to assign himself control of Dachau. Similar moves by other Nazi party leaders fused the state and the party, accelerating the disintegration of German law.

On April 10, while raids and arrests exploded across Bavaria, a group of SS men marched into Dachau. Prisoners listened as guards lined up in the compound and were told by their commander that anyone who felt averse to bloodshed or inclined to treat the prisoners as human beings should remove himself immediately. The next day the SS took control away from the police who had been managing the prisoners, shifting it overnight away from the familiar framework of internment and labor camps of the First World War and further into the realm of sadism and horror.

While the Nazis sought to ensure undisputed control of government across Germany, their foremost goal was the annihilation of political opposition. With the Communist deputies of the Reichstag held in protective custody or forced into hiding, they rammed the Enabling Act through the legislature, which allowed Hitler to implement new laws and even to change the constitution at will.

As with the early Gulag, the first camps were publicly celebrated.

An emphasis on the punitive nature of the camps was paired with a contradictory insistence on the state's mercy and its civilizing role. Newspaper accounts told of cigarettes and special food being given to inmates on Hitler's birthday and described educational plans intended for the prisoners: "It is hoped that work, adequate meals and fair treatment will make the internees usable again for patriotic ideas."[17]

Even as educating and civilizing missions served as justification for the camps, tensions developed over those people the Nazis had already deemed defective or inferior. The treatment of targeted groups inside the camp reflected an intensified version of their treatment on the outside: during his first months in power, Hitler began to impose his dream from the 1920s of subjugating targeted minorities as alien races.

A new law in April prohibited Jewish and politically suspect individuals from civil service, eliminating Jewish doctors from public hospitals and Jewish professors from teaching posts, as well as limiting the number of Jewish students at universities. At Berlin's Opernplatz the following month, forty thousand people gathered to hear Minister of Propaganda Joseph Goebbels speak and to burn books by Jewish and prodemocracy authors.

Student groups took up the Nazi banner to reclaim a mythical Germany for an imaginary racially pure subset of Germans. Describing the strange Nazi mythology that developed over time, linguist Max Weinreich wrote, "The Jew could be represented as the embodiment of everything to be resented, feared, or despised. He was a carrier of bolshevism but curiously enough, he simultaneously stood for the liberal spirit of rotten Western democracy. Economically he was both capitalist and socialist. He was blamed as the indolent pacifist but by strange coincidence, he was also the eternal instigator to wars."[18]

Jewishness was not usually the primary trigger for arrest and detention in 1933, but Jewish prisoners nonetheless found themselves singled out for abuse in the camps. Segregated on arrival, some Jewish prisoners did not survive their welcome beatings.

Accused as a group of smuggling letters out of Dachau, they were run through exercise drills then put under strict arrest as punishment.[19] Sometimes detainees would try to hide their ancestry on arrival in order to remain invisible in the main body of prisoners, paying a brutal price if the subterfuge was later unearthed.

Surviving the welcome beating was not always enough. The day after the SS took control of Dachau, four Jewish prisoners were separated after roll call, taken outside the gate, and shot. Three of the four detainees were killed immediately; the fourth died later in the hospital. The reports that were filed claimed, as they would later for many compliant prisoners, that the dead had been killed "while trying to escape."[20]

5. Two weeks after Dachau fell into SS hands, Hans Beimler spent his first night in the camp. Sitting alone in his cell, he heard the SS coming. They began with cell number one and the prisoner they believed to be an informant. From the sounds of the assault, more attackers were present than had joined in during the afternoon session.

Sometime after the first prisoner lost the ability to scream, they moved on to Götz's cell and repeated their drill. After Götz, they came for Beimler. Four men flogged him with both ends of the whip, while two more spit insults and mocked Communist slogans as he was struck. After dozens of blows from each attacker on his trunk, arms, and legs, he was forced to hold out his fingertips and the back of his hands, so they could be hit, too.

When the men finally finished with him, he hoped there might be peace on the cell block, but they brought a column of Jewish prisoners to the empty fourth cell next to his and beat them the same way, one after the other. The violence ended well before midnight, but Beimler was in too much pain to sleep.[21]

In the morning the beatings began again. Beimler felt revulsion at the sounds of blow after blow striking bodies, and laughter in the hall afterward. This time they stopped after the first cell. Hours later, a commission of inquiry arrived to look into how the prisoner in cell number one had managed to hang himself.

For Beimler, the days passed by in the same fashion, but now the attackers had only two special prisoners left to focus on. He was told over and over that it was a sign of his cowardice that he had not yet used his rope. On the fourth day he asked for food and water, and was given a slice of sausage, tea, and bread. On the fifth day he developed severe stomach pains and after some internal debate asked to see a doctor. A Jewish prisoner who was a physician examined him and gave him a referral to what turned into a three-day ordeal. He went from the sick bay at the prison to the hospital, then back to police headquarters in Munich, and finally to the bunker at Dachau, this time passing through the maze of barbed wire in rain and mud.

He was again segregated from the group of prisoners about to join the camp population, and again given two weeks of strict arrest. This time, three newcomers—including Fritz Dressel, a friend and fellow party member—accompanied him to the camp's arrest section, where he was once more herded into cell number 3, with Sepp Götz still alive next door.

An hour after his arrival, the beatings began and were repeated that night, as the men moved from cell number one toward Beimler. He was told he would be hanged the next morning at 7 a.m.[22] But morning came and went, and the cycle of torture and waiting continued as before, except that he was moved to a new cell where all the windows were covered with wood nailed on from the outside. After two more days of this treatment, Dressel, who was confined next door, was said to have slit his wrists. The warden would not let the injured man stay in the sick bay but ordered him brought back to his cell.

Steinbrenner came into Beimler's cell the next morning and repeatedly punched him in the chest, asking how many more days he intended to remain alive to report "present" at inspection. Beimler, who had been plotting an escape, delighted in the possibility that his captors might soon come in and find him gone. Briefly taken for questioning, he worried that his cell could be searched in his absence and that the board he had loosened over his window might be discovered. But when he returned, he found everything untouched.

Visiting again that afternoon, Steinbrenner pointed out a table knife sitting on a small bench. The commander dragged Beimler out and took him into cell number 4, where his friend's corpse was splayed. Beimler feared he would be left with the body until he killed himself, but he was soon returned to his own cell, as the departing Steinbrenner said, "So! Now you've seen how it is done." Shortly afterward, his captor came back and tore a four-inch strip the length of the prison blanket, knotting a loop in one end and observing that the other end could be tied to the window. The rest, he suggested, was up to Beimler, but he demanded that the deed be done that day. Beimler put him off, explaining that it was his son's birthday, so he would wait until the day was over.

Götz told Beimler it was foolish to try to escape, that their friend Dressel was the third in a row to die in strict arrest at Dachau, and that such violence would not long be tolerated. Things would surely improve. If Beimler tried to escape, Götz believed he would be shot.

By then, Beimler was convinced he would die either way, believing Steinbrenner's promises that they would never get out of the bunker alive. He preferred to be shot while trying to escape rather than have someone string him up by the neck in the filth of Dachau and claim that he had killed himself.

The night of May 8, a friend who was a prisoner outside the bunker managed to slip him a tool to unscrew the grate over his window and tin snips to help manage the barbed wire.[23] Later reports claimed that he strangled a storm trooper and took his clothing, but Beimler simply crawled out of his high window, taking a board with him.[24] He navigated three layers of barbed wire—the middle one electrified—using the wood for insulation, and climbed onto the six-foot wall around the camp's exterior. Waiting there a moment to make sure he had not been seen, he jumped down on the other side and made his way into Munich.

The next morning, Steinbrenner arrived to find an empty cell. Frantic searches were made, prisoners were interrogated. For some time, guardhouse staff remained certain that Beimler was hiding somewhere on the grounds. Dogs were used to search, and a hundred-mark reward was posted in the local paper *Amper-Bote*. But Beimler remained in hiding until he could safely get to Berlin and cross the border to the east.

Once out of the country, he mailed a postcard to Dachau telling the camp commanders to kiss his ass. Some three months after his escape, he was sitting in Moscow, writing a searing indictment of Nazi atrocities. It was printed in three languages and circled the globe.

Beimler became an international hero of the left. He humiliated the Nazis and played an indispensable role in informing the world what was happening in the camps—and how badly the German justice system was foundering mere months into Hitler's rule.

Yet his escape stood out so markedly in part because it was set against a landscape of expanding horror. While he wrote from the relative freedom of Moscow, Beimler's wife was still held in protective custody in Germany. Götz—who stayed behind and relied on his faith in the legal system to halt the violence—was shot for "assaulting a guard" just after Beimler's escape.[25] And a local councilman transported to Dachau on suspicion of having aided Beimler's flight was executed point-blank on May 17, while "trying to escape."

In his public account, Beimler protected his friend by obscuring the means by which he had pulled off his vanishing trick, but his success taught the SS to add another layer of security—one devoted to keeping prisoners in.

While other escape attempts took place, none were successful. Later in the war some prisoners managed to flee and join the local resistance, but they were eventually found and killed. After Beimler, until Dachau's final days, no other prisoner would escape from the main camp without being caught.

6. Dachau quickly grew notorious in and outside Germany, through published articles, rumors, and a children's rhyme ("Dear God, make me deaf and dumb, / so I will not to Dachau come"). A month after its founding, and in the wake of the shooting of three Communist prisoners, the commandant allowed a *New York Times* reporter inside—the first journalist to see the camp. He noted the electrified barbed wire, the four-tiered pallets of bunks in the sleeping quarters with a four-inch board between prisoners on each side. He described the prisoners' overalls and shaved heads, tracked their work schedules, and reported on the food being prepared (sausage and sauerkraut). He even managed to question detainees—always, he noted, in the company of officers. One man protested that he had no idea why he had been arrested, as he had done nothing wrong. The commandant smiled and replied, "You all say you did nothing."[26]

The reporter turned to familiar institutions to try to put the camp into perspective, pegging camp life as falling between "a severely disciplined regiment and a hard-labor prison." He conveyed gently and deliberately that he was not getting the whole story—the prisoners playing instruments ostensibly for their own recreation started up just as the reporter arrived among them. And he felt sure that some portion of the detainees must have been arrested due to nothing more than Nazi grudges. Nevertheless, sharing a eugenic viewpoint common in both Europe and America at the time, he acknowledged that some of the prisoners did look like those whom society might be better off without.[27]

On the heels of Dachau, new camps rose at Oranienburg, Lichtenberg, and Sachsenburg in the east, as well as Esterwegen in the north. Some camps were founded in abandoned breweries, former textile mills, and one in a Renaissance castle, while others were built from the ground up. Enterprising local SS even set up rogue concentration camps on their own initiative.

Despite neighbors' reports of screams and the way names like Dachau became punch lines to grim jokes, reporters and the public could not have imagined the range of abuse visited on prisoners in the early Nazi concentration camp system. Family members allowed to visit their loved ones in detention, an intermittent practice in the first years, could see the signs of torture. Others received prisoners' messages, smuggled out in code via letters, and realized that life in the camps was brutal. The knowledge of terrible things happening that could not be discussed underlined the sense of helplessness, emphasizing that a detainee could do nothing to save himself, and neither could anyone else.

As rumors increased, and detainees who had been released described their experiences, more journalists pressed to visit the camps. Eager to showcase the rehabilitative aspects of detention, commandants instead found themselves forced to deny the use of corporal punishment.

They were roundly disbelieved. One *Times* of London correspondent permitted into camps during the summer of 1933 reported the usual denials from commanders but then described prisoners showing him the wounds on their backs from flogging. Leaving the camp, he felt indecent after being "permitted to witness such inhuman treatment imposed by ruthless men on their own flesh and blood."[28]

Not all prisoners faced the kind of abuse Hans Beimler received. Detainees in early camps who were not singled out for mistreatment often faced harsh but less lethal conditions, alternating between set hours of manual labor and military discipline. As in prior camp systems, prisoners' reactions to extrajudicial detention varied widely. Some became ill, some had mental breakdowns. Old political hands— many of whom had faced arrest together before Nazi rule—built solidarity among their comrades. And as always, they tried to find ways to regain a sense of normalcy and some feeling of control.

At Börgermoor, one of the northern marshland sites that visibly recalled the camps of the First World War, prisoners decided to put on a concentration camp circus—what they called a "Zirkus Konzentrazani." Despite fears that the SS would decide that captives were being coddled, inmates assembled a weekend spectacle packed with acrobats, gymnasts, singers, and jugglers performing for prisoners and camp staff alike. On the day of the event, a brave detainee walked through the camp—even past the commandant's office—carrying a poster advertising the circus ("Great gala performance!" "Gigantic animal show!").[29]

The circus sold out. Risky moments included a sketch in which clowns dressed as concentration camp prisoners commented on their forced labor. A year later, professional actor Wolfgang Langhoff was released from the camps and made his way to Switzerland, where he included details of the performance in his 1935 memoir, *Rubber Truncheon: Being an Account of Thirteen Months in a Concentration Camp.*

One side of the Nazi argument abroad was to claim the prisoners were well treated. The other was to argue that the prisoners were subhuman and dangerous to society. Concern over the need to mitigate international condemnation was such that they distributed photos of physically unusual or disabled prisoners to highlight the career criminals they portrayed as "asocial" elements threatening society. They also shot propaganda footage aimed at depicting life in the earliest Nazi concentration camps as idyllic.

Footage from the first months of Oranienburg concentration camp survives today. As with Dachau, Oranienburg quickly gained an international reputation for brutality. Yet staged scenes depict prisoners relaxing outside listening to violin and guitar, washing clothes, eating dinner, doing calisthenics, and performing manual labor. The awkwardness of everyone involved as they pretend the camera is not present reveals the images as propaganda—but amateur propaganda. The camp officers play at fussy military bureaucracy with lists, while the prisoners stiffly pretend to be at ease in the detention of a benevolent state, all against a backdrop that looks more like a rustic campsite than a concentration camp.

The images of Oranienburg roll call were shot on an enclosed field. The men are called to line up, and they scramble into rows, hopelessly civilian in their posture and stance. A middle-aged man in a business suit stands next to one in shirtsleeves in front of another in a collared sweater, the prisoners wearing whatever they had on at the time of their arrests. Even though it is likely that some of the prisoners in the film had faced interrogation, seeing them in retrospect lends a naïve character to the camp as an institution. The future—its rows of prisoners in striped uniforms and shaved heads lined up with military precision by the thousands, harangued by officers in crisp Death's Head attire—does not yet exist.

There was, in fact, a moment when that future might never have come to pass. After the death of German president Paul von Hindenburg in August 1934, Hitler gained uncontested power and took the title of Führer. Two visions for the Third Reich emerged. In one, instruments of terror and extrajudicial detention such as the camps would diminish in importance and fall under the control of traditional institutions. In their place a Nazi government would rely principally on normal channels of law, rendered more aggressive and more brutal but still within Germany's existing judicial framework.

The other model brimmed with reflections of Dachau. Calling for the continued use of protective custody, Himmler advocated keeping control in the form of SS authority that would supersede laws and courts. In this way, Hitler's coterie, accountable only to itself, could rule through permanent extrajudicial terror.

Amid these contesting visions—one playing out mostly in the Prussian north, the other in the Bavarian south—came a purge of the SA and its leader, Ernst Rohm, who stood second only to Hitler. The SA had provided the brute muscle to help the Nazis grow and take power, but with power secure, the more sophisticated SS, which had begun as protection squads under SA control, became ascendant.

The summer purge culminated in almost two dozen SAs being transported to Dachau as prisoners and shot, followed by the execution of Rohm in Munich's Stadelheim Prison on July 1, 1934. The decimation of the SA strengthened Himmler's hand and brought Germany closer to a lawless abyss.

7. At Kemna concentration camp near Düsseldorf, reports of brutal beatings, smoke blown into metal lockers used to confine prisoners, and detainees forced to eat vomit led to the camp's closure after just six months. On the initiative of the state's attorney, twenty-five sadistic SA guards were locally charged and convicted in 1934.[30] Hitler pardoned them the following year, effectively discouraging future court intervention in camp atrocities.

SS men often contested the stories of abuse that circulated. In his first months as commandant at Dachau, Theodor Eicke flew into a rage, haranguing prisoners about the vicious rumors in the community about conditions there. Reminding them that detainees had already been killed for spreading word about the camp—including Dr. Katz, who had helped so many prisoners—Eicke threatened that more could be executed at any point. He seemed especially offended by any suggested comparison to Soviet tactics. "There are no atrocities and there is no Cheka cellar in Dachau!" he insisted. "Anybody whipped deserves to be whipped."[31] The atrocities continued without interruption, but SS men went to greater lengths to hide their crimes, in one case setting a shed on fire to burn tortured bodies beyond possible identification.[32]

If those running the camps refused to recognize the parallels between Soviet secret police brutality and their own, a handful of prosecutors were more attentive and tried to bring cases of early crimes to justice. In a 1934 letter to then minister president of Prussia Hermann Göring, one state prosecutor complained about a concentration camp created independently by an SS officer who was also head of police: "In Stettin there has been...a rule of absolute arbitrariness, rightly compared by the presiding judge with Communist Cheka methods."[33] A regional court convicted seven SS men for abuses committed in the nearby camp. In July 1934 as part of the larger purge of "wild" elements in the party, Hitler announced that three of the seven were executed due to their "disgraceful abuse of prisoners in protective custody."[34]

While the German legal system did not on the whole resist concentration camps or the abuses taking place in them, neither did it immediately surrender judicial authority over them. After the April 1933 shooting of the four men ostensibly trying to escape Dachau, Joseph Hartinger, a local prosecutor, investigated the killings as a serial murder of Jews. He got autopsy reports that detailed the shredded skin, whip marks, and guns fired point-blank. He filed indictments against the camp commandant and three of his SS men.

His moral clarity in defying the early concentration camp system nearly provoked the Nazis to murder him.[35] Continuing his investigation, he found that reports filed by guards on the circumstances of shootings did not match the wounds on the bodies of the dead. Autopsies on ostensible "suicides" revealed horrific evidence of torture. It was clear that captors were out of control. The Nazis, however, would not brook such audacity, and provoked a disturbance that triggered a federal assumption of local powers in order to restore order. Weeks later, the case was quashed.

Though a scattered handful of attempts to bring perpetrators to justice could not subvert the entire Nazi camp system, pressure resulting from public attention did succeed in transforming the early savagery of the camps into a more regulated state. Named inspector of concentration camps in 1934, Dachau commandant Theodor Eicke helped enforce the rules he had already created in Bavaria, which limited the tactics guards could employ. Random, improvised punishments were discouraged for a smaller set of more consistently applied measures, such as floggings, "punishment exercise drills," loss of food, confinement, and "pole hanging," a practice in which prisoners' wrists were bound behind their backs, then used to hoist them onto a chain and hook suspended from a pole or crossbeam. Prisoners assaulting guards or trying to escape were to be shot instantly, with no lesser measures permitted.[36]

In the wake of the SA purge, Himmler had transformed himself into one of Hitler's closest advisors and effectively gained control over the camps. Yet for a time, a future without concentration camps remained possible. In August 1934, Hitler put limits on protective custody ahead of an election in which he ran unopposed, proclaiming an amnesty that set thousands of prisoners free. Consideration was given to reducing the role of the camps, diminishing the general terror, and making use of more traditional institutions in their place.

But Dachau itself still held almost two thousand detainees, and Himmler, who felt the Third Reich was under constant threat from inside and abroad, had no intention of reversing his course. The larger the role of the camps and the greater the number of people involved in running them, the more power both he and the SS would wield. Referring to the earlier amnesty, Himmler wrote that "we...in total misjudgment of the opponent, cleared all but an insignificant part of the concentration camps. This was one of the gravest political mistakes the National Socialist State could have made."[37]

More than once, officials tried to bring Himmler to heel over the number of detainees and hold him accountable to Hitler's directions regarding protective custody, to no avail. Despite the reprieve given by Hitler months earlier, Himmler arrested a thousand Communist prisoners—many of them detainees who had just been released under the amnesty—and authorized the arrest of thousands more suspects. He then misrepresented the number of prisoners he held. Later, he simply dealt with letters of complaint by meeting with Hitler, who sided with him, writing direct replies on the letters themselves. Camp prisoners, Hitler announced, did not need to be released. Further, Himmler wrote in a letter to the Reich minister of justice, "The Führer has forbidden the consulting of lawyers, and has charged me with informing you of his decision."[38]

By 1935, Himmler's ambition for a state of permanent terror, along with Hitler's approval of his methods, guaranteed a future for the Nazi camps. Germany had abandoned the path that might have seen the rule of law return, transforming the camps into another system entirely.

8. Even for those who had not yet seen the inside of a camp, Nazi rules placed devastating restrictions on daily life. "The time has come," Hitler said, introducing new provisions in September 1935, "to openly oppose Jewish interests to those of the German nation."[39] The Nuremberg Laws built on existing anti-Semitic decrees and worked to strip Jews of German citizenship, leaving them stateless and without legal rights. Anyone with at least three Jewish grandparents was officially considered a Jew, whether they were observant or not. Nazi race theories advanced a more extreme reading of a eugenic theory already popular in the United States and Europe, viewing degeneracy, disease, and deformity as fully inherited through aberrant genes that should not be allowed to reproduce. Anyone born a Jew was said to be incapable of assimilation into the new Aryan order.

Further, it was made a race crime for Jews to marry or have extramarital relations with German or Germanic peoples. In time, officials would add a red *J* to the identity papers of German Jews, and many were forced to change their middle names to "Sara" and "Israel" for easier identification. They would be prohibited from having typewriters, purchasing periodicals, going to the movies, riding buses, taking taxis, using radios, talking on the telephone, owning bicycles, and going to the barber, among many other rules.[40] The Draconian measures and the small inconveniences alike combined to make Jews' legal existence in Germany impossible.

Germany's Jews were not the only minority seen as suspect. Nazi race ideology also considered the "Gypsy," or Roma and Sinti, populations a stain on the new Reich. In November 1935, the government extended the provisions of the Nuremberg Laws to apply to black and Gypsy residents as well as their children.

With these measures, the Nazis took the first steps toward a repudiation of basic human rights that would in time become the foundation of their camp policy—the idea that some people were not fully human.

In Germany, those deemed Gypsies had long been subject to special legal provisions, with Bavarian police logging a special registry of them decades before the Nazis seized power.[41] A later 1926 Bavarian law "Combating Gypsies, Vagabonds, and the Work Shy" had become standard throughout Germany by 1929.

Using camps as a collection point for unwanted elements also predated Hitler's rule. Four years before the first Nazi camps opened, the city of Frankfurt established what it called a "concentration camp" for Gypsies. With wide public and political support, the city council tried to force traveling Roma into the camp in order to keep them away from town.[42]

In 1933, with the Nazis in power, systemic harassment of Gypsies quickly expanded to include even those assimilated into German communities. Famous for his footwork and good looks, Gypsy boxer Johann Trollmann fought his first bouts in Hanover. His ringside nickname Rukeli, from the Romani word for "tree," played on his strength. As a teenage amateur, he had won several regional championships. In his four years as a professional, he had gone on to build a solid record as a fighter. Some papers dismissed him as "un-German" and "the Gypsy in the ring," but his elegant style and speed made him a crowd favorite.

After the German boxing association had stripped Jewish light-heavyweight Erich Seelig of his national title in 1933 and expelled him from the profession, Trollmann decided to make a bid for the position. Trollmann fought his title match against Adolf Witt at the Bock Brewery in Berlin on June 9, 1933. On the night of the contest, Trollmann and his opponent battled twelve rounds, with Rukeli outboxing his opponent until a Nazi boxing official called the fight and pressured the judges to rule "no decision."

Spectators who had watched Trollmann dominate the match were outraged and began to riot. As the crowd grew rowdy, the judges avoided a confrontation by overturning their initial decision and declaring victory for Trollmann. But a week later, he received a letter nullifying the result, reinstating the match as a draw due to "the inadequate performance of both fighters." He was stripped of his title.

Before his next fight, he was informed that if he wanted to keep his boxing license, he would have to adopt the German style and not "dance like a Gypsy." Embracing the inevitable, he turned the match into a brutal parody. On July 21, the night of his second title fight, he entered the ring as an Aryan—covered in white flour, with his hair dyed blond. He tried to fight standing toe to toe without using his footwork and withstood his opponent's blows for five rounds before he was knocked out. It was the last title fight of his career.[43]

9. After Hitler made it clear that the Nazi concentration camp system would be a permanent fixture in the Third Reich, Himmler embarked on ambitious plans. He started by eliminating several camps, closing rogue and unsuitable sites, strategizing instead toward a long-term, consistent detention system. Yet he did not rush. For the time being, Nazi concern for world opinion took precedence over the National Socialist agenda.

Before Hitler had been appointed chancellor, Berlin had won the right to host the 1936 Olympic Summer Games, and the event was meant to showcase Germany's return to greatness on the world stage. The Olympics would serve as the Nazis' debutante ball.

Not everyone wanted to be part of the orchestrated propaganda. Calling for a US boycott of the games, Church of Christ minister Samuel Cavert wrote in 1935, "What we now witness is not violence, but a cruel and systematic effort to relegate the Jews to a position of recognized inferiority....If present tendencies continue there is the possibility of actual pogroms against the Jews."[44]

Reporters in Germany required to pass material through censors had a more difficult time warning readers against misinformation from the propaganda minister Joseph Goebbels, but still managed to slip in cautionary notes: "The visitor to Germany this Summer who wants to avoid becoming Dr. Goebbels's unconscious tool will have to possess an unusual amount of sales resistance."[45]

Publicly acknowledging the Draconinan image they had created, Nazi leadership leaked word to reporters that they were calling off their focus on "State enemies" and easing suppression of Jews and Catholics.[46] Even as homeless people and vagrants were taken into custody to clear the streets, a show was made of releasing some prisoners. Dramatic expansion of camps was postponed, lulling many into believing that international pressure had affected German policies.

Yet following this hibernation period, establishment of the Nazi concentration camp system began in earnest. A year after the Olympics, a metal gate bearing the legend *Arbeit Macht Frei* ("Work Sets You Free") was placed at the west entrance to a completely rebuilt Dachau. The new camp formed a rectangular grid, with a long avenue running between rows of barracks, seventeen on a side, with a capacity for more than six thousand detainees.

A new camp at Sachsenhausen, designed in a triangular shape to maximize watchtower surveillance, had opened twenty miles north of Berlin even before Dachau was complete. Its gate carried the same motto, and soon the facility's elegant wedge shape would need remodeling in order to accommodate more prisoners. In time, *Arbeit Macht Frei* would be welded to metal bars or painted on signs for camps at Flossenbürg and Auschwitz as well. Buchenwald's gate, finished in 1937, read *Jedem das Seine* ("To Each His Own," but also "Everyone Deserves What He Gets").

The emergence of slogans and military structure reflected a more disciplined image for the camps, with Himmler lauding the birth of the "modern, up-to-date, ideal and easily expandable concentration camp."[47] Universal standards were set. Each prisoner was assigned a mattress, a blanket, aluminum cutlery, a towel, a shoe brush, and a metal locker.[48] In a 1937 speech, Himmler declared that the vast majority of those in the camps were "slavish souls," "the scum of criminality, of failures." Since they were largely incapable of instruction, he argued, "Education is therefore [achieved] by orderliness."[49] A Death's Head Unit (*SS-Totenkopfverbände*) of guards and administrators with a skull-and-crossbones insignia was established, and going forward, Death's Head units staffed all Nazi camps. Himmler justified large numbers of guards for the system by arguing that because they dealt with criminals and villains, "no other service is more devastating and strenuous for the troops."[50]

At this time, Jewish detainees still constituted a minority of prisoners in the camps. Yet after the promulgation of the Nuremberg Laws and the end of the Olympics, Jews faced increasingly worse treatment across the country. Not satisfied with the anti-Semitic regulations in place, Goebbels—perhaps the most rabidly racist of Hitler's inner circle—launched a multimedia campaign to educate the public.

A traveling exhibition called "The Eternal Jew" began circulating in November 1937, reaching more than four hundred thousand Germans in Munich alone. Displaying images and invented "facts" attributing mythical corruption and depravity to Jewish people across the centuries, the exhibition blamed Jews around the world for everything from capitalism and Bolshevism to filth and disease. The film industry, too, was bent to the service of the Nazi cause, lauding Hitler and the party while slandering Jews worldwide.

Restructuring German society toward a perverted notion of purity also brought more homosexuals into the camps. More than five thousand gay men would be sent to camps on the basis of Paragraph 175, a revision of earlier law that targeted any "male who commits lewd and lascivious acts with another male."[51] The Reich likewise targeted Jehovah's Witnesses, who refused to salute Hitler or report for conscription.

In the mid-1930s, large numbers of chronic criminal offenders were added to the rolls of those detained on the basis of new preventative custody rules. It was a tactical attempt to gin up a more menacing camp population for the public, as well as diluting the percentage—though not the numbers—of political prisoners held by the Nazis.

In addition, internment camps outside the formal *Konzentration-slager* system detained Gypsies across Germany. During the Olympics, as part of the street sweeps of vagrants, Gypsies had been rounded up and held at Marzahn, an open field away from competition sites. Detainees who had jobs were permitted to leave during the day but had to return at night; others were forced to provide labor for government construction projects.

In 1936, a Munich headquarters to "Combat the Gypsy Nuisance" was opened, cataloguing a national database of Roma. In Berlin the same year, psychiatrist Robert Ritter was installed at the head of the Research Institute for Eugenics and Population Biology. Ritter collected data on Roma and Sinti genealogy and decided that all but a few "pure-blooded" Gypsies were alien and incapable of being assimilated into German society. Therefore, he suggested that they should be subject to permanent "preventive detention in work camps or guarded closed settlements."[52] He further recommended their sterilization.

By the end of 1937, four new purpose-built German concentration camps existed: Dachau, Buchenwald, Sachsenhausen, and Lichtenburg—a camp specifically for women. By that time, Jews and Gypsies were facing repression, but many still lived in German communities.

When Hitler had announced the Nuremberg Laws, he said that he hoped they would successfully address the issue of race in Germany, but if they did not, the problem must "be handed over by law to the National-Socialist Party for a final solution."[53] In the interim, the Nazis used propaganda and eugenics to shift public opinion. The full force of exclusion from German daily life would soon fall on Jews and Gypsies alike.

10. In the wake of his defeat in the first months of the Third Reich, Gypsy boxer Johann Trollmann lived in Berlin and Hanover, his childhood home. No longer able to compete professionally, he resorted to fighting at fairground matches. In June 1935, he married

a non-Sinti woman with whom he had a daughter. Living in a work-house at Rummelsburg in Berlin that July, Trollmann faced involun-tary sterilization at the request of the workhouse director. Told he suffered from "congenital idiocy," he refused to accept the diagnosis or that it could be inherited. In the legal proceedings that followed, three doctors ruled against him, and the judges at the Court of Hereditary Health appear to have agreed. He was sterilized on December 23. As persecution increased, Trollmann began to fear for his family's safety and ended up divorcing his wife.

When war came, the former boxer was called up for military ser-vice and went off to serve the country that had put him in a work-house and sterilized him. Johann Trollmann fought in Belgium, Poland, France, and then on the Eastern Front before the Third Reich decided that Gypsies no longer had the privilege of dying as soldiers for the German cause. When race became an enemy to be destroyed as thoroughly as any opposing country, he was dishonor-ably discharged, along with all other Roma and Sinti.

After returning to Hanover, he was arrested in June 1942 and tor-tured. Sent north to Neuengamme, a vast concentration camp outside Hamburg, he was likely assigned to a hard-labor brigade. The boxer officially met his fate in the form of heart failure in February 1943.

But a secret prisoners committee at Neuengamme may have killed Trollmann in the hopes of saving him. A year after his official death, he was seen at Wittenberge, a subcamp of Neuengamme some seventy-five miles away.

For all the brutality of the *Konzentrationslager* system and the pow-erlessness of the prisoners, detainees still managed to accomplish striking feats. It was sometimes possible for committees of prisoners to help a living detainee switch identities with the dead if it might shorten a sentence or better position someone for survival. The audacity of the moment is hard to imagine. The exchange of uni-forms, the report of the death, the burning of the corpse of Johann Trollmann who was not Johann Trollmann. All to help one prisoner survive for a little bit longer, or as long as any of them might hope to.

If that was the hope, the ruse did not buy him much time. According to another prisoner who was sent to Neuengamme and then the factory quarry at Wittenberge, Trollmann was recognized. Forced to fight other prisoners even at Wittenberge, he wound up in a match with Emil Cornelius, a former criminal and widely loathed *kapo*.

Trollmann defeated his opponent, but soon afterward the *kapo* demonstrated his own power outside the ring, bludgeoning Trollmann to death with a shovel. The Neuengamme book of the dead—one of the few camp records that survived the war—lists his death as February 9, 1943. But it seems that Sinto boxer Johann Trollmann survived another year as another man, even though his second life failed to shield him from the fury inspired by the brilliance of the first.

11. During the summer of 1938, the Nazis cracked down on vagrancy, arresting itinerant workers, including hundreds of Gypsies, and sending them to concentration camps. It came as a surprise to many of those arrested but was merely the next step in the slow elimination from society of groups deemed undesirable.

That fall, however, Nazi violence reached new heights. In Paris on November 7, a seventeen-year-old Jewish teenager named Herschel Grynszpan shot German diplomat Ernst vom Rath, triggering a cascade of terror. After Rath died of his wounds, chief of police and Gestapo head Reinhard Heydrich unleashed waves of reprisals against synagogues, businesses, and cemeteries, calling for widespread arrests of young, healthy Jews, with notifications sent to concentration camps.[54]

On November 9 and 10, across Germany and Austria—which had been annexed by the Reich that spring—party members and storm troopers in plain clothes destroyed property, smashing windows, defacing buildings, burning synagogues, and looting. Jewish men were swept up and subjected to harassment and torture. Jewish women were sexually humiliated and made to strip. Approximately forty thousand Jews in the Reich were arrested in the immediate wake of what would come to be called Kristallnacht. Some thirty thousand were sent to concentration camps, many of them pulled out of their homes at night in pajamas and slippers.[55]

Paris newspapers condemned the reprisals, pointedly noting that Goebbels had made no public call to order and that the vandals had been allowed to riot for more than twenty-four hours.[56] The Netherlands proposed the creation of two refugee camps to allow Germans to cross the border, the Dutch premier calling events in Germany "the most distressing tragedy in our times."[57]

Many other countries joined the chorus, but most balked at accepting Jewish refugees, arguing that their countries were in no position to increase immigration quotas. Nations around the world had offered the same platitudes months before at the Evian Conference on refugees, when they had likewise refused to accept any more Jews fleeing Nazi Germany. The German government used the failed conference to claim that the world did not want Jews in their midst any more than Hitler did.

The Nazis had invented a modern pogrom. They had learned that the violence and dislocation of riots could be harnessed and institutionalized by funneling prisoners into concentration camps. Under Nazi rule, Jews had long been on the receiving end of discriminatory treatment in both concentration camps and German society. But Kristallnacht marked the moment when German Jews were taken out of society en masse, without even the pretense of individual culpability, and moved beyond legal protection.

German Jews were assessed a billion-Reichsmark fine for the trouble they had caused by being attacked. Many of the Jews arrested during Kristallnacht were released after promising to emigrate, the last wave to have that privilege.

By autumn 1939, only fifteen hundred Jews would remain in the Nazi concentration camp system.[58] The Nazis did not want to detain Jews indefinitely; they wanted the Jews gone. The tidal wave of detentions in November 1938 had been halted and even temporarily reversed. But Germany's realization that it could move to destroy the Jewish community and that the world would do nothing about it opened a new window into possible futures.

The population of the *Konzentrationslager* stabilized after the release of the Kristallnacht prisoners. With an amnesty for thousands the following April on Hitler's birthday, the entire concentration camp population fell to just over twenty thousand.[59] And yet the physical machinery of the camps grew. In the spring of 1938, Flossenbürg opened in Bavaria, followed by the new women's camp at Ravensbrück in May 1939.

Other priorities took precedence for a time. After the Anschluss in Austria, a bloodless takeover of Czechoslovakia, and a buildup of German forces in the Rhineland, observers understood that war was imminent. Yet in this arena, too, Hitler shocked the world, when Nazi Germany and Soviet Russia, totalitarian states and deadly enemies, put aside their differences to divide Poland between them. Nazi forces invaded Poland on September 1, 1939.

12. As Poland was dismembered, Germany negotiated the return of its citizens held in the Soviet Union before the start of the war. Thus it happened that after passing through Butyrka Prison twice and enduring the misery of Karaganda in the Gulag, Margarete Buber-Neumann was not set free but delivered from the border crossing at Brest-Litovsk into the hands of the Gestapo.

Taken to Poland's Lublin Castle for questioning, she heard her interrogator wonder aloud why Russians would let the wife of a Communist leader leave for Germany unless she happened to be a spy for the Soviet secret police. After interrogation, Buber-Neumann was locked in a cell with Polish Communists, who were plotting their escape to the promised land of Soviet Russia. Buber-Neumann vacillated over whether to let them know what they would find if they managed to get away. When she finally told them her story, her cell-mates refused to believe her.

Photographed and fingerprinted, she wound up escorted by Gestapo agents on a transport headed for Berlin. On the way to the Alexanderplatz, the police presidium, she rode through the streets of the city she had dreamed of seeing again, but felt no joy in return-ing. Turned over to the women's department with a piece of paper, she watched the administrator copy her familiar personal details, as well as one new piece of information. The charge against her, she discovered, was high treason.[60]

Her next cellmate had been an activist for the Socialist Workers' Party, and, like the others, dreamed of a Soviet paradise to which she might escape. This time, Buber-Neumann's account of her stay in Russia was believed, and the young woman began to weep, asking, "What have we got to live for now?"

After months at the Berlin police station, Buber-Neumann was taken to Stettiner Railway Station and put on a prison train with fifty women—political prisoners, prostitutes, and Jehovah's Wit-nesses, all packed in together. On arrival in Fürstenberg, they heard the barking of dogs and guards outside. As the locked door opened, prisoners were hounded off the train and run through corridors with German shepherds snapping at their legs.[61] Herded to a gate, they were delivered to a woman who checked their names off a list and took charge of them. They had arrived at Ravensbrück.

The largest women's concentration camp in the Nazi system at the time of Buber-Neumann's arrival, it had begun with the transfer of just under a thousand women in 1939. During her last days in the camp, its population would exceed fifty thousand.

Neat flower beds, saplings, and raked gravel paths led to a vast aviary in which Buber-Neumann could glimpse peacocks wandering at ground level and monkeys swinging limb to limb overhead. In the distance stood a barbed-wire fence. Rows of women streamed by in lockstep, barefoot and expressionless. In columns of five they filed by, singing marches as guards hectored them.

By 1940, entry into a Nazi camp had become a consistent, regimented experience. Each new prisoner's information was registered on a card and she was photographed, whereupon she surrendered her clothing and showered. One white-clad attendant—also a prisoner—relentlessly examined newcomers for head lice, another for pubic lice. The price for hosting a single louse was being shaved to the skin; sometimes shaving was done regardless.

At Ravensbrück, after a doctor conducted a cursory medical exam (and called Buber-Neumann a "Bolshevist shrew"), the newcomers were issued camp uniforms, nightclothes, utensils, and bedding. New arrivals quickly learned the color code of triangles on prison uniforms. Criminals got green patches, and political prisoners wore red. Asocials (prostitutes, alcoholics, addicts, vagrants, the mentally ill, and some Gypsies) got black, while political Jews were given two triangles to form a red-and-yellow star. Jews who had committed "racial offenses" got black-and-yellow ones, while those of Jehovah's Witnesses were lilac.

Avenues ran between rows of barracks for prisoners. Each building contained two wings that had a common room and a dormitory meant for one hundred that would eventually house up to five hundred detainees. Despite the later addition of two avenues of barracks, the prisoner population continued to grow and conditions became more crowded as the war dragged on.

Buber-Neumann's first Ravensbrück meal of porridge, fruit, bread, margarine, and sausage astounded her. This was like no camp of the Gulag. But she soon found the better food offset by the demand for order, which dictated complex rules and punishments around bed inspections. The convoluted ritual needed to prepare a bed—including using two boards and a stick as tools—led her to declare the whole process a "typically Prussian piece of chicanery," a phrase she used for almost every unreasonable Nazi demand.[62] After repeat offenses, those who had not adequately prodded their sacks of straw and blankets into shape were reported as violators. Reports could lead to official punishments in levels of increasing severity depending on the offense. "Bed-building" infractions generally meant going eight days without one of two daily meals and spending several hours standing at attention in front of the Punishment Block. The intermediate level of discipline led to solitary confinement in darkness, and the third was a brutal twenty-five lashes with a whip, a legacy of the regulations developed at Dachau.[63]

After she was integrated into the main camp population, Buber-Neumann was visited by three prisoners, who drew her into the dormitory to question her about her past. Again, she told the unvarnished story of political events and her fate in the Soviet Union. As she did, she realized that the interview represented some kind of tribunal of Communist prisoners within the camp. One of the three—a senior prisoner for Buber-Neumann's block—declared the new detainee a Trotskyite. She had not even adjusted to life in a Nazi camp before being labeled a counterrevolutionary and ostracized by other Communists.[64]

13. Germany's war effort drew on its concentration camps, and in return, concentration camps fed on the war. Weeks before the invasion of Poland, the Gestapo pulled a group of male prisoners from the *Konzentrationslager* system and placed them in solitary confinement in a jail to await the start of hostilities. The day before the invasion, they were dressed in Polish uniforms, taken in black Mercedes limousines to the border station at Hochlinden, and shot.[65]

Germany broadcast its planned announcement that "Polish insurrectionists and soldiers" had besieged the custom house in darkness, and an hour-and-a-half battle had been required to regain it.[66] SS major Alfred Naujocks later testified that he had taken part in the setup, arranging the bodies of the corpses for the operation nicknamed "Canned Goods."[67] The staged photos of battered, unrecognizable bodies of men who had merely been concentration camp inmates became the sham justification for the invasion of Poland.

The war likewise drew on camp staff for its execution. Former Dachau commandant turned concentration camp inspector Theodor

Eicke was reassigned to combat duty and commanded SS Death's Head divisions and cavalry largely drawn from concentration camp guards. In Poland, the Death's Head divisions terrorized the population at large and eliminated targeted individuals in the wake of invasion.

The camps reaped the bounty of this destruction, as deportations to Germany soared. During the first month of battle, Buchenwald's population nearly doubled. Among the new arrivals was a group of 110 Polish prisoners denounced as the "Bromberg snipers." Accused of atrocities, they were brought in from the front, tortured, and put in a cage of barbed wire and boards nicknamed "the dungeon," where all but one died in the following weeks.[68]

Even early in the war the influx of Poles at Ravensbrück was so vast, Margarete Buber-Neumann wrote, "It seemed almost as though Hitler had determined to wipe out the Polish people altogether."[69]

Long before 1939, Hitler had embraced the idea of *Lebensraum*—living space—for the German people. In *Mein Kampf,* published in 1925, Hitler took up and promoted this preexisting concept of German expansion into "new land and soil" in order to escape "the danger of vanishing from the earth or of having to enter the service of others as a slave nation."[70] Through war, he hoped to enslave other nations instead.

To carry out his plans, Hitler embraced not only camps for those deported from occupied territories, but also the historical precursors of concentration camps. He rationalized the removal of populations in Eastern Europe by making analogies to the eradication of Native Americans from North America. "The struggle we are waging there against the partisans resembles very much the struggle in North America against the Red Indians," Hitler wrote in a note to soldiers on the Eastern Front. This message was placed inside three hundred thousand copies of Wild West novels by Karl May, the best-selling writer in German history.[71]

In a colonial settler fantasy, the Nazis likewise adopted the idea of reservations. Very early on, they had considered deporting Jews to Madagascar. Later, the plan had been to send Polish Jews to live on a reserve in the area of Lublin. Adolf Eichmann, then head of the

Central Office for Jewish Emigration for the Protectorate of Bohemia and Moravia, had in fact begun deportations to the region. It quickly became apparent, however, that for Nazi purposes, reconcentrating populations would not suffice to provide *Lebensraum*.[72] There was not enough territory to go around.

Mass deportations of Poles to existing camps proved just as problematic. It is one thing to remove people from society; it is quite another to maintain them in camps. Himmler fetishized his camp system as a modern marvel run on discipline and precision. If those deemed disruptive or degenerate could not function in normal society, they could at least be quarantined in a system that would contain them with fierce structure and rules.

But Himmler had realized even before the war began that the current camps would not be able to keep up with the quantity of prisoners, telling the SS, "We won't be able to make do."[73] Using the existing system to absorb all the newcomers would be like drinking from a firehose.

As the German army rolled through Belgium, Denmark, and France, and then invaded Russia to the east in June 1941, camp conditions deteriorated precipitously. Barracks were filled to two or three times their capacity. Food rations were cut. Sick wards were constructed, in which the contagious were often isolated and left to die. Meanwhile, the system continued to expand. Neuengamme, where Johann Trollmann had been sent after his torture, was promoted from a subcamp to a major camp in 1940, receiving prisoners from across Europe. But even the establishment of new camps, combined with locally improvised detention facilities, would prove inadequate.

The answer, suggested Richard Glücks, who had succeeded Theodor Eicke as concentration camp inspector, was to expand the camp system eastward. In February 1940, Glücks was authorized to hunt for an appropriate location. Later that month, he wrote to Himmler, advising him that a place had been found in the town of Oświęcim, some thirty miles due west of Kraków. Rows of two-story barracks on the site had previously housed an Austrian cavalry unit and, before them, immigrant workers. Except for the nearby town of some twelve thousand residents, the area was isolated. The town square had already been renamed Adolf Hitler Place, and the town itself forced to revert to a preexisting German version of its name: Auschwitz.

After getting approval from Himmler, Glücks appointed Rudolf Höss commandant of the camp. The German mayor sent some 250 Jews from town to carry out additional construction work. The first thirty prisoners, who were German criminals, arrived on May 20, 1940.[74]

14. Though many detainees were taken to Auschwitz, Polish prisoners continued to arrive at Ravensbrück. Two weeks into her stay there, Margarete Buber-Neumann was prompted by a group of Poles to become the block senior of their hut. Horrified, she explained that she was unwilling to administer the cruelty and bullying that accompanied the job. When they told her it would be a cooperative arrangement for everyone involved—she would not abuse them, and they in turn would not give her trouble—she agreed.

But their scheme went awry, and Buber-Neumann instead found herself assigned to supervise a barrack filled with "asocials," including prostitutes, bed wetters, and mentally ill prisoners who refused to follow rules. Amid nightly arguments and betrayals between different factions, she lived in despair of protecting from the SS those she saw as her charges. She suddenly came to appreciate roll call, a mind- and body-numbing tedium that stretched on for hours, as a haven of relative peace in which she was responsible only for herself.[75]

A more cordial arrangement prevailed after she was moved to supervise a block of Jehovah's Witnesses. Doing all their assigned tasks ahead of orders, the "Bible Students" complied rigorously with the rules. Buber-Neumann acclimated herself to illicit theological discussions over whether it was biblically permissible to eat the camp's blood sausage and ignored their repeated attempts to convert her.[76]

Learning that Jehovah's Witnesses could sign a declaration renouncing their religious activities and gain release from the camp, she was baffled by their refusal to do so. When one of the prisoners in her block was slated for transfer out, which was suspected to be a preliminary to execution, Buber-Neumann convinced the woman to renounce her faith and save her life, only to earn condemnation from everyone in the hut. She was impressed by their religious discipline, but after captivity in Russia and Germany she had lost any enthusiasm for martyrdom.

She spent two years in relative calm running their block. But in the spring of 1942, the atmosphere in the camp began to shift. One afternoon, after the grounds were cleared and prisoners sent to their huts, a group of ten Polish women were marched through the broad expanse of the square. Following the 6 p.m. siren, when camp prisoners lined up in row after row for roll call, a spray of gunfire sounded outside the camp wall. Afterward, a series of individual shots scattered crows overhead. Executions had come to Ravensbrück.

The process was repeated regularly, with an outside SS detail brought in to serve as the firing squad. Sometimes, however, work assignments or camp medical staff did the executioners' work for them. Walking through the camp, Buber-Neumann saw a block of new Jewish prisoners returning from offloading shipments of brick. The fierce sun had scalded their skin, and the rough work had shredded their soft palms. Buber-Neumann saw them day after day at the sick bay, where the attending doctor refused to treat the "Jewish cows."[77] By the time their rough bandages were replaced, the prisoners were fevered and their open wounds brimmed with maggots.

Even those with access to the sick bay balked at going. Jewish patients and badly ailing prisoners would find themselves assigned to a stretcher in the corridor and narcotized into a stupor, eventually dispatched via lethal injection to the heart. Women accused of "intercourse with foreigners" underwent forced abortions well into their third trimester of pregnancy. Himmler's personal physician,

Karl Gebhardt, had a special operating room in which he conducted medical procedures on prisoners, testing bone and muscle grafts and experimenting with gangrene.[78]

After being moved to work in the office of the senior supervisor, Buber-Neumann began altering paperwork, misrouting reports, and protecting prisoners from a stay in the dreaded punishment bunker. When the senior supervisor was removed under a cloud of suspicion, however, Buber-Neumann was likewise accused of conducting "Communist agitation" and interfering with official documents.

Ending up in a dark cell in the bunker from which she had tried to save others, she spent her first days without food. Squatting in her sleeveless dress on the cold stone, she scrounged an old newspaper to sit on. She faced her interrogator's vague intimations of public hanging without fear, but his threat to send her to Auschwitz demoralized her.

Left alone again, she was so sure she could smell burnt flesh that she whispered to her neighbor in the next cell to ask whether the woman could smell it, too. "Yes, of course," her neighbor replied, explaining that since her arrival in the bunkers, a crematorium had been installed.

After ten weeks, she was released, only to wind up back in punishment for discussing a British propaganda leaflet that had been dropped by a plane and found outdoors by a prisoner. Spending five more weeks in solitary, she began hallucinating and completely lost touch with reality. By the end of her second stay, she was so far gone she had no wish to leave the punishment cell at the end of her sentence. She could be coaxed back to life only by a friend who took over her care.

Upon recovery, Buber-Neumann was assigned to run a sewing machine in the three-thousand-person Ravensbrück factory that produced SS uniforms. Amid the hundreds of seamstresses running the electric machines, she was always behind, often breaking needles and regularly rescued by other prisoners, who rethreaded her machine, replaced her needles, and left extra pieces of completed work to fill her basket. A Ukrainian girl taught her Russian folk songs, and they sang them together, the noise of the machines covering their transgression.

As the camp expanded, and winter came on again, roll call grew worse. The more prisoners there were to count and the sicker they grew, the harder it became to maintain perfect formation while the SS accounted for everyone. Women collapsed, frostbite began to take its toll, and amputations followed.

Buber-Neumann managed to weather the duress of roll call, but in the fall of 1944 she developed boils from the endless filth of the camp. The boils led to blood poisoning in January 1945, when a Communist medical assistant took pity on her and saved her life by administering stolen medication. For her pains, the girl was ostracized by the Communist prisoners for helping that "Trotskyite Grete Buber."[79]

In the spring of 1945, bombing runs increased in frequency and the electrical grid grew less and less reliable. It became clear that the German military lines had disintegrated. In full rebellion, the women stole back cigarettes originally confiscated by the SS, walking around the camp furiously smoking at will. Eventually the prisoners were lined up and sent out the front gate, the overseer telling them, "You can do what you like and go where you like. From now on regard yourself as fugitives."[80]

Aware that Soviet forces were coming in from the east, Buber-Neumann knew she had to go the other way. Hiking to the train station, she and her companions gathered items from thousands of stolen Red Cross packages that littered the ground, thrown away by fleeing German soldiers. Cigarettes, chocolate, and a wonderland of delicacies lay sprinkled across a landscape of desolation. She headed out to resume the life that had been interrupted seven years before.

15. By late 1941, the camps had grown dense and squalid from the flood of detainees arriving from abroad, yet the war placed still more demands on the camps. Unlike the early frivolous labor projects in the first *Konzentrationslager*, in which meaningless work was

sometimes ordered simply to punish prisoners, a complex network of labor projects emerged, spread across thousands of sites. Every camp and subcamp used prisoner labor in some fashion. Prisoners working for the I. G. Farben rubber plant lived in a dedicated compound at Auschwitz. Fur linings in the coats of the SS came from hutches of rabbits under the administration of prisoners at Dachau. At Neuengamme, detainees were set to work clearing rubble from bombed roads and buildings outside Hamburg.

Forced labor was endured by millions outside the camps as well, with Nazis diverting populations in occupied territories to meet labor needs elsewhere. But prisoners in the camps were often assigned the worst jobs—brutal work in quarries or endless hours digging in wet clay, which quickly drove inmates to collapse.

Both the Nazis and the Soviets conducted the war on the backs of their concentration camp prisoners. Forced-labor Gulag efficiency expert Naftaly Frenkel had suggested that the system be optimized to get the most out of prisoners in their first three months, after which they were disposable. He would have been ideally placed to appreciate that before the end of the war, average life expectancy at Neuengamme concentration camp had dropped to twelve weeks.

The long blocks of barracks at Auschwitz-Birkenau had originally been built to house such slave labor. But in 1942 the magical, almost infinite supply of Soviet POWs had thinned and then evaporated, leaving Birkenau underpopulated.

At the start of Hitler's rule the German Jewish population had been less than 1 percent. After Kristallnacht and the emigration that followed it, that number had dropped further. Jews were still subject to abuse and at risk of worse inside Germany, but in the wake of Kristallnacht, the issue of Jews in the Third Reich had not generated the same urgency. Even in early 1942, they made up less than 7 percent of the overall concentration camp population.[81] For comparison, at Auschwitz in 1941, Poles represented the vast majority of detainees.

Nazi anti-Semitism, however, had not vanished; it had merely been preoccupied for a time outside the confines of the camps. Einsatzgruppen and Order Police battalions were sent behind German armed forces invading the Soviet Union, working as mobile assassination squads. They targeted local officials on an individual basis but also carried out mass executions of Jews, Gypsies, and disabled noncombatants.

In August 1941, Himmler witnessed one such execution of one hundred Jewish prisoners at Minsk. Standing at the edge of a mass grave, he grew queasy after being spattered with the brains of a dead man. Concerned about the effect of the killings, he wondered how they might be done in a way that would not traumatize the executioners.[82]

Months later, senior Nazi officials gathered at Wannsee to discuss the resolution of the Jewish question. Following the trajectory of much that had already been discussed, attendees decided on January 20, 1942, to reconcentrate the Jews of Europe in eastern territories and destroy them there. Initially, the Nazi turn toward genocide was not framed in terms of the concentration camp system, but weeks after the conference, Himmler saw his opening. If the anticipated supply of Soviet forced labor had run dry, concentration camps had another role to play.

The *Konzentrationslager* system had already pioneered many approaches to mass killing that would be used during the three-year period that followed, from the bullet to the back of the head in a "doctor's" office to the use of Zyklon-B. These extraordinary measures had previously been applied on other populations, such as Soviet prisoners of war and the disabled; they had not yet been used systematically to exterminate Jews. "It is striking," writes historian Nikolaus Wachsmann, "how many structural elements of the Holocaust had emerged inside concentration camps before the SS crossed the threshold to genocide."[83]

Nazi concentration camps had begun as a tool to suppress Hitler's political opponents but had soon moved on to isolating whole classes of people. During the war, they expanded to make use of vast populations of slave laborers. All of these types of camps had been seen elsewhere. But in its final years, the Third Reich would invent a new category of camp, one aimed at eradicating not just political identity or legal standing, but all the Jews of Europe.

If Dachau had been the first permanent camp, the ur-camp through which the Nazis established a camp culture, recognizable physical features, and a training method, the death camps would represent the evolution of the concentration camp to its logical end point, reducing the individual detainee not to a number but to nothing. And one camp, Auschwitz, would encompass the alpha and omega of the Nazi *Konzentrationslager* system, carrying out every camp function simultaneously.

16. By the time she was loaded into a cattle car bound for Auschwitz, Krystyna Żywulska had endured multiple traumas in the destruction of her native Poland. Born Sonia Landau to a Jewish family in the city of Lodz, she had been forced out of law school by the Nazi invasion in 1939. Fleeing with her family to Warsaw two years later to escape rising anti-Semitism in her hometown, she soon found herself driven into the Warsaw Ghetto.

Not every ghetto is a camp, but the Nazis found ways to use ghettos as adjuncts to the camp system. By the time Żywulska entered the Warsaw Ghetto in 1941, it had become a deliberately lethal setting— a way of segregating hundreds of thousands of Polish Jews into a quadrant just over one square mile and starving them to death. Realizing that they were likely to die, Sonia Landau and her mother took the audacious step of escaping with the help of a woman from the Polish Home Army.

Landau hid her roots by adopting a non-Jewish identity. She tried to rent a room with false papers that even her landlord recognized were forged. The two ended up an unlikely pair working together in the Polish underground. They were later arrested and held together in Pawiak Prison in Warsaw, just blocks from the ghetto she had escaped. Under interrogation by the Gestapo, she took up a third identity: that of a Christian Pole named Krystyna Żywulska.

By 1943, Krystyna and the other prisoners in the women's section at Pawiak had years of rumors and experience to draw on. So when they were told to line up and herded into the transport cell knowing they were headed to Auschwitz, they believed they were going to their deaths. Pawiak had flea infestations, brutal daily interrogations, suicide attempts, and even killings, but it lacked the finality of Auschwitz. As they prepared to leave, a cellmate broke the gloom, saying, "At least you'll get a beautiful haircut."[84]

They sped in trucks through the city to the train station, watching residents headed to work. Driven onto cattle cars, the prisoners waited for the train to move, and finally arrived in an open field after dark. The snarling dogs, the columns of five, the frightening march toward the barbed wire and sentry boxes on high towers visible from a distance—now she had seen a death camp. Standing next to her, Zosia, her former landlord and sister in the underground, spoke: "We've entered hell."[85]

In this hell there were barracks, and people, and work. At registration, a new arrival asked, "Do we die here immediately?" An irritable senior German prisoner brandishing a stick replied that she herself was an eight-year veteran of the *Konzentrationslager* and was now the only one left out of eighty women who had arrived with her. Asked what the rest had died of, she said, "A cold, you stupid asshole. In a concentration camp, you die of death."[86]

Żywulska was tattooed with prisoner number 55908. Her head was shaved, and she was deloused. Each detainee suddenly seemed indistinct and unrecognizable. After two days with no food or water, they were given turnip soup and four ounces of bread, a full day's ration. They ate everything without thought, as quickly as they could, which spurred the realization that they had already turned into animals.

They squatted in a large field for the day, waiting to be let into the quarantine hut to sleep. A woman who had been arrested during her wedding still wore her gown and held her bouquet as she comforted one of the guests brought to Auschwitz with her. Another detainee, who had been tortured daily at Pawiak Prison, expressed optimism that at least so far things at Auschwitz were better than that. Veteran prisoners moved around them in the field, trading hoarded food for rags, underwear, or sweaters. Finally allowed into the barrack, they were stampeded toward the lowest platforms of bunk beds, where they shoved their way in amid deafening chatter. The moment they looked away, their clogs were stolen.

Woken at 2 a.m. for morning roll call, Żywulska stood for more than three hours under a star-filled navy sky until the count was done and dawn came. Permitted to relieve themselves, the women sat in two long rows over the holes of the latrines as the shithouse matron walked along beating them from behind with a stick. Veteran prisoners offered advice on navigating Auschwitz, telling newcomers not to expect a bath more than once a month, not to worry about menstrual hygiene because their cycles would soon vanish, and not to go to the hospital, as those who went rarely came back.

During her month of quarantine, Żywulska learned to sleep in the crowded bunks and how to navigate the guards. She found that bread could buy a constellation of things, because there was never enough of it. Hunger at Auschwitz was a constant state. Out of earshot of camp administrators, prisoners were perpetually in conversation aimed at distracting themselves from the longing for food.

Contraband entered the camp through the prisoners who processed the belongings of Jewish transports. Family members could send parcels of approved items to prisoners, too, though Jewish prisoners were not permitted to receive packages. Żywulska imagined a magical day when she, too, might get a package from home. In the meantime, Zosia plotted how she could steal a sweater to keep her friend warm.

One morning, detainees heard a shrill whistle and were told to get to their block and stay inside. Soon afterward, a midmorning roll call was announced—but only for Jewish prisoners. Żywulska watched as women from the adjacent building were forced to line up, each one trying to avoid the front row. A familiar, hated SS executioner, unsteady on his feet and apparently drunk, proceeded to point with his cane at individual women. After they undressed, he directed each one to his right or his left. In time, it became clear that the small percentage of healthy prisoners went to the left. A thousand women in the bright sunlight stood in total silence. The prisoners in rows, the detainees still in their blocks spying through windows, the hundreds of women who had just been sent to the right—everyone understood that they had just witnessed a selection.

The larger group of women was herded by the camp *kapo* to Block 25. Within hours, the women inside began calling out for water, but once prisoners were slated for execution, they no longer received anything. The other prisoners could hear them, but no one would risk visiting. Night fell, and still the prisoners remained suspended between the living and the dead. Eventually truck headlights passed over Żywulska's block. After a time, they heard the engines start again and a wailing that vanished in the distance as the women from Block 25 were carried to their death.[87]

In the weeks that followed, Żywulska received a first parcel from her mother, which she could hardly open for weeping. Because she found roll call unbearable, she began to compose poems in her head, a thing she had never done before. Yet setbacks occurred continuously. She watched as a new acquaintance who had survived interrogations and torture at Auschwitz was taken away for good by the Gestapo. She and Zosia had to flee their barracks and hide to avoid being chosen for service in a camp brothel. Another prisoner's ill-timed diarrhea resulted in collective punishment of kneeling in the mud—which led to widespread fever. For the first time, she was separated from Zosia, who fell ill.

After nearly succumbing to work in the fields, Żywulska was assigned to the camp office. Her salvation came through the intervention of a still-human *kapo*—one who had admired a poem she had written about morning roll call.

Assigned to process new arrivals, Żywulska learned to corral and reassure them. She could not bring herself to hit prisoners with a stick. Children came in with their mothers and lined up with them at roll call, only to be taken away for denationalization and integration into German society. A Ukrainian woman gave up hope and made a run at the barbed wire perimeter fence, knowing she would be shot.

One night during a concert performed by prisoners for administrators, *kapos*, and guards, Żywulska stopped in to watch a Jewish violinist from Vienna play and conduct. Just before the concert, she had seen the detainees of Block 15 kneeling for punishment. She had watched the elegant, dark-haired Greek Jews sifting through the kitchen garbage for bones to chew on. As the orchestra played, Żywulska used the distraction of the performance to slip into the typhus-ridden hospital ward and bring warm water to Zosia. The surreal beauty and the horror of the evening struck her, but it was Zosia who stayed foremost in her mind. Zosia, who had endured alongside her since the trip from Pawiak Prison, who had wondered if they would roast together in hell, soon died anyway.

Anything was possible at Auschwitz, and nothing made sense. Żywulska came down with typhus, too, and lay unconscious for several days.[88] The violinist from the performance swallowed poison and killed herself. A former Soviet parachutist screamed in the night and was tied to her bed. Żywulska's scabies began to itch, and she clawed herself, hoping to die. Yet after she was clandestinely sent medicine by a male prisoner who had kissed her during outdoor duties in her first weeks at Auschwitz, Żywulska recovered. An intervention by the same *kapo* who had admired her writing helped keep her, once again, from brutal outside labor.

Soon after her recovery, a group of French women were taken in trucks to their deaths singing "La Marseillaise." A patient in the hospital hid among corpses in order to avoid being selected for death with the sickest detainees, though she would surely be chosen in the next round. Another prisoner wondered at the effort everyone was making: "Why do we want so much to live?"[89]

After weeks in the hospital, Żywulska finally joined her new block for roll call. Back in the tiny universe of the camp, she watched a prisoner beaten for stealing potatoes. An SS man on a bicycle paused for a moment to attack an old woman. The crematorium chimney spat fire into the sky. The *kapos* were the same, the endless routines of the camp remained, but new prisoners lined up in place of the dead.

17. In the last half of the war, new Nazi strategies arose to make use of distant concentration camps. On December 7, 1941, Hitler issued the *Nacht und Nebel* (Night and Fog) decree, designed to instill terror into anyone still opposing the Nazis. Particularly targeting conquered and occupied territory, the decree mandated that political activists, resistance fighters, and their suspected associates who were arrested were to be killed quickly or, barring speedy execution, brought from outlying regions to Germany. The standard approach of giving detainees trials by military tribunal in the field now was seen by the Führer as having been too lenient. Field Marshal Wilhelm Keitel clarified: "In case German or foreign authorities inquire about such prisoners, they are to be told that they were arrested, but that the proceedings do not allow any further information."

The following spring, Keitel expanded the directive to apply to all arrests. The Gestapo generally came for prisoners clandestinely and at night. Their families—and even some German officials— had no way to trace them or to know whether they were even still alive. Those who survived their initial interrogations and sentences could quickly find themselves at hard labor with fifty thousand other prisoners in Natzweiler-Struthof, a concentration camp on the French-German border.

Night and Fog detainees such as Jean Améry, a member of the Belgian resistance, sometimes faced torture, then after interrogation were demoted from prisoner to Jew and sent to Auschwitz. Additional decrees allowed violence committed by a non-German—or any action detrimental to German interests—to be considered an act of terror. Some seven thousand prisoners were abducted under the secrecy of Night and Fog.

Inside the camps, Germany's use of terror against its own people fell into a gray zone of international law, which in general restricted reprisals against civilians but was not intended to address a country's treatment of its own citizens.

Measures taken by Nazis against prisoners of war, however, broke sharply with established law on the conduct of warfare. During the second half of 1941, the SS would further violate the Geneva Conventions at several concentration camps, experimenting with an execution chamber for Soviet POWs at Gross-Rosen in occupied Poland and a gas chamber using Zyklon-B in Block 11 at Auschwitz.

By the first months of 1942, individual camp commandants had worked out their own approaches to mass extermination, but it was the Auschwitz method that triumphed as Germany launched genocide. Gas chambers were built not just at Auschwitz, but also at Birkenau, Ravensbrück, Stutthof, Mauthausen, and Sachsenhausen. Even before the Wannsee Conference had committed to the Nazi plan of thorough extermination, Jews and Gypsies had been killed in mobile gas vans at the first extermination camp at Chelmno, where some 150,000 people would eventually die. In 1942, death camps—*Vernichtungslager*—rose at Sobibór, Belzec, and Treblinka, where stationary gas chambers killed more than one and a half million people. Auschwitz alone would kill over a million more, nearly 90 percent of them Jewish deportees.

In most of the dedicated extermination centers, prisoners would be brought in and processed, their valuables taken from them. Told to strip, they were sent—women, men, children, the elderly, and invalids—naked along a path that led to a room labeled "showers," where the doors were closed and they were killed.

At Auschwitz, trains dropped prisoners off on a path that ran down the center of Birkenau, where they faced immediate selection. Some of the younger or healthier adults were kept for administrative duties or camp labor; the rest were sent down the long path, around a corner, and by a thicket of trees to the gas chambers.

They often died trying to break down the doors, or clawing at one another to escape, or covering their mouths to keep from breathing in the gas. The screams were audible from some distance. A *Sonderkommando* squad drafted from the prisoner population dealt with the corpses, burying them at first and later burning them.

The Nazis also pursued genocide through careful calibration of food rations, attempting to feed and starve people in equal measure to maximize work output before death. German industries sometimes partnered in these labor projects. In 1942, the main camp at Auschwitz and the death camp at Auschwitz-Birkenau were supplemented with a third facility, Monowitz, planned and financed by the private sector and housing prisoners who worked at a nearby rubber plant.

In 1944, fifteen-year-old Romanian Jew Elie Wiesel and his father worked there together sorting electrical components. Wiesel had lost his mother and sister on arrival, when women and children were sent off so quickly that he did not even have time to realize he would never see them again.

Though the forced laborers at Monowitz understood that Jews were being starved at Auschwitz, many would not realize until after the war that mass extermination was taking place just minutes away at Birkenau.[90] They faced their own obstacles to survival, living in what detainee Primo Levi called the Grey Zone, where people learned to press for every advantage, at whatever cost or detriment to others, in order to stay alive.

Wiesel passed his days in hunger, living through a series of nightmares, from having the gold crown ripped out of his mouth by another prisoner to watching a small child hanged.[91] In time, he was removed from his father's block and sent to haul heavy slabs of stone twelve hours a day on a construction crew, all the while trying to get through additional selections in which the workers most incapacitated by hard labor were taken away. In midwinter, the barracks were evacuated to Buchenwald on a forced march to stay ahead of advancing Soviet forces. Wiesel's father survived the journey only to die at Buchenwald in January 1945.

More than 270,000 Romanian Jews, over a third of the prewar population, died between 1939 and 1945. Working at the Reich Security

Main Office, Adolf Eichmann supervised a complex network of com-
puter punch cards, using data from local censuses of Jewish families
(often abetted, sometimes stymied, by community leaders) to organize
rivers of deportations from France, Belgium, the Netherlands, Slova-
kia, Greece, northern Italy, and Hungary. More than a million and a
half of these deportees were sent to extermination camps.

18. No one wanted to go to Birkenau, but soon after her recovery
from typhus in Auschwitz, Krystyna Żywulska's SS supervisor
announced that their office would be moved there. The next day,
she was taken a mile and a half northeast from the main camp to
the death camp, where there was more room to process the high-
volume human traffic.

By the time she was assigned there, Birkenau was fully operational. It was the part of Auschwitz prisoners tried not to think
about. After barely sustaining the will to live at the main camp,
Żywulska wondered how she could withstand the proximity to endless extermination. Aware that tracking the belongings of those not
sentenced to die was one of the safest, best jobs and that her good
fortune should not be wasted, she tried to steel herself to live.

The intake staff worked in an office barracks, processing the
possessions of prisoners kept alive as laborers. Nearby stood the huts
of "Canada," the nickname given to the vast storehouse of possessions stolen from Jewish transports sent to their deaths. Just outside
the gate of Żywulska's sector at Birkenau were flowers, and a pictur-
esque white cottage whose interior walls were covered with blood
from mass executions. The house also served as a provisional gas
chamber, but by the time she arrived, four new purpose-built crematorium chimneys stretched toward the sky, visible over fencing and
lower buildings.

In her new barracks, the group of sixty women had a block senior
who was kind, as well as windows that let light in. Żywulska could
continue to work on her poems. She no longer had to share a bed,

and she got a clean straw mattress of her own. Her new bunkmate gave her a nightgown stolen from Canada. They debated the decency of wearing clothing belonging to Jewish prisoners who had been gassed but decided that the clothing was better used by prisoners than sent with the rest of the goods to Nazis back in Germany: "Let's sleep in nightgowns as long as we're alive."[92]

Their second day at work at Birkenau, the women opened the window and saw a column of prisoners being led to the gas chambers just before the crematorium chimney lit up. They could smell the smoke.

Żywulska soon ended up even closer, in the room during a selection for a transport of Italian families, watching a girl jumping rope to entertain herself as her mother was chosen to die. In all innocence, the girl skipped over to her mother, sealing her own fate. Asked by one of the men where they were being taken — he took off his hat to ask politely — Żywulska lied, hoping to give them a few more minutes of peace: "Disinfection."[93]

The intake crew developed affection for their Nazi overseer, Janda, which made them uncomfortable. She expected them to obey her but never yelled at them or beat them, for which they were grateful. Still, Żywulska had trouble reconciling her warmth toward Janda with the overseer's adoration of Hitler. Asked about the extermination of the Jews going on all around them, Janda replied that she was sure Hitler knew nothing about it.[94]

At night, the group debated what should happen to the perpetrators of annihilation, including Janda. Żywulska occasionally advocated for the death of all Germans. Another said she would not herself assault their overseer, but that Janda was as guilty as the other Nazis. Some said they would kill her themselves, but with the sorrow one would feel over a losing a sister who had done grievous wrong.

Meanwhile, cattle cars arrived group by group, delivering their passengers to be gassed. On October 23, a woman in a Jewish transport from Bergen-Belsen managed to grab the pistol of a senior squad leader and shoot him in the dressing room of the crematorium before wounding a second guard. Other members of the transport rallied to

General Valeriano Weyler, the Spanish Governor of Cuba who adopted *reconcentración,* establishing the first concentration camps in 1896. (Photograph courtesy of Library of Congress/Corbis/ VCG via Getty Images)

Tanauan reconcentrado camp, angas, the Philippines, circa 1901. (Image courtesy of University of chigan Digital Library Collection)

Activist Emily Hobhouse, who condemned wartime detention of Boer civilians and fought for humane conditions in British Concentration camps, 1902. (Photograph by Henry Walter Barnett, copyright National Portrait Gallery, London)

Bloemfontein concentration camp for Boer civilians, Southern Africa, circa 1902. (Image courtesy of National Archives, United Kingdom)

Shark Island, site of a German detention camp for Nama and Herero peoples, German South-West Africa, 1906. (Photograph from the album of Lieutenant von Düring, 1906)

Paul Cohen-Portheim, detainee in British internment camps from the First World War. (Photograph courtesy of Duckworth Publishers)

Knockaloe Internment Camp, a British camp for enemy aliens on the Isle of Man during the First World War, circa 1915. (Image courtesy of Manx National Heritage)

The expulsion of the A
nian people into the d
Ottoman Empire, 1915
(Photograph by Armin
Wegner; image copyrig
Wallstein Verlag)

Dmitri Likhachev, former Solovki forced-labor camp detainee, 1990. (Photograph by Igor Palmin)

Monastery buildings at Solovki. Solovetsky Islands, Russia, 1993. (Photograph copyright Gulag Archives by Tomasz Kizny)

Alexander Solzhenitsyn, the Gulag detainee who would later chronicle the entire Soviet detention system, at the beginning of his ordeal, 1946. (AP Images)

Hans Beimler, Communist Party member, Reichstag representative, and Dachau concentration camp prisoner. (Photograph courtesy of Ullstein Bild/Getty Images)

Basement detention cells, Dachau bunker, Germany, 2015. (Photograph by Andrea Pitzer)

Johann Trollmann, Sinto boxer who defied Aryanization and was murdered as a concentration camp prisoner in Nazi Germany. (Photograph courtesy of Documentation and Cultural Center of German Sinti and Roma)

Women inmates working at the concentration camp near Ravensbrück, Germany, circa 1943. (Photograph courtesy of Ullstein Bild/Getty Images)

Margarete Buber-Neumann, detainee in both the Gulag and Nazi camp systems. (Photograph courtesy of Ullstein Bild/ Getty Images)

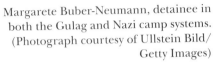

A transport of Hungarian Jews undergoes selection for extermination, Auschwitz-Birkenau, circa 1944. (Photograph from Sovfoto Archive/ UIG via Getty Images)

Inmates of the German concentration camp at Buchenwald shortly after liberation by U.S. troops. The young man seventh from left in the middle row is Elie Wiesel. April 16, 1945. (AP Images)

Train tracks leading to the main gates of the former Auschwitz-Birkenau extermination camp, 2015. (Photograph by Andrea Pitzer)

Former internment camp detainee and political theorist Hannah Arendt, 1949. (Photograph from Fred Stein Archive/Getty Images)

Detainee barracks at Gurs internment camp, southern France, 1940. (Photograph courtesy of Ullstein Bild/Getty Images)

Entrance stele memorializing groups detained between 1939 and 1945 at Gurs concentration camp. Gurs, France, 2015. (Photograph by Andrea Pitzer)

Fred Korematsu, Japanese American camp detainee and U.S. Supreme Court litigant, 1940s. (Photograph courtesy of Fred T. Korematsu Institute)

Two children in Minidoka concentration camp, Idaho, circa 1943. (Photograph from the Hatate Collection/courtesy Wing Luke Asian Museum)

Mitsuye Endo, camp detainee and U.S. Supreme Court litigant, seated at her desk in the administrative office at the Central Utah Relocation Center, 1942. (Photograph courtesy of U.S. National Archives)

Harry Wu, former prisoner in Chinese labor camps and founder of the Laogai Research Foundation, 2000. (Photograph by Damian Dovarganes/AP Images)

A work detail in transit at Tuanhe labor camp outside Beijing, China. (Photograph Agence France-Presse)

Reeducation camp in Tay Ninh Province under the provisional Revolutionary Government of South Vietnam, 1976. (Photograph from Sovfoto Archive/UIG via Getty Images)

Jane Muthoni Mara, former detainee in Kenyan camps who became a litigant at Britain's High Court addressing Mau Mau treatment, October 5, 2012. (Photograph by Ben Curtis/AP Images)

Guards detain Mau Mau suspects while their huts are searched. Kariobangi, Kenya. (Photograph from Bettmann Archive/Getty Images)

French regroupment camp in the mountains of Kabylie, Algeria, 1962. (Photograph by Philip Jones Griffiths/Magnum Photos)

Felipe Agüero, who was detained in Chile's national stadium after a 1973 military coup. Santiago, Chile, 2016. (Photograph by Andrea Pitzer)

A soldier guards detainees at Chile's national stadium in the wake of the military coup. Santiago, Chile, 1973. (Photograph from Bettmann Archive/Getty Images)

The officers' casino at the Navy Mechanical School (ESMA) in Buenos Aires, Argentina. Thousands of detainees were tortured on the basement level under the dictatorship that ruled from 1976 to 1983. (Photograph by Andrea Pitzer)

Camp X-Ray, the first detention camp for prisoners at Guantánamo after the 9/11 attacks, falling to ruin. Guantanamo Bay, Cuba, 2015. (Photograph by Andrea Pitzer)

Camp 6, the main facility housing prisoners at Guantánamo, Guantánamo Bay, Cuba, 2015. (Photograph by Andrea Pitzer)

Courtroom sketch of February 2015 pretrial hearings in the case of the five Guantánamo detainees charged in relation to the 9/11 terror attacks. Guantánamo Bay, Cuba. (Drawing by Andrea Pitzer)

Children at Dar Paing Camp, near Sittwe, Myanmar, 2015. Denied citizenship, residents are not allowed to leave Rohingya areas and are classified as refugees in the wake of 2012 riots and arson. (Photograph by Andrea Pitzer)

her side and fought, too. The prisoners were all killed in the end but managed to take the squad leader, an SS man, with them. A funeral was held at the camp, and Żywulska toasted the death in secret.

From their perch near the processing huts, the women who did prisoner intake did not go hungry. Thanks to parcels they received from families, items they pocketed to trade for food, and indoor work duties, the threat of slow death from conditions in the camp was eliminated. For those working outside, still subject to starvation and manual labor, the time and energy required to conduct a philosophical debate over the assassination of a Nazi overseer would remain impossible.

Yet the easier life led by Żywulska and those in charge of prisoner intake did not eliminate all danger. They broke rules constantly and were sometimes caught. When the block senior was in a bad mood and saw one of them with a cigarette, the unfortunate prisoner was demoted to manual labor at the main camp.

At one point, Żywulska feared that she, too, would be sent back, or worse. She had become celebrated among prisoners for her ironic, fierce poems. One day a messenger ran to warn her that a prisoner had been caught with some of her verse. After translating the poem, the authorities were furious—and determined to find the author.

Friends at the barracks destroyed all copies of her writing before anyone could come for them, but knowing that the woman would face brutal interrogation over the poem, Żywulska could not imagine that she would hold out. A young prisoner on the squad promised that in the event that anything happened to Żywulska, she had memorized her work by heart—which only reminded them the poet might soon vanish.

Word came that a second woman, someone Żywulska knew from Pawiak Prison, was also being interrogated. She lost hope. Awake all night, she learned in the morning that under questioning, the prisoner had attributed the poem to a detainee who had already died. Żywulska was safe.

But other horrors awaited. In August 1944, the Gypsy sector of the camp, in which whole families had been segregated from other prisoners but not gassed, was suddenly liquidated. Hungarian and Romanian Jews, including young Elie Wiesel's mother and sister, met the same fate. The Jews of the Lodz ghetto also burned. Dr. Josef Mengele, chief camp physician at Birkenau, attended selections, sending prisoners to their deaths and always looking for twins to use in monstrous medical experiments.

After months of frantic activity at the camps, air raids began. Transports slowed, then ceased. Packages sent to the Reich were returned. In the absence of new prisoners, Żywulska's block not only had nothing to trade for extra food, they themselves were superfluous. Overhearing radio broadcasts—sometimes even sneaking to listen to the SS radio—they were thrilled by the Allied advance but began to wonder how long it would be before they would be murdered for knowing too much.

When Himmler ordered the dismantling of crematoria, she could hear prisoner crews dynamiting their foundations. Żywulska spent long, frantic days updating prisoners' cards in preparation for the camp's closure. To her surprise, she was not killed in the mayhem of retreat.

Pressed into the march to Buchenwald as Birkenau was emptied that January, she escaped the column of prisoners and hid under an overturned hay wagon. She waited until the long body of the march had snaked its way past her. Then she crawled out, asked for directions from a passerby, and made her way to a Polish village two miles away.

19. The Soviet Army liberated Auschwitz on January 27, 1945, arriving to find crematoria demolished, records gone, and only a few thousand prisoners left behind. There were, however, indications of what had taken place at the camp. Many storehouses had been destroyed, but among the remains of the Canada processing area, hundreds of thousands of suits and women's clothing were discovered, along with more than seven tons of human hair harvested for wigs.

Given the fast-moving war news elsewhere, it would take more than two months after its liberation before the *Washington Post* and the *New York Times* published stories even mentioning Auschwitz.[95] They did, however, follow horrifying accounts from the April 4 arrival of the US Army's 4th Armored Division at Ohrdruf, a sub-camp of Buchenwald, where guards had killed many of those left behind. On a visit a week later to the camp, General Dwight Eisenhower and General George Patton were taken on a tour by former prisoners past the half-burned bodies of those who had died or been shot. Patton refused to enter a barrack filled with corpses of those who had starved to death for fear he would vomit.

The sight of piles of dead and dying not on the battlefield but lying behind barbed wire in the dirt of a concentration camp was horrifying. The photos and film footage stunned the world. Yet the details had been known in the abstract for some time. A report sent out through the Polish underground announced that seven hundred thousand Jews had been killed with machine guns, hand grenades, and in mobile gas chambers. Covered widely in Western newspapers, the report appeared in 1942, during the first months of the Holocaust and nearly three years before the war's end.

A shortage of information on the camps was not the issue, as is apparent in a bit of editorializing that the *New York Times* appended to its description of the report, declaring that its sources were said to be reliable, yet "the stories seemed too terrible and the atrocities too inhuman to be true."[96] The Polish underground had sent Jan Karski to London and Washington to share firsthand reports on the death camps, to which Supreme Court justice Felix Frankfurter famously replied, "I did not say this young man is lying. I said I am unable to believe him." By 1943, newspapers were reporting credible stories that more than three million civilians had been killed in Poland.[97] The truth is that the general public in the West had enough information to realize that concentration camps lay at the heart of something terrible—but by and large they lacked the capacity to imagine that it was all true.

People would later ask why many of those sent to the camps

seemed to resign themselves to going. It might be more useful to wonder why the detainees of the First World War did so decades before. Though several items had turned out not to be true, during the prior war, atrocity stories about the concentration camps had been plentiful in the French and English newspapers. And yet, when enemy aliens were called to register and then asked to turn themselves in during that war, they had generally done so without a fuss. They were called monsters in the street, and were spat on and vilified by many members of the press. But they knew they were innocent, and hoped that if the government distrusted them as a group, it might hold no malice toward them on an individual basis. The war would pass, and they would be released. That was their expectation, and with few exceptions, it was exactly what had happened. This concentration camp model was the one the world had seen in operation around the globe just two decades before.

Bloody as the Stalinist purges had been, Soviet camps eventually released the vast majority of their detainees. In the *Konzentration-slager* after the terrifying events of Kristallnacht, most Jewish prisoners who had been arrested were released within weeks. Both systems were horrific, but there was nothing in the recent models of concentration camps that pointed toward wholesale extermination. As people began to hear rumors that deportees were not headed to reservations, some did resist. Uprisings took place in the ghettos; prisoners assassinated SS men in the camps. But once the extermination mission became clear, it was often too late. By the time wholesale extermination had begun, the Nazis had spent eight years developing a network of camps, torture, and repression, with staff trained toward brutally imposing each. Escape had become almost impossible, and acts of resistance were met with massive reprisals.

It is worth recalling, too, that if some knew what was happening, not everyone did. Upon hearing rumors of the Warsaw Ghetto uprising in the spring of 1943, Elie Wiesel's mother, still living at home in the Romanian town of Sighet, asked, "Why are our Jewish brothers doing that? Why are they fighting? Couldn't they wait quietly until the end of the war?"[98] Loaded onto trains a year later, the passengers in Wiesel's transport arrived at a station and saw the sign labeled "Auschwitz." They should have been terrified, but as Wiesel writes, "No one had ever heard that name."[99]

20. Allied liberation of the camps, which had begun on the Eastern Front in the middle of 1944, lasted until May 1945. Thrilled as they were to see enemy troops at the gates of their camps, many prisoners experienced a kind of half liberation that left them trapped in detention. Forced laborers were kept in internment camps for months until they could be rerouted home on railways that were damaged or requisitioned for immediate postwar needs. With a food crisis raging across Western Europe, getting adequate rations was difficult, and many who were already ill or severely malnourished died.

There were widely publicized pogroms against Holocaust survivors in Poland, and many Jews from there and elsewhere were unwilling or unable to go home. Hundreds of thousands ended up routed to displaced persons (DP) camps in Germany, Austria, and Italy. Though the camps had little in common with the *Konzentrationslager*, many detainees waited months or years to learn their fate.

Even former prisoners who went free were not always liberated. Roma and Sinti populations continued to face prejudice and legal restrictions as Gypsies in Germany after the war. Antihomosexual statutes stayed on the books as well, leaving gay survivors doubly in the closet, avoiding references to their time in the camps or the reason for being sent there, and staying silent about sterilizations. Krystyna Żywulska, who had been born Sonia Landau, would keep her adopted name after leaving Auschwitz, not coming out as a Jew until almost two decades later, perhaps for good reason: she was eventually kicked out of the Polish Writers' Union in an "anti-Zionist" purge.

Margarete Buber-Neumann, who had survived both the Gulag and the Nazi camp system, went on to testify about her experiences in the Gulag as part of a libel suit that pitted a Soviet émigré against a French Communist newspaper trying to discredit him. She herself was libeled by a German reporter, who dismissed her account of her time in Russia and called her a Nazi sympathizer. Her case went all the way to the German Supreme Court before she was victorious. She became a leading anti-Soviet crusader, monitored by the East German secret police.[100]

Other postwar judicial proceedings had more historic significance. At the Nuremberg Trials in 1945, the charge of "crimes against humanity" was brought for the first time. Under the auspices of an International Military Tribunal, prosecutors charged several of the architects of the war and those who promulgated anti-Semitic policies. Twelve death sentences were handed down, and seven defendants were sentenced to prison for ten to twenty years. At the Neuengamme War Trials held in Hamburg in March 1946, the British tried fourteen men in a military tribunal that ran for two months, handing down eleven death sentences and three prison sentences of ten to twenty-five years. After the Auschwitz trials held in Krakow in 1947, twenty-one former camp staff members were hanged and eighteen sentenced from three years to life in prison. More than seven decades after the end of the war, individual trials continue to bring convictions, most recently a five-year sentence handed down to former Auschwitz guard Reinhold Hanning in June 2016.

In its entirety, the Holocaust killed as many as six million Jews, seven million Soviet civilians, nearly two million non-Jewish Poles, and up to two hundred thousand Roma and Sinti. As with nearly every concentration camp system, no complete death total exists. Setting aside Auschwitz-Birkenau and the extermination camps, which murdered nearly three million Jews, the non-death camp *Konzentrationslager* system killed approximately seven hundred thousand people out of 1.2 million prisoners of all races and nationalities, the vast majority of them after the start of the war.

Today a museum operates at the main Auschwitz site and at

nearby Birkenau, hosting a million or more visitors each year. Restaurants across the road court tour buses and individual visitors with signs and specials. As at most Nazi camp memorial sites, a bookstore sells memoirs, academic texts, and collections of documentary photography. Guided tours are offered in eight languages, and in the middle of the entryway to the former camp sits a snack kiosk. None of these things diminish the power of the place.

In 2013 Yad Vashem, the World Holocaust Remembrance Center, provided an exhibition that was installed in Block 27 of the main Auschwitz site, where it remains today. The displays contain a series of commemorations, including a room mourning the 1.5 million children lost in the Holocaust. Toward the end of the stops on the guided tour, in a nondescript area of the former concentration camp, a book of the dead has been mounted chest high in the center of the room. Its black base stands just over six feet tall and perhaps twenty feet in length, but the thousands of white pages protruding from each side like wings run nearly the length of the room and almost seem to float.

On those pages appear the names of all the Jewish dead of the Holocaust that have been collected to date. As of this writing, the book contains more than 4.2 million names. Each page includes five hundred individuals, and each entry lists the hometown, life span, and place of death of those lost. The names are arranged alphabetically.[101] Opening pages to look for someone reveals not only the names of the dead, but also a bright light that shines from the center of the book, illuminating each page.

Though the remembrance is beautifully prepared and moving, it seems almost cruel to keep the names of the dead locked inside Block 27 forever. Yet it also is appropriate that the details do not vanish into the ether of abstract tragedy or some forgotten field, and are instead anchored to the setting in which the worst of modernity's crimes took place.

After the Second World War, concentration camps became the symbol of genocide. That camps were not actually required for genocide was proven by the deaths of more than a million Eastern

European Jews in forests and mass graves, killed by mobile death squads or enthusiastic local citizens in pogroms. Yet Nazi death camps gained their reputation because they did something unprecedented: they systematized the killing, anesthetized the killers, and created an efficient bureaucracy of execution.

The death toll and the virulence of Nazi camps became so expansive as to make other concentration camp systems recede in the panoramic view. It is easy to think that the Nazi system—the *Konzentrationslager* and the death camps together—was singular not only in its final, apocalyptic stage but also in its beginnings. In reality, what happened in Germany started in a familiar way. As with the Gulag, and the camps of the First World War, preemptive arrests of thousands who had been declared a national threat led to a framework of arbitrary detention that became entrenched. In the case of Nazi Germany, tyranny fed the system, and the system normalized brutality; in time, it became possible to take terror and extrajudicial detention further than anyone could have imagined. Under Hitler and Himmler, concentration camps incorporated centuries of human progress, modernization, and civilization, and transformed them into something not glorious but heinous.

As the apotheosis of horror, death camps inspired the vow "Never again." Yet concentration camps themselves did not disappear; they multiplied. The Gulag continued, having not yet reached its zenith, and new camp systems holding millions of prisoners in Africa and Asia were only a few years away.

CHAPTER SIX

Increments of Evil

1. IN THE FIRST MONTHS after Hitler came to power in 1933, refugees from Nazi repression fled both east and west. In Paris, refugees poured into the city at a rate of two hundred a day. Some still held German passports; others carried striped green Nansen booklets issued to stateless people. Jews leaving Berlin could bring only two hundred marks with them — barely enough to travel with, let alone live on. Most were destitute within weeks.

Germany's baleful metamorphosis stunned refugees, leaving some shattered by the speed of their descent. Realizing that they might never go home, the exiles were gripped by depression. "At my age it is too late to make over one's life," wrote former Prussian Supreme Court judge Arnold Freymuth from the Paris apartment where he and his wife committed suicide on July 14.[1] Freymuth was representative of many of the first arrivals. Despite their sudden poverty, the refugees included many of Germany's leading cultural figures. Paris alone hosted filmmaker Max Ophüls, composer Kurt Weill, philosopher Walter Benjamin, anti-Fascist crusader Arthur Koestler, and rising political theorist Hannah Arendt. German enclaves likewise sprang up in Zurich, Prague, Vienna, and London.

As the decade neared its end, Germany annexed Austria via the

Anschluss. Czechoslovakia was dismembered and its western regions made into a German protectorate. Those who had already avoided Nazi persecution by heading east to Prague or Vienna had to escape again. With France one of the last accessible havens, a second wave of displaced people flooded the country, and the Paris refugee community outgrew its welcome.

France offered temporary sanctuary but no work papers to the newcomers, leaving them without means to survive. The specter of possible German invasion, high unemployment at home, and political tensions between French socialists and right-wing parties contributed to the suspicion with which large sectors of the population viewed the new arrivals. By the time Germany invaded Poland in September 1939, the French had begun to resent their guests.

During the "phony war," the quiet first months of the conflict on the Western front, no immediate threat of invasion appeared, and France turned to a policy of selective internment of some newcomers. Stalin's alliance with Hitler prompted France to ban the Communist Party and target current or former party members for internment. Hungarian writer and former Communist Arthur Koestler was arrested in October 1939. Told at the prefecture that he was being taken to detention, he made one of many protests, arguing that he was a journalist. He got nothing for his trouble but a pair of handcuffs and a punch in the back.

Koestler knew that even solitary confinement in a French prison was preferable to a Nazi camp, but the former could be bad enough. He was therefore delighted to find himself not taken to prison but classified as an "undesirable alien" and driven across town to Roland Garros tennis stadium, which had been surrounded in barbed wire and converted into an internment camp. Sleeping alongside hundreds of men in grottoes under the stairwells, they became "a tribe of present-day troglodytes at the mouth of their concrete cave."[2] He would eventually be moved south to a camp at Le Vernet.

In that moment, French camps were still a fluid enterprise. Hannah Arendt's partner Heinrich Blücher, a once-active member of the German Communist Party, had broken with Stalin in 1928 but was nonetheless arrested.[3] Released from detention in a barn in the countryside at Villemalard through the intercession of a friend, he returned to Paris after just two months. In the midst of war, Blücher and Arendt married. He was forty-one and fascinated by the collapse of democracies; she was thirty-three and obsessed with political ideas. They had four months together as husband and wife before Germany invaded Belgium on May 10, 1940.

France had begun to brace for the inevitable. Five days ahead of the invasion, a broader net for internment was cast, with German aliens of every political background summoned to detention. Newspapers announced a schedule for foreigners to turn themselves in. Arendt was sent to the women's reception center at the Vélodrome d'Hiver, a cycling stadium near the Eiffel Tower. Blücher went with the men, who were required to present themselves at the Stadion Buffalo. Internees were to bring no more than sixty-six pounds of belongings, along with two days of food and eating utensils.[4]

Arendt took the metro to the velodrome with a friend. Processed into detention, she sat on the stone seats of the stadium above its curved track. The women slept on straw mattresses, not knowing where they would be sent or what would happen to them. Like Margarete Buber-Neumann on the train heading west from Russia just months before, they feared that they might be repatriated to Nazi Germany. But they were not badly treated by the guards, and they began to think deportation unlikely.[5] Reminding themselves that at least they were not surrounded by SS men, they hoped for mercy from the French.

After a week under the stadium's glass roof, fearing bombs from every passing airplane, they were herded onto buses and driven to the Gare de Lyon. An eight-hour ride south to Toulouse gave way to a five-hour trip to the tiny station at Oloron-Sainte-Marie, at the base of the Pyrenees Mountains. From there, eleven winding miles remained before arrival at the internment camp at Gurs, a little over twenty miles from the Spanish border. The voyage was nearly as far as one could travel from Paris without leaving the country.

As Germany brought the world to war again, France was not the only nation to resurrect its camps. Enemy alien laws from the First World War led to widespread civilian internment in the Second, with varying degrees of deprivation and abuse. Some governments repeated mistakes from the prior conflict; others would make new mistakes altogether.

Keeping faith with an unfortunate theme in concentration camp history, leaders often turned to internment out of panic, ignoring the advice of well-informed dissenters. In the Pacific theater, wartime needs produced forced-labor camps for civilians and POWs alike. In the West, they led to unnecessary hardships for minorities and refugees, sometimes also for citizens of the detaining power. In each case, civilians paid a price.

In Europe, one difference in midcentury internment was the nature of who faced detention. The overwhelming majority of people held by Western European nations in the First World War had been innocent civilians without divided loyalties to their country of origin. During the Second World War, most aliens interned by Allied forces not only lacked any overriding loyalty to their native land, they were fleeing persecution in it. Many were Jews; some were early Nazi concentration camp survivors.

Hardly alone in resurrecting an enemy alien camp system, France was joined by Japan, Britain, and the United States—along with dozens of other belligerents. Even Germany administered a set of camps for enemy aliens. Called *ilags*, they were run according to Geneva Convention protocols for foreigners only, and remained separate from both the domestic *Konzentrationslager* system and the prisoner of war camps for captured combatants.

With so many nations involved, the internment camps of the Second World War ran the gamut from refugee camps and detention centers to brutal interrogation sites and antechambers to execution. But in the first half of the century, no camp better represented the fluid possibilities for change and the dangers of internment than Gurs.

2. When Arendt arrived in southernmost France in May 1940, Gurs had already been open for more than a year. The camp had been built to house refugees flooding across the Spanish border from a civil war that had raged since the middle of the decade. Well away from any large town, the camp featured a lone road that began near a guard post and ran through the center of camp, with perpendicular paths splitting clusters of barracks into blocks.[6] Each block had its own kitchen and toilet area, and was cordoned off from the next by barbed wire. Though detainees were guarded, Gurs was not constructed as a prison fortress—the barbed wire was not electrified, and the fence stood only six feet high.

Gurs was a novelty to those first Spanish detainees, but many had previous experience with concentration camps. When Spanish Republicans and soldiers of the International Brigades were battling General Francisco Franco's Falangist forces, both sides had made use of camps. The Republicans had set up a ragtag collection of probationary labor camps that held over a thousand prisoners in all. But Franco's concentration camps became notorious around the world, with prisoners describing arbitrary detention, "pig sty" dormitories, and nights during which a hundred or more prisoners were taken out to be shot, with cleanup trucks clearing the ditches of human "sausages" in the morning.[7] Falangists held seven hundred thousand prisoners in some thirty-five camps in a system that extended from North Africa to San Sebastián, almost on the French border.

In an era of dictatorships, Franco's system operated concurrently with Nazi camps and the Gulag. A sometimes open, sometimes secret German partnership in the war extended to the arena of detention as well: Nazi expertise had helped fine-tune Franco's concentration camps, leading to the use of high exterior walls, barbed wire, and watchtowers. Tens of thousands would remain in detention under Franco's regime for more than a decade after the end of the Spanish Civil War.[8]

Spanish Republicans had made headway against Franco, but assistance from the Germans and a massive offensive led to crushing defeat in the spring of 1939. Fleeing detention in Franco's camps or worse, nearly half a million Republican refugees made their way across the French border in a period of weeks. Dispersed to camps around the country, they ended up at Le Vernet, Rivesaltes, and elsewhere—dozens of sites, some of which were still under construction as they arrived.[9]

Before the flood of refugees began, France had debated how to handle their arrival. The country was split between socialist sympathizers and law-and-order citizens, many of whom loathed the Spanish Republicans. French politicians worried that a flood of radicals could destabilize the government, and they did not want to be seen by Franco as actively abetting his opponents. Filtered through "welcome centers," refugees were directed to temporary pens where they received little in the way of food and had to sleep on the beach. After the first camps on France's southwestern coast descended into overcrowding and dysentery, sites were constructed farther inland.

Gurs was born in that moment. More than fifteen thousand new arrivals in April 1939 strained the capacity of the camp. Barracks in rows stretched over the flat field nearly as far as the eye could see. From a distance the camp looked crisp and regimented; a closer view revealed chaos. A-frame interiors built of flimsy boards were covered in tarpaper, which leaked water as it wore through. The clay soil did not drain, and in the rain, ankle-deep mud or worse churned up. Rudimentary toilets and overcrowding led to disease. Gurs and its sister facilities were technically refugee camps, but the lack of adequate food, sanitation, and medical care plunged detainees into punitive internment.

3. Hannah Arendt's arrival in France as a refugee six years earlier had been a quieter flight, though just as desperate. For most of the

Weimar era, the unconventional, cigar-smoking Arendt had been interested in political philosophy without actually practicing politics. Realizing that German Jews were increasingly unwelcome and in danger in Germany, she embraced Zionism as the Nazi Party gained strength. She traveled across Germany to give lectures on her country's anti-Semitic history and the possibilities of emigration.

During the weeks after the Reichstag fire in Berlin in early 1933, the stakes were raised. Arendt dedicated herself to fighting the Third Reich. She helped those fleeing the country by opening her home as a way station while others coordinated border crossings for the refugees, most of whom were Communist Jews. She also helped Zionist friends by going to the Prussian State Library to copy anti-Semitic articles from German newspapers, to show how the spirit of Nazi policies extended down to the level of small towns, councils, and businesses.

This work was illegal, and Arendt was soon caught and taken to the police presidium at Alexanderplatz. Her mother, too, was arrested, and would give no statement beyond saying that whatever her daughter had been caught doing was the right thing to do, and she herself would do the same.

The police officer who detained Arendt was a newcomer to the political desk, and she was not a garden-variety detainee, with no membership in the Communist Party and no official history of Zionism. He bought her cigarettes and kept her for eight days without mistreatment before letting her go.[10]

Arendt knew she would not be as lucky a second time. She fled the country without papers, crossing Germany's eastern border via the same networks she had helped coordinate for others. By visiting a helpful German family whose house straddled the border, she made her way from one country to another without setting foot outside.[11] From Prague she went to Geneva, where she worked briefly at the League of Nations. In the fall of 1933, Paris received her as a stateless refugee.

She was traumatized by the separation from her country and culture. Worst had been her realization that the problem of the Third

Reich was not only Hitler and his cohort, but also many German friends and acquaintances of Jews who had decided to go along with the Nazi program.[12]

In Paris she addressed the very circumstances that had shaken her. Lacking an identity card, she was nonetheless able to get secretarial work with a French agricultural organization training Jews to be sent to Palestine. She continued to lecture on the history of anti-Semitism in German and French, a defiant stance amid the rising prejudice in Paris and across the country. When Jewish medical student David Frankfurter assassinated a Nazi party leader in Davos in 1936, Arendt joined the legal team defending him, conducting interviews and doing research.

The tidal wave of refugees that followed the annexations of Austria and Czech territories heightened French anti-Semitism, and far-right and pro-Fascist newspapers began decrying the Jews and supposed traitors in their midst. Anti-Semitic legislation was passed, limiting Jewish involvement in specific professions and calling for the deportation of those without proper work permits, though deportation would mean death for many. Germany funded much of the propaganda, but the seeds fell on fertile ground. Xenophobic, Jew-hating newspapers were everywhere. Even inside the Chamber of Deputies, the rallying cry "Death to the Jews!" rang out.[13]

Arendt had grown accustomed to navigating anti-Semitism, but to be sent to Gurs in May 1940 was still heartbreaking. She was interned alongside other Germans living in France at the beginning of the war, including civilian Nazi Party members and their sympathizers. She was separated from her new husband and faced an uncertain fate. And after long years living and working in France, she felt abandoned by the country she had turned to in the wake of the loss of her home.

4. Gurs was a bitter awakening. By the time Arendt arrived, the Spanish Republican soldiers and International Brigadists who had been the first inmates of the camp were almost all gone. The decla-

ration of war in September 1939 had mobilized local Frenchmen, leaving openings for many kinds of labor. Detainees with technical skills had been integrated for work into the local communities. Thousands more had returned to Spain despite the risk of interrogation, imprisonment, or death.

The influx of enemy alien women to Gurs that May immediately re-created the miasma of the previous year, as the camp population swelled from fifteen hundred to more than twelve thousand detainees. Ten thousand who had been rounded up at the velodrome were joined by more than a thousand equally unwanted Communists, syndicalists, pacifists, and Muslims—including children. Prisoners generally did their best to avoid associating with the hundreds of Nazis also detained in the camp.

With the arrival of the Germans, who were mostly Jews, Gurs transitioned from a quasi-voluntary refugee camp to a dedicated detention camp. New arrivals were termed *indésirables* and viewed as useless baggage. There were no beds or closets for possessions. Detainees slept sixty to a barracks, thirty down each side, atop straw-filled sacks on the floor, with a sentry for each block.[14] Food rations amounted to some 1,100 calories a day—half a standard allotment, and not enough for long-term survival.[15] Arendt despaired; she felt herself solidly part of a pariah class. In addition to the miserable conditions of the camp, no one knew what would happen to the detainees if Germany continued to advance into French territory. She considered suicide.

Less than a month after Arendt's arrival at Gurs, German forces rolled through the streets of Paris. By June 22, France had fallen. The formal surrender took place at Compiègne—not by accident, since it had been the site of the German surrender in the First World War. Now a symbol of Nazi victory, in time Compiègne, too, would became a concentration camp.

In the chaos of surrender, the routine at Gurs fell apart. Along with hundreds of other detainees, Arendt managed to acquire papers authorizing liberation. Trying to sound the alarm about the terrors that might await those who did not take the opportunity to flee, Arendt left many unconvinced. Others chose to wait out the French surrender in the camp.

A few weeks later, local authorities gave the "Gursiennes" who had left the camp but were still in the area twenty-four hours to quit the Pyrenees region or be interned again.[16] Soon after, the Gestapo came and released Nazi women who had been held as enemy aliens. They pressed the camp commandant to turn over the other prisoners, but were refused for the time being. Meanwhile, the commandant destroyed the camp log, the only record listing those who had escaped, to keep it from falling into German hands.

Even after the Gestapo made an appearance, many former prisoners remained nearby, uncertain of where to go and not wanting to leave the only place to which their friends and family might be able to trace them. Arendt did not wait to find out what would happen. She walked out of the camp and began hitchhiking to a friend's house near Montauban, not far from Toulouse. Several days later, she had covered 140 miles, reuniting with her friends from Paris, who were also safe.

The French press largely backed the internment of Jews. Koestler marked the irony of the reversal in France's portrayal of them, writing, "A few years ago we were called the martyrs of the Fascist barbarism, pioneers in the fight for civilisation, defenders of liberty, and what not; the Press and statesmen of the West had made rather a fuss about us, probably to drown the voice of their bad conscience. Now we had become the scum of the earth."[17]

The socialist mayor of Montauban wanted to stick a finger in the eye of the collaborationist Vichy government, so he hosted as many "undesirables" as could be accommodated in houses left behind by those who had fled. By chance, Arendt ran into her husband on the streets of the town. Heinrich's camp had been emptied before the Germans took Paris, and detainees had escaped their French guards on the forced march southward when Germans bombarded the evacuees. Heinrich had emerged with nothing more than an ear infection; Arendt suffered only rheumatism from her long days of walking.[18]

Others were less fortunate. Walter Benjamin had already been interned as an enemy alien in French camps, first at Nevers and then in a furniture factory at Vernuche, where he had been freed in 1939. With the invasion of France, he fled south from Paris to avoid being extradited to Germany. He tried to make his way on foot with a group of other refugees, with the possibility of visas waiting across the Spanish border—visas that might get them into Lisbon and across the Atlantic. But the day they were to go into Spain, the visas had fallen through. Benjamin committed suicide by swallowing morphine capsules he had hoarded.

Arendt became a different person after Gurs. She was no longer an émigré; she had become a refugee. Contemporary history had created new human beings, she wrote, "the kind that are put into concentration camps by their foes and into internment camps by their friends."[19]

5. Arendt's experience was repeated again and again, not just in France, but around the globe. Despite the British government's assessment that internment of civilians in the First World War had been a mistake, the mistake was apparently too tempting and politically convenient not to duplicate.

As German forces rolled through Western Europe with ease, British leaders lived in fear of amphibious invasion. It was not an outlandish concern for England during the summer of 1940, but the government's hysterical response followed the same route taken after the sinking of the *Lusitania* in 1915. If anything, the government's response was worse in the Second World War, because Britain had, in theory, learned from its prior experience. The nation had surveyed the internment program in place during the First World War and decided that a better policy would be to assign a board to assess the risk posed by each enemy alien instead of committing to mass internment.

Under that policy, German and Austrian aliens in the United

Kingdom had been required to register at the beginning of the war, after which they were segregated into three classes. Category A included 569 known Nazi sympathizers and those who had been assessed as espionage risks. This group faced immediate internment. Category B held approximately 6,700 aliens whose status was not clear. This group was monitored and was refused permission to own cameras and other items. Assigned to Category C were more than 66,000 enemy aliens judged to be no threat at all. More than 50,000 of Category C aliens were specifically understood to be Jewish refugees in flight from the Nazis.[20]

The policy of selective internment was followed for the first nine months of the war despite rising calls for mass detention. Critics of this more cautious policy believed that Norway had fallen due to a fifth column of spies and that the same strategy could topple Western Europe and Britain. Even normally level-headed journalists folded spy fever into their copy, offering observations that "now it is difficult to separate the genuine refugee from Nazi persecution from the Nazi agent posing as such."[21]

When Germany invaded France in May 1940, the measures protecting refugees were abandoned. Neville Chamberlain resigned, and Winston Churchill became prime minister. Two days later, British security forces arrested some 3,000 German and Austrian enemy aliens, regardless of their categorization.[22] In short order, the total number of German and Austrian detainees had doubled. The following month, when war with Italy became official, Winston Churchill told officers to "Collar the lot!" adding 4,000 Italians to the interned population.[23] The hastily improvised arrangements led to prisoners arriving before facilities were completed, as well as misunderstandings about the identities of the internees. The sight of Orthodox Jews in their distinctive clothing on their way to a camp near Liverpool led an adjutant to observe, "I never knew so many Jews were Nazis."[24]

The Isle of Man, home to tens of thousands of internees during the First World War, opened its gates again. This time, however, Brit-

ish authorities decided that the island was not sufficient for detention purposes. Over the next month, more than 7,500 enemy aliens
were shipped to internment in Canada and Australia. Some faced
catastrophe en route to overseas concentration camps. One refugee
vessel, the *Arandora Star*, was torpedoed on July 2 by a German
U-boat en route to Canada, sinking the ship and killing more than
600 passengers and crew. Despite the tragedy, Britain instructed the
Dunera to set sail for Australia the following week, carrying some
2,000 enemy alien passengers on a ship designed for 1,600. The ship
was hit by a torpedo, which struck "with a loud bang" but did not
explode. By the time it pulled into harbor, prisoners' luggage had
washed overboard, guards had stolen their personal effects, and
abuse was rampant.[25] The overcrowded conditions jammed Fascists
into tight quarters with Dachau survivors, with predictable results.
On arrival, the captain of the ship and some of the crew faced court-
martial for mistreatment of the refugees. Winston Churchill later
called the incident "a deplorable mistake."[26]

Between 1939 and 1947, more than two dozen camps sprang up
in Canada from New Brunswick to Alberta, most of them located in
Quebec and Ontario.[27] Prisoners in Canada remained stoic for the
most part, though depression afflicted many. Fascists and Germans
loyal to Hitler were once again housed in the same barracks as Jewish refugees, leading to intimidation and threats. "Here we have
honest English soldiers as guards," one refugee from Vienna said,
"but we are forced to live in close proximity to people who persecuted our relations and whose principles we have fought all our
lives."[28] The issue became a problem on both sides of the Atlantic,
but over time, camp commanders took a stronger hand in segregating population groups.

Britain did not entirely fail her refugees. A public outcry over the
internment of Jewish refugees began in the first days of the revised
policy. Sir Norman Angell, who had won the Nobel Peace Prize in
1933, publicly took the side of the refugees. H. G. Wells, Oxford scholars, and members of Parliament followed suit, with one conservative

MP calling the new policy "totally un-English" and the British home secretary agreeing that universal internment represented "a matter which touches on the name of this good country."[29] By August, the government had begun to reverse its policy. Prisoners' cases were reviewed, and some Category C detainees began to be released during the fall of 1940.

6. After France's surrender, the country faced a second invading army. Just as the armistice was signed, the Italian army crossed the border and took Menton on June 21, 1940. As part of the larger agreement, Fascist dictator Benito Mussolini's forces occupied the territory around Nice and Grenoble, eventually expanding out toward Toulon. That September, Italy invaded Egypt, and in October, it moved into Greece. The following spring, Mussolini's soldiers helped to dismember Yugoslavia. Italy would end up establishing detention camps for civilians and prisoners of war in all these occupied territories as well as on the mainland.

Though Mussolini's National Fascist Party allied itself with Nazi Germany and some strongly anti-Semitic individuals were counted among its leadership, Jews had long been an accepted part of Italian society and were less subject to the bitter resentment that reared its head in Germany and France. In addition, Italian Fascism was authoritarian rather than totalitarian and did not have anti-Semitism at its core. As a result, the nation had no deep-rooted commitment to extermination.

Mussolini, however, was not above appeasing Hitler on occasion. On November 17, 1938, a series of Italian Racial Laws were set forth. The new code barred Jews from holding public office, serving in the military, receiving higher education, working as journalists, and marrying non-Jewish Italians. In addition all foreign Jews who had arrived in Italy after January 1, 1919, were to be interned.

While individual Jews were selected for detention, no mass internment took place at first. Those detained were guaranteed time on the beach each day and a daily allowance if they ran out of money. But in the month between the German and Italian invasions of France, word came to the Italian ministry of the interior that Mussolini had requested the preparation of "concentration camps for the Jews in case of war."[30] On June 10, Jews around the country began to be arrested, a move the government described as a security measure. By November, the Italian government held 5,500 foreign and native detainees in detention, half of them Jewish. Of that total, more than 3,000 were held in camps.

Violence was not normally part of the Italian camp regime. In fact many of the camps were not even traditional camps; small groups of prisoners were often held in homes, at schools, and on estates. Later in the war, as prisoners were brought in from other territories, hunger and conditions of confinement became severe. The camps, however, were not laboratories of cruelty, as Nazi camps were. Cultural activities were not only tolerated, they were organized. Unlimited numbers of letters and packages could be received, and very few deaths occurred.

In time tensions grew over the fate of Jews in areas occupied by Italian forces. With its Final Solution in place, Germany demanded that Jews in Italian-held territory be assembled and deported for extermination. But Mussolini's military perpetually refused to take up Germany's murderous mission. Recognizing that Italian forces were not committed to Hitler's cause, Jewish refugees often fled from German-occupied territory into areas held by Italy when they could. For over a year, more than forty thousand Jews found refuge in places from Dalmatia and Croatia to Tunisia that were under Italian occupation.

Ferramonti, the most traditional concentration camp on the Italian mainland, held thousands in barracks behind barbed wire. Yet officials often issued passes for detainees to leave the camp in cases of medical or family emergency. Barracks chiefs were elected, and they in turn elected a head of the prisoners who had access to the camp commandant. By and large, Mussolini had resurrected the internment-style camps of the First World War.

Yet outside Italy's borders, the results were sometimes less neutral. More than a thousand prisoners suspected of sympathizing with the resistance, including children, died from starvation and amid bitter conditions in an Italian camp on the island of Rab in what is today Croatia.[31] In addition, pressure from Nazis to surrender Albanian Jews led Italian forces to eventually hand over hundreds of detainees from camps in Pristina and elsewhere; some sixty Jews were effectively sent to their deaths.

Mild as its bigotry was in comparison to that of Nazi Germany, Italy's anti-Semitism and mass detention on its territory established a vulnerable framework. When Mussolini's military failures led to his removal as leader and imprisonment in July 1943, his successor negotiated a surrender to Allied forces. That September, a German unit managed to free Mussolini and spirit him away to Germany for a meeting with Hitler. Installing him as the ostensible leader of a puppet Fascist Italian Social Republic in the northern half of the country, they quickly began to round up Italian Jews for deportation.

In the south, the concentration camp system for civilians was dismantled after the armistice. Most internees were freed as Allied forces moved in. In a strange bid to sidestep traditional immigration procedures, President Franklin Roosevelt sent a ship to bring a thousand refugees, mostly foreign Jews, to an army camp in Oswego, New York, in June 1944. They thought they would be set free on arrival. In a gesture that made sense to no one, even in subsequent decades, they were put on trains and held behind barbed wire—much to their initial alarm—until seven months after the end of the war.[32]

Events in northern Italy remained grimmer. Nazi transit camps were set up to funnel detainees to Auschwitz. Even under Nazi direction, however, Italians did not hold enough animosity toward Jews to make the deportation plan work. Local officials, police, and residents alerted area Jews to imminent arrests, allowing most to hide or escape. Of some 43,000 Jews living in the puppet republic, about one in ten were actually sent to Auschwitz. But of those 4,300 who were put on trains headed to occupied Poland, only 314 survived.[33]

7. Risky as life could be in June of 1940, getting out of an internment camp in southern France was perhaps the easiest step in the process of escaping the Nazis. Acquiring papers and crossing the border presented greater challenges. Out of a fear of losing neutral status or a wish to appease Hitler, Switzerland, long a haven for radicals and refugees, had begun to turn back people at the border long before the war started.[34]

France's northern neighbors were under Nazi occupation, so the southern route into Spain remained the obvious choice. Though Spain was sympathetic to Nazi Germany, it had not officially entered the war. Border guards could be bribed, but the Gestapo could bribe them, too. For those who could get through Spain to Portugal, Lisbon was a haven. But even in Lisbon, refugees were not permitted to stay indefinitely. Foreigners, mostly stateless people, needed visas that would allow them to go abroad. Refugees were arrested in each stage of attempting to escape, and to be caught would mean more punitive detention and perhaps death.

Hannah Arendt spent the fall of 1940 stateless and trapped with friends in the south of France. Sensing the hand of German bureaucracy at its most threatening, Arendt persuaded the group not to report to local police or register for the census of Jews. If they had to be stateless, they were better off invisible—as long as they were not caught.

Foreign observers began to help. Varian Fry, a thirty-two-year-old American writer and editor, had been sent to France by the Emergency Rescue Committee, a charity group organized to help those endangered by the fall of France. Fry started out following official procedures and quickly discovered he could accomplish next to nothing. Creating a legitimate French organization to provide cover, he quickly built a network of people to work on the black market, obtaining false papers as well as legal ones, and arranging clandestine border crossings. Hiram Bingham, a visa officer in the US consulate at Marseille, collaborated with Fry. After visiting internment camps and recognizing the danger refugees were in, he issued travel documents in complete contravention of the standard American policy of the day. The son of a former governor and heir to the Tiffany fortune, Bingham sometimes hid refugees in his home.

The Vichy regime put Fry under surveillance and held him for questioning several times. Overstaying his allotted term, he could not get his passport renewed by the US government and lost his job in America.[35] In the long run, uninterested in going to war over a crusading writer dabbling in saving refugees, the US State Department and the Vichy government eventually sent him home.

Hiram Bingham was soon relieved of his visa duties at the consulate. In all, Fry, Bingham, and the Emergency Rescue Committee helped some two thousand refugees escape, among them Marc Chagall, Max Ernst, Claude Lévi-Strauss, Marcel Duchamp, Max Ophüls, Arthur Koestler, and Hannah Arendt.

Arendt emigrated with her husband, Heinrich, through Lisbon and on to New York City, carrying Walter Benjamin's papers with her. At the recommendation of theologian Paul Tillich, who had arrived in the city before her, she applied for a two-month home placement with an American family in order to learn English. Within six months, she was hired as a columnist for the German-language newspaper *Aufbau*. A decade later, after eighteen years as a stateless person, she became an American citizen.[36]

After the war, Arendt began work on *The Origins of Totalitarianism,* which would become one of the first attempts to wrestle with the links between anti-Semitism, ideological extremism, and concentration camps. Via her portrayal of internment camps, the Gulag, and Nazi death camps as analogous to "Hades, Purgatory, and Hell," Arendt would address both the universal motivations and the distinct qualities of each system. "The real horror of the concentration and extermination camps," she wrote, "lies in the fact that the inmates, even if they happen to keep alive, are more effectively cut off from the world of the living than if they had died."[37]

8. Six months after Arendt's arrival in New York, more than three hundred Japanese planes bombed ships stationed at Pearl Harbor in Hawaii, triggering the US entry into the war. Japan had joined the Axis powers more than a year before, but until December 7, 1941, they had fought only in China.

Within forty-eight hours of Pearl Harbor, however, Japan attacked Thailand and US territories in Guam and the Philippines, as well as British possessions in Malaya, Hong Kong, and Singapore. As Japanese forces swept south and west through Asia and the Pacific, they obliterated Allied defenses for the first several months, getting as far as making a bombing run on northern Australia. During these initial victories, many enemy aliens from Allied nations suddenly found themselves in Japanese-controlled territory.

Japanese troops had gained a reputation for atrocities even before the war. The death toll from Japan's seizure of the city of Nanking in 1937, along with widespread rape and other violence that unfolded during it, has never been finalized, but the total sits somewhere between tens of thousands and hundreds of thousands. Emperor Hirohito's soldiers soon became notorious for their treatment of Allied prisoners of war as well. Japan had promised that during the conflict its forces would observe the 1929 Geneva Convention, which guaranteed the humane treatment of captives, including protection from public humiliation and reprisals. But in practice, they rarely complied.

Of some 140,000 POWs in Japanese custody, more than 30,000 died.[38] The brutal Bataan Death March—later testimony recounted mass executions, maiming, and starvation—was prosecuted as a war crime after the Japanese surrender in 1945.

Along with POW camps, Japanese forces also administered concentration camp systems for civilians in territories they occupied.

Lacking the central coordination and universal policies of the Nazi *Konzentrationslager* system, Japanese camps fostered a range of outcomes, from neutral to stunningly lethal. Mary Previte, a young British Girl Guide (the equivalent of a Girl Scout), recalled the days when her whole school, along with its teachers, became detainees in the Japanese camp at Weixian, China. Wearing armbands to indicate their nationality, they lived behind barbed wire, undernourished and consuming eggshells for extra calcium.[39] Armed guards patrolled with bayonets and dogs, and prisoners stood for roll call daily. Previte remembers singing songs and earning merit badges to keep busy.

Conditions in some camps for Westerners were indistinguishable from the kinds of hardships and fundamental injustices present in detention camps around the world during the Second World War. But at least two types of civilian camps reflect the official Japanese embrace of atrocity during the conflict. Even before the war began, Japan had a tradition of labor conscription, and had asserted its position while governing Korea to extract civilian workers for hard labor on infrastructure or for private companies. In wartime, this approach expanded and accelerated, and as in Nazi Germany, millions of civilians were subjected to abuse and forced labor. In addition, hundreds of thousands of workers were forced to leave their home countries to live in harrowing conditions while performing lethal work elsewhere.

A complex calculus of paid and unpaid workers, recruited by deception or force, took part in each project, but the disregard for working conditions and horrendous abuse of workers was a recurring theme. Beginning in 1942, tens of thousands of civilian laborers died constructing the Burma–Siam railroad, which came to be known as the "Death Railway."[40] Rife with beatings, malnutrition, and tropical ulcers that ate away at workers' skin, labor on the railway line was eventually included in war crimes trials against Japanese military officials. Thirty-two death-sentence convictions were handed down for the mistreatment of the POWs involved.

Military courts did not have jurisdiction to impose justice on behalf of the much larger number of civilian deaths resulting from Japanese labor projects. However, lawsuits seeking compensation for both prisoners of war and civilians who worked in a wide range of forced-labor camps have appeared continuously since the 1990s, with corporations making payments to workers who had been pressed into involuntary service by Japanese forces decades before.[41]

The most fraught legacy of the Japanese civilian concentration camps lies in the government's role in creating "comfort stations"— ostensibly brothels—for the use of Japanese soldiers. The number of women involved is still sometimes contested by Japanese scholars, but elsewhere it is accepted that between 80,000 and 100,000 women were trafficked to work as sex slaves in these facilities at some point during the war.[42] As with forced labor, coercion and deception played key roles in finding workers.

Some fifty years after the surrender, the Japanese government apologized for "a grave affront to the honor and dignity of a large number of women."[43] Although civilians ran several stations, Japan acknowledged that its representatives had solicited their creation and had operated others. An official report outlined that officials were heavily involved in setting prices, checking for sexually transmitted diseases, and managing "customer" workloads for the women.[44] Military officials had helped obtain workers by intimidation and force when necessary and transported the women to the camps.

Over many years, archival material in China and Japan has bolstered the accounts of the women held at comfort stations, underlining the role of the military in authorizing and maintaining the facilities. Former comfort women described being raped by dozens of soldiers a day and being forced into intercourse even if they were ill or infected with a sexually transmitted disease. Hwang So Gyun testified in 1996 that she had been lured away from home with the promise of a factory job, only to find herself in a comfort station.

"One day, a new girl was put in the compartment next to me," Gyun said. "She tried to resist the men and bit one of them in his arm.

She was then taken to the courtyard and in front of all of us, her head was cut off with a sword and her body was cut into small pieces."[45]

For more than three decades, apologies and stuttering resolutions of the controversy laying out Japanese responsibility have often been followed by revisionist remarks from Japanese officials. In 2015, South Korea and Japan negotiated an $8.3 million fund for survivors in exchange for an end to public South Korean denunciations of the Japanese. Yet payments to survivors have not put the matter to rest.[46]

9. One day after the bombing at Pearl Harbor, the United States declared war on Japan. The question of what to do with enemy aliens if the country entered the war had been planned long before the attack, and the events of December 7 jolted the FBI into action. With deportations largely off the table, options were limited to detention, surveillance, or liberty.

FBI Director J. Edgar Hoover's agents had been conducting surveillance on foreigners and keeping rosters of suspects for years. Within forty-eight hours, Hoover's office had distributed lists by teletype, and agents had taken 1,291 Japanese Americans into custody, many simply on the basis of being leaders in their communities.[47] Agents soon moved on to bringing in Germans and Italians. Each individual had already been categorized by descending level of threat, in the style of the British enemy alien program.

Three-person tribunals were set up to review detainees' cases and decide whether to keep them in custody, release them on parole with a sponsor, or free them completely. Sometimes the tribunals overrode FBI requests—in at least one case, refusing to provide liberty to a Nazi sympathizer who had aided the bureau.[48] In all, more than 31,000 enemy aliens from European countries were detained for the course of the war, some because of evidence and others on the basis of speculative allegations. Among them were Jewish refugees who had managed to escape the Nazis only to end up behind barbed wire in America.[49]

For the first time, the United States provided other nations with a list of enemy aliens living in Central and South America and pressured these countries to deport the suspects to the States for detention, often on the basis of minimal or spurious information. These Japanese, German, and Italian nationals were brought north as part of a plan to trade them and their families for high-profile American detainees trapped abroad. Under pressure from Washington, during the war more than six thousand detainees were sent from Bolivia, Colombia, Honduras, and other regions to the detention camp at Crystal City, Texas, where guards in cowboy hats and chaps patrolled ten-foot-high barbed wire fences strung between watchtowers.[50]

On the assumption that even stricter measures might be necessary for Japanese Americans on the West Coast, President Roosevelt issued Executive Order 9066 in February 1942, claiming authority for commanders to designate "military areas" in the country and to control all conditions inside those zones. Leading the Western Defense Command was Lieutenant General John L. DeWitt, who publicly argued that espionage by Japanese Americans lay at the heart of the Pearl Harbor disaster. He made his first proclamation on March 2, suggesting that certain groups might be exiled from the West Coast in the interest of stopping "espionage and acts of sabotage."[51] Congress quickly passed legislation assigning penalties to anyone convicted of violating regulations in these areas, over the objections of Senator Robert Taft, who took the floor to say, "I think this is probably the 'sloppiest' criminal law I have ever read or seen anywhere."[52]

A curfew specific to Japanese Americans was set at 8 p.m., and Roosevelt signed another executive order creating the War Relocation Authority. The government then began issuing Civilian Exclusion Orders that forced everyone of Japanese ancestry into temporary detention centers while permanent concentration camps were built. Americans like Mitsuye Endo, a clerk with the California Department of Motor Vehicles, were hounded out of their jobs. Fred Korematsu, who had tried to join the army, was turned down for medical reasons and then found himself barred from work because he was Japanese American. Refusing to obey the exclusion order, he was arrested in San Leandro and held in jail. With help from the American Civil Liberties Union, he brought a legal case contesting the government's right to detain him. Quickly convicted, put on probation, and transferred to the processing center at Tanforan horsetrack, he was sent to the Central Utah War Relocation Center in Topaz.

Within a matter of months, Japanese Americans on the West Coast had been sent to concentration camps. They sold their vehicles and homes, their businesses and farms, sometimes with only forty-eight hours' notice. After relocation plans were complete, more than 120,000 Japanese Americans—some two-thirds of them US citizens—were put on trains and shipped out of the restricted area into indefinite detention. Scattered to Northern California, Wyoming, Idaho, Arkansas, and Utah, they arrived to find camps located on plains, in swamps, or among mountains.

For their trouble, they got barbed wire and barracks and not much else. On the front page of the first issue of the *Denson Communiqué* published for residents of Jerome War Relocation Center in Arkansas, an article informed US citizens in concentration camps "How To Vote by Absentee Ballot."[53]

Conditions in US internment camps included spare accommodations, harsh weather, and unsympathetic guards. A typical shoddy tarpaper-and-plywood barrack measured twenty feet wide and a hundred feet long, and had to house four families for two years or more. American camps did not resort to torture, and physical discipline was not part of any official agenda. But the very framework of the camps was difficult to square with the idea that they were not intended to be punitive. In one early tragedy, two sick prisoners who had been assigned a special medical detail were shot "trying to escape" on arrival at a New Mexico camp in 1942.[54] Brought before a court-martial, the shooter was acquitted.

After administering a confusing questionnaire to detainees in

an attempt to assess their loyalty to the United States, camp administrators segregated prisoners on the basis of their answers—or their
refusal to answer. Asking detainees who had just lost everything and
were isolated in detention centers whether they were willing to serve
in the armed forces was a ham-handed way of assessing threat. The
"No-No" crowd, those who answered two key questions in the negative or left them blank, were shipped off to the concentration camp
at Tule Lake, which became the main site for "disloyal" detainees.
The most troublesome prisoners there were banished to a single-
story, low-slung cinder-block prison with no comforts and little light,
sequestered from the rest of the camp.

Many continued to protest their detention. After the initial court
decision against him, Fred Korematsu's lawyer filed an appeal. A
lawyer for Mitsuye Endo, imprisoned at Tule Lake, filed a habeus
corpus petition challenging her detention as interference with the
right of a state employee to go to work. The court offered to release
her if she stayed out of the exclusion zone, but she refused on principle, remaining in detention until the case was resolved. The US
Supreme Court eventually accepted her case, along with Fred
Korematsu's.

In what would come to be seen as one of the most shameful decisions in US legal history, the court in January 1944 upheld the lower
court's verdict in the Korematsu case. Ruling that "exclusion of large
groups of citizens from their homes, except under circumstances of
direst emergency and peril, is inconsistent with our basic govern-
mental institutions," the court somehow managed to rationalize that
this time, the practice might be acceptable.[55]

In Endo's case, however, the court ruled almost a year later that a
non-Japanese-speaking Christian who was a US citizen and whose
brother was serving in the US Army could not be indefinitely
detained as a disloyal citizen. To accept the government's arguments, the court said, "would be to assume that the Congress and
the President intended that this discriminatory action should be
taken against these people wholly on account of their ancestry even

though the government conceded their loyalty to this country. We cannot make such an assumption."[56]

American democracy had tried to absorb the idea of legal concentration camps for whole races or classes of people, but ultimately the two concepts were incompatible. The executive and legislative branches had swallowed the idea, but in time the judicial branch coughed up the mess it had been handed. Nine months ahead of victory against Japan, the government began to release detainees.

Writing about Japanese internment in the United States, Hannah Arendt suggested that by effectively revoking the citizenship of Japanese Americans on the West Coast, the detainees had for all practical purposes been rendered stateless. The US government had left innocent citizens with fewer rights to protection under the law than they would have had as criminals.[57]

10. While US military officials first began to contemplate the idea of universal internment for Japanese Americans in January 1942, top Nazi leaders were meeting at Wannsee to commit to the Final Solution. The Wannsee decision reverberated throughout Europe, with immediate repercussions in France. German authorities had long been working with the Vichy government there to pave the way for more complete attention to the "Jewish problem" through a series of statutes and internment camps run by French administrators.

Months after Hannah Arendt's departure from France in 1940, German officials ordered the deportation of more than 6,500 Jews from Rhineland areas to Gurs, bringing the camp population to more than 12,000 inmates. Given no advance notice about these new arrivals, the commandant could provide rations for only a little more than half the detainees. As overcrowding and hunger took their toll, children began to die, seven-year-old Arne Herze, six-year-old Rolph Neumann, and four-year-old Evelyne Blum the first among them.[58]

A rabbi permitted access to Gurs during the summer Arendt had left was shocked by the hunger, vermin, and despair that dominated daily life. Organizing internal committees of prisoners to set up a post office, synagogue, and cultural center, he appealed to French and American Jews for support.[59] Within weeks, the French Red Cross, Swiss Jewish communities, and Quakers began to funnel aid to prisoners, but they could only do so much. First-person accounts of visits to the camp began to appear in foreign newspapers, describing swollen faces, bleeding gums, teeth falling out, and detainees' "intense desire to die."[60] By late November, eight prisoners on average were buried every day.[61]

As a distraction from hunger, detainees organized cultural evenings of performances and lectures. With outside assistance, musical instruments were brought in, and prisoners entertained each other. Among Gurs detainees were the organist for the Strasbourg Cathedral and the first chair violinist of the Vienna Philharmonic.[62]

Introducing a "Law on the Status of Jews" that fall, the Vichy government somehow managed to come up with an even more severe statute to determine Jewish identity than the Germans had produced. Only two Jewish grandparents, not three, were necessary to designate someone as Jewish, if that person was also married to a Jew. In practice, it might not matter whom they had married; two grandparents would effectively label an individual Jewish.

By the time the law was enacted, seven camps in the Free Zone held foreign Jews, anarchists, Communists, anti-Fascists, Gypsies, and the remainder of the International Brigadists from the Spanish Civil War. Three more camps were added that January. Two months later, six thousand children were held at Rivesaltes in slightly better conditions, with US newspapers recounting a description of Gurs as "Hell."[63]

At Paris, in the Occupied Zone, censuses of Jews had already allowed authorities to begin a slow segregation. Jews first were denied radios and refused permission to travel within the country. They had to observe a curfew, and in the event of aerial bombardment, they were prohibited from entering bomb shelters. Expected to pay a billion-franc fine for anonymous assassination attempts on German soldiers, they were told they would be preferentially executed in reprisal for any successful assassinations.[64]

When Germany invaded Russia, the rupture of their alliance provided cover for Occupation forces in France to attack Jews as Communists and go door to door rounding them up. Many French Jews were included. Within two weeks more than four thousand had been interned at the concentration camp at Drancy, a repurposed police building in the northeastern suburbs of Paris. The typically horrific conditions of overcrowding, poor sanitation, and limited food prevailed, with many prisoners losing thirty to forty pounds in a matter of weeks.[65]

Publications of the far-right French press were happy to support the rising tide of anti-Semitic laws, claiming that previous restrictive legislation had not gone far enough. However, France was not yet Germany. When French proxies received help from the Gestapo to carry out bombings of seven synagogues in October 1941, the attacks failed to trigger the massive Kristallnacht-style violence the Nazis had hoped for. A German military paper reported the response of the French public with apparent disappointment: "Although they do not like the Jews, the French are displeased when they see Jews massacred and when their places of worship are blown up."[66]

As the Final Solution became official policy, annihilation swept Europe. Multiple citizen registries with addresses and lists of property had already been completed. Deportations began in earnest. The Parisian metropolitan bus company reserved fifty buses for French police to use in roundups.[67] In 1942 the Vélodrome d'Hiver, where Arendt had stayed before being transported to Gurs, degenerated into a nightmare of more than eight thousand men, women, and children trapped with no food.

Around the region, children whose parents were taken away stayed alone or were taken in by neighbors. In some cases they were too young to speak or know their names. "So many babies on the straw, totally alone and helpless!" wrote Marie-Louise Blondeau of the chaos in the camp at Pithiviers.[68]

The prefect of the Paris police took over the camp at Drancy, with a French police chief as camp commandant. The prisoners' daily food ration was negligible. They could leave their quarters for only one hour a day, but many were too weak to do as little as that, even for mandatory roll calls. "There was one bar of soap for ten people, one comb for twenty," writes Renée Poznanski, "one toothbrush for five, and one razor for ten."[69] The authorities displayed no great concern over meeting the needs of prisoners who would soon be in German hands.

Some did not make it that far. In December 1941, an SS commander came to the camp and began taking prisoners away. Ninety-five of them were shot in retaliation for resistance elsewhere that had nothing to do with them. In the months that followed, when assassination attempts were made on German soldiers, Drancy became a hostage depot for use in reprisals.[70] More than five hundred other detainees were soon put on trains with inmates from Compiègne. They knew that they were heading east, but they were not told their final destination.

The world would ask later how it was possible that these things happened, but at that moment no proper language existed for it. The spare lexicon that had formed had yet to convey its full meaning. In January 1943, the *New York Times* ran the headline "Liquidation Day Set for France's Jews," informing readers that it had received word from relief agencies that "gradual elimination is planned." Yet even as the reporter heard and wrote down the words "liquidation" and "elimination," he explained that the policy "aims at the progressive internment of Jews and their expulsion to the Eastern territories."[71] Some thoughts were still unthinkable.

France did not kill the Jewish population trapped in its territory when the country fell, but many of its newspapers, police, bureaucrats, camp administrators, and railway workers actively abetted their detention at home or sent them abroad to their deaths. Other Western European countries under Nazi occupation played similar roles.

Yet some did not. There were those few countries that resisted, adopting children, hiding whole families, and setting up intelligence networks to get word of atrocities out to the world. In Denmark during September and October 1943, given only three days' notice of impending arrests, the authorities and the civilian population managed to evacuate more than 95 percent of the country's Jewish residents and refugees, sneaking them to the coast and ferrying them across open water to Sweden at night.

France would offer no such salvation. Almost all the prisoners at Gurs—those who stayed when Hannah Arendt fled or were corralled by the Gestapo after she escaped—ended up on trains headed for Drancy. On orders of the French ministry of the interior, Gurs had been made a transit hub for deportations from the south. Traveling north from Oloron-Sainte-Marie through Pau to Toulouse and up to Drancy, Jews were then put on trains that crossed the German border, headed into Poland, to Kraków and on to Oświęcim, where they were forced out onto the ground between the vast, fenced blocks of barracks at Auschwitz-Birkenau. They made their way around to the tiny forest, where they may have had to bide their time, and then on to the gas chamber and crematorium. Out of more than 60,000 Jews sent east from Drancy, fewer than 2,000 would survive. More than 3,900 Jews were sent to their death from Gurs alone.

11. The world would be slow to come to terms with the less obvious evils perpetrated by both Axis and Allied countries during the Second World War. Thousands of camps were emptied and shuttered; but even outside the Gulag, some camps remained open for years.

The toll from the Nazi camp systems was unprecedented and unfathomable. But the damage resulting from British and American internment was also tragic. Hundreds died on the *Arandora Star* on their way to overseas internment. Some US soldiers shot or beat Japanese Americans who were American citizens. Vast towns of detention were built in unlivable areas; millions of dollars were spent. Immigrant communities and the lives of hundreds of thousands of citizens in England and America were dislocated or shattered, despite all the prior experience indicating that internment would serve no useful purpose.

It is easy to dismiss internment as a mistake perpetrated in ignorance by frightened decision makers. But this would be a fundamental misreading of how internment tends to occur. In early 1942, weeks after Pearl Harbor, naval intelligence officer Kenneth Ringle submitted a report to the War Department assessing the threat from Japanese-born residents and Japanese American citizens on the West Coast. Ringle, who had broken up a Japanese spy network three years before, was considered the most informed analyst on the issue of potential Japanese disloyalty. In his report he clearly laid out that there were probably fewer than three hundred dangerous individuals of Japanese ancestry left in the country, and almost all of them were already known to intelligence services through their involvement with nationalist cultural societies. "The entire 'Japanese Problem,'" he wrote, "has been magnified out of its true proportion, largely because of the physical characteristics of the people....It should be handled on the basis of the individual, regardless of citizenship, and not on a racial basis."[72]

Another report submitted before the bombing of Pearl Harbor had come to the same conclusion. FBI director J. Edgar Hoover himself found mass detention problematic.[73] Sensational, unfounded allegations in a congressional report of espionage rings in Hawaii, of cane fields being cut into arrow shapes to signal Japanese aviators, and sabotage on the ground at Pearl Harbor had likewise been debunked by the FBI.[74]

Ringle's report had been seen and shared at the time among military leaders. It was known by those with the power to decide that relocating those of Japanese ancestry was unnecessary. But key politicians used the issue to grandstand for the public, and the general in charge of the Western Defense Command, who had been uncertain about how to proceed, caved to public pressure, concluding that "a Jap is a Jap to these people now."[75]

The original reports assessing that the Japanese population as a whole represented no threat were hidden by the US Solicitor General's office before the Supreme Court case that ruled in favor of wartime detention. It would take nearly thirty years for the truth to come out. Standing in a courtroom in November 1983, Fred Korematsu asked the judge to overturn his initial conviction for violating military orders. "As long as my record stands in federal court," he said, "any American citizen can be held in prison or concentration camps without a trial or a hearing."[76]

A writ of coram nobis was granted, acknowledging that the prior legal judgment in *Korematsu* had been based on flawed evidence that, had it been revealed as erroneous at the time, would likely have precluded the earlier decision.

In the matter of accountability for the millions killed in Europe, trials of key architects of the Holocaust gave way to charges against lower-level officials and negotiations for compensation to refugees and survivors. Yet surprises remained. In 1960, Israeli agents kidnapped Adolf Eichmann in Argentina and took him to Israel to face justice. Hannah Arendt's account of his trial appeared as a five-part series in *The New Yorker* in 1963, eventually becoming the book *Eichmann in Jerusalem: A Report on the Banality of Evil.*

Ahead of the trial, she wrote to her mentor-turned-friend Karl Jaspers, fretting, "I'm afraid that Eichmann will be able to prove, first of all, that no country wanted the Jews... and will demonstrate, second, to what a huge degree the Jews helped organize their own destruction."[77] Arendt believed that the extent to which Jewish leaders in the ghettos had provided information to Nazi officials and permitted, or even encouraged, residents to go along with deportations had played a key role in augmenting the death toll from the final stages of the Holocaust.

She was prescient about the questions the case would raise even before she went to Jerusalem ("we need a court for criminal cases in The Hague"[78]), and later wondered whether the process had at times been unjust, as Eichmann was not permitted to call witnesses for his defense. She felt the judge had erred in his argumentation and wished that he had instead condemned the defendant for proceeding "as though you or your superiors had any right to determine who should and who should not inhabit the world."[79]

Arendt's book on Eichmann became her most famous, but it would blight her reputation permanently among a significant portion of the audience that had once admired her. Running excerpts of the book, French newspaper *Le Nouvel Observateur* asked, "Is She a Nazi?"[80] Furious readers made two charges against her. She appeared to suggest that Eichmann was not especially hateful toward Jews and had functioned as an ambitious *apparatchik* without any deeper motive in the Nazi system. Further, and more disturbingly, she publicly reiterated her thinking from the private letter to Jasper, once more sitting in harsh judgment of the Jewish Councils over their cooperation with their executioners.

As for her perception of Eichmann's banality, others had noted that the trait was present in many Nazi functionaries. Her insight that willing servitude rather than evil genius is all a totalitarian society requires has become widely accepted. In Eichmann's case, however, he managed to appear so normal due in part to his active deception on the stand, and in part to the Argentina Papers, notes and interviews related to his ties to a group in Argentina dedicated to a Nazi restoration. Some of these materials had not yet been unearthed by the time of the trial, while others could not be vetted and confirmed as legitimate in time to be admitted as evidence.[81] He effectively duped the observers and the court into believing he had the soul of a lackey but was executed anyway.

Arendt's focus on the role of the Jews in their own destruction is more complicated. When witnesses against Eichmann were asked why they did not rebel, she called the question "silly and cruel." Yet she seemed to ask the question herself, and to have decided to assign partial blame to Jews for the Holocaust, with the surprising declaration that "to a Jew, this role of the Jewish leaders in the destruction of their own people is undoubtedly the darkest chapter of the whole dark story."[82]

The letter to Jaspers before the start of the trial showed that she had been thinking about the issue well before she went to Jerusalem. But in condemning the *Judenräte*—the Jewish Councils in Nazi-occupied territories—as a whole for not doing more to resist or at least stall the deportations, she missed the mark. Others have taken detailed issue with her arguments, including those who say the councils' actions included both resistance and collaboration, and likely had little overall effect.[83] But the point that has perhaps not been made to counter Arendt's accusation is the degree to which the already decades-long history of concentration camps made individuals worldwide more compliant with regard to detention and allowed the Nazis to sow confusion even among the defiant.

In raising the issue of resistance, Arendt also failed to consider her own history. She had helped many Jews escape before leaving Germany in 1933, and had seen the angel of death approaching the detention camp at Gurs. She had spent years of her life stateless, and by the time of the Eichmann trial had done as much original thinking on concentration camps as any thinker to date. Yet she seems not to have recalled that when brutal anti-Semitism had risen in France, and war had been declared in 1940, and summons were printed for enemy aliens to appear, Arendt had promptly reported when and where she was told to do so. She had taken her belongings on the metro to the velodrome along with thousands of others. By this point in time, accounts of early Nazi camps and of the persecution of Jews were widespread throughout Western Europe. Yet Arendt had stayed a week sleeping in a stadium under armed guard with no word on what would happen to her, despite her realization that France could hand her and the other detainees over to Germany.

France in 1940 was not Nazi-occupied Poland in 1942. Yet to surrender oneself for detention in a concentration camp without hesitation in a moment of political crisis was exactly what pariah classes had been trained to do. And during the Second World War, they did it worldwide, in Germany and Poland, in France and England, in China and Italy, and in the United States.

Only the chaos in Gurs after the fall of France gave Arendt another opportunity to resist. Otherwise she, too, would in time have been put on a train north to Drancy and delivered to the gates of Auschwitz. Many others who complied—council leaders, observant Jews, and apostates alike—never got a second chance.

CHAPTER SEVEN

Stepchildren of the Gulag

1. AT NIGHT IN WARSAW, the streets rang with gunfire. Five months after the German surrender, secret police haunted doorways in Poland, staking out buildings and arresting anyone who showed up. Auschwitz had reopened, and the electric current on the fences had been turned back on. Rjeszow Kojder, a regional leader of the Polish Peasants Party, gave a speech at a rally, only to vanish in the company of four uniformed men the next day. Soon after, his corpse was found.

By October 1945, a new political landscape was evolving. On a ten-day tour of Poland that fall, Gladwin Hill—one of the first Western reporters to visit Warsaw after the war—reported on the violence that had seized the liberated nation. He noticed that along with arrests and murders, officials were quietly mounting a disinformation campaign. His interpreter, a former member of the underground and a concentration camp survivor, disappeared without explanation after irritating party officials with his candor. A program director who failed to broadcast propaganda on schedule was dismissed over a trivial offense.

Other, more obvious attempts at distorting reality began, with the police insisting that only a thousand political prisoners were in custody, while other members of the government acknowledged that the number was actually between sixty thousand and eighty thousand. Equally disturbing was the government's initial announcement that security forces were being trained by Russian experts, followed by a denial that any such thing was under way. Soon even Americans were being taken into custody without charges or trials. Uninterested in getting a personal tour of the new Polish prisons, Hill waited until he was out of the country to file his story.[1]

This new political order would soon spread. In the wake of the war, through intimidation, strategic financial support, and international collaboration, the Soviet Union extended its reach around the globe. Military interference would drive the formation of puppet governments in some nations, while softer tactics would come to dominate existing revolutionary movements in others. As Communism became the ruling ideology in more than a dozen countries around the world, from Eastern Europe to China and Southeast Asia—and even Cuba—the Soviet Gulag offered a model for extrajudicial civilian detention for those seen as unfit for Communist society. What resulted was a generation of camps that were not carbon copies of the Gulag but that to varying degrees embraced the Russian model.

Detention in these camps was nothing like the end stage of the Nazi concentration camp system. Even at Auschwitz, prisoners were no longer gassed: detainees had been brought in to dismantle the I. G. Farben plant where Elie Wiesel and his father had worked, so that its parts could be shipped to Russia.[2] Yet oppression was in the air. Poland, Hill wrote, was experiencing "a subtle reign of terror."[3]

Despite a promise to allow the emergence of a free Poland, the Soviet Union kept the provisional government under its thumb. Anyone voicing opposition to Moscow's influence was at risk. After gaining control of the newly reconstituted army, Polish Communists began locking up dissidents. On the eve of the elections held in January 1947, *Time* magazine reported that "in a spirit of partisan exuberance tempered with terror...the Communist-dominated Government ventured to predict an 'overwhelming' victory."[4]

A Communist Polish People's Republic did not officially arrive until 1952, but during those postwar years, all of Eastern Europe felt the heavy hand of Moscow. In Czechoslovakia, the new Communist government held espionage trials in 1948 to eliminate its leftist rivals and over the next six years sent twenty-two thousand people to labor camps, including a deadly uranium mine at Jàchymov.[5]

Many of the unofficial rules in the new regime echoed those inside the USSR. In a letter dated 1951, a neighbor denounced a local merchant, testifying that she had heard him call Stalin an imbecile and say that he would never put a picture of "that cursed mustache" in his display case.[6] Other reasons sufficient for detention included a "failure to understand the goals of the Five-Year Plan."

Yugoslavia, Hungary, and Romania followed suit, launching their own detention systems under the auspices of local Communist leadership, supported by Moscow. German civilians (many of whom had emigrated before the war) were forced out of Eastern Bloc countries under duress or kept as involuntary labor, working for the state or private industry. Meanwhile the *"deutscher Blick,"* the reflex to look over one's shoulder under Nazi rule, remained a survival skill under the new order in Warsaw. And with good reason: the regime of secret police and Soviet influence that Gladwin Hill reported witnessing in Poland in 1945 would stay in power for almost half a century.

In the Baltic states—Latvia, Estonia, and Lithuania—which had been directly annexed as Soviet republics after occupation, massive forced relocation began in the wake of the war. Operation Spring deported almost fifty thousand Lithuanians to the Soviet Union in 1948. During Operation Priboy the following year, more than forty thousand Latvians and twenty thousand Estonians were sent to Siberia by their new Soviet governments.[7] In the meantime, the Soviets had created the "Cominform"—a Communist Information Bureau—to help coordinate official Communist Party ideology among the fledgling "revolutionary" states.

As the Iron Curtain divided Europe, Western newspapers began to address the wave of police states rising in the East. "Their goals are dictated by Soviet Russia, their methods are those of Hitler," wrote the editorial board of the *New York Times.* "They are establishing a new totalitarianism with the concentration camp, slave labor and a tremendous propaganda effort as the characteristic features of the new ruling technique."[8]

Civilians in nearly every country ruled by a Communist Party in the postwar period endured extrajudicial detention borrowed to varying degrees from the Stalinist system. Yet it was not in Eastern Europe but in China that a genuinely revolutionary state and a system built on forced labor and propaganda managed to dwarf the Soviet model and other Communist systems combined. Only in China did the new concentration camps outgrow the Gulag, using civilian detention and Communist ideology across generations to reshape society for more than a fifth of the planet's population.

2. When Mao Zedong took power after the 1949 Revolution, it was perhaps predictable that he would impose a nationwide Gulag-style system of concentration camps. He had long advocated an arbitrary period of mob justice and extrajudicial punishment, saying that those who felt revolutionaries were "going too far" did not realize that "proper limits have to be exceeded in order to right a wrong."[9] And he had approved of Leninist revolutionary terror from the first years of Soviet triumph, writing in the 1920s, "To put it bluntly, it is necessary to create terror for a while in every rural area."[10]

Chinese concentration camps also reflected longstanding domestic traditions. Imperial China had never accepted the idea of individual rights that eclipsed obligations to the government. Instead, imperial subjects were heavily subordinate to ruling dynasties, with frequent use of civilian labor conscription stretching back more than two millennia.[11]

Yet Mao had a long history of adopting outside legal influences, embracing the 1928 Soviet legal code that made counterrevolutionary charges applicable to almost everything. An early 1933 draft statute on the treatment of counterrevolutionaries made clear that if any particular behavior had been overlooked in the list of offenses, individuals could be punished under a statute addressing analogous crimes.

Parallels also existed between the Soviet and Maoist approaches to concentration camps. Linguist Yenna Wu traces Mao's adoption of "remolding" through hard labor to the Soviet "reforging" concept embraced at the dawn of the Gulag. And some officials of the People's Republic of China openly emulated disturbing figures from the Soviet system itself. Luo Ruiqing, the first minister of public security for the PRC, hung a picture of Felix Dzerzhinsky, the first director of the Russian Cheka, in his office.[12]

In the 1950s, Soviet legal statutes served as a source in the drafting of a criminal code for China. Though it would not be formalized for another two decades, the Chinese code came to reflect the Soviet obsession with the use of law as a political weapon. The rehabilitative and reeducative approaches of China's attempt to "learn from the Soviet big brother" were likewise embraced, with Soviet advisors and specialists initially collaborating with Chinese legal and security officials in the new regime.[13]

But long before Mao's forces had won victory, he had already made use of a loose network of labor camps during decades of fighting with Nationalist Guomindang forces in the Chinese Civil War. America had backed Chiang Kai-shek and his Nationalist Army, while Russia had supported Communist guerrilla fighters led by Mao. Under Mao, political opponents in Communist-held territory faced summary executions, with a small percentage assigned to forced-labor camps. In Jiangxi Province in the 1930s, detainees in Communist-held territory were also sent to compulsory labor on the front lines of battle for military projects. By 1932 Communist administrators had included forced labor at the provincial and local level to "educate and reform" as a key part of economic plans. Communist forces also began integrating not just behavioral change but also "thought reform."[14]

By that time, the First World War had legitimized reflexive civilian detention and made it ubiquitous; the Guomindang under Chiang likewise made use of camps. Guomindang forces held thousands of prisoners across a decade in what at least one US diplomat, and even Guomindang leaders themselves, referred to as a system of "concentration camps."[15]

Most detainees were captured enemy combatants, but several sites held intellectuals, high school and college students, Communist Party supporters, and critics of the government—all of whom were subject to political indoctrination sessions and forced labor in an attempt to reform them. The Guomindang also launched forced-labor projects conscripting hundreds of thousands of workers, who suffered under terrible conditions.

Communist forces prevailed after four years of open civil war, with Mao proclaiming the People's Republic of China on October 1, 1949. Concentration camps were already part of his plan. The summer before, he had explained that "remolding through labor," by force if necessary, would be the party's primary method for dealing with internal enemies.[16]

The October Revolution in Russia had inspired its Chinese counterpart, and just as camps had been present at the genesis of the Soviet Union, mass civilian detention found deep inscription into the DNA of the People's Republic. Those seen as unable or unwilling to accommodate the country's new ideology would discover that they, too, would be cast into the same abyss of extrajudicial detention, backbreaking labor, and a release date that might never come.

3. The year Mao Zedong took power, Hongda "Harry" Wu was a twelve-year-old baseball fan living in the wealthy western district of Shanghai. His father, a college graduate educated by missionaries, worked in banking. As People's Liberation Army forces drove Nationalist soldiers out of town, many of his father's associates fled the country, but Wu's family stayed.

Little changed in Harry's life at first. Political curriculum appeared in the schools, promoting Marxist thought. And when the Korean War broke out, patriotic messages against US interference became a constant. But Wu grew up protected from the harsh conditions endured by much of the country, only finding out about the endemic starvation and suffering of China's poor from photos he saw in Western magazines. Too young to volunteer to fight in the Korean War, he embraced the idea of the Communist state and hoped to contribute to its success. So after reading a 1955 appeal in the *People's Daily* for young scholars to become geologists, Wu headed to college.

He found a different world in Beijing. Political instructors took students in hand and organized them into military-style brigades. Unlike Wu, most classmates were already politically active. On his third day at college, he was assigned to write an autobiographical essay that gave his family's background and information on his friends and relatives. He was asked by his Communist Youth League leader whether his father had been a "capitalist running dog."

Soon after, his university stipend for meals and expenses was cut in half.[17] His girlfriend back home began to avoid him. Pressured repeatedly to join the Communist Youth League, he resigned himself to the idea, only to learn that because of his background he would have to publicly criticize his family and confess that his father had betrayed the people by serving as a lackey to capitalism. Deferring membership out of anxiety, he focused on his baseball training and the softball team he had founded at the school.

Meanwhile, Mao launched the Hundred Flowers campaign, encouraging different schools of political thought and welcoming criticism of the Communist Party. Wu and his classmates—along with citizens across China—were instructed to offer thoughts about how to improve the party in the final stages of revolution.

Egged on to express opinions and let ideas flourish, Wu explained that the party had persecuted his brother with five months in detention, an example of how innocents had been hurt in the campaign against counterrevolutionaries. He told his Youth League leader that she treated some members preferentially although Chairman Mao had declared that all socialists were comrades. He presented a ten-point list of grievances while the leader took notes.

Months later the campaign was rescinded, and those who had spoken up were targeted as "Rightists." Wu was forced to turn over his diary and again told that he would have to write a detailed history explaining the roots of his counterrevolutionary thought. He was denounced on the university bulletin board, with a six-page list of his crimes.

The university let him stay for a time, assigning a minder who followed him everywhere, even to the bathroom. He was not allowed to go home for vacation break. Assigned to catch rats on campus, he could not find any. He was told to catch fifty flies a day; eventually, everyone involved agreed maggots would count toward the quota. He could not imagine how he could stand years of such treatment and feared he would follow the path of five students who had been expelled and assigned to hard labor the previous spring.

He made a plan with friends to escape across the border to Burma, but before they fled, one of the plotters stole money and forged Wu's name. Confronted by accusations of theft and under increasing scrutiny, he blindly broke rule after rule, neglecting his research, escaping his handler, and violating restrictions on curfew and travel. It became impossible to imagine any future for himself in the unthinking slogans and obedience demanded by the Chinese state. He knew he was endangering himself but felt helpless to stop.

As graduation approached in the spring of 1960, he was called into a classroom, where he saw the words "Meeting to Criticize Rightist Wu Hongda" written on the chalkboard. After twenty minutes of denunciation by the group, he was expelled. A security officer came into the room to announce that Wu had been sentenced to reeducation through labor.[18]

4. In the decade between the founding of the People's Republic of China and Wu's arrest, Chinese labor camps exploded in size. Prisoner

population estimates for the first years of PRC rule—a period known as the Founding Terror—range from four million upward, with at least two million executed in the same period.[19]

At first, "remolding through labor," abbreviated as *laogai*, promised a semblance of legal process as prisoners ostensibly went before tribunals for judgment. But it is not clear that this process always occurred, and when it did, there was no brief for the defense and no protection of prisoners' rights. A guilty verdict was inevitable, with standard sentences lasting five, ten, or fifteen years.

Unable to keep up with the expanding waves of arrests, these first *laogai* facilities quickly grew overcrowded. The inability of courts to clear their dockets resulted in the development of a short-cut for detainees charged with minor offenses. From the mid-1950s forward a second system, "reeducation through labor," was used for those lesser charges, crimes of attitude rather than deed.

This second system, which came to be known as *laojiao*, was officially administrative—a detainee would become a prisoner without formal charges or any official review of his case. Ostensibly a three-year term, *laojiao* sentences could stretch to ten years or more and be extended without warning.

The term *laogai* came to refer generically to both kinds of detention. Both were arbitrarily determined; both offered no justice to the prisoner. In Wu's case, the latter was applied without review or warning, or even formal charges. He demanded to see the accusation against him before he was taken away, but the arresting officer did not need it. He was a student one day, a prisoner the next.

In April 1960, Wu was put in a jeep and driven an hour away to the Beiyuan Detention Center. Stepping into the prison yard, he saw more than a thousand detainees sitting cross-legged in the dirt. During his stay there, it would become even more crowded, with sleeping prisoners pressed so tightly one to another that no one could move without disturbing his neighbors. Guards gave a formal order twice a night for everyone to roll over simultaneously.

Wu was given food but could not bring himself to eat the thin soup with bits of leaves swimming in it or the small dark sorghum-and-chaff *woutou* buns that were standard camp fare. He handed his *woutou* over to a peasant next to him who introduced himself as Big Mouth Xing.

When prisoners were paired off for a hygiene exercise, he was assigned to Big Mouth and told to pick lice off his partner. Revolted by the peasant's dirty ears, rotten teeth, and snot-encrusted nose, Wu protested that he had never seen a louse and so would not recognize it. He was pulled onto a platform before the whole prison yard and mocked for his ignorance, while another prisoner waved a louse in his face.

Big Mouth later revealed that he had first been arrested while on his way to Beijing to steal food. The famine was so bad in his home village that he no longer had hope of surviving if he stayed. His mother had died, and, lacking the strength to bury her, he had covered her face and left her body where she lay. Sometimes he had nightmares that starving dogs had found her. Trying to walk to Beijing to hunt for food, he wound up arrested en route.

An intellectual protected from many changes in Chinese society over the past decade, Wu had foolishly packed useless, even dangerous reminders of his past to bring along with him, including volumes of Voltaire and Dickens. But from the beginning, he recognized Big Mouth's greater sophistication in their new environment. Big Mouth stole whatever he needed when he could, swiping unguarded bread and tripping prisoners carrying soup.

Sent off to a brickworks camp two weeks after Wu arrived, Big Mouth had managed to escape, only to end up back with Wu months later. Finally reaching Beijing, he had found everyone in the city starving, too. There was no food to steal. He turned himself in and was sent to Beiyuan for a second time.

His willingness to take whatever he needed without hesitation shocked Wu. But Big Mouth was unembarrassed, saying, "Nobody here will take care of you. You have to take care of yourself."[20]

Wu had arrived at Beiyuan in the midst of the Great Leap Forward, the disastrous effort to industrialize during China's second Five Year Plan. Peasant farmers had been forced to merge their private plots of land into agricultural communes, with shared kitchens and propaganda sessions replacing traditional religious and mystic practices. Food rationing and taxation were established, along with staggering steel quotas aimed at surpassing the United Kingdom's annual industrial output. The government pressed its citizens to build "backyard furnaces" in which to forge metal at home out of scraps and household pots and pans. The effort diverted vast numbers of hours from agricultural production, which became a factor in the massive famine that resulted. These and other strategies devastated the economy, forcing the government to abandon the plan midway through.

Wu later recalled that his first exposure to the Great Leap Forward while he was still at the university had marked the beginning of his realization that he could not be a good member of the revolutionary state. The program's goals and methods seemed insane to him. And he was not wrong in his assessment. As with the Soviet Union during collectivization and industrialization, the era on which the Great Leap Forward was modeled, millions died due to catastrophic decision making in an attempt to modernize.

5. Six months into his detention in the suburbs of Beijing, Harry Wu climbed into an open-bed truck with thirty prisoners and rode north into the mountains. Looking for ways to increase his rations, he had been anxious for a labor camp assignment. But once the truck was on its way, he had second thoughts. The guards on the convoy showed only hostility to the detainees. Wu realized he had no idea what he had gotten himself into. His hope turned to dread.

Arriving in October 1960 at the Yanqing Steel Factory, at the bottom of a freezing, desolate canyon, Wu found his fears confirmed. The many crises unleashed by the Great Leap Forward had led to a loss of electricity to power the plant. Workers were idle and waiting to be transferred. The new group had been brought to the factory only to relieve overcrowding at the detention centers.

After they counted off and their files were handed over, the prisoners waited in the snow for further orders. A guard directed them to their barracks in an abandoned building partway up the hillside and then walked away. There were no fences or walls or barbed wire. They were allowed to walk unsupervised.

Wu briefly relished the freedom to move around, but the long-shuttered living quarters were cold and without fuel. The shack measured some fifteen by fifty feet and had windows but no panes, leaving residents at the mercy of the wind. The prisoners asked for something to burn and were told to scavenge outside. They were allocated wheat paste to paper over the windows. And after that, they would have to make do.

It was the tenth anniversary of Chinese troop deployment to North Korea. Wu remembered how patriotic he had felt as a teenager when the war was under way, knowing that China had moved into northern Korea to help expel Western imperialists in the south. At the time, he had longed to be old enough to join his country on the battlefield; now he was an enemy of the state.

Lacking vegetables, the flour and chaff of the *woutou* effectively cemented the prisoners' intestines, making unassisted bowel movements nearly impossible. When he was sent to harvest cabbages, Wu was the only prisoner in the group who was not caught eating them. As a result, he was given sole responsibility for gathering the cabbages, several of which he stole and ate each week. The vegetable matter eased digestion of the sorghum buns but exposed him to harassment from other prisoners, who demanded he steal for them, too.

After he was knocked down and kicked by his fellow detainees, Wu reported the assault. A second, worse beating convinced him that he would have to come up with a solution on his own. On his next trip back from the cabbage patch, Wu ambushed the gang leader and cut him on the head with a rock. He had learned Big Mouth Xing's lesson. He would take care of himself.

6. China had not been alone in embracing the Soviet model. After three years of occupation by Russian troops in the wake of the Second

World War, the northern half of the Korean peninsula proclaimed its independence, establishing its capital in Pyongyang in 1948. Kim Il-sung, a revolutionary who had resisted Japanese occupation in Manchuria during the war, was declared the first premier of the Democratic People's Republic of Korea.

From its birth, North Korea was a garrison state. Kim had trained in Russia, and joined the Communist Party before becoming a Soviet Army captain commanding a battalion of Korean and Chinese soldiers.[21] After independence, massive support from Stalin helped to establish security forces for the new nation, with equipment for an army that would come to number more than a million troops. Forged in the crucible of Cold War conflict, the state could cast itself as permanently threatened by the West.

In the wake of the split, both North and South Korea quickly moved to repression and massacres, arresting and executing political dissidents. United Nations recognition of South Korea as the only official Korean government prompted the North to begin planning an invasion that would reunify the country under a Communist banner. After three years of war fought by troops from China and the Soviet Union in the North, and the United Kingdom and United States in the South, the Korean War ended in a stalemate in 1953. The two Koreas had polarized into Cold War proxies.

Korea's independence movement had fused with a Communist framework. But other influences also played a role in North Korean ideology and the camp system that arose there. Patriarchal Confucian tradition and more than three decades of colonial rule promoting Japanese emperor worship combined to foster eugenic obsessions with bloodlines and purity reminiscent of Nazi race theories.[22]

When Stalin died in 1953, just months before the end of the Korean War, North Korea turned further in on itself. The subsequent thaw in Russia to reconsider Stalin-era repression—as well as uprisings in Yugoslavia and Hungary against Communist governments—motivated North Korean leadership to bulwark itself against any such revisionist thinking. Tilting toward the Chinese model, it broke from Soviet orthodoxy and doubled down on government control of every aspect of citizens' lives.

Kim Il-sung's Korea wove disparate influences into a deification of the nation and its leader, cloaked in an ideology of independence and self-reliance called *Juche.* In place of the historical economic forces at the center of revolution, he put the agency of the people themselves. And as the embodiment of the workers stood the infallible great leader who would personally provide for every need.

Complete control of information in the country soon allowed a cult of personality to develop. It first mimicked the cults surrounding Stalin and Mao, building on Kim's guerrilla experience fighting the Japanese occupation. As in China, citizens soon took to wearing images of Kim on a badge pinned over their hearts. In North Korea, however, the cult had solidified within a generation into a quasi-theological construct in which the Leader possessed purity, divine power, and unquestionable dynastic authority.[23]

The Soviet Union had been the first to develop a camp system integrating Marxist theory with terror and forced labor, but North Korea's system would prove to be longer-lived and more opaque. During the Korean War, the North had been reluctant to divulge even the names of combatants it had captured, telegraphing a single list of 110 detainees to the International Red Cross headquarters in Geneva at the start of the conflict, after which it sent nothing.[24] A parallel silence would carry over to concentration camp detainees.

From independence forward, the government moved to arrest those associated with organizations seen as hostile to Communist rule, including Christian groups and competing socialist factions. Tragedy could result from a citizen's smallest misstep. Households had to keep a residence book of who had visited, and authorities might appear at any moment asking to see it. Failure to keep it updated could lead to detention.[25]

In addition to any past association with organizations or individuals opposing Kim's interests or the Workers' Party of Korea, prisoners could be arrested for owning land or businesses, or having emigrated to Japan and then returned after the war. Sometimes it was enough simply to know personal information about the Kim family that the Leader wished to keep private.

As with Stalin and Mao, the mildest criticism of general policy could lead to retaliation. Citizenship was effectively revoked for those who were sent to detention. Widespread surveillance led to arrests by security forces, and many were executed.

By the late 1950s, Kim's government had established an extensive system of camps for political prisoners, a system that has never closed.[26] Using a quarantine model for isolating politically or culturally dangerous citizens, North Korean leaders would eliminate the message of redemption and return to society offered at least obliquely by the Soviet and Chinese camp systems. The overwhelming majority of those taken into custody could rightly expect to die in detention.

Though firsthand accounts remained elusive for many years, eventually the collected stories of defectors, escapees, and former prison guards began to offer a more complete picture. Kang Chol-hwan was nine years old when his grandfather was taken from work and sent to a hard-labor camp. The rest of his family was arrested at home in 1977, the children with the adults. Kang was driven in a truck out of Pyongyang through the Pass of Tears with his grandmother and sister, and sent to Political Prison Camp No. 15 in Yodok County.[27]

Recent satellite imagery reveals that the concentration camp at Yodok covers more than 140 square miles. Unlike most such facilities, Yodok is divided into a total control zone, from which no one is released, and a "revolutionizing zone," where well-connected families or their relatives are given the opportunity for rehabilitation.

Kang was fortunate to belong to the latter group. At the whim of the state, he lived behind barbed wire, assigned to carry bags of minerals from the mines on his back, to work in the cornfield, and to bury corpses. The camp had informants—including one who specialized in reporting on juveniles. As prisoners had done in Nazi camps, children at Yodok raised rabbits whose fur was harvested to line officers' jackets. Insufficient food meant that children often stopped growing.[28]

To stave off starvation and pellagra, Kang learned to steal corn and soybeans to supplement his rations, and also to catch rats and frogs. After five years he transitioned to the life of an adult prisoner, working an all-day hard-labor schedule and attending self-criticism sessions. After ten years his family was freed from the concentration camp to work on a collective farm.

Today camp life remains dangerous. Through testimony from a handful of refugees detained at Yodok or whose family members were sent there, we know that its victims include children as young as three.[29] Adults find their rations cut; they are sent to solitary confinement in the sweatbox, a tiny cell in which it is possible only to kneel or crouch. Detainees are repeatedly told that in the event of military invasion, the guards have been instructed to kill all inmates. But at least those on the rehabilitative side of the camp believe they might one day leave.

Most detainees in North Korea are not so lucky. Prison Camp No. 14 in Pyongan Province, open since the 1960s, holds tens of thousands who have no chance of release. Like Yodok, it is run by the national secret police.[30] Former guards and prisoners point to Kim Il-sung's repeated instruction to eliminate class enemies and their descendants across three generations. The practical form this elimination takes is rescinded citizenship, execution, or life imprisonment, in a radical program dedicated to removing anyone perceived as a political threat.

Traditional twentieth-century eugenics has a place, too. Disabled citizens are expelled from cities, and parents are encouraged to turn minors over to state institutions, after which the children are never seen again. An obsession with racial purity mandates forced abortions and sterilizations for women suspected of having sex with foreigners.

Detainees live at the mercy of the officials who run the camps. As former guard Ahn Myong-chol from Hoeryong prison testified, "The inmates are no longer registered citizens, so you do not need a law to decide the sentences. The [secret police] agent is the person who decides whether you are saved or you are executed. There are no other criteria other than his words. [The inmates] are already eliminated from society."[31]

In recent decades, the North Korean political prisons have been estimated to hold 150,000 to 200,000 detainees, out of a total estimated population of 25 million. But analysis from the past few years suggests a large drop, with political camps now holding perhaps 80,000 to 120,000 prisoners.[32] The reduction in numbers may reflect some releases, but there are other, grimmer possibilities.

In a 2014 report on North Korean concentration camps, the United Nations Human Rights Council noted that part of such a decrease can be attributed to periods in which "the inflow of new inmates does not keep up with the high rate at which prisoners are dying due to starvation, neglect, arduous forced labour, disease and executions."[33]

Kang Chul-ho described how as a child, he witnessed his father's execution for setting fire to a secret police building in 1976. His mother committed suicide afterward, leaving him an orphan. Eleven years later Kang was sentenced without charge or trial to Prison Camp No. 19, where he lived with five thousand other detainees behind electric fences, digging for ore using a pick and shovel from 6:30 a.m. to 10:00 p.m. each day. Gulag-style formulas for rationing food based on meeting labor quotas were still in use, with prisoners expected to survive on approximately half a pound of food a day. Many ate bark to keep from starving; nevertheless, Kang watched dozens of fellow inmates die from lack of food. In 1990, after three years in detention, he escaped from the camp hospital and made his way on foot to China.[34]

Under the leadership of Kim Il-sung's son Kim Jong-il and then his grandson Kim Jong-un, the government has continued the camps' legacy. Along with traditional detention in camps, families determined to be low in *songbun*—an official, inherited rating of political allegiance and loyalty to the regime—often face forced relocation to the rural, mountainous northern regions of the country.[35]

Few people have escaped detention, and some former prisoners who have told their stories were later forced to revise them after inaccuracies were found in their accounts. Detainee Shin Dong-hyuk described the execution of his mother and brother, confessing later that it was he who had betrayed their escape plan to camp authorities.[36] He eventually also admitted to distorting the time line of events in his memoir.

Hyeonseo Lee, a North Korean defector who slipped across the Chinese border, expressed sympathy for Shin despite his inconsistency, noting that no one has contested the marks of torture on his body or his physical deformities due to a childhood spent at hard labor. She explained the bind faced by those who escape such horrors and must start new lives: "It's easy to see how Mr. Shin was tempted to obscure the truth. For defectors, sometimes doing so is the only way to survive."[37]

Every punitive camp system to one degree or another has relied on pitting inmates against each other to break down solidarity, often pushing detainees to lies, collaboration, or worse. The North Korean system appears to have followed this tradition and raised the bar. Shin's distortions and revisions reveal how difficult it is to escape the system without being morally compromised.

During the seven decades of North Korea's existence, an estimated four hundred thousand people have been sent to its detention camps. The government continues to deny their existence. Satellite imagery, however, has confirmed the existence of buildings and compounds corresponding to former prisoners' accounts, as well as revealing that they are still in active use as detention sites.

While North Korea took its inspiration from the Soviet camps and follows its own philosophy of *Juche*, it is the Chinese camps under the cult of Mao that the system most resembles, the camps born from the same Soviet ancestor in the same years, having persisted alongside them decade after decade.

7. As in North Korea, forced labor in the mines and quarries of Chinese labor camps led to illness and starvation. Prisoners were rarely

allowed to shower, and water was often in short supply—which meant washing in a shared tub of water or eating with dirty hands. Lice infested the barracks. Mosquitoes, too, were endemic, and as in the Gulag were sometimes used to torture prisoners left naked outside.[38]

Hongda "Harry" Wu escaped many of these dangers at the Yanqing Steel Mine in 1961. When production was cut off because of the economic crisis generated by the Great Leap Forward, Wu sat idle for three months before he was pulled from the regular labor pool by a captain who had seen him work at the detention center. Assigned to keep prisoner files updated, he not only escaped hard labor but also began to get special perks, such as cigarettes. Happy that he was not expected to inform on other detainees, he nonetheless felt uneasy as he overheard beatings in the interrogation room next to the captain's office.

One morning he was sent out with three duty prisoners—detainees who had been promoted to overseeing their fellow prisoners—to search for two escapees. Guards went out with dogs, while the prisoners searched on foot. Although they came in empty-handed at the end of the day, they were rewarded by the captain anyway, given vegetable soup and all the *woutou* they could eat. The dogs were fed next to Wu, and also ate *woutou*. Wu suddenly realized he had finally been transformed into a running dog, serving his jailors in return for bits of food and the small advantages that would keep him alive.[39] He was filled with self-loathing.

Lecturing prisoners in study group and hearing their mandatory confessions, the captain told his charges that they were criminals who deserved a full three-year sentence, the maximum applied to those sent for reeducation through labor. Wu had by then served one year and had already lost twenty pounds.

Soon he was transferred with other prisoners to work on a farm, where he was reunited with Big Mouth Xing, much to his delight. Disappointment struck, however, when he learned that the major food source was ground, twice-cooked corncob, a fibrous, nonnutritional filler that had a purging effect on the intestines. Prisoners regularly succumbed to chronic diarrhea.

Believing they would not survive if they stayed in the camp, Big Mouth asked Wu one day whether he would be willing to partner on an escape attempt. Wu promised not to divulge the plan but pointed out that they had no food to take with them and nowhere to escape to. He was not willing to take the risk.

In the wake of his refusal, Wu watched Big Mouth decline. His friend had never exercised much restraint, but now he began constantly grabbing food from other prisoners, persisting until he was finally sentenced to solitary confinement—a small cell with reduced rations and complete isolation. He had been sent to solitary before and knew that in his debilitated state, this was a death sentence. He begged not to go, cutting deep into his little finger with a spade to swear a blood oath promising good behavior.

Big Mouth succeeded in avoiding confinement, but his finger became infected. After two weeks of fever, Wu's mentor in the art of camp survival died of tetanus. Big Mouth had no education or political affiliation, but Wu had come to see him as the most skilled and influential teacher of his life.

In August 1961, starvation devastated Chinese camp populations nationwide, and regional authorities stepped in to lift morale and stanch the death toll. Prisoners in more advanced stages of inanition were transferred to another camp, receiving special attention to help them recover. But provisions in the invalid section of the camp were not adequate to nurse anyone back to health. Detainees got only a tiny packet of powder in addition to their previous rations. Wu's weight dropped to just over eighty pounds.

Conversation was minimal—to walk a few feet seemed impossible. Prisoners could barely move to relieve themselves. While in the sick camp, Wu saw only one fight—an ineffectual, slow-motion affair, "as if paper men were trying to strike each other when they could have just blown each other down."[40]

When men died, other duty prisoners wrapped each corpse in its own quilt and dragged it outside, where it was loaded on a cart drawn by an ox. When death came for his friend Chen Ming, imprisoned as a thought reactionary, Wu could not bear to let him leave. Despite the captain's protests, Wu was helped onto the cart, which already held half a dozen fresh corpses. The cart bumped along a path, then out into a field, jostling over mounds and ruts until Wu finally realized they were crossing a graveyard. He looked around and saw the field covered in hillocks, some settled, some fresh, perhaps thousands of them, a vast cemetery as far as he could see.

8. Asia was home to the most established and expansive Communist camp systems, but it did not host them all. After revolutionaries in Cuba overthrew dictator Fulgencio Batista in 1959, the charismatic Che Guevara was named head of La Cabaña Fortress in Havana. The romantic hero of the Left, Che was pressed into actual governance between revolutions. As supervisor of La Cabaña, he was ultimately responsible for the judicial fate of Batista officials and enforcers taken before military tribunals in the days after victory.

Che's title for the first six months of 1959 was supreme prosecutor. As such, he heard appeals, reviewed cases, and approved verdicts. He did not sit on the tribunals, but as a believer in harsh revolutionary justice neither did he did mitigate the verdicts that came before him for review. He saved any qualms he felt for his diary, but publicly he expressed no doubt.

Rationalizing the tribunals, his partner in revolution and new prime minister of Cuba Fidel Castro explained that they would bring justice to the worst perpetrators of atrocities under the previous regime. But many of Batista's immediate subordinates had already fled, leaving only smaller fish to be prosecuted. Rebutting further criticism, Castro compared the approach to the Nuremberg Trials and claimed that the procedures were actually intended to shield suspects from mob justice.[41]

The tribunals, however, became mob spectacles. The most notorious took place in January 1959 at Havana's Sports City stadium, with the crowd shouting "Kill them!" while the trial was under way.[42] The death penalty was forbidden under the Cuban Constitution, but the revolutionary movement had already made use of it during the fight for independence. And after victory, the provisional revolutionary government included capital punishment among the penalties available in military tribunals.[43]

In the immediate wake of the revolution, hundreds were shot and many more wound up in detention under summary justice. Major Jesús Sosa Blanco, who had been tried in the Sports City stadium, was sentenced to death, made an appeal, and won another trial before being resentenced and shot by a firing squad the following month.

At the end of the following year, Che circled the world, traveling to other Communist states. He met with a delegation in Moscow, visited Kim Il-sung in North Korea, and saw Mao Zedong in China. He had been impressed by the Maoist concept of work brigades carrying out voluntary labor, and back in Cuba enthusiastically encouraged Cuban citizens to dedicate their free time to building the workers' utopia. He himself began volunteering with labor projects on the weekends.

After his return from Asia, Che was named head of the Ministry of Industries. In that capacity, he inaugurated the first Cuban postrevolutionary concentration camp at Guanahacabibes, on the western tip of the island.[44] It hardly belonged in the same universe as Solovki or Kolyma, but given Soviet history—which Che knew well—a rehabilitative labor camp set a dangerous precedent.

People who had, in Che's view, committed offenses "against revolutionary morals" were sent to administrative detention, spending weeks or months atoning for their errors without any legal process. Che tried to justify the practice in a 1962 ministry meeting, saying, "We only send to Guanahacabibes those doubtful cases where we are not sure people should go to jail."

Sometimes detainees lost their positions; in other cases they were allowed to return to their jobs after their stint in the camp, once they had been "reeducated through labor." Work included everything from mining coal to felling trees, which Che acknowledged was "hard labor."[45] A popular columnist with the publication *Revolución* once challenged Che to justify it.[46]

While many detainees returned to their lives without further judgment or penalty after their stay, the abuses of the camp's commander became notorious over time, raising concerns among managers. He was eventually dismissed for misconduct, and after Che's death in 1967, Guanahacabibes was shut down.[47]

During the prior dictatorship, Batista had tried his hand at reviving concentration camps. Under his rule, the army had been frustrated in its effort to hem in the guerrillas and had swept thousands of peasants into *reconcentración*, repeating the strategies instituted by Valeriano "Butcher" Weyler sixty years before. The memory of the Butcher still had power in Cuba, and Castro made the comparisons between the two men.[48]

Yet in history's strange spiral, Che, like Trotsky, provided the initial spark for concentration camps as part of the revolutionary struggle. Trotsky helped carry the modern concept of extrajudicial internment from Canada back east. And after his 1960 trip, Che carried the inspiration of voluntary and not-so-voluntary labor from China and Russia westward back to Cuba, where concentration camps had been born. Trotsky wrote a memo recommending the use of concentration camps; Che went a step further by inaugurating a camp and sending prisoners directly to it himself, providing not just an inspiration but leadership.

In both cases, the apparatus and history of detention were larger than any one person. It is likely that in Russia, China, and Cuba, forced-labor camps would have risen in some form without a Trotsky or a Che. Russia and Cuba both had a prerevolutionary tradition of camps before either man had appeared on the historical stage. But exposure elsewhere planted seeds in fertile soil.

Building on Che's early experiment, Castro institutionalized the use of civilian labor camps in 1965 in the province of Camagüey. Called Military Units to Aid Production (UMAPs), the camps were billed as a requirement for those who were not able, willing, or (in the case of homosexuals) permitted to perform mandatory military service. During their three years of operation, the camps held tens of thousands of detainees in harsh conditions.

In practice, the UMAPs provided an opportunity to put nonconformists and nonproducers—conscientious objectors, Jehovah's Witnesses, the illiterate, homosexuals, and others targeted for particular offenses—to work harvesting fruit and cutting sugar cane for up to twelve hours a day. Canadian journalist Paul Kidd managed to visit one in 1966, for which he was deported. Kidd estimated at the time that there were some two hundred "forced-labor camps" on the island holding perhaps thirty thousand people.[49]

Detention and repression continued even after the fall of the Soviet Union cut off financial subsidies to the Cuban economy. In 1996 the Cuban Commission for Human Rights and National Reconciliation, an independent organization seen as illegal by the state, estimated that in addition to its brutal prisons, more than two hundred forced-labor camps still existed on Cuban soil.[50]

The following year a decree limited the free movement of citizens, a move that aided the authorities in cracking down on dissidents coming to Havana. Though sporadic reform has taken place, preemptive arrests, particularly of political prisoners, has surged again in recent years with reports from the first ten months of 2015 alone listing more than 6,200 cases of arbitrary detention.[51] In March 2016, when Barack Obama made the first official visit by a US president to Cuban shores in almost ninety years, Cuban president Raúl Castro was caught off-guard by press inquiries about political dissidents held captive by the state.

9. In the early 1960s, while Che visited workers sentenced to the camp at Guanahacabibes in Cuba, Hongda "Harry" Wu was finishing his third year of detention in the company of some twenty thousand prisoners working at Qinghe Farm southeast of Beijing. Wu and other prisoners in the invalid ward had survived the winter by

digging up a patch of carrots workers had failed to harvest the fall before and gathering bits of cabbage similarly overlooked. A generous captain had let them eat everything they could find. Their reward was improved health, which got them sent back to a labor squad, where Wu was assigned to repair irrigation ditches.

Then twenty-five years old, Wu was still a virgin. He watched with confusion as prisoners who had been sexually active before their arrests grew tense and frustrated. For most prisoners, starvation conditions led to food becoming a more fundamental—and less fraught—obsession. Talk of physical intimacy occurred, but in Wu's camp detainees more often lingered over step-by-step discussions of how to cook favorite foods. Those who did not know how to cook made up recipes.

Discussions also turned to what each prisoner would do on his first day of freedom. One fantasized about eating several pounds of pork head meat. Another imagined confronting the party secretary responsible for his arrest. A third hoped to buy strings for his lute. Wu said he would buy a kite, put a long tail on it, fly it as high as the string would allow, and cut it loose.[52]

More time was spent on the regular ritual of struggle and study sessions, in which detainees sang Mao quotations, read from party literature, and discussed proper political ideology.[53] Confessions and denunciations were followed by prisoners beating other prisoners in supervised rituals aimed at keeping rigid control over the group.

Some prisoners used struggle sessions to exact revenge on others or as payback for petty quarrels. When an informer accused a quiet, respected prisoner of declaring that history would prove he was not guilty, a special session was organized to beat him and force him to confess his criminal thinking. Only after the initial beating and partway through the confession was another prisoner able to interject that the accused had been reading aloud a pamphlet in the barracks titled "History Will Pronounce Me Not Guilty," a landmark speech given by Fidel Castro and published by the Chinese Communist Party.[54]

In 1963, Wu was transferred to Tuanhe Farm on the outskirts of Beijing. Despite its proximity to the city, the camp had no armed guards or watchtowers—only a six-foot-high barbed-wire perimeter fence. Starvation conditions began to ease, and detainees were given more food each day, as well as modest wages deposited in their prisoner accounts each month.

As some detainees were transferred out to resettlement camps, Wu and his fellow rightists grew more expectant about their own impending release. May 24 marked the third anniversary of the government announcement that prisoners in administrative detention should be released within three years. Even though many of them, including Wu, had already been in detention for longer than that, they felt certain that on the third anniversary of the policy, the government would free them.

The evening of May 23, prisoners were told that they did not have to report for work details the next day and that they should expect a special announcement. But when the administrator came to speak with them, he acknowledged that though they had served their intended sentence, no release order had yet been received, so they would remain at the camp. Reminding them that "thought reform is a lifetime effort," he dismissed them abruptly.

The prisoners were furious. As the weeks went by, their disappointment did not fade. Wu wrote a letter to his family explaining that he had not been released. He received a response from his brother telling him that their stepmother was dead and their father had been labeled a counterrevolutionary rightist. The family as a whole was cutting itself off from Wu, and he should focus on following the example of Chairman Mao.

Reading his assigned articles in *People's Daily* during evening study sessions, Wu tried to understand the politics of the day, in which China formally denounced the reform measures that were unfolding in the Soviet Union since the death of Stalin. Mao declared that the Communist Party in Russia had deviated from the true path, and only China followed Marxist ideals. On the local level, this crackdown on revisionism played out as a witch hunt for reactionary ideas and ideological heresy.

A year passed after they had expected to gain their freedom, and still they were not released. Prisoners in the camp felt very remote from all the party intrigue; Mao was the only one they were certain had the power to help them. A young prisoner approached Wu to talk about writing to Mao, to inform him that prisoners were not being released even though they had served their sentences. Two other friends who were equally outraged joined the effort, and together, with the help of a former newspaper editor, they drafted a letter to the most powerful man in China asking why they had not been set free. For good measure, they also wrote letters to the Central Committee of the Communist Party and the Beijing Municipal Party Committee.[55]

Wu recalled seeing a mailbox on a section of the farm that had no perimeter fence. Told by the captain to gather a crew to harvest peaches, he took his letter-writing accomplices along. He worked with a partner while two other prisoners waded across a canal to put the letters in the mailbox. Everything went smoothly, and after the men finished picking peaches, everyone returned to the camp.

Like Margarete Buber-Neumann's impulsive appeal to Soviet courts in the Gulag, Wu's letters had been doomed from the start. The next night after dinner, the captain appeared before the assembled prisoners and held up all three letters, demanding that the culprit turn himself in at the main office. Leaving the camp was a serious offense. They had all agreed ahead of time that if the letters were discovered, they would not admit to writing them. One by one, however, Wu's collaborators were called out for questioning. When only he and the newspaper editor were left, the two men discussed what they should do. The editor told Wu that the only hope was for him to confess. If he took responsibility for the entire project, only one person would end up in solitary confinement. If he did not, they might all suffer.

When Wu was called, he quickly confessed before he could second-guess his decision. His collaborators were sent back to the barracks, and the captain ordered him into solitary confinement. The cells stood in a row at the edge of the compound, their entrances shielded from view by a brick wall. The guard shoved his shoulders down as he stepped through a barred gate into an open cell. Trying to stand after entering, he hit his head on the low cement ceiling and fell. A guard pushed his feet inside and locked the door.[56]

The cell was three feet high, three feet wide, and the length of a coffin. Its dank cement floor had no straw. Eventually, he needed to relieve himself and saw a latrine bucket outside the cell, out of reach from the door. He yelled for someone to come, but no one appeared. He tried unsuccessfully to urinate on all fours, then sat and sprayed the iron bars.

A second day passed, and no one brought food or water. A duty prisoner appeared around midday the third day, checked on him, then walked away. On the fourth day, he was briefly let out of the cell and given a bowl of water. Soon after, he was fed gruel and a pickled turnip. He asked to be allowed to confess.

When the captain came, Wu tried to explain that he had only wanted to end his detention after three years and become a productive member of society. His confession was mocked, and he found himself alone again. On the fifth day, his body started to shiver and he stopped noticing when he soiled himself. The next day, he began to hallucinate. He asked to speak to the captain again.

On the seventh day, the captain returned and sat on a stool at the gated opening of the cell. Wu pulled himself near and began to speak, but his confession was again rejected. He was told he would have to fully account for his counterrevolutionary clique, or he would never get out of solitary confinement.

The eighth day, Wu refused to come out to eat. Dragged from the cell, he knocked over the bowl of gruel. The guard returned later with more food, but again Wu refused to eat. The captain came back the next day with a squad of prisoners and a health worker who told him that the government's revolutionary humanitarianism would save him from death.[57] They pinned him down and held his head while the health worker forced a tube into his nostril then poured the gruel through a funnel into the tube.

Force-fed again on the tenth day, he realized that one of the prisoners holding him down had slipped a note into his hand. He read
it when he was alone again. The editor who had collaborated on the
letter to Mao wrote to advise Wu to confess to part of the plot, assur-
ing him that no one else would be harmed if he did so. Wu called
for the captain again, and on his eleventh day in solitary, his confession was deemed adequate. He was returned to the regular detainee
population in September 1965, five and a half years into a three-year
sentence.

10. The disputes between Communist China and the Soviet Union
that Wu read about in his study sessions did not keep either country
from aggressively expanding its sphere of influence. As former colonies became new states, Chinese and Soviet approaches to concentration camps began to appear elsewhere in Asia.

When US forces evacuated the American embassy in Saigon amid
pandemonium in April 1975, Western strategists predicted that Communist North Vietnamese forces would slaughter city residents.
Instead, a new socialist order was gradually imposed. Some unsettling
events did occur: a few thieves posing as Vietcong were shot. More
often, journalists seemed bemused by the idea that there was any danger. Western reporters who had stayed behind sent winking dispatches
noting that yes, there were reeducation camps being set up, but so far
they had only noticed barmaids being sent to them.[58] Instead of a
massacre, correspondents informed readers, "the hysteria and panic
of the first days ebbed as it became apparent that the blood bath
promised by the American Embassy was not going to happen."[59]

But taking time to reinvent Saigon was a North Vietnamese strategy. "All problems are important," an anonymous member of the
new leadership told a reporter, "but some are immediate, and others
can wait."[60] In place of blood in the streets, a radical transformation
had begun.

A month after the fall of Saigon, whole groups of people associated directly and indirectly with the former government were asked to register with the new authorities. Weeks later, in June 1975, the government at Hanoi sent letters instructing more than a million former South Vietnamese officials—male and female military personnel, civil servants, translators, clerics, and their associates—to turn themselves in for reeducation and integration into the new Vietnam under Communism. Recipients of the letters were told to pack clothes and money to last from a few days to a month, but they had no idea what to expect. Some who received the letters fled the country. Others decided to turn themselves in, hoping the indoctrination would not involve mistreatment.

In the absence of punitive annihilation, announcements about reeducation camps rang fewer alarm bells. Commentators described how the transfers of people would, in some cases, reunify family members who had not seen each other for decades.[61]

The new camps were divided into levels, the mildest of which involved staying at home and attending political and educational indoctrination sessions during the day. Other camps demanded months of on-site reeducation in centers away from home. Those suspected of counterrevolutionary thought were sent for longer-term detention.

After years of aid and military advisors contributing both training and institutional planning to North Vietnam, it is perhaps no surprise that principles from both Stalinist and Maoist detention made their way into Vietnamese concentration camps. As in Chinese *laojiao*, prisoners in Vietnamese camps were by law not supposed to be under administrative detention for more than three (or sometimes five) years, depending on their sentence. The statute, however, was as widely ignored as it had been in China, and overall life in the camps followed a Maoist pattern.

Detainees were sent to labor sites without trial. Forced to read texts by Marx, Lenin, and Ho Chi Minh, prisoners had to repeatedly confess their faults in public. Evenings were spent listening to anti-American propaganda broadcast over loudspeakers and publicly denouncing the laziness of co-workers.

Those in the most severe camps faced solitary confinement in five-foot metal shipping containers. The reeducation for unification that had ostensibly been the point of the camps turned into simple hard labor, with torture and beatings for minor infractions. Days turned into weeks, weeks to months, and still there was no mention of release. As many as a hundred thousand political prisoners were held for seven years or more, with unnumbered thousands dying in the concentration camps of the Socialist Republic of Vietnam.[62]

Doan Van Toai, who had fought to overthrow the South Vietnamese government and been imprisoned under its rule, later found himself sentenced by his fellow revolutionaries to a reeducation camp after infuriating leaders by advocating a slow transition to a socialist economy.[63] He spent years there asking himself how revolutionary fighters who "had struggled so heroically to rid the nation of bloody oppression" could become just as oppressive, once given a turn as wardens. He came to the conclusion that the answer lay not in the individuals themselves: "For the most part they were just ordinary human beings. Some were vicious, some were not. And the more you studied their viciousness, the more it seemed it was mostly due to indoctrination. Conditioned to regard their prisoners as wicked enemies, they simply believed any brutality was justified."[64]

Yet, like most revolutionary states, Vietnam did not operate death camps. It was willing to kill recalcitrant prisoners, it was willing to starve and neglect others, but it kept a façade of perfunctory privileges inconsistently made available to prisoners, such as the right to receive packages and the right to family visits. Through such means, the government could cling to the illusion of rehabilitative labor and the even older concept of the concentration camp as a civilized and civilizing force.

11. No such pretense of a civilizing mission remained after the Khmer Rouge took power in Cambodia under Pol Pot during April

1975, the same month Saigon fell. Here the revolution responded to the very idea of civilization with chaos and destruction.

In a massive dismantling of the economy, Khmer Rouge leadership ordered all city and town residents, as well as anyone living near a road, to report for agricultural labor in the countryside, telling them, "To keep you is no gain; to lose you is no loss."[65] Their homes were burned or destroyed, leaving them nothing to return to and committing the country to the path the Khmer Rouge had chosen. The literate, those with glasses, and anyone with experience in finance or any sign of Western education were selectively targeted for harassment and often executed in a ruthless attempt to create a classless agrarian utopia.

Nearly all the government's actions were clandestine and went unnoted until long after the country had descended into horror. As Samantha Power wrote, "The Khmer Rouge may well have run the most secretive regime of the twentieth century."[66]

Even experienced journalists could not agree on what was happening in the moment. Elizabeth Becker, sent by the *Washington Post* into Cambodia in 1978 to find out whether the rumors of labor camps and executions were true, found her views pitted against those of a *St. Louis Post-Distpatch* reporter traveling with her, who saw no signs of genocide.

The trip was so stage-managed, there was no way to be sure. Becker would later compare the effort to successful Nazi attempts to fool the Red Cross when the agency inspected the concentration camp at Theresienstadt in 1944. In the same way, the Khmer Rouge had hidden most signs of violence and suffering from the visiting journalists, but Becker had lived in Cambodia for two years before the group had come to power. She had seen Phnom Penh, the capital city of more than a million people, thriving and vibrant even in wartime. During her return visit, she was struck by dread on discovering that it had been turned into a ghost town.

"Pagodas, mosques, and churches were shuttered. All commercial life was forbidden: There were no more markets, no stores, no banks, no cafés," she wrote. "The old art-deco Central Market where farmers and artisans once sold their wares was empty."[67] Asking about the shuttered schools, she was told that all the children had been sent into the countryside. Catching a single glimpse of "thin children, barefoot and in rags" carrying firewood near the highway only reinforced her suspicion that the rumors of camps and genocide were true. After escaping an assassin who killed another journalist in her group, she filed her stories for the *Post*, which were largely ignored by policymakers.

By the time Becker arrived, it was not only forced-labor camps in agricultural areas that citizens had to fear. In 1976, the Khmer Rouge leader known as Comrade Duch had installed himself on the grounds of a former high school. Adding barbed wire and bars, he converted the grounds into Tuol Sleng, one of more than a hundred torture camps where people were held both communally and in isolation. Beginning in September, the Communist Party of Kampuchea (the new name for Cambodia) purged its members, using torture and interrogation to extract confessions and denunciations. By December, remaining party leaders started to prepare for war with Vietnam, first purging diplomats and intellectuals with ties to their eastern neighbor or its supporter, Soviet Russia, then arresting, torturing, and executing intellectuals.

Former Pol Pot protégé Siet Chhe was taken to Tuol Sleng—also known as S-21—for interrogation in April 1977. Writing to senior party officials to beg for his life, he stated, "I have always understood without any firsthand knowledge...that once entering S-21, very few leave; that is, there's only entering; leaving never happens. Brother, if this is the case, I have no way out."[68] After months of interrogation and a demand that he write out in detail an account of (nonexistent) sexual relations with his daughter, Chhe cracked and began denouncing dozens of former associates.[69]

As with the paranoia over Trotskyite sabotage unleashed in Soviet Russia in the 1930s, detainees were forced to invent complex, impossible accounts of Vietnamese infiltrators, CIA spies, and hundreds of co-conspirators.

Untethered from contact with the Soviet and Chinese advisors and ideology that had shaped other postwar Communist states, however, Cambodia would never develop a sustainable Gulag-style system of detention. Instead, paranoid and insular leaders applied themselves to the literal destruction of the country. Some fourteen thousand detainees were taken for interrogation at Tuol Sleng. Only seven survived.[70]

The massacres and death by starvation ended in December 1978, when Vietnam invaded, forcing the Khmer Rouge from Phnom Penh and occupying the country for a decade. By the time the Vietnamese arrived, instead of using camps to slough off or reconstruct the elements that did not fit into their version of an ideal society, Khmer Rouge forces had immolated the society as a whole. Between 1975 and 1979, almost two million people died—nearly a quarter of the entire population of Cambodia.

As chair of the US President's Commission on the Holocaust in 1980, Elie Wiesel traveled with a delegation to Cambodian refugee camps built for those fleeing the Khmer Rouge. The sight of 160,000 Cambodians massed on the Thai border moved Wiesel to describe the camps as "spectacles of horror." He was especially grieved over some Cambodians' conviction that their people as a whole might be eradicated. Yet Wiesel pleaded for the delegation not to use the word "holocaust" in relation to the event, insisting that such terrors must be related but never compared: "Every tragedy deserves to have its own words."[71]

The idea of a society devoured and defined by camps did not arrive with Pol Pot. The metaphor of omnipresent concentration camps turning an entire country into a prison dates back to 1922 with the pre-Gulag Cheka camps in Russia. According to newspapers, after a show trial and executions of intellectuals, dissidents, and political thinkers, many of Russia's most creative and accomplished citizens were being imprisoned and exiled, and the entire country was at risk of becoming an Arctic prison. That image held through many iterations of totalitarian states in different times and places, including China and North Korea—wherever the threat of concentration camps was used as part of the background repression that affected all citizens.

But in Cambodia, nearly the entire population was sent to the coun-tryside into what would have been a labor-camp system, except that the camps could no longer be distinguished from society. Survivor Sophe-line Cheam Shapiro later described her experience digging earth in the killing fields from dawn to dusk as a nine-year-old after losing her father, two brothers, and a grandmother, along with uncles and cous-ins. "I am no different," she wrote, "from most of my generation."[72] She recalled the thin rice soup workers tried to subsist on, the Khmer Rouge songs about ruby blood sprinkling the towns and the plains, and those working in the fields, millions of whom would never return, victims of what would come to be called a self-inflicted genocide.

No gas chambers were required, just torture, massacres, starva-tion, and the complete annihilation of everyday life. "Cambodia, in fact," wrote Southeast Asia correspondent Sydney Schanberg, "was transformed into one giant forced-labor camp."[73]

12. China did not murder a quarter of its citizens. And its per capita rate of concentration camp incarceration remained lower than the peak years in the USSR. Yet its vast population meant detention poli-cies had outsized effects.

Beginning in 1966, in a paranoid grasp to reestablish control, Mao Zedong triggered violence to purge the party. His Cultural Revolution would persecute tens of millions in the years that followed. Estimates of the death toll range from half a million to three million people.

With repression launched in urban areas first, some of those already in labor camps were not initially affected. Still at Tuanhe Farm, Harry Wu had been more aware of the conflict in Vietnam than of the Cultural Revolution until a squad of Red Guard youths appeared at the camp and stormed the compound, singling out a prisoner to whip with their belts.[74]

Later, zealotry and fever to purify the party through violence consumed the camp staff. Called to a struggle session, Wu saw guards holding two detainees with their arms wrenched high behind them and their heads pulled forward. Other prisoners began kicking and beating them with a belt. Wu could hardly fathom the cruelty of prisoners torturing one another. Mao's saying "The revolution is not a dinner party!" had become the mantra for a new kind of terror in captivity.

Wu would soon get his own turn. He had managed to keep his books—his Tolstoy, Twain, and Dickens—with him since his arrival in the camp. They had first been concealed in his trunk in a communal storage room; then he had wrapped them in a plastic sheet and buried them near a toolshed. A year later, he had tucked them back into his trunk before he was moved to another labor site. But when guards conducted a surprise search, Wu knew his trove would be found. He realized the books had no real value in any life he was likely to be able to lead, but he was determined not to give them up.

After smuggling them under the sleeping platform at his barracks, Wu noticed that he was being watched by an informant. Soon enough, his name was called, and then he was subjected to the kind of beating by prisoners he had seen before. As they kicked and punched him, a duty prisoner he had once offended swung a spade handle toward his head. Wu managed to block the strike with an arm, but a bone shattered. Beatings were permitted, but broken bones were out of bounds for a struggle session. Wu's torture ended.

A doctor sewed up the gash and set the bone between wooden splints, but Wu remained in shock. He gave up caring about what happened to him. So it was with utter surprise but not much feeling that he learned in the fall of 1969 that he had been assigned a job and would be departing in three days. After nine years as a prisoner, he was freed from the surveillance and brutality of detention.[75]

He was sent into exile nine hours away, required to live and work in the mines of Shanxi Province. He was not entirely free, but many things changed. He married a former prisoner and was allowed to live with his wife in a cleared-out cave away from the miners' quarters. He could take a passenger train to visit his family in Shanghai. When he did, one sister was frightened by him; another ran to the police station to get a security officer. After the officer had reviewed his papers, they all sat together, drinking tea and making small talk, unable to address the events that were still too perilous to discuss.[76]

In all, Wu spent nineteen years at hard labor for the state, not fully released to live and work on his own until 1979. Months before his final release, he received a letter from the friend who had forged his name to steal money twenty years before and launched the cascade of offenses that had sent him to *laojiao*. The friend had heard that some counterrevolutionaries might finally be released, and he wanted to clear Wu's name.

Wu was reinstated at the Geological Institute but found himself unable to move on. After his father's death, he was invited to California as a visiting scholar. Four years of paperwork later, issued a passport and permission to travel, he ended up at the Hoover Institution at Stanford University.

He had been released from the camps, yet he could not let the camps go. In 1991, still a Chinese citizen, he traveled with his wife to China, posing as a potential investor while surreptitiously recording video of conditions at the forced-labor sites where he had worked. Asked by *60 Minutes* correspondent Ed Bradley why he would take such a risk, he said, "Because I think the world has to realize there's a camp system in China."[77]

Returning again to his homeland, he was arrested in 1995 and charged with stealing state secrets. Wu was sentenced to fifteen years in prison. After protests by US politicians and human rights groups, he was deported back to America in 1995.

13. Camps in Russia, China, and North Korea alike were part of systems that lasted four decades or more. North Korean camps are still fully operational. The Gulag is long gone in Russia, yet show trials and sentences for political enemies of the state persist like a recur-

rent low-grade virus, with detention in hard-labor camps continuing to the present day. China sits somewhere between the two, with *laogai* camps folded into the prison system, but still demanding hard labor from those convicted.

Laojiao, the system entirely outside the legal process that led to Harry Wu's stay in concentration camps, was technically abolished in 2013, but arbitrary detention of dissidents, public irritants, and members of religious sects has not stopped. In recent years, psychiatric treatment sites, drug rehabilitation centers, and other unregistered locations have been used as ad-hoc "black jails," allowing for less public, more nimble extrajudicial detention.[78] Well into the twenty-first century, Chinese leadership has decried criticism of human rights violations as "foreign infiltration."[79] The former and current Communist states are caught between shuddering in the light and staggering back into the past.

In 2002, Harry Wu established the Laogai Research Foundation — and later a museum — to publicize details of the Chinese concentration camp system in all its forms. From his first years in the United States, he was called the "Chinese Solzhenitsyn" for the single-minded dedication with which he pursued his cause.[80] Yet as with Solzhenitsyn, who alienated many supporters through later reactionary diatribes and support of Vladimir Putin, the stubbornness and self-interest that Wu developed in order to survive in the camps may have hurt him after release. He died in April 2016 amid allegations that a multimillion-dollar grant he administered had focused more on benefitting the museum he treasured than on supporting the families of jailed dissidents.[81]

His meticulous documentation of camps and their prisoners remains the cornerstone of his legacy, as do his accounts of his years spent in detention. As a result of Wu's lobbying efforts, the word *laogai* now appears in the *Oxford English Dictionary*.

CHAPTER EIGHT

Echoes of Empire

1. JANE MUTHONI MARA WAS thirteen years old and living in the village of Gatiko north of Nairobi in 1952 when Mau Mau guerrillas began fighting for Kenya's independence from Britain. She had briefly attended school, writing her lessons in the dirt, but the death of her father when she was young meant an end to formal studies. Her brother's schooling was provided for by their uncle, while she stayed home.

Even as a child, Mara was told that white people ruled Kenya and that some black Kenyans worked with them against "ordinary Kenyans." She had also heard that her people's land was being taken by Europeans, who hired them to work what had once been their own property.[1] But her father's land had not yet been seized, and she knew that Mau Mau forces had organized to fight the thieves.

Many Kikuyu, the largest ethnic group in Kenya, had already been pushed off their land through a series of regulations aimed not only at acquisition of territory but at forcing them to serve as low-cost labor.[2] In the fall of 1952, Mau Mau rebels, on a mission for independence, executed a loyalist chief and a European woman, sending the settler community into a frenzy.

On October 21, the day after the governor authorized a state of emergency, Kenyan policemen launched Operation Jock Scott, sending three thousand African soldiers and the 1st Battalion of the Lancashire Fusiliers to hunt to down Mau Mau suspects.[3] Troops came for Jomo Kenyatta, head of the Kenyan African Union, along with nearly two hundred other people suspected of holding leadership posts in the Mau Mau. The Moscow- and London-educated Kenyatta was no Mau Mau leader—or even a known supporter. He had denounced the group months before, but none of the facts mattered. He was convicted of "managing and being a member of the Mau Mau terrorist society."[4] The judge further identified him as the "mastermind" of the group. He was sentenced to seven years' hard labor, revealing that the colonial government either did not know or did not care who their declared enemy was.

Jane Muthoni Mara did know the Mau Mau. She had first come face-to-face with the guerrillas around 1953, when fighters slipped into her village from the forest at night and brought residents out of their homes to stand together in a clearing in the dark. They separated the older children from the younger, gave them something to drink—Mara could not sense what it was—and made the older children take a loyalty oath and promise to never tell that they had done so.[5]

Others who took one or more of several levels of oaths administered by the Mau Mau would later describe drinking animal blood, or drinking blood from an incision made on their head or arm. For many Mau Mau, the blood ritual was a binding ceremony seen as a way to build loyalty and an underground network in support of independence. It also served as a pretext to punish those later deemed to have violated their oaths. For British authorities who began to hear about the ritual, it underlined what they already believed to be the savage nature of the Mau Mau.

Mara's parents eventually told her that they had left the door to their home open the night she took the oath so that she could be brought out with the others to join. Her brother, three hours away at school, had been taken with the Mau Mau into the forest and stayed with them there.

He made an appearance soon after in the village, arriving with several other Mau Mau and saying they were being hunted. Mara cooked food for him and the other men, which drew out more arrivals. With some fifty people to be fed, she organized help from neighbors. Her brother spent the night, though she hardly got a chance to talk to him. After he left with the other men, she never saw him again.

2. At the end of the Second World War, Fascism fell into disrepute, retreating to South America with several thousand Nazis. But Western imperialism lingered on worldwide in a bellicose invalid state. The British Empire alone still held more than three dozen colonies, while defiant subjects continued to resist imperial rule. Fierce independence movements exploded after 1945, some with deep domestic roots, others amplified by geopolitics.

The British Empire, along with Soviet Russia, had never stopped using concentration camps in the wake of the First World War. While camps like Solovki rose steadily to become an integral part of Russian society by the end of the 1920s, the British experimented with overseas systems of detention and repression. From the *lagers* of the Boer War and enemy alien internment during the First World War to the 1916 Easter Rising arrests, concentration camps had become a standard component of British police and military campaigns. Carried out under cover of various states of emergency, these camps and their attendant abuses operated in fundamental opposition to the rule of law.

India, like Ireland, was a laboratory for these tactics between the world wars. As the movement for independence flourished there under Mahatma Gandhi's leadership, Britain began arresting not just radicals suspected of assassinations and bombings, but also thousands of protesters, detaining them without trial in a network of camps at Buxa Fort, Deoli, and elsewhere.[6]

After a coverup of killings at Bengal's Hijli Detention Center in 1931, when guards opened fire on unarmed prisoners, Hijli itself became a rallying cry. The Indian writer Rabindranath Tagore, who had been knighted by King George V, led a protest denouncing "the concerted homicidal attack, under cover of darkness, on defenseless prisoners undergoing the system of barbaric incarceration."[7] Guards maintained they had shot prisoners trying to escape, but it emerged that camp staff had lied to investigators.

One wing of the independence movement embraced assassination. On the heels of the murder of a local policeman, John Anderson was appointed governor of Bengal and took full advantage of security measures that allowed preemptive detention. He quickly gained a well-deserved reputation for repression.

These strategies were not new to him. As undersecretary for Ireland more than a decade before, he had played a key role in the inauguration of mass detention there. He had also helped introduce the Black and Tans—temporary constables who scandalized England by brutalizing Irish civilians, conducting raids that carried them into concentration camps, and burning the city of Cork. Indians predicted the detention and violence to come when he took his post in Bengal, nicknaming Anderson the "Black and Tan governor."[8]

By the 1940s, individual acts of violence, or even nonviolence, were often met with severe measures by colonial governments. Yet how the ruling power interpreted the resistance was key. Liberation movements contained fighters who might or might not fit the evolving Cold War binary. Clerics declared "holy war," Marxists called for revolution, unaffiliated peasants skirmished with occupying forces, and committed democrats wanted elections, all simultaneously defying the legitimacy of the imperial yoke. In 1945, independence fighters in Indonesia took weapons from defeated Axis forces, repelled attacks by the British, and asked for help from President Truman, the British prime minister, and Stalin—all in the space of one week.[9]

The rise of Communist nations inspired fear in the West, which in turn attempted to keep revolution from spreading. Many regions were seen only through this binary view, when in reality some were unrelated to Communism, while the politics of others were more complex than merely being pro-Soviet or pro-Western. There were dozens of Indonesias around the globe over which world powers might seek influence only to find themselves in the middle of an armed uprising. In many of them, concentration camps became part of the arsenal to defeat independence movements or fight Communism.

3. After the Mau Mau's first visit to her village, Jane Muthoni Mara became part of a support network in which other guerrillas would occasionally appear looking for food. The village would get advance notice from a scout, and residents would begin to cook. Sometimes laundry would be sent ahead, and the women would wash clothing that was carried back to the fighters. More than once, Mara helped coordinate preparation and delivery of meals to a scout at a drop-off location. The fighters she saw act as the go-betweens were never men she knew.

She later thought she was designated "a leader" by the Mau Mau because of her brother's role as a fighter. After a year of helping them, however, her village was relocated. The new village held ten times as many homesteads and concentrated larger groups of people into houses made of upright logs, mud, and thatched grass roofs.

One of the men running the new village, a member of the home guard working with British authorities, had residents dig a trench circling the village and line it with sharpened bamboo spikes. A single bridge over it left one highly visible path in and out of the village. No longer allowed to leave unescorted to draw water from the river, the inhabitants had effectively become detainees.[10]

The British, trying to cut off exactly the kind of support Mara had been giving the Mau Mau, forced more than a million Kikuyu into protected villages under surveillance and restrictions.[11] The colonial authority had implemented a modified version of the oldest camps—the kind of *reconcentración* that had been applied under

Weyler in Cuba, in which rural sympathizers were detained in fortified towns.

The historic parallels were not lost on Europeans. Forcing Kikuyu
off their land and into reserves, part of a prior strategy of dealing with
the guerrillas, had required massive dislocation and suffering. Shirley
Cooke, a settler representative on the Kenya Legislative Council, recognized even in the early stages that the plan was brutal, telling fellow
council members, "These Transit Camps...will probably get the reputation of the concentration camps after the Boer War."[12]

Mara and her neighbors' new villages were secured with armed
home guard sentries. In all, some eight hundred villages were built,
predominantly holding women and children. After a year or so of
feeding the Mau Mau, she could no longer help them.[13]

Sometimes home guards took men from the village for labor
projects on white settlers' properties. They also did spot checks
inside homes to look for Mau Mau fighters in hiding. For a time, villagers were safe from harm, though patrols routinely shot anyone
wandering outside the settlement on foot. Then home guards began
taking villagers to another compound for questioning. They were
beaten with truncheons, interrogated about whether they were part
of the Mau Mau, and asked repeatedly about taking the oath. Mara
recalled being beaten once and witnessing others' beatings, and
realized that the abuse was in no way dependent on whether an individual villager denied or admitted to taking the oath.

After several weeks in the new location, Mara's neighbors came
to her home and took her to the compound of the home guard
chief. They denounced her as a Mau Mau sympathizer. She was put
under arrest by armed guards and driven in a truck with other prisoners to Gatithi screening camp.[14] It was July 1954, and she was fifteen years old.

4. In Kenya, the harshest measures had begun with the October 1952
state of emergency. Two months later, the Mau Mau killed six-year-old

Michael Ruck in his bed with a machete, also executing his European settler parents, triggering a massive protest and calls for vigilante action against the Kikuyu. British forces would be responsible for the military defeat of the guerrillas, but the colonial government, with its open racism and fear of annihilation at the hands of Africans, was left to manage civilian forces and populations.

The state of emergency mirrored tactics adopted during a conflict that had begun in 1948 in British Malaya. Fighting armed insurgents of the Malayan Communist Party, who were aided by Chinese squatters in jungle regions, the British spent more than a decade revising and refining their strategies. Though army divisions battled the guerrillas, mining and rubber interests pushed to declare the conflict an emergency rather than a war, because the latter would have voided the insurance claims of corporations whose property was destroyed.

It was during this emergency in British Malaya that the idea of introducing positive incentives to win "hearts and minds"—in combination with the use of concentration camps—became widespread. The phrase came to represent the modern reboot of counterinsurgency strategies used fifty years before in South Africa and the Philippines. Despite variations in interrogation methods, punitive measures, and styles of camps, most anti-terror operations carried out by Western nations in the second half of the twentieth century would come to be modeled on the arsenal of strategies refined during the twelve-year campaign in British Malaya.

The influence of the Malaya campaign can be attributed to its apparent success in putting down an insurrection against colonial authority: the guerrillas were isolated and killed, the population became compliant, and violence subsided. But as with the Hijli shooting coverup in India, the official narrative was not always an accurate picture of events on the ground. Even in Malaya, victory was not clean. "It is in fact impossible," wrote Sir Henry Gurney, the high commissioner of British Malaya at the time, "to maintain the rule of law and to fight terrorism effectively at the same time."[15]

During the first stage of the conflict in Malaya, troops suppressed the independence movement by burning villages and removing food from areas suspected of aiding Communist insurgents. Forced relocation as punishment for perceived rebel sympathizers was common. Eventually, broad-based *reconcentración* was put in place, and half a million civilians were herded into carefully controlled camps as part of a "New Villages" program.

Atrocities, such as a massacre of twenty-six civilians ostensibly shot while trying to escape a camp at Batang Kali in 1948, were kept quiet.[16] As with the Boer War and in the Philippines, the punishment of vast numbers of noncombatants was presented as the deliberate, necessary price of waging real war. High Commissioner Gurney's strategy for combating terrorism, which would become the boilerplate response given by democracies facing violence overseas, was that "to maintain law and order in present conditions in Malaya it is necessary for the Government itself to break it for a time." He added that during the Emergency, "the Police and Army are breaking the law every day."[17]

After guerrillas were isolated from the Chinese squatters who provided them support and intelligence, the insurgency struggled to maintain a foothold. The same tactics of relocating the population and clearing rural areas region by region used in Cuba and South Africa proved more effective in British Malaya. In many cases, the "new villages" provided humane living conditions and better security than residents had faced outside the camps.

By the time independence was granted in 1957, the remaining guerrillas no longer had a cause with which to rally the population. The most problematic portions of the rebellious Chinese population had been deported to China, already a Communist nation, where they were hailed as heroes. The British use of concentration camps in Malaya was sold as a great success. Carried on a wave of enthusiasm, the forced-relocation approach to detention camps would quickly be incorporated into counterinsurgency gospel in other conflicts even before the fighting in Malaya had ended.

In time, however, grainy photos from Malaya of limbs cut off as battle trophies or British soldiers holding aloft the severed heads of their enemies would begin to circulate. Journalists would track down survivors and witnesses who swore that soldiers shot unarmed civilians without provocation.[18] The question of what success had cost, or whether it had really been success, would eventually rear its head. With the destruction and concealment of official records that might have given a fuller picture, it would become impossible to fully document atrocities committed in British Malaya by government and colonial forces. Britain's success in quelling the uprising and isolating or deporting the Chinese Communist squatters who had launched it ensured that forced relocation of civilians into camps would take place again and again around the world, with evidence of abuse mounting in the repetitions, beginning in Kenya.

5. Kenya's immolation proceeded quietly at first, as more and more people were brought into protected villages and faced interrogations during arbitrary "screening" sessions. Gatithi, the camp that the teenage Jane Muthoni Mara was brought to after her arrest, was located very close to her home village. The ride lasted just minutes yet deposited her in an unfamiliar landscape; climbing out of the truck at the screening camp, Mara descended into a horror show. Kenyan detainees sat on the ground with their legs extended in front of them. A home guard soldier in army boots walked over their legs under the supervision of a European district officer. Prisoners who cried out in pain were hit by other guards. A little more than a stone's throw from her home, she had entered another world.

Women and men lived in separate sections of the camp, sleeping five to a small, crowded tent. On her first day, Mara was taken for torture. Divided into groups of five for this as well, Mara's group was beaten where they sat on the ground, while the district officer and the chief home guard walked over their legs just as she had seen them do to the other prisoners. She spent her first day at Gatithi facing constant abuse, given water but nothing to eat by the guards. Families who had learned the prisoners' destination brought them meals from home. Sometimes guards passed it along, sometimes they stole it. Prisoners could see family members coming and going, but Mara was not allowed to talk to her sister.

The second morning, she was asleep when home guards began beating the tent's occupants with truncheons and ordering them all outside. Standing next to the shelter with the guards still in a frenzy, she realized they were telling her they would beat her to death. Taken to a new tent, she was put inside with three other women and several home guards. The district officer told her to sit on the floor in the middle of the tent and asked her how many oaths she had taken. She denied taking any oath at all. He asked again about the oath, and then demanded that she tell them where her brother and the other Mau Mau fighters were hiding, as they knew he had visited her village.

While she was questioned, the guards struck her with long wooden sticks and kicked her. After she repeated that she knew nothing, three guards pinned her to the ground while a fourth forced her legs apart. The chief home guard sat on a chair facing her spread legs, pressing his studded hobnail boots onto her bare feet. As she fought and swore she had never taken the oath, the men proceeded to rape her with a glass soda bottle filled with hot water. Wounded and bleeding from the assault, Mara was relieved that at least the bottle had not broken inside her. She saw more than a dozen women assaulted the same way during her time at the camp. The guards, she realized later, used a larger bottle on the adult women.

Living in gender-segregated sections of the camp, Mara did not see the men, but sometimes there were screams from their compound unlike any she had heard before. She had no way of knowing at that time, but many men underwent a parallel sexual torture during their interrogations, facing castration with foot-long pliers. A typical case was Paulo Muoka Nzili's, a man taken by the Mau Mau in the middle of the night who had managed to desert a few months later. He walked two weeks toward the capital and was eventually picked up by policemen in Nairobi. Taken to a nearby detention center, he was stripped in front of other prisoners and castrated by a traffic policeman who doubled as a senior officer at the camp. More than half a century later, he would tell the British High Court, "It took years for me to find any hope but I have never really recovered from what was done to me."[19]

Guards at Gatithi passed the time by having prisoners jump into a deep, cold river and beating them as they came out of the water. They would also burn prisoners with hot spades, leaving wedge-shaped scars on their backs, sometimes crippling detainees. Mara never saw medical treatment dispensed at the camp.

When she did not line up quickly enough to suit a guard at Gatithi, she was struck with the butt of a rifle, permanently damaging her lower back. Still in pain from the blow, Mara was put in the bed of a large truck and carried off to another camp. She had just finished her first week in detention.

6. In the same year, Algerian insurgents on the northern coast of Africa made a bid to rid their country of French rule. The French had again refused to offer Muslims either citizenship or independence after the end of the Second World War. What followed, beginning in 1954, was eight years of revolutionary terror, increasingly matched and then exceeded by counterterror on the part of French forces, with civilians targeted by both sides.

As guerrilla assassinations and bombings expanded, the French combined mass arrests and detention with a deliberate embrace of torture. The French also adopted the "night and fog" tactics used earlier by Nazis against French resistance fighters.[20] To the Nazi methods of detention and disappearance, the French added their own flourishes, loading bodies of interrogated suspects onto helicopters and dumping them over open water during death flights.[21]

When extremists continued their executions of moderate and loyalist Muslims, government reprisals mounted. Employing superior knowledge of the vast Algerian terrain, guerrillas could not only disappear but also summon willing or coerced support from rural populations. In a classic effort to isolate insurgents, French authorities in 1957 launched a massive policy of civilian relocation into *camps de regroupement* similar to the protected villages in Kenya and the Malayan new villages. Barbed wire went up as soldiers evacuated families in the forbidden zones, laying waste to homes and crops.

By 1959, French concentration camps held more than one million Muslim detainees. Two years later, the total would approach two million, in a country with a population of less than ten million.[22] Residents forced to move were promised electricity and running water, in the "civilizing mission" tradition of turn-of-the-century camps. When they arrived, they typically discovered that no plumbing existed and electrical wiring extended only as far as outside lights that helped guards monitor their movements.

While regroupment camps were not extermination camps, the wide variety of sites encompassed nearly every other manifestation of detention camps that had existed to date. Some barracks-style camps recalled German *Konzentrationslager*, while elsewhere, fortified towns resembled Cuban *reconcentración*. For nomadic populations in the south, historian Alistair Horne writes, barbed wire surrounded clusters of tents where "infants were often found dead of cold in the morning."[23] Some encampments held five times their intended capacity, and newcomers were relegated to sleep on open ground for lack of shelter.

Forced into new surroundings with strangers, detainees often found it difficult to know who was an informant. In any case, they were under perpetual surveillance from nearby military posts and watchtowers. Officers who visited the camps were routinely horrified, but little was done to change policy.

A scathing dispatch from the camp at Bessombourg near the Mediterranean coast appeared in the July 22, 1959, issue of *Le Figaro*, describing detainees "crammed together in unbroken wretchedness" amid starvation, overcrowding, filth, no soap, and nothing but semolina to eat. Many of the nearly two thousand children could not attend classes because they had no clothes. Other critical dispatches followed, with journalists and returning soldiers reporting organized rape in the camps as well as torture using dogs.[24]

Even after the shocking conditions were publicized, concentration camps remained in place. But the shift in public perception took a toll. The French had opened relocation camps before, in Indochina in 1946, where the policy had incurred less destruction after gaining the support of a Cambodian nationalist prince. In Algeria, however, the French were moving farther and farther from their stated ideals and the civilizing mission they claimed.

Regroupment camps shattered the colony. Moving people away from relatives and communities into quarters designed for French nuclear families or, more often, into overcrowded hovels or open fields took a tremendous toll on social structures. Those accustomed to living off the land had no work and little food. The worst aspects of *reconcentración*—helplessness, starvation, and disease—were repeated, this time accompanied not by benign neglect but by widespread torture.

In a variation of the water cure in the Philippines, French police ran hoses from sink taps into the mouths of restrained detainees, distending their stomachs, then bending their knees to their midsections to press it back out again. Interrogators competed with each other to invent new torture techniques. Left to their own devices by commanding officers, they used electroshock, gang rape, and even murder.[25]

A group of Soviet and Nazi camp survivors operating as the International Committee against Concentration Camp Regimes went to investigate the situation in Algeria. Though they did not find the system as oppressive as the Gulag or German camps, they were stunned by the widespread evidence of physical abuse by French authorities. Germaine Tillion, a survivor of Ravensbrück and a member of the French Resistance, despaired for the future of the colony, stating, "All the Algerian elite was in prison. All those who, among the Europeans and the Muslims, could have made up the first core of a true Franco-Algerian community were imprisoned, tortured."[26] With estimates as high as 30 to 40 percent of men facing arrest at some point, Tillion noted that nearly everyone arrested was destined to be brutalized.

The crisis was not limited to Algeria. The threat of losing another colony after the nation had just surrendered Indochina represented for many the loss of French honor. Officers declared their lack of confidence in the government in Paris, with the implicit threat of military action behind their disapproval. The French Fourth Republic fell, triggering a constitutional crisis.

The conflict dragged on until 1962, when Charles De Gaulle, who had effectively been given dictatorial powers, cut a deal with the revolutionaries for independence. France pulled out, and the *harkis*— Muslim loyalists who had supported or fought alongside French forces—were left to fend for themselves, facing massive retaliation in Algeria, from detention to execution.

Those who made their way to France were refused any productive place in the new republic, and many were detained in decommissioned military areas or reopened concentration camps, including Rivesaltes, a deportation camp for Jews during the Vichy era. Not until the 1990s would legislation begin to address the prejudice against them and the destitute conditions that plagued them for decades after their release from the camps.

7. In Algeria, the independence movement was not Communist but did have the backing of the French Communist Party, which galvanized the French military to fight it. In Kenya, the Cold War dynamic was absent. Some British propaganda tried to portray the Mau Mau as a Communist movement, but it was widely understood that the shoe did not fit.

Elsewhere, however, anti-Communist campaigns would begin in earnest. On October 1, 1965, the assassination of several generals in

Indonesia led to a coup and the seizure of power in Jakarta by a pro-Western government. The country had gained independence more than a decade before and in the interim had veered toward closer relations with Russia and China. After the coup, the new government under Suharto immediately began purging suspected Communists via a combination of detention camps and mass executions. The policy of strategic massacre would swell quietly into a tidal wave of death, taking the lives of some five hundred thousand Indonesians in just over five months.

Though the Suharto government carried out the purges, Cold War drama heightened Western interest in the campaign, and the United States played a key role in making targeted killings possible. Membership rosters of the Communist Party of Indonesia and other suspected leftists were provided by US analysts after a two-year collaboration between the State Department and the Central Intelligence Agency, with the implicit understanding that those on them would be killed or held in camps.[27] The United States also shipped jeeps, field radios, and small arms to those carrying out the operation.[28] According to Howard Federspiel, an Indonesia expert at the State Department in 1965, "No one cared, as long as they were Communists, that they were being butchered. No one was getting very worked up about it."[29]

In the wake of the executions, more than a million suspected leftists and members of the Indonesian Communist Party were herded into temporary camps and prisons until long-term detention facilities could be completed. Eventually prisoners ended up in purpose-built concentration camps, assigned to forced-labor projects building highways, harvesting bamboo or timber, and cultivating land for their own subsistence and for the military.[30]

Just as in the enemy alien camps in both world wars, detainees were divided into three classes of prisoners. The vast majority were considered Class C, those simply suspected of political opposition but who had no involvement with the coup. Class B was reserved for detainees the government believed had been involved in planning or advocating violence but against whom it did not have usable evidence. Class A prisoners were those for whom the government had both what it saw as reasonable evidence and certainty of involvement in the coup.

Buru Island, more than four hundred miles from the capital city of Jakarta, functioned as the Solovki of the Indonesian camp system and held many Class B detainees. In 1969 more than twelve thousand suspected Communists were deported to the island, where they were forced to find means to survive for a decade. Prisoners lived behind a six-foot fence in wooden barracks and ate rats and snakes to stay alive. Harassed by the authorities, they were also often attacked by the island's native population for being Communists, though many had been mistakenly detained.

The country's most celebrated intellectuals, writers, loyalists, and artists were among those exiled to Buru. Novelist Pramoedya Ananta Toer had first been imprisoned by the Dutch before Indonesian independence, and later on Buru Island for being a Communist, though he denied ever joining the party. During his second imprisonment, initially refused pen and paper, he composed a cycle of novels in his head—the "Buru Quartet"—to tell as stories to other prisoners.

The stigma of detention left former prisoners and their families vulnerable to harassment and abuse even after their release, when many were too afraid of persecution to go home.[31] Hundreds more died in captivity from torture, executions, or malaria, victims of what the government called the Buru Island Humanitarian Project.[32]

8. More than a decade before Indonesia imprisoned a million suspects, however, British detention in the protected villages, interrogation camps, and labor camps of Kenya hit the same mark and then surpassed it. And before she reached adulthood, Jane Muthoni Mara would experience each kind of detention during the state of emergency in Kenya.

After the rape and beatings during her stay in Gatithi camp, Mara was driven in the bed of a large truck through the green landscape to

Kerugoya camp, at the foot of Mount Kenya. Clubbed on the head by guards in transit, the prisoners were made to line up as they came off the truck. Once roll call was finished, the men and women were again separated, with 150 women given mats to sleep on and locked in two rooms. They were provided food, and the camp had toilets and running water. Women branded with the hot spade during their interrogations and men who had been castrated were allowed to seek treatment at the hospital.

The next day the prisoners were called from their cells, and as at Ravensbrück, they were lined up in columns of five. The camp's entire population, 250 to 300 prisoners, found itself summoned before a judge who had been invited to the camp by its district officer. Standing behind a table, the judge surveyed the group and simultaneously sentenced them all to three years and six months' imprisonment for being members of the Mau Mau. He asked if anyone had anything to say in the way of a defense, but no one replied.

Noticing some ailing prisoners in the back, he had them brought forward. They had open wounds and infected sores, and some could barely walk. The judge asked each of the injured what had happened. When the prisoners described their tortures, the judge said he wouldn't have sentenced them if he had heard their stories beforehand. He ordered the obviously injured detainees to be taken to the hospital. Guards took the wounded away. The rest of the prisoners had no such luck. It was as much of a trial as Mara would get. After a week at Kerugoya, another truck took her to another prison.

In addition to the million or more living under surveillance in protected villages, historian Caroline Elkins records that at least 160,000 suspected Mau Mau were sent to detention camps.[33] Novelist Ngugi wa Thiong'o, a teenage student at the time of the Mau Mau rebellion, saw both the villages and the camps as essentially the same scheme. Everyone was forced to move, everyone had to live where they were told. "The whole of central Kenya was displaced, and the old order of life destroyed," he wrote, "in the name of isolating and starving the anticolonial guerrillas in the mountains."[34]

Ngugi's brother, Good Wallace, had spent years with the fighters before eventually burying his gun and going home. Upon his return he had been sent to a detention camp, but was released in 1959.

Soon after, however, Ngugi was stopped by the police on a bus returning from boarding school to show his mother his college acceptance papers. Mocked for putting on airs—the college papers were the only identification he had with him—he was detained overnight behind barbed wire. The next morning, Ngugi ended up standing before a young white district officer, pleading for release. He was nothing more than a student, he explained, and would soon be leaving for college. Without glancing up, the officer reached for the acceptance papers. Reading through them, he sat back and looked at Ngugi. He was waiting to hear about his own acceptance, he explained. The two young men had gone to rival boarding schools.[35]

They chatted about sports, but Ngugi was not yet free. As he was leaving the building, one of the policemen concocted a story that he had resisted arrest. Reversing course, the white district officer ordered him brought back, held, and charged. Ngugi waited for days for trial before a judge. Once inside the courtroom, he was not allowed to tell his own story, only to ask questions of the arresting officers.

When the officers said he had assaulted them, the audience in the courtroom was shocked. During the court recess, the crowd grew. Who would assault a policeman? Who would go against the police in court? Interrogating his accuser, Ngugi recast every moment of the arrest in the form of a question, to which the officer replied more and more sullenly. Ngugi confounded the man; the officer could not keep his lies straight. In the end, the judge acquitted Ngugi.[36]

He was free to leave. Yet it was a limited freedom, paper thin. In the screening camps, conditions were awful. The protected villages, too, were just another kind of detention. In them families considered loyal received larger homes spaced farther apart, with tin roofs and durable construction. Families believed to be disloyal lived crowded together in mud-and-grass huts. At bottom, Ngugi found the villages and the camps similar: residents in both places were trapped and at the mercy of the colonial government. They all sat under the constant gaze of the watchtower flying a Union Jack. "For all practical purposes," Ngugi wrote, "the line between the prison, the concentration camp, and the village had been erased."[37]

9. After her group sentencing before the judge, Mara was sent to Embu prison, a brick complex with several buildings. She was weighed, measured, and handed a prison uniform. Prison staff gave the convicts porridge.[38] Each morning around 4 a.m., guards entered the prisoners' cells to beat them with whips and sticks for an hour. After the daily beatings, they were fed breakfast. They were then ordered to carry heavy bricks on their heads to a nearby school. Malaria was endemic; hunger and typhoid, too, were common.

After six weeks, guards transferred Mara from Embu to Kamiti prison. A trumpet blew reveille each morning. Prisoners had nowhere to wash up, and a bucket took the place of a latrine. The work was harder, with no exemptions for illness. Guards beat prisoners just as before, but at Kamiti, a European woman joined in, too. Mara watched as all around her prisoners died from disease. Detainees sentenced to ten years wore blue tunics. Those sentenced to life wore red. Blue and red tunic prisoners were responsible for burying the dead. She would spend two years there quarrying rock before she was moved again.

At Athi River, she carried stones to help build a dam for nine or more hours a day. And then she was slowly transferred back along the same route she had already traveled. From Athi River, she returned to Kamiti prison for a month. From Kamiti—the worst of her detention sites—she went back to Embu, where she had four months left to go.

Near the end of her sentence, Mara was sent back to the office she had visited on her way into the prison system after her conviction. She was measured and weighed, just as before. Pictures were taken. Prison staff gave her old clothing back, but in three and a half years she had grown. Her things no longer fit, but she wore them anyway.

Driven to Kerugoya in a car, she was taken to the district officer's headquarters, where she was handed a letter. She had to turn the letter and photos in and report twice a week to her police station at home. She was forbidden to visit anyone, and the police warned that she should consider herself still in jail. Not free but no longer a prisoner, she could go home. She was released on September 27, 1957, at the age of eighteen.[39]

10. Though the rebellion was put down in 1956, the Emergency remained in place in Kenya for four more years, during which abuses continued. In an ocean of atrocities—any of which seems capable of generating public outrage—one incident drew international attention to the colonial government's brutality.

Wambugu Wa Nyingi, a local leader with the Kenyan African Union, had been picked up and taken to a screening camp. During interrogations, some prisoners were beaten and some were stabbed. Later he saw detainees beaten to death, after which their genitals were cut off. But he was spared death. Sent instead to a labor camp, he ended up at the same Athi River location where Jane Muthoni Mara had helped to build the dam.

After a year he was moved to Lodwar prison, where guards kept ankle manacles on him for two years. Taken back to Athi River with a group of prisoners, he noticed guards taking prisoners singly for interrogation. When Nyingi's turn came weeks later, he was asked about the Mau Mau oath. Guards turned him upside down and held him by his shackled feet. After his captors beat and whipped him, they poured water over his face until he could no longer breathe. The water torture continued during the entire beating.[40]

None of these events might have sufficed to draw attention were it not for what happened next. Nyingi was transferred with eighty other men to Hola Camp, some sixty miles inland from the coast. He was held communally with other prisoners in a section called the "closed camp." Its detainees were said by the administration to be the most resistant of all the guerrillas, generally refusing all work assignments or attempts at rehabilitation.

In March 1959 he was taken out of the camp with a large group of prisoners by a squad of as many as fifty home guards. They were handed shovels and told to start digging. After they refused, the guards beat them continuously, disemboweling one man. Nyingi was struck hard on the back of his head and passed out.[41] He was found unconscious two days later in a room filled with the corpses of his fellow detainees. Examining the bodies, a European doctor realized that Nyingi was alive and had him taken to the hospital. He regained consciousness after two more days. He had no broken bones but had terrible headaches and was racked with pain all over his body.

The injuries on the corpses did not match the accounts of camp administrators, and an inquest was opened in which surviving detainees gave their stories—including hours of testimony from Nyingi. After testifying he was sent to other detention sites, including a three-month stint in solitary confinement. The results of the inquest were initially covered up, the men's deaths blamed on contaminated drinking water.

The cordon, the protected villages, the detention camps, and the interrogations that had been used in British Malaya had worked again—the Mau Mau Rebellion had been put down. But this time the dirty laundry of colonial war was revealed to the public. The Mau Mau, who also committed brutal violence in their quest for independence, had been thoroughly outsavaged by the purveyors of progress and civilization. Even before the Hola Massacre, the Anglican Church had publicly referred to the atrocities committed by the colonial office's Europeans and their surrogates as "the Government's Mau Mau."[42]

Others had likewise been trying to publicize abuses in Kenya.

Member of Parliament Barbara Castle had made reforming colonial affairs a personal and Labour Party mission starting in the mid-1950s. Castle took up her crusade in the wake of accounts like that of Kamau Kichina, a detainee in interrogation who had died after five days of torture in which he had been "flogged, kicked, hand-cuffed with his arms between his legs and fastened behind his neck, made to eat earth, pushed into a river, denied food," and more.[43] Castle's key source inside Kenya, the assistant police commissioner, confided to her that what he had seen in Kenyan camps was worse than the conditions he had survived as a Japanese prisoner of war.

It was not, however, until the Hola Massacre, which took place years after the rebellion had been put down, that the nation was gal-vanized toward reform. Addressing the House of Commons on July 27, 1959, Conservative member of Parliament Enoch Powell denounced the idea of the Emergency justifying abuses, as well as another mem-ber's condemnation of the dead as "subhuman." It was too easy to argue "special circumstances," he said, even if one were willing to accept the designation of the victims as monsters.

If the policy of rehabilitation were in any way to be taken seri-ously, he argued, it meant that the men could be made fully human again: "No one who supports the policy of rehabilitation can argue from the character and condition of these men that responsibility for their death should be different from the responsibility for any-one else's death." In an appeal that moved the room, Powell carried on until well after midnight, declaring, "We cannot say, 'We will have African standards in Africa, Asian standards in Asia and per-haps British standards here at home.'"[44]

11. Britain was not alone in its application of the double standard mentioned by Powell. In 1953—early in the Mau Mau conflict— Thomas Askwith, the former commissioner of community develop-ment in the colonial government, had visited British Malaya to review the new villages there and study the campaign by which

hearts and minds of those opposed to colonial rule could be won over. The following year, under the auspices of NATO, French officers were invited to visit Kenya to observe tactics used against the Mau Mau. In 1956 the British ambassador in Paris also fostered exchanges of French and English staff to strategize on the expanding rebellion against French rule in northern Africa. Soon after, British officer A. J. Wilson traversed Algeria, encouraging the use of colonial methods applied in Kenya against the population there.[45] With the disintegration of the French and British empires in the postwar era, this kind of ad hoc exchange of advisors led to an informal network of countries collaborating to minimize Soviet influence and develop more effective counterinsurgency programs.

But the French may have embraced British methods too thoroughly—or perhaps too publicly. Noting the brutality unleashed after the battle of Algiers in 1956 and 1957, London ended the staff exchanges, concerned about being associated with such harsh treatment of Arabs. Paris was left to develop its own counterrevolutionary war theory, one that shifted from isolating guerrillas to dictatorial control over every aspect of the lives of the civilian population. "Call me a fascist if you want," said French army colonel Roger Trinquier, "but we have to bring the population to heel."[46]

Algeria had its debacles, but in no colonial territory did concentration camps find more frequent implementation—or more frequent failure—than in Vietnam. While still vying for control of Indochina (modern-day Cambodia, Laos, and Vietnam) in the early 1950s, French forces moved peasants from contested areas into *agrovilles,* new, US-funded agricultural villages set up to isolate civilians and cut off support to Ho Chi Minh's guerrilla fighters. War correspondent Bernard Fall visited several of the first *agroville* settlements in 1953, noting that the villages mimicked the British Malayan camps "line for line."[47] It proved to be a short-lived program.

The following year, France headed to Algeria after surrendering Indochina, leaving North Vietnam to Ho Chi Minh's forces and the South to what would soon become the fledgling, doomed government of Ngo Dinh Diem. The quick scuttle from one counterinsurgency conflict to the next linked the two in the minds of French soldiers, who called Algerian rebels "les viets."

By 1956, Western-allied Diem had expanded systematic detention in Vietnam to include anyone suspected of being dangerous to the government. Tens of thousands of detainees were eventually sent to political reeducation camps, which the Pentagon Papers described as "little more than concentration camps for potential foes of the government."[48] Many of the Vietnamese held in them had little or no connection to Communism, and were simply those targeted as potentially opposing Diem. After a dramatic escalation in attacks by Communist forces, military tribunals were authorized in 1959 to try state security cases without appeal.

The same year, Diem's government launched its own *agroville* program, one that repeated many aspects of the earlier effort, pressuring peasants to move into modern villages with the promise of schools and hospitals. Yet residents were reluctant. They were expected to dismantle their old homes for materials to use in building their new shelters, and they had to take out loans to purchase plots of land in the *agroville*. The program was a disaster and had to be shuttered in its second year.

Trying to develop a better approach to counterinsurgency, Diem went to British Malaya to get advice and in turn hosted British advisors who came to Saigon. He noted that unlike British Malaya, where the insurgents were Chinese squatters easily distinguished from the general population, in Vietnam the guerrillas could move through the countryside undetected.

Despite his hesitations, Diem adopted the British approach also favored by President John F. Kennedy. Diem had additional early support from the CIA under Allen Dulles—who had written so fiercely as a child against putting Boers in concentration camps.

Dulles soon fell from grace in the wake of the Bay of Pigs Invasion, but under his successor, US financial aid continued. In 1962, Diem appointed his brother to relaunch a mass reconcentration effort that came to be known at the Strategic Hamlet Program. For a third time, Vietnamese peasants were forcibly relocated into barbed-wire compounds, theoretically secure areas in which they could be isolated from insurgents.

But the government did not have the resources or the commitment to isolate them effectively. As a result, they were vulnerable to insurgent troops and lost faith in Diem's government. In 1962, two RAND Corporation researchers went into the field to talk to peasants in one of the villages and encountered a volcano of fury over the program. Villagers did not get lunches, as they had been promised. No one paid them for their labor building the settlement. The government had not reimbursed them for the land they had lost by moving, and it expected them to pay for the bamboo, the fence posts, and even the barbed wire that were to be part of the fortifications. Meanwhile, they could not attend to their regular farming, by which they made a living.[49]

Taking this bad news back to the Pentagon, the researchers found officers unwilling to listen. One general turned his back on them as they spoke. Another told them that the United States would make the peasants "do what's necessary for the strategic hamlets to succeed."[50] Mass civilian relocation failed the French in its first iteration, the Diem government in its second, and US aspirations in its third, dashing American hopes of avoiding the deployment and massive airstrikes that would come from fighting a conventional war.

Bernard Fall, who had visited the earliest *agroville* program, saw the same Malayan model replicated in the 1960s strategic hamlets.[51] The program, branded Operation Sunrise, was declared a failure. The concentration camp strategy in Vietnam sputtered in 1963 amid rising American troop levels. With the collapse of reconcentration, the dream of saving South Vietnam without engaging large numbers of US troops died, cementing the fate of nearly sixty thousand American soldiers who would never come home.

In South Vietnam, as in Algeria, forced relocation of civilians into secure compounds was a failed cornerstone of counterinsurgency. Yet in Vietnam, even after the relocation efforts flagged, civilian detention in the form of reeducation camps persisted. The Red Cross visited groups of some twenty thousand undifferentiated civilians and POWs in camps and hospitals in the South in 1968 and noted disturbing conditions.[52] By the end of the decade concentration camps, along with coercive interrogation, had become the dark side of a connected, global counterinsurgency strategy floating in the wreckage of colonialism.

In the fever for detention camps, there were some government officials who managed to bring colonial counterinsurgency tactics home to the United States. In 1950 the House and the Senate passed the McCarran Internal Security Act over the veto of President Harry Truman. The act gave the president discretionary powers—powers he did not want—in the event of an "Internal Security Emergency." Most alarming was the government's ability to preemptively detain citizens for the duration of the emergency, if there was "reasonable ground to believe" they would engage in "acts of espionage or of sabotage."[53] Socialist Joseph Hansen, running for a New York Senate seat that year, wrote a public letter stating that the measure "legalizes concentration camps in America," which was accurate. Truman denounced the act as a "long step toward totalitarianism."[54] Nevertheless its detention provisions remained in place and available to subsequent presidents for twenty-one years.[55]

12. Viewing every geopolitical question of the day through the distortion field of Cold War politics led to blinkered decision-making that destroyed good governance and devastated the lives of millions. In Kenya, historian Frank Furedi described the colonial government's successful portrayal of the Mau Mau as "an irrational force of evil, dominated by bestial impulses and influenced by world communism."[56] Yet the success of this portrayal doomed the colonial government's ability to understand the long-term implications of its actions, which were ultimately self-defeating.

The lesson that was taught and taught again but not learned in the postwar era of concentration camps was that emergency laws in combination with demonization of military or political opposition led to a downward spiral and systemic atrocity. Moreover, when these counterinsurgency tactics appeared to succeed, they tended to deliver only temporary victory and in fact exacerbated the larger crises that initially triggered the conflict.

Some officials would continue to insist on Mau Mau depravity as the defining element in the conflict, and for decades they would successfully shape the public memory of events in Kenya. By 1970, the verb "mau-mau" had entered the English language as a general term for intimidation and terror.

But in the twenty-first century, the ways in which the British response had dwarfed the crisis began to emerge. The Mau Mau lost their outlaw status in Kenya in 2003, sparking the formation of a Kenyan Human Rights Commission and Mau Mau veterans' groups. A London law firm agreed to look for plaintiffs, and it involved historians who had already made discoveries sharply undercutting official accounts of the Emergency.

When Britain granted Kenya its independence in 1963, it had promised to transfer all relevant files to the new government. Yet historians learned that key sets of files were missing from Kenyan records, as if they had been selectively pruned for inflammatory material. The Kenyan government put in a request for the files, and later on researchers working in London had asked for them as well, noticing references to the missing documents in other records. Nonetheless, the Foreign and Commonwealth Office came up empty-handed in response to the queries.

In 2009 the British law firm Leigh Day brought a claim on behalf of five plaintiffs against the Foreign and Commonwealth Office before the High Court of Justice in London over the torture and abuse of Kenyans in detention camps during the colonial era. The government's position was that the current administration should not be held accountable for the actions of the colonial government during the Emergency. In the midst of legal preparations for the claim in 2011, the Foreign and Commonwealth Office announced that it had found many of the missing files and apologized for its previous failure to produce them. The trove spanned more than one hundred feet of records, including 8,800 files on sensitive government matters in thirty-seven colonies and offered broad support not just for the Kenyans' allegations of abuse but also for the government's awareness of it.

The documents made clear that the colonial government took measures to have guards change their tactics in order to carry out abusive techniques while limiting legal liability and evidence. Oxford historian David Anderson declared that these documents showed that officials had "decided to use torture and abuse as normal, systemic practices."[57] Having accepted that they would turn to torture, the officials tried to put lipstick on the pig of illegal conduct. The attorney general of the colonial administration wrote to the governor in 1957 instructing that prisoners should not be struck on the kidneys, spleen, or liver. "If, therefore, we are going to sin," he wrote, "we must sin quietly."[58]

In 2009, Jane Muthoni Mara, then seventy years old and living in rural Kahuhoni Village north of Nairobi, traveled to London with other camp survivors to file a claim in person. The following year she provided a witness statement about her rape by home guards and the European district officer who supervised the assault. While she was in detention she lost her father's land, and today lives illiterate and landless in a remote homestead without plumbing or electricity. She acknowledged that she had sometimes fed the Mau Mau, but said, "I do not understand why I was treated with such brutality....I killed no one, I harmed no one, all I wanted to do was to help those who were fighting for the dignity and the freedom of our people."[59]

Wambugu Wa Nyingi, who spent two days among corpses after the Hola Massacre, was also brought to London as a plaintiff in

2009. He added his own statement a year later, at the age of eighty-two. He ended his testimony with an address to Queen Elizabeth II, who had ascended to the throne a year into the Mau Mau rebellion:

> I want the world to know about the years I have lost and what was taken away from a generation of Kenyans. If I could speak to the Queen I would say that Britain did many good things in Kenya but they also did many bad things. The settlers took our land, they killed our people and they burnt down our houses. In the years before independence people were beaten, their land was stolen, women were raped, men were castrated and their children were killed. I do not hold her personally responsible but I would like the wrongs which were done to me and other Kenyans to be recognized by the British Government so I can die in peace.[60]

In June 2013, British foreign secretary William Hague acknowledged "that Kenyans were subject to torture and other forms of ill treatment at the hands of the colonial administration" and expressed regrets for the abuse, acknowledging that it had "marred Kenya's progress towards independence." A settlement of £19.9 million was designated for allocation among 5,228 Kenyan victims, precluding the need for the High Court to render a decision on the case.[61]

The trove of missing documents that suddenly appeared from obscurity was vast and offered other insights, including the fact that concerns about the brutality of the response to the Mau Mau were raised in the first year of the rebellion, with the solicitor general describing government actions as "distressingly reminiscent of conditions in Nazi Germany or Communist Russia."[62] Not all the files were found. Others had simply been destroyed, leaving lingering questions about what price may have been paid by those in British Malaya whose suppression became the template for using relocation camps as part of a larger counterinsurgency strategy. Perhaps sensing the ramifications, Foreign Secretary Hague made sure to announce that his office in no way meant the Kenya settlement to establish a precedent.

The delay in accountability for colonial abuses came with a cost. In the postwar era, Western democracies fused turn-of-the-century *reconcentración* tactics with institutionalized torture programs, resurrecting the use of concentration camps in colonial conflicts. The detention of millions in these colonial outposts divided entire societies into victims and collaborators, creating rifts that remained long after independence. "It was the European officers," said Jane Muthoni Mara in her testimony to the court, "who were responsible for my torture and the torture of other prisoners."[63] But only Kenyans suffered the consequences.

In the next phase of concentration camp evolution, techniques used in colonial outposts to fight guerrillas and Marxists would be imported into the capital cities of once-democratic nations to turn them into police states. The informal exchange of counterinsurgency tactics between countries during the colonial era would solidify into multinational collaboration. Drawing on support from the United States and Europe, military juntas in South America would use detention and torture to take over a continent.

CHAPTER NINE

Bastard Children of the Camps

1. On September 11, 1973, Hawker Hunter jets belonging to the Chilean Air Force streaked low over downtown Santiago, dropping bombs on the presidential palace. Plumes of smoke blossomed from the roof after each pass as flames leapt skyward from second-story windows. The jets winged in one after another, strafing the building's neoclassical façade before pulling up to bank away. After releasing his payload, one pilot nosed up and over in an acrobatic flip. They made it look easy, just another day's work, toppling an elected government.

Twenty-one-year-old political science student Felipe Agüero Piwonka watched the explosions from the window of a stranger's home. He had been a few blocks from La Moneda when he had seen tanks with their guns pointed at the palace. Soldiers were everywhere, and there were rumors of snipers. He left his car and tried to get out of the area on foot, only to freeze on a residential street amid the pandemonium. Looking up, he saw a group of people motioning to him from the second floor of their home, beckoning him to safety. He made a dash to their doorway and slipped inside.[1]

They sat and had sandwiches while the radio relayed the news that final warnings had been given to the president to surrender. From the small talk, Agüero, a member of a leftist party and a supporter of the government of Salvador Allende, quickly realized that the people who had saved him from being shot were in favor of the coup d'état.

Jet fighters were already overhead, and soon afterward, the explosions began. While they watched the bombers strafe La Moneda from a small window, his hosts cheered. Terrified that he might be turned over to the police, he went along with their celebration until a lull in the gunfire outside gave him an excuse to leave.

Anyone paying attention had known for months that the military intended to seize power. In June of the same year, a group of colonels with broad support from the army had driven a regiment of tanks through the streets toward the palace before their attempted coup was put down. Members of the opposition to Allende's government had also passed a bill authorizing the military to enter civilian areas to search for and seize weapons at will. By the time the Chilean congress passed a resolution denying the legitimacy of the government in August, it seemed to Agüero that a military dictatorship might be inevitable.[2]

When picturing a coup, Agüero had somehow imagined some civilized transfer of power, but the brutality of the actual moment was terrifying. Clouds of smoke rose skyward as pillars were spliced and the roof collapsed. Allende had given a series of radio addresses from the palace that morning, saying, "Surely this will be the last opportunity for me to address you." His cabinet surrendered, and Allende committed suicide as soldiers stormed the palace. The Chilean army, which had not seen battle for nearly a century, found an enemy it could defeat.

Within forty-eight hours, army general Augusto Pinochet, whom Allende had believed was against the coup, made a statement as president of the four-man junta and announced his intention to "exterminate Marxism."[3] Another curfew was imposed and a state of siege declared, ending a three-year experiment with elected socialist government in the Western Hemisphere.

Allende had run on the Popular Unity coalition, an unapologetic alliance of socialists, Communists, and (later) the Christian Left, but he faced resistance early on from Chile's business and military sectors. Active Cold War opposition from outside the country likewise damaged the administration's ability to govern, with US national security advisor Henry Kissinger announcing in 1970, the year of Allende's election, "I don't see why we need to stand by and watch a country go communist due to the irresponsibility of its own people."[4]

After Fidel Castro established a Cuban revolutionary state in 1959, the US government was terrified that Communism would spread and give the Soviet Union additional footholds in the West. The Nixon administration brought heavy pressure to bear on Chile, directing the CIA to prevent Allende from coming to power and "make the economy scream."[5] Encouraging an early coup attempt that led to the kidnapping and death of the head of the army, the CIA plotted against Allende as if the threat to democracy were so significant that anything was permitted.[6]

Blocks away from La Moneda on September 11, Felipe Agüero had more cause for worry than most Chileans. It was understood that all members of Marxist and socialist groups were now targets, and Agüero belonged to the Popular Unitary Action Movement (MAPU), part of Allende's coalition. He also had direct associations with Allende's government. Spending the following days lying low with friends, he burned Marxist books and other texts that might be seized as evidence. As soon as the curfew was lifted for a few hours, he made his way to the hiding place of one of the MAPU leaders.

Agüero later ventured out in a blue Peugeot with his friend Fernando Villagrán, carrying the party's typed response to the coup and a handwritten list of party contacts hidden in his underwear. Trying to leave the area, the two men were briefly stopped by the police, who ran a check on their records and then, to their surprise, let them go.

On his way again, Agüero's luck deserted him as they ran into the perimeter of a military sweep in a working-class neighborhood. The car was searched; letterhead from a government ministry was found. Agüero caught a rifle butt to the head, and the soldiers kicked him with their combat boots. When they were frisked, the police found the statement intended for party members and supporters. It was read aloud, and soon there was no question of getting released a second time.

Agüero was taken to a nearby factory yard, where hundreds of workers who had been attacked by guards were lying on the ground, their hands over their heads. Everything suddenly registered: the curfew, the sounds of gunfire, and now, before him, a vast carpet of people held facedown at gunpoint. The magnitude of the coup struck home.

Badly beaten and limping, Agüero was put back into the car with Fernando and driven to El Bosque Air Force Base at the southern end of Santiago. "From then on," he recalls, "it was just deeper degrees of hell." He was assaulted again, with rifle butts and other objects. Blindfolded, he was forced to run in a courtyard, crashing into trees and walls. And through it all came the terrible recognition that his captors were not improvising but instead employing actual counterinsurgency tactics for use against revolutionaries. He knew very well from his readings that the military studied such techniques, but it was another thing to have them applied to his own body. Separated from Fernando, he was left facedown, bleeding and shirtless.

Under interrogation, he invented an explanation out of whole cloth. Later, one of his captors let him know that his friend had also talked, and their stories did not match. He was taken into a room and his blindfold removed. Before him sat a classroom of young, blond, elite-looking junior officers from the Air Force Academy located on the base. They seemed eager for blood. While the observers called out for harsher techniques to be used, Agüero was treated with unexpected humanity by the lead interrogator, a captain who provided him water and a blanket. Then Fernando was brought into the room. Inexplicably given a chance to reconcile their accounts, the friends concocted a story that they were merely couriers of the documents discovered in their possession. They invented a street corner destination where they said they had been instructed to turn over the documents. The interrogator decided that the two men would be taken there the next day so the intended recipients of the party message could also be arrested.

Herded to a gymnasium afterward, Agüero again saw a large open space filled with people from the surrounding neighborhood lying facedown. Amid the sounds of kicking and punching, and the moaning of those beaten, officers who had observed his interrogation informed him that there would be no more gentle treatment. He took a hard hit to the ear, lost consciousness, and woke up lying on the floor.

After spending the remainder of the day under assault in the gymnasium, Agüero was loaded on a bus, where the assault continued. Blindfolded, he nonetheless had the sense of traveling as part of a caravan. Climbing down off the bus to more abuse, he was turned over to an officer. At the prospect of additional blows, he and Fernando spoke up to say that it would not do to beat them any more, because they were to take part in an intelligence operation the next day. "We have to look good," they said. The friends were separated from the rest of the passengers, who were treated to further savagery.

By this point Agüero's blindfold had been taken off, and he was standing in a gallery with concrete walls and gated broad exit ramps. It was a place he knew well. As with Germany's Ruhleben racetrack in the First World War and France's Vélodrome d'Hiver in the Second, the Chilean junta had turned the country's sporting venues into impromptu concentration camps. Agüero realized he had been brought to Chile's national stadium.

Imprisonment there meant a homecoming of sorts for Agüero. The arena was famous for its World Cup matches, and as a youth he had gone to the Estadio Nacional with his father to watch the Pan American Games and other track and field competitions. During a meet for children, Agüero had competed in a relay event on the same track at the age of twelve.

From the gallery he saw the Marathon Avenue gates through which competitors arrived. He had once rounded the lanes that enclosed the grass pitch, running on the track past the press box, past the long-jump pit and the *disco negro*, that black circle against which timekeepers watched for smoke rising from the starter pistol.

But now he was trapped under the stadium seating. He heard the sound of rifle butts hitting prisoners' heads. Some of the prisoners could no longer stand. Blood covered the floor. The rest of the captives were marched off while Agüero was taken just a few feet, where he and his friend lay down on the floor. Fernando said, "If you could just see what you look like." Exhausted, they fell asleep.

Early the next morning he saw more people, including some he knew: Ángel Parra, the son of Chilean folksinger Violeta Parra, and Vicente Sota, a leader in Agüero's own party. A calculus of caution emerged over whom to talk to and for how long. Uncertain of what would happen next—would there be trials? executions?—friends pretended to be strangers to protect themselves and each other.

A set of doors in one side of the hallway opened to reveal a locker room packed with prisoners. They began streaming out to get food. A man in military gear called Fernando's name and took him away. Agüero was left on his own, to become a resident in one of the dozens of locker-room detention cells set in a circle around the base of the stadium, which was also filled with people, as were the eight entrance gates that held hundreds more.

2. Though Chileans had known the coup was coming, and some Communist intelligence operatives even got wind of its launch a few hours early, the existing government and its allies on the left failed to mount an effective resistance.[7] Four soldiers died storming La Moneda, but government administrators fled or were quickly rounded up, with dozens of Allende's cabinet members taken into custody. Even self-declared militant wings of extremist parties found themselves woefully unprepared and quickly overwhelmed. Students and

leftist party members who gathered at Santiago's State Technical University to oppose the army held out only a little more than twenty-four hours.

Along with attention to campuses, army units had been premobilized to raid working-class neighborhoods and factories. Soldiers were met with violence at a few locations and even suffered some fatalities, but resistance was largely extinguished in the first days of the coup. In the weeks that followed, sweeps and targeted grabs aimed at capturing Allende supporters, party members, and community organizers. Factories were searched. Hospitals were raided. Afterward, bodies were found along the highway, on bridges, on a soccer field. Some had been summarily executed on the spot, more were interrogated and then killed. Many ended up, like Agüero, at the Estadio Nacional.[8]

Overwhelmed by the expanding numbers of prisoners in the stadium, two generals asked the United States for assistance and a dedicated advisor who had experience in constructing mass detention facilities. They also requested tents for temporary housing.[9] The US ambassador suggested that it would be risky to associate his country with the junta's human rights violations but noted that donated tents might be perceived as a humanitarian gesture.

Unlike the Communist camps that had risen during the Cold War, in South America detention under anti-Communist governments would evolve more and more toward hidden sites, becoming the unclaimed, illegitimate offspring of Western democracies. For the moment, the generals had little choice but to continue using public stadiums and other locations that had become ad hoc concentration camps.

3. By the time Agüero took up residence in one of the locker rooms under the stadium seating, it was still mid-September, only a week after the bombing of La Moneda. Routine quickly set in. Now he was

one of the horde streaming down the hallway and through the doors for a small roll and something to drink each morning.

Quarters were tight; the doors on the concourse opened onto a narrow entrance hall, which led to a rectangular changing area with lockers, which in turn led to toilets, sinks, and showers. Sleeping was complicated because there was not enough room for everyone to lie down. Detainees lay on narrow wooden rails attached to the wall that were meant to store duffel bags. Organizers emerged via initiative and consensus to conduct the symphony of bodies. On the floor, prisoners arranged themselves alternately head to toe in order to reduce nighttime crowding. Those unable to sleep gave their spaces to the ill and the newly interrogated, and an orderly arrangement emerged.

Detention at the stadium remained unpredictable. One day the locker room doors opened to reveal Cardinal Raúl Silva Henriquez, the Roman Catholic archbishop of Santiago. Silva had long advocated on behalf of the poor in the deeply Catholic country of Chile, and when Allende's leftist government had come to power, the cardinal had tried to act as a neutral facilitator with some opponents, to no avail.

A welcome sight to the locker room detainees, Silva explained that the Church was pained by the recent violence. He promised to follow events closely and do everything in his power to ensure prisoners' well-being. Agüero felt relieved to realize that someone other than the military and the prisoners knew they were being detained.

After days of confinement, guards began to let the detainees out into the stands for a few hours each day, where they could stand in the sun and fresh air. They had to stay in their assigned sections but were permitted to wander within those confines or to sit on the wooden bench seats. Detainees embraced the relative freedom but often maintained a cautious distance from one another. After several days, Agüero finally spied Fernando in another section of the stands and waved to get his attention.

Along with the cardinal's visit and the outdoor time, spirits were buoyed by packages that began to arrive. Red Cross representatives had been permitted into the stadium. Agüero's name was called. He was given a small parcel he realized must have come from his family. Subsequent days brought additional packages. A few cigarettes or a little bread, maybe some chocolate. He felt the pleasure of the small luxuries but realized that taking so much trouble to send so little likely meant that his family was facing its own hardships under the rule of General Pinochet.

If it was not surreal enough to be wandering the stands of the national soccer stadium in broad daylight with thousands of men, bruised and shirtless and having been visited by the cardinal, Agüero soon noticed men in suits walking onto the field, checking the grass and making measurements. Remembering that a World Cup match was to be played in the stadium that November, Agüero assumed the men were soccer officials from FIFA, soccer's governing body. In that moment they represented another possible connection to the outside world. Although some prisoners had been taken below, others were left outside. Wandering through the stands, beaten, hungry, and frightened, they watched the guests with fascination, hoping to get their attention or make an impression on them, willing them to make eye contact. Agüero never saw the men look up.

Not all interruptions were welcome. Some days brought visits from young and obviously elite officers wearing elegant jackets— men Agüero nicknamed "Pierre Cardin guys." Entering the locker room, they called certain prisoners out for interrogation. Many detainees returned in noticeably worse shape. Eventually an officer came for Agüero. Speaking privately, he said, "I'm going to interrogate you. But I'm going to try to help you out. I'm a friend of a friend of yours." He mentioned the name of one of Agüero's high school classmates.

Agüero suspected a trap but played along. He was taken to an area on the far side of the stadium above the regular seating, where luxury seats and the press box were located. Once there, a low-key interrogation began in which Agüero was allowed to answer carefully and at length. Meanwhile, he saw other prisoners standing splay-legged with their foreheads pressed against the wall, absorbing brutal treatment as they were questioned. Horrific sounds came from nearby rooms.

The disparity in treatment made an impression not only on Agüero, but also on a ranking officer, who came over to ask what was going on. He ended the interrogation, sent the junior officer away, and marched Agüero back to the locker room. Rather than a sense of relief, Agüero felt dread that he had caught the attention of someone in charge who was clearly displeased with the gentle treatment he had received.

A day or two later, just after prisoners had returned from the stands, Agüero heard his name called over the stadium's public address system. A disembodied voice told him to report to the *disco negro*. His heart sank. He debated ignoring the summons but thought it could only make matters worse if he made them come for him.

The *disco negro* had been set up by the long-jump pit, and there was no direct way to get to it. Agüero headed from the gallery to the closest entrance gate and waited for the guard to let him through. Stepping onto the track he had run as a child, he walked the straightaway and the curve as he circled the soccer field. At his assigned spot he stood waiting for his torturers, taking in the grass, the sky, and tens of thousands of seats, row after empty row.

4. With the bombing of La Moneda as an overture, the junta immediately gained the attention of the world. The *New York Times* alone ran more than a dozen stories on September 12, the day after the coup, plastering a triple-decker, all-capitals banner headline atop page one. The same day, tens of thousands of Europeans protested in the streets, carrying signs reading "Allende Lives" and denouncing reports of US sponsorship of the violence.[10] A shoving match broke out in the General Assembly of the United Nations when the

Chilean delegate took offense at allegations that detainees were slated for execution.[11]

Within two weeks, Red Cross observers from the outside were allowed to visit Dawson Island, a detention camp in the Strait of Magellan where three dozen of Allende's most prominent supporters—and later, hundreds more prisoners—were kept in crude barracks in a brutal Antarctic climate.[12] On the heels of that visit, more than two hundred members of the press were allowed to accompany the Red Cross onto the main field of the Estadio Nacional, where the government reported holding more than five thouand prisoners.[13]

While the Red Cross continued to investigate, foreigners who had been allowed to leave the stadium and the country spoke of witnessing mass shootings of thirty to forty people at a time.[14] A government spokesman took issue with the accounts, protesting to reporters that "not even one person...has been executed."[15]

Within weeks the government would pivot to defiantly announcing military tribunals and subsequent executions, with sixteen "extremists" shot on one day in October.[16] Later that month, desperate for some public justification of government terror, the junta released a 264-page white paper describing "Plan Zeta," a massive assassination conspiracy that had supposedly been planned by militant leftists for mid-September. It accused the Popular Unity coalition of not being "satisfied with trampling upon the majority will of the country" after "ruining the country economically and financially." It alleged that extremists had been "prepared and ready to carry out [a] self-coup designed to conquer and absolute power based on force and crime, and installing the 'people's dictatorship.'"[17] The junta claimed that it had staged the coup to save the country from tyranny.

Foreign correspondents quickly noticed that the hundreds of pages seemed to offer no actual proof of the plot. "Nothing is said about where the plan was discovered by military officers, no names or political organizations are directly linked to it," wrote journalist Jonathan Kandell, "and no strong evidence is presented to connect it to President Allende." He noted, however, that anti-Communists in Chile ate up the unlikely story, swearing that they themselves had been among those targeted for assassination.[18] Before the consequences of the coup had become clear, many people instructed to report for questioning had turned themselves in, never to be seen again. Others went underground or fled the country, if they could. In all, more than twenty thousand were taken in September or October to the Estadio Nacional to face interrogation and torture.

5. Felipe Agüero stood alone for a time by the long-jump pit, feeling that he was being watched. Eventually two soldiers came for him. They slipped a hood over his head and made him run up the stadium stairs, stumbling and falling as he went. As they pushed him on, he had a sense that he had ended up back in the press box, where his earlier, truncated interrogation had taken place. Now he was the one positioned as he had seen others before, wrists bound with wire behind his back, forehead planted against the wall, legs spread. He realized with dismay that he had failed to imagine how painful this position would be. Again he heard frightening sounds nearby.

Then his turn came. Taken into another room, his hands were freed and he was told to undress completely, except for the hood. Naked, he was placed against one wall in the same position as before, except that his hands were now braced against the wall.

His interrogators began to ask questions that made it clear they knew a few things about him: that he was a student at Catholic University, that he was a leftist, that he was affiliated with the university's student council and sociology department, and that he had worked with people who were in the Ministry of Foreign Affairs under Allende. And they asked the same question asked of all prisoners: "Where are the guns?"

Despite the horror of it all, he was fortunate. Still hooded, he thought there were three interrogators in the room, but none of them seemed to know that he was a member of MAPU who had been arrested carrying party documents—which would have made him a high-value prisoner. However bad the questioning would get, he realized that his position could have been much worse.

Yet it got bad enough. They asked questions and gave him little time to answer. It was very hard to remain consistent. They beat him with nunchaku, two clubs connected by a short chain. The blow from the first baton would land on his back, and the chain would act as a hinge allowing the second stick to wrap around his torso and strike his stomach—two blows for every hit. They ground their boots on his bare feet. They pressed lit cigarette butts onto his fingers. They used metal instruments on his genitals.

The session felt interminable, but Agüero later thought that it might have lasted an hour or less. He was hustled through the tunnels in terrible shape, taken outside, and told to sing Popular Unity songs. Other people heard the singing and came over to hit him as he sang.

After his inquisitors decided that he had performed long enough, they took him back to the press box, and the interrogation began all over again. His hood was made of a type of burlap, and sometimes when it was pulled or stretched, Agüero could glimpse his surroundings. He had already recognized the voice of one of the interrogators—it belonged to a soldier who had come to his locker room before. At the second session he got a clear look at a second torturer through the hood, but the vision of a tall man with dark hair did not feel like a triumph. Agüero was frightened to see the face of someone willing to do these things to him.

At the end of the second session, they told him they would start up again the next day. He was taken downstairs, but instead of ending up back with the other prisoners, he was locked alone in a tiny dark room filled with objects. His hands no longer bound, he was able to take off the hood and get a sense of the space. He made out the shape of a pommel horse and realized he was in a gymnastics equipment storage room.

His initial thought that he was alone proved incorrect. There were rats in the room. Agüero had on his pants, shoes, and jacket, but his shirt had been torn off him before he had arrived at the stadium. His bare torso was covered with bruises and cuts in various stages of healing. To stay clear of the rats, he climbed onto the horse.

It was not easy, but he managed to sleep a little on his perch despite his fear that someone might come for him at any moment. Then the quiet of nighttime outside the doors dissipated, and he heard activity again. But no one came. He had to relieve himself in the closed space. A full day passed, and he remained happy to have been forgotten by his interrogators, but he began to get thirsty.

Night came again, and he heard voices outside. After a while, they opened the door. Since these soldiers were not the men who had interrogated him, Agüero thought perhaps they would give him food and something to drink, but they only harassed him and forced him to do pushups, then put him back in the room and locked the door again. At some point after that—hours or a day, Agüero had lost any sense of time—he was found by an army medic who seemed to be going around the stadium collecting stray prisoners. He was given food and water on the spot and was taken to another locker room.

The other prisoners looked at him askance—shirtless, his injuries and torture were on obvious display. Why had he suddenly appeared in their midst? Maybe the military junta had labeled him particularly dangerous. Whether he was a high-value detainee or an informant, they wanted little to do with him and kept their distance, adding to the loneliness of the ordeal. Agüero tried to settle back into his previous routine while keeping out of sight of anyone who might notice the marks of his torture and start the process all over again.

6. Chile's overthrow by military junta was not the first South American coup spurred by fears of Communism. The United States had backed right-wing military coups that subverted democracy in Guatemala and Paraguay in 1954, nearly twenty years earlier. And during the 1960s, Brazil's army had blazed a trail of civilian arrests, clandestine abduction, and torture to eradicate opposition.

The coup in Brazil was pulled off almost without bloodshed, but the United States had been prepared to play the role of enforcer. Arranging to ship 110 tons of weapons and ammunition into São Paulo, including tear gas for use on crowds, the State Department coordinated with US forces for possible military backup.[19] As he reviewed preparations in the opening hours of the coup on March 31, 1964, President Lyndon Johnson instructed Undersecretary of State George Ball, "I think we ought to take every step that we can, be prepared to do everything that we need to do."[20]

By then, the United States had already done quite a bit. The CIA had funded nearly a thousand anti-Communist candidates running for state and local offices in Brazil, as well as supporting the rise of paramilitary groups that opposed the government.[21] But after the coup's success, American offers of assistance went beyond political machinations and munitions. The CIA was widely understood by Brazilian officers to be heavily involved with the establishment of Brazil's new Serviço Nacional de Informações, a secret intelligence organization.[22] And US attachés signed in on dozens of visits to a São Paolo interrogation center in a single year, sometimes on days when extended torture sessions of high-value prisoners were conducted.[23]

Thousands of prisoners in Brazil were detained without charges in state prisons, city jails, and special police headquarters. Reports leaked abroad detailed a variety of abuses, including standard electrical tortures; a method of hanging detainees upside down from a pole with arms and feet bound together; an eardrum-rupturing technique called "telephone" that involved striking both of a prisoner's ears simultaneously with cupped hands; and a special room in which the floors were electrified.[24]

In time, the CIA would receive significant blame for encouraging abuse and training torturers, but French counterinsurgency training methods adopted in Algiers also provided a model. Later, British intelligence received specific credit for introducing Brazilian generals to techniques used on Irish Republican Army suspects in detention.[25]

Faced with increasing repression and expanding arrests, thousands fled Brazil for Chile in the 1960s to take refuge under Allende's socialist rule. But once democracy fell in Chile, leftist refugees were trapped. Intelligence networks in both countries began tracking and trading information.[26]

7. For the rest of his detention at the Estadio Nacional, Felipe Agüero managed to avoid getting called back to the press box for interrogation. But out in the stands one day, he noticed a large group of people—perhaps a hundred—coming into the stadium through the Marathon Avenue gates. The prisoners, looking at the ground and covered with blankets, appeared markedly worse than any prisoners he had seen thus far. Their shattered aspects brought to mind images of Nazi camp survivors. He wondered where these people had been and what they had gone through to look like that.

Not long afterward, Agüero was told to join a large group standing on the track. They were handed blankets, lined up in formation, and marched from the stadium through the Marathon gates. On the way out he saw another group of people coming in, also with blankets, looking just as bad as the first group he had seen. He noticed his friend Fernando among them and realized that wherever they had been, his turn was next. He caught Fernando's eyes in passing, and his friend made a face to warn Agüero that what was coming was horrible.

Soon the group was told to put the blankets over their heads, and after that all Agüero could see were his feet. They walked for some distance, and then were taken up into stands again—but not the seats of the Estadio Nacional. Agüero deduced that he was in the velodrome, which sat on the stadium grounds. Prisoners were seated on benches between entrances, several to a row, and made to wait with their blankets still over their heads. The sound of horrific screaming erupted, like nothing Agüero had ever heard, even during the press box torture. He tried to imagine what could cause such screams.

While he wondered, the prisoners were told to remove their

blankets. A naked young man was carried out of one of the velo-drome tunnels, and they were told that he was going to identify people. The naked man faced them and started pointing randomly, wildly, as prisoners tried desperately to avoid being targeted. Agüero remained lucky for the time being—he was not selected for special attention. Once the spectacle ended, the blankets went back on and the process continued. One row of prisoners was taken at a time while the others waited. The horrible screams started up again, and then the next row went.

Agüero's turn came. He moved into the tunnel and two guards held him upright facing an officer seated on the edge of a table. He was asked the pro forma questions about where the guns were hidden, and when his answers were deemed insufficient, a guard bent him double and ran him headfirst into the wall.

Yet he was grateful. They were asking generic questions, which meant that his captors still had not connected him to the original reason for his detention—the party documents in his possession when he had been caught.

It also dawned on him that the interrogators had no idea what they were doing. There appeared to be no real strategy; the men simply seemed set on inflicting massive punishment. He was leaned against the wall, and one of the men slammed a fist up into his testicles. Then he was taken to the area where the screams were coming from.

He was told to undress again, and once naked, he was made to lie down. As the men began attaching wiring to his wrists and testicles, he understood what had triggered the screams. After the setup was complete, they repeated the same questions and turned the electricity on. The voltage ran through the circuit they had made of his body, and he heard the inhuman screams coming from his own mouth, beyond restraint or suppression.

Without a doubt, it was terrible to be electrocuted, and Agüero knew that if it went on very long, he would be in serious trouble. Yet he felt relieved to realize that screams were an involuntary response of the body—that was what had made them sound so different. For him at least, this new torture fit within the universe of pain inflicted during prior interrogations. He could release his mind from the most horrific imaginings of what they might to do him. He believed that he would live.

8. Others did not survive the first weeks of the coup. While Agüero was detained at the stadium, General Sergio Arellano Stark, a member of the Chilean junta, handpicked a death squad and flew on a Puma helicopter across northern Chile, massacring detainees at various detention sites, first in the south and then across the north. To instill terror and show that mercy would not be tolerated, Arellano's men brutally interrogated detainees and executed them using tactics designed to maximize their suffering. Limbs were shot off prior to execution. Machetes were used to slice prisoners open. Others were shot "trying to escape." Some lost noses or ears prior to death.[27] At least seventy-five prisoners were executed through September and into October in the raids, which came to be known as the Caravan of Death.[28]

Among the prisoners, torture became the shared experience of the dead and the survivors. But as with so many camp detainees before them, prisoners tried to insist on their humanity where they could. Jorge Escalante, a young leftist who had been monitoring a naval station for signs of the coup, was caught snooping and briefly detained. He was rearrested early in October 1973 and tortured until he lost consciousness.

Kept in detention afterward, he was thrown with other prisoners into the hold of a ship.[29] The captain of the ship turned out to be the father-in-law of one of the detainees and was sympathetic to the men. One day they asked for ribbons, paper, and colored pencils. To alleviate their suffering and to mock the legitimacy of their detention, the inmates quickly produced a circus, with clowns, stand-up comics, impersonators, and singers.

Escalante remained the director of a weekly performance even after he was moved to Melinka, a public resort that the junta later

converted to a concentration camp. Each Sunday guards, camp officials, and inmates alike came to watch the show. Prisoners mounted
a production with new material every weekend, except for the one
Sunday that Escalante spent in solitary confinement, when the cast
refused to perform.[30]

As detainees began to build community within the camps cobbled
out of the stadium grounds, vacation cabins, merchant ships, jails, and
private estates around the country, some Chileans on the outside tried
to intervene. Cardinal Silva, who had visited Agüero and the other
detainees at the national stadium, helped launch the Committee for
Cooperation for Peace in Chile. A nondenominational, multifaith religious group, the committee sought to help refugees who had fled violence in other countries as well as Chileans most at risk after the coup.

In time, Pinochet would move against the committee and shut it
down, but a defiant Silva immediately launched a new organization—
the Vicariate of Solidarity—with the same mission, this time under
the auspices of the Catholic Church.[31]

9. After Agüero had undergone electroshock, fellow detainees back
at the stadium admitted that they had believed him to be an informant, but no longer. He had felt the isolation from other prisoners
keenly, and was comforted by his return to whatever one could call
the normal, mutually cautious society of the locker room.

That society was soon to disperse. Soldiers began calling out
groups of detainees, with new people chosen each day. Those who left
did not return. About a week after his torture in the velodrome, Agüero's name was also called, and he was herded onto a bus. Not beaten
this time or forced to wear hoods, prisoners could look out the windows as they rode through the streets of Santiago, taking in the everyday world that had carried on in their absence. Although their
existences had been completely upended, they had been in the stadium only about a month.

Agüero wound up in the Santiago jail, where he was reunited

with Fernando. The food was bad, but there was enough of it, so he no longer went hungry. Prisoners could receive visitors; those with money could even order delivery food.

In line at the jail one day, they saw the captain from the air force academy who had conducted their first, gentle interrogation after their initial arrest. Insufficient enthusiasm for the coup had resulted in his becoming a prisoner himself. They later learned that by sending them to the Estadio Nacional, he had intervened in a plot to kill them. Their first interrogator had saved their lives.

The last prisoners were taken out of the stadium after two months, just weeks ahead of Chile's World Cup qualifying match against the Soviet Union on November 21. By then, reports had slowly made their way out of Santiago, and the world was aghast. Faced with rising accounts of killings in the stadium, published photos of injured prisoners, and even covert footage of an execution, the Russian team requested a new World Cup venue. When this request was denied, they refused to show up despite pressure from FIFA. On the day of the match, the Chilean team came out onto the field of the stadium, so meticulously checked by officials weeks before. From his seat in the Santiago jail, Agüero watched a Chilean player kick the undefended goal that officially won the game.

Although Agüero had escaped the inferno, he remained at risk. Arrests were still under way. He read a story about the death of a close friend of his brother's as part of the executions in northern Chile. Newspapers were filled with accounts of military actions. Even at the jail, detainees were still sometimes called out in the middle of the night never to return, the staff collecting their belongings the next day.

One evening Agüero was sent for and loaded into a van, one wrist shackled to his ankle. Driven to the Ministry of Defense, he rode upstairs in an elevator filled with armed soldiers. Bracing himself for another interrogation, he was instead left alone with General Pinochet's closest advisor, Jaime Guzmán, who asked him to explain what had happened. The two had met once in connection with a university speech, and Guzmán claimed to want to help him, but Agüero was not forthcoming. He was returned to his jail cell only to find a note hidden in a sandwich sent by his family, telling him to cooperate with Guzmán because Agüero's brother had asked him to intervene.

Given another chance to meet, Agüero provided details of what he had experienced and seen in detention. Guzmán tried to arrange his release, only to be told that General Arellano, leader of the Caravan of Death, planned to bring Agüero up on charges before a military tribunal. In response, Guzmán threatened to serve as Agüero's attorney at trial. The military relented. Both Agüero and Fernando went home in mid-February, five months after the coup began.

10. The initial wave of violence, involving mass arrests of thousands per day, ended after the first months. The Estadio Nacional, as well as nearby Chile Stadium, had been permanently emptied of prisoners before the end of November. But for others the terror continued, and a long-term system of torture and detention was evolving.

More traditional camps were constructed or improvised out of existing spaces. Melinka, under the control of the navy, was established on the site of a former seaside resort that Allende had made available to the poor. Not far away, wooden fencing and barbed wire gave birth to Ritoque, another former resort reclaimed as a detention site—this one run by the Chilean air force and police units. Tres Alamos, on the southeastern outskirts of Santiago, housed hundreds in extrajudicial purgatory, ostensibly under the control of the police. Smaller, clandestine sites devoted to interrogation and torture fed into or drew prisoners back out of more traditional camps as needed.[32]

Within months of the coup, a National Intelligence Directorate (DINA) began to form under General Manuel Contreras. Even before its formal establishment in June 1974, DINA had become the heart of state terror in the new regime. Acquiring officers from the Carabineros, the Investigations Police, and the military, Contreras scrambled to set up a DINA torture school at Las Rocas de Santo Domingo, repurposing yet another beach resort Allende's government had dedicated to working-class families. At Las Rocas, the DINA began using detainees as guinea pigs to train officers in torture techniques.[33]

Prisoners there slept in cabins, which were also later used for interrogation. Ana Becerra, a teenage militant, was arrested in the first days of the coup, given a trial by military tribunal, and released with time served. Arrested a second time near Santiago early in 1975, she was taken to Las Rocas, where she was singled out for extra punishment by her previous interrogator. In addition to the standard tortures, she was blindfolded and tied to her bunk bed for a month. During her captivity, she was cut with instruments and shocked with electricity until she bit her tongue and her mouth filled with blood. She was tortured so extensively that for a time after her transfer to another camp, she lost all memory of who she was. She believes that a dying prisoner who alerted a Red Cross observer to her presence saved her life.[34]

The seizure of workers' resorts for use in detention and torture was part of a pattern. Using the very buildings Allende's government had dedicated to improving the standard of living of the poor gave the detention sites practical and symbolic power.

Along with Las Rocas at Santo Domingo and the vacation cabins at Melinka and Ritoque, the DINA and branches of the armed forces took over other iconic sites from Allende's rule and repurposed them. Londres 38, an elegant building in Santiago that had served as socialist party headquarters, was employed for detention and torture within days after the coup.[35] Former safe houses for radicals and the site of a printing press for a Communist newspaper became miniature detention and interrogation outposts as well.[36]

The DINA also took control of Villa Grimaldi, an estate on the outskirts of Santiago that had been a cultural home for the intelligentsia. Like Las Rocas, it was turned into a torture training center. Over three years, more than 4,500 people were taken inside the gated enclosure there. Some were shut into niches in the two-story tower. Others were held in tiny cells less than a yard wide, which guards mockingly named "Corvi houses" after the affordable housing program of prior administrations. Still other detainees were locked four or five at a time into closet-size "Chile houses," without room for inmates to sit or stand at the same time.[37]

Prisoners were raped, subjected to bestiality, burned, run over with automobiles, and worse. All were blindfolded and tortured; many were never seen again. One DINA victim's fate was finally determined after a button from her sweater was found. It was still attached to the railroad tie that her tortured and burned body was bound to before being thrown from a helicopter into the sea.[38]

Not all detention areas were clandestine. At some sites, like Tres Alamos, the Vicariate of Solidarity managed to gain access. Prisoners were permitted to do handicrafts, which the organization took and sold to benefit their families.[39] Occasionally, the Vicariate could supply larger items, like a sewing machine. Outside observers could occasionally visit detainees. Meanwhile, at other sites in the network—sometimes at hidden locations adjacent to the camps—electrocutions, torture, and rape continued.

As Pinochet's forces tried to extinguish all opposition, their human rights abuses continued to draw rebukes worldwide. From Dawson Island to the Estadio Nacional, the phrase "concentration camp" surfaced in reports during the first weeks of the dictatorship.[40] With the Nazi baggage the phrase carried and growing accusations abroad, the generals could not indefinitely afford the public relations burden of a system of visible camps. Even the detainees they released and forced into exile haunted them by writing accounts of their abuse and torture once they were safely out of the country.

The first months of military rule would end with the closure of improvised concentration camps holding thousands under the control of the armed forces. The second phase in Chilean civilian detention favored systematized camps holding hundreds. With repression institutionalized and international pressure increasing (and many known leftists in exile or dead), the need for mass arrests dropped. By the time of the DINA's dissolution in 1977, even midsize camps had been closed.

Four years into the military dictatorship, the new intelligence agency that rose from the DINA's ashes continued abusive arrests and interrogations, but it would carry them out largely without mass detention. Even though its camps chapter had closed, however, the reckoning for the death of thousands and the torture of exponentially more Chileans would not come for decades.

11. Many detainees were released in the first months after the coup only to face arrest again, but after his torture in the Estadio Nacional and his time in jail, Felipe Agüero remained at liberty. He was allowed to return to his university. One day while in the economics department, he saw one of his torturers. He froze in fear and then left, having failed to get any identifying information about the man. A newspaper wedding announcement accompanied by a photo later solved the mystery. He had gotten the man's name. But what could he do? Still required to check in weekly with the authorities, Agüero felt unsafe in his own country. He finished his degree and moved to the United States in 1982, earning a PhD at Duke University.

Meanwhile, much of South America had descended into terror. Argentina, Chile's neighbor to the east, was the last country in the continent's Southern Cone to fall. After a trio of generals took over in March 1976, anti-Communist death squads quickly began executing people and dumping mutilated bodies in ditches around the capital.[41]

After witnessing Chile's transition to dictatorship, the Argentine military knew well enough not to herd thousands of suspects into open-air stadiums and allow Red Cross observers to visit them. From the beginning, the junta operated a network of hidden concentration camps. Via rapid-fire "night and fog" kidnappings by unidentifiable agents and clandestine seizures that sometimes captured witnesses for good measure, thousands soon vanished without a trace.

In transit to oblivion, the *desaparecidos*—the "disappeared"—were taken to hundreds of detention sites across the country. At La Perla, a military installation outside Cordoba, some two thousand endured rape, electrocution, or execution, with only 137 surviving.[42] In the basement of the nondescript officers' casino on the grounds of the Navy Mechanical School (ESMA) in Buenos Aires, some five thousand detainees suffered torture amid the stench of blood and feces while the Rolling Stones' "Satisfaction" played over and over to cover their screams. In a birthing room upstairs, pregnant prisoners delivered more than four hundred babies, who were taken from prisoners and given to associates of the junta or its officers and raised as their own.[43]

The complexity of the stolen-infant enterprise was an Argentine innovation, but functionaries of the junta also enthusiastically recycled history in its camps. In the Athletic Club of the capital, prisoners were interrogated under photos of Hitler. Elsewhere swastikas hung on the walls. Some prisoners were forced to say "Heil Hitler" and salute.[44] Except those conscripted to work for their jailers, most lived with blindfolds, bandages, or hoods over their eyes. In extreme cases, perpetual covering of the eyes resulted in infection, infestation by maggots, or blindness.[45]

During the seven years of dictatorship that followed, detainees were selected for death flights similar to those pioneered by the French in Algeria. A dedicated army air battalion was formed, manned by personnel from five companies chosen for the unit. Told that they were being vaccinated for a trip to a rural southern detention center, one with better conditions, detainees were instead sedated. They were driven in trucks to a nearby airfield, their bodies loaded onto planes and thrown out over the ocean. One sedated detainee woke up and was offloaded before departure, but not before he saw the other bodies in the plane. Brought back alive, he managed to inform others.

They could hardly absorb the implications of what he had seen. "If we had known we were in danger of dying every Monday, we wouldn't have been able to go on," explained ESMA survivor Miriam Lewin in a Buenos Aires café in 2016. "We tried to convince ourselves that what the guards told us was true. Sometimes they would even let us see our families. You assume being in touch with your family would guarantee your life. But it was not true. They killed them anyway."[46]

American support for anti-Communist measures took precedence over any expectation of democracy. The junta was urged to continue with repressive measures as needed.[47] After the bloodshed and civilian detention in Brazil, Uruguay, Paraguay, and Chile, there were few illusions that Argentina's coup would be civilized.

Only months into the junta's rule, the US embassy in Argentina had rebuked the country for human rights abuses, delivering a formal statement to that effect. But Secretary of State Henry Kissinger opposed the embassy's approach. As he prepared to give a speech on human rights at a meeting of the Organization of American States that June, Kissinger encouraged the generals to ignore his public message.[48] He met privately with Pinochet, and likewise had meetings with representatives from Paraguay and Guatemala.[49] The newly minted Argentine junta's foreign minister, who came to the meeting expecting condemnation for the detention and torture of civilians, instead found encouragement. "If there are things that have to be done, you should do them quickly," Kissinger suggested. "We want you to succeed."[50]

Refugees who had fled dictatorship in neighboring countries — radicals, professors, artists, intellectuals, students, trade unionists, and their family members — now found themselves hunted in Argentina. Some who managed to escape were caught by Operation Condor, a collaboration between intelligence services of several countries that led to thousands of arrests and renditions.[51] Operation Condor was accepted as a legitimate counterterror organization by US military representatives, who compared it to a US Special Forces Team.[52]

Argentina represented the new face of mass civilian detention. Without large, purpose-built camps, officials instituted a cycle of covert kidnapping, interrogation, and execution to make room for additional prisoners, most of whom would also eventually be killed. The officers' casino at ESMA, the site to which the largest number of detainees were taken under the military regime, was no bigger than a middle school. Although only the upper floors were set aside as sleeping quarters for prisoners, it still managed to swallow thousands of them during the years of the dictatorship.

The ESMA torture site proved that it was possible to run a large program of detention, interrogation, and execution in a leaner, more covert fashion, bringing in suspects from scattered small locations on a just-in-time basis. More narrowly focused waves of arrests, hidden detention sites, and the systematic execution of captives after interrogation combined to create a stealth system for detaining civilians that was very hard to document. Yet in the end, hiding prisoners and killing nearly all of them would not be sufficient: even in Argentina the junta's crimes would be revealed.

12. Arrests and detention continued until the government, facing internal instability, tried to gin up public support by picking a territorial fight with Great Britain over the Falkland Islands. Popular unrest culminated in an unpopular war, which led to elections the following year.

Amnesty laws passed later in the decade were meant to prevent lawsuits against the state for any actions taken in the fight against terrorism. But two decades later, amnesty was rescinded, launching years of investigation. The Abuelas de Plaza de Mayo, grandmothers of the babies stolen from female prisoners, began to hunt for these children, eventually using DNA technology to prove their cases.

Given the hundreds of detention sites, and prisoners who had routinely been hooded, a painstaking process of identifying what had happened began. If any records of extrajudicial detention still existed, no military officers surrendered them. It was only through piecing together survivors' and witnesses' memories that investigators could begin to know where to look for evidence.

Neighbors who lived adjacent to what had once been a private home remembered hearing screams through the walls at night.[53] A prisoner recalled her small cell and seeing distinct floor tiles from the gap beneath her hood. Eventually investigators visited the site next door to the neighbors who had heard screams and discovered the floor pattern the prisoner had described—so much effort just to find one clandestine site.

More accounts were matched over time. Prisoners recalled hitting their heads or being forced to duck when they were taken into the basement of one detention site. A low cement beam in the bottom level of the casino at ESMA fit their descriptions perfectly. As pieces of the puzzle came together, megatrials of the generals and collaborators that involved hundreds of witnesses handed down convictions to thirty-eight defendants in August 2016. A similar megatrial in Buenos Aires was still under way in 2017.

Not saddled with the internal chaos triggered in Argentina by the Falklands War, Chile's dictatorship outlasted the junta next door. But the seams of dictatorship had started to give way there as well. In the 1980s street protests began, calling for workers' rights and an end to repression. Both peaceful and militant opposition forces gathered steam. After an unavoidable 1988 plebiscite proved that a majority of the population wanted him gone, General Augusto Pinochet surrendered the presidency. He stayed on as head of the Chilean army, his presence dogging the nation for another decade during its slow steps toward full democracy.

A Truth and Reconciliation Commission opened an investigation into the disappearances under the dictatorship. The government's Rettig Report carefully avoided naming perpetrators while trying to account for the thousands killed by the government since 1973 through extralegal means. Prepared under Pinochet's long shadow, the report met with criticism over the number of sites it had missed, what were felt to be undercounted executions, and its refusal to name murderers or acknowledge the tens of thousands of survivors of torture.

Once democracy had been fully reestablished, a second report tried to address the deficiencies of the first, finding that more than thirty thousand people had been arbitrarily detained and the over-whelming majority of them tortured.

13. As changes large and small transformed Chile, Felipe Agüero continued to visit his native land from his new home in the United States. Occasionally returning to Santiago for conferences, he once looked up his interrogator's phone number in the local directory and sometimes crank-called him during these visits.

One day in Santiago, he entered a small hotel conference room for a foreign affairs meeting with perhaps fifteen people and found himself face-to-face with a man he was sure was another one of his torturers—the tall, dark-haired man he had glimpsed through the gap in his hood at the stadium. The man came over and spoke to him as if they did not know each other, but Agüero felt certain that he had been recognized and that the small talk was an attempt to defuse the encounter. This man, Emilio Meneses, had apparently become a professor, too, and had joined the faculty of Catholic University, Agüero's alma mater.

When Agüero returned to Santiago on future visits and met with colleagues at Catholic University, he continued to run into Meneses. At one point, Agüero went to Meneses's office to try to speak with him privately. But no one was there, and he found himself waiting, alone and afraid. Why, he wondered, should he be the one who was afraid? He had no idea what to do, and tried not to think about it.

Yet the past had a way of inserting itself into the present. In 1993, Manuel Contreras, the head of DINA, was tried for his role in the Washington assassination of Orlando Letelier. Five years later, General Pinochet was arrested in England after being indicted by a Spanish court, charged with committing atrocities against Spanish citizens.[54]

The trials felt like a window opening onto broader accountability, though some lawmakers wanted to consider only cases with symbolic importance rather than rehashing all the abuses under dictatorship. "But who decides what are the most emblematic cases?"

Agüero asked himself. "All cases of torture are emblematic. Why not all of the cases?"

The decisive moment came when Agüero heard the details of the fate of a friend of his brother—a prisoner who had been executed during the Caravan of Death. The government death squad had systematically tortured the young man, breaking his back in several places and slicing off his ears. His execution was one more horrendous loss among many that might never receive justice.

In early 2001, Agüero sat down in his office at the University of Miami and wrote a letter to Catholic University denouncing Emilio Meneses as his torturer. The letter somehow made its way into *La Segunda*, an evening newspaper, igniting a firestorm. Academics in the United States and abroad took sides. Later that year, Meneses filed a libel suit against Agüero. He said that it was widely known that he had been at the stadium in fall of 1973 as a naval reservist but insisted he had neither seen nor participated in atrocities and so could not have been Agüero's torturer. The navy threw its support behind Meneses.

Agüero returned to Chile for the trial despite the risk of imprisonment if he lost. When he testified, he gave the details of his torture. Many of Meneses's statements about the events of 1973 were discredited. Thirty years after Agüero's detention in the Estadio Nacional, the judge ruled in favor of the former prisoner and dismissed the libel suit. Under the Pinochet-era revision of the constitution, the statute of limitations for abuses at the stadium had already ended. Meneses lost his job at the university but would not face trial himself.

The case was nonetheless a watershed moment for Chile. After years in which people could only discuss the dead and the disappeared, finally the reality of perpetrators and survivors of torture living together in cities and towns across Chile began to be publicly acknowledged.

14. The move toward clandestine camps in South America allowed whole sectors of the public to be insulated from the broader view of

what was being done by their country in their name. Governments insisted that no abuses were happening, and when presented with contrary evidence, each argued that only true terrorists were being detained.

The generals of the juntas also learned that repression could be atomized. A network of smaller, flexible sites could work alongside — or even in place of — compounds and barbed wire. Illegal detention, it turned out, could be tucked away in the everyday world, carried out with few people being the wiser.

Yet even clandestine detention could not stay hidden. The grandmothers of babies stolen from detainees marched on the Plaza de Mayo in front of the presidential palace in Buenos Aires every Thursday, year after year, decade after decade, until the thefts were acknowledged. Jorge Escalante, who had served as circus director in the Chilean camp at Melinka, in time became a journalist investigating the Caravan of Death. Years after his detention, he confronted the former director of the DINA face-to-face, saying "I was tortured" even as the man was denying that any such abuse had taken place.[55]

Perpetrators would eventually be brought to justice, and citizens across South America filled courtrooms to watch proceedings against those who had terrorized society for years. Although they would be held accountable for their specific crimes, the innovations they had made in camp logistics and interrogation would endure. Cross-border renditions, counterinsurgency strategies applied across a whole continent, and torture as the cornerstone of clandestine detention combined to create something new. In the wake of September 11, 2001, some of the worst aspects of military dictatorship would be taken up by the United States and Europe as counterinsurgency strategy for fighting terrorists at home and abroad. A twenty-first-century model for global concentration camps had entered the world.

CHAPTER TEN

Guantánamo Bay and the World

1. AT THE END OF December 2003, Khaled El-Masri, a naturalized German citizen and unemployed car salesman, traveled nearly a thousand miles on a southbound bus headed for Skopje, Macedonia. Asked to step off the bus at the Macedonian border, he was questioned by an official who kept his passport. While he waited for its return, the bus left without him, and he soon found himself detained without explanation. Taken to a hotel in Skopje, he was held and interrogated in English about links to places and people he said were unknown to him. During his Macedonian captivity, hours turned to days and days to weeks, and still he was not allowed to call his family. He started a hunger strike to protest his detention.[1]

After twenty-three days, El-Masri recalls, agents made him record a video saying that he had been well treated. Afterward he was blindfolded and handcuffed before being taken somewhere else. His captors began to beat him, and cut off his clothes and underwear before throwing him facedown on the ground. He could not see what was happening but would later describe a boot on his back pinning him down and some kind of stick or object forced into his rectum. A diaper and clothes were put on him. A new set of agents placed a bag over his head and shackled his ankles. Frog-marched onto a plane and forced to lay on the floor, he was tied, limbs splayed, to the sides of the aircraft and given two injections.

A series of hazily remembered plane flights later, he woke up in a filthy concrete cell in Afghanistan, accused by interrogators of possessing a forged German passport and attending a terrorist training camp. El-Masri spent weeks demanding to meet with a representative of the German government before starting a new hunger strike, which lasted more than a month. As his weight plummeted, he was eventually force-fed via a tube inserted through his nostril.

In May, a German man calling himself "Sam" was brought to meet him. Sam promised El-Masri he would soon be free. Near the end of the month he was handcuffed again and taken by jeep to an airport. He was chained to the seat of a plane and accompanied by Sam on the flight. El-Masri described learning that he was being flown not to Germany but to another country in Europe, though he was told he would eventually arrive back home. At the end of this flight he was blindfolded and handcuffed, and driven for hours before being taken from the car. Agents removed his blindfold and cut the restraints from his wrists. Returning his wallet, passport, and suitcase after he had spent almost six months in detention, they pointed out which direction he should walk and left him alone on the side of the road.

In time, *Washington Post* journalist Dana Priest would write about El-Masri's detention, as well as the CIA network of covert rendition flights that delivered terrorism suspects to third countries for detention. And in fact, the records of a Boeing private jet owned by what was identified as a CIA front organization suspected in these renditions logged travel from Skopje to Afghanistan on the date El-Masri reported being transported.[2] El-Masri would also identify a photo of an official from Germany's federal police agency as the man who had paid him a visit in Afghanistan.

Berlin would deny that the official he identified could possibly be "Sam," but German chancellor Angela Merkel stated that the George W. Bush administration had admitted that El-Masri's detention was a case of mistaken identity.[3] NBC News would report that a CIA "black renditions" team had taken him from Macedonia to a site in Afghanistan called "the Salt Pit," and that American officials had known for months that El-Masri had been detained in error yet failed to release him.[4]

El-Masri's case against the US government would be quashed on the grounds of "state secrets privilege," but several years later the European Court of Human Rights would find that he had been brutalized and demand that Macedonia pay him sixty thousand euros for handing him over to the CIA.[5]

Set free in what would turn out to be Albania on May 28, 2004, El-Masri at first feared that he would be shot in the back as he walked away. But no shot rang out, and he continued on foot down the road and around a bend, where he encountered three armed men who seemed to be expecting him. They walked him to a small house, where he spoke with an Albanian official. Driven to the airport at Tirana, El-Masri gave them cash to buy his plane ticket to Germany, where he went home to find his family gone. After months had passed, his wife assumed he had abandoned them, and she had returned to her native Lebanon with their four children.

El-Masri had not been caught on a battlefield or arrested due to involvement in any terror plot. He had been swept up without evidence and held without reason long after the government's error was clear.

As an unintended casualty—and there were many others—he had witnessed firsthand the new model for counterinsurgency that the United States was imposing worldwide in the wake of the September 11, 2001, terrorist attacks. He had lost sixty pounds through hunger strikes while surviving a traumatic ordeal of torture and extrajudicial detention. Yet as harrowing as his treatment had been, El-Masri had also been lucky. Not only had he been released, but one terrifying possibility he contemplated just before being shackled to the floor of the plane had not come to pass. He'd had to survive the Salt Pit, but he had not ended up a prisoner in the crown jewel of the new American detention system. He had not been sent to Guantánamo.

2. After American Airlines Flight 77 slammed into the west wall of the Pentagon and the twin towers fell, after passengers had managed to foil the other plot by crashing their plane into a Pennsylvania field, all the hijackers were dead, but the hunt for those who had colluded with them began. In a televised statement the night of the attacks, President Bush announced, "The search is under way for those who are behind these evil acts. I have directed the full resources of our intelligence and law enforcement communities to find those responsible and to bring them to justice."

A domestic manhunt began in which the government arrested thousands of foreigners and federal law enforcement then looked for crimes with which to charge them. Out of more than five thousand arrests, only three detainees were ever charged with terrorism-related violations.[6] In 2002, a National Security Entry-Exit Registration System was set up to fingerprint, photograph, and question men from twenty-five countries, all but one of them majority Muslim. More than ninety thousand individuals' records were gathered, yet they failed to generate a single terrorism conviction before the program was suspended nearly a decade later.[7]

Abroad, the response was even more dramatic. On September 14, Congress passed an "Authorization for Use of Military Force against Terrorists" that approved action against those responsible for the recent attacks and any government sheltering them. Six days later, President Bush addressed Congress, declaring a "war on terror," condemning the Taliban regime for repressing its own people and for harboring Al Qaeda. "By aiding and abetting murder," he said, "the Taliban regime is committing murder."

Delivering an ultimatum to the Taliban, he described a global network of organizations in places like Egypt and Uzbekistan that was complicit in sending people to training camps in Afghanistan. "Our war on terror begins with Al Qaeda, but it does not end there. It will not end until every terrorist group of global reach has been found, stopped, and defeated."[8] The framework Bush had provided would have far-reaching consequences. The United States had launched a global counterterror campaign.

The first twenty prisoners arrived at Guantánamo on January 11, 2002. Wearing what would become iconic neon-orange jumpsuits along with an assortment of ski masks, headphones, goggles, ankle shackles, and surgical masks (said to be due to fears of tuberculosis), the men were escorted off an airplane in view of a pool of reporters chosen by lot. A small group of journalists were allowed to watch from a nearby hillside only because some among them had refused to get on a plane when told to leave the previous day. A few detainees appeared to reporters to struggle and to be pushed to their knees in retaliation, though a Pentagon spokesman said that the guards were merely bracing prisoners wobbly from the flight.[9]

Prisoners were ferried to the windward side of the base then driven along a desolate road that led to kennel-style chain-link cages at Camp X-Ray. A cement floor and corrugated metal roof provided little protection from the elements. There were no prisoner latrines. Buckets were used, until sanitation was improved by the use of gravity tubes—metal pipes with an opening in each cell that ran downhill to allow sewage to flow away from the cages.

Past the prisoner cells stood plywood sheds for interrogation. More than a decade later, in 2015, public affairs staff at Gitmo informed visitors that airconditioning at Camp X-Ray had been reserved for guard dogs, which were sensitive to the heat.[10]

Who were these captives? Publicly, there were mixed messages over whether they were detainees or enemy prisoners of war. Geneva Convention protocols would be observed, the Defense Department insisted in the moment—though that would not turn out to be the case. For the time being, military spokesmen explained, the men were detainees. As if it would clarify anything, commander of the detention project Brigadier General Michael Lehnert called the captives "EPWs"—enemy prisoners of war—and explained that they would be held in conditions that were "humane but not comfortable."[11]

The confusion over the status of the new arrivals had serious ramifications. Debates over what rights the prisoners had and how they would be treated had already caused headaches for Lehnert. He had included provisions for Geneva Convention Article Five hearings—which would officially determine the status of the captives—in his initial action plan, but the Pentagon had scrapped them. Defining the 9/11 attack as a global war on terror, and thus an "armed conflict," allowed the government to trigger all the benefits of executive power in wartime, even as the executive branch repeatedly ignored accountability to international human rights conventions.[12]

A heavily redacted February 2002 memo from a CIA official to the Counterterror Center developing plans for detention and interrogation made clear that "if a detainee were granted POW status, and therefore is covered by the Geneva Convention, there are few alternatives to simply asking questions."[13] Fearing another imminent terror attack, officials did not want to limit their options. Six days later, President Bush declared that the United States would not be bound by the Geneva Conventions in handling the detainees.[14]

The moment the Pentagon turned away from Article Five hearings, the tilt of US detention in the war on terror shifted toward concentration camps. Committing to Geneva Convention protections might have resulted in rulings that protected the prisoners from torture and harsh detention. In the wake of the unprecedented terror strike, however, the government appeared to be less worried about who was legitimately detained than about preserving absolute control over prisoners for purposes of interrogation.

Abandoning the Geneva Conventions was crucial, because the interrogations, military commissions, and executions without appeal that were planned by the administration could not take place without extrajudicial, offshore internment.[15] Detention within the normal legal framework and protections provided by the US Constitution would never have allowed the tactics American leaders wanted to adopt.

In time, John Yoo, a thirty-six-year-old attorney in the Justice Department's Office of Legal Counsel, would build on an earlier memo justifying torture to redefine abusive interrogation in a manner that amputated whole sections of existing legal protections. For torture to occur, he wrote, addressing the Pentagon's general counsel, a "victim must experience intense pain or suffering of the kind that is equivalent to the pain that would be associated with serious physical injury so severe that death, organ failure or permanent damage resulting in loss of significant body function will likely result."[16] Even if "a government defendant were to harm an enemy combatant during an interrogation in a manner that might arguably violate a criminal prohibition," Yoo continued, "he would be doing so in order to prevent further attacks on the United States by the Al Qaeda terrorist network. In that case, we believe that he could argue that the executive branch's constitutional authority to protect the nation from attack justified his actions."[17]

Previous writing by Yoo had maintained a certain nostalgia for the virtues of absolute monarchy. Yoo wrote that the Founding Fathers of the country had not intended to break from the kind of unbridled power held by a king—they only wanted their own version of it.[18] In a November 2001 memo, Yoo had further hypothesized that the Bush administration could exert exactly that kind of power based on a 1942 case, *Ex parte Quirin,* in which the Supreme Court authorized President Franklin Roosevelt to summarily dispatch a group of Nazi saboteurs via military commissions. The *Quirin* decision had come down after two days spent on arguments, in acknowledgment of wartime needs. Only months later did the court appear to come up with a rationalization for it.[19] The decision looks more than a little suspect in hindsight, as the executive branch appeared to have used a military commission and capital punishment in order to avoid a public trial that would embarrass the FBI for failing to uncover a Nazi plot on its own.

But *Ex parte Quirin* could still serve as a precedent for a far-fetched argument—one that would sell surprisingly well in the midst of national trauma over 9/11. Hoping to assert the same wartime powers for President Bush to use in the fight against Al Qaeda, American officials realized that interrogations and military trials needed to take place in a location where the Supreme Court was already disinclined to support constitutional protections. The point of such places—Devil's Island for French political prisoners, New Caledonia for the Communards, and Ceylon for captured guerrillas during the Boer War—was to be punitive, and to make more punishment possible.

Many stories exist about who first suggested Guantánamo, but it is clear that the government was nervous about using other countries for such controversial conduct—especially when America's new partners in clandestine detention wanted extravagant amounts of cash for their trouble, or were skittish over the possibility of discovery.

The government had become so wedded to a narrative that required torture and secrecy that it was willing to try to invent a place of detention under US control but outside US and international law—a place to which an unlimited number of people could be sent without legal recourse to protection or aid. This is the definition of a concentration camp, and Guantánamo fit it perfectly.

The Supreme Court had already ruled that for legal purposes, Guantánamo was not automatically US territory. Just as several camps used in the Vichy era were rehabilitated during France's Algerian conflict, so too had Guantánamo's latest and most severe incarnation been preceded by prior problematic detentions. In 1991, thirty thousand Haitian refugees fleeing a coup in their homeland set sail for Florida on ramshackle boats, hoping to touch land and gain asylum, only to be detained at Guantánamo.[20]

Three years later, another eighteen thousand Cuban and Haitian refugees were likewise intercepted by the Coast Guard on their way north. As *Wall Street Journal* correspondent Jess Bravin noted, "some of the migrants were humiliated and beaten, or hooded, handcuffed, and left to swelter in the tropical sun, or held for extended periods in painful positions."[21] After migrant riots in 1994, two guard units were investigated for detainee abuse.

Meanwhile, a federal judge had ruled against the Clinton administration's decision to hold 158 Haitian refugees infected with HIV in a detention camp on Guantánamo, citing their current status behind barbed wire without sufficient access to medical care or legal advice.[22]

A second judge, however, would decide that for purposes of seeking asylum, the Haitians who had landed there a decade before were not guaranteed consideration. Leased from Cuba, Guantánamo was not, the court ruled, US soil. The earlier ruling had originally gone the other way, but the architects of US post-9/11 detention policy were able to seize on the second decision, isolating the island base from constitutional guarantees.[23] "Fenced off from Castro's Cuba," one official later said, "it is the 'legal equivalent of outer space.'"[24]

As with most key moments in concentration camp innovation, there were people who could not yet see the runaway train but could hear it coming. Colonel Miguel Supervielle, talking with Brigadier General Mike Lehnert about preparing to open the site, grew concerned over the army's inexperience with detention operations and the potential for human rights violations. The two men asked for permission to bring representatives from the International Committee of the Red Cross onto the island—standard operating procedure in any overseas detention setting. One rejection had already been received from the Pentagon; they waited through dithering in response to a second request. Just days before the first prisoners arrived, Supervielle himself picked up the phone to invite the Red Cross.[25] The call was one of the few heroic moments in Gitmo history, but those still interested in the rule of law were swimming against the tide.

Two days after Christmas, during an early press conference about Guantánamo in 2001, a reporter asked Secretary of Defense Donald Rumsfeld about the choice of venue for the detention camp. "Mr. Secretary, we've gotten into trouble every time we've tried to use

Guantánamo Bay in the past to hold people," she asked. "Why use it? Why is it the best place?" It was not necessarily the best place, Rumsfeld replied, but it was "the least worst place we could have selected."

3. When the United States got into the business of extrajudicial detention with Guantánamo, it joined a dismaying gallery of powers that had been using camps in recent decades. Bosnian Serb forces had created detention camps in hundreds of towns across a disintegrating Yugoslavia in the early 1990s, where they conducted widespread "informative conversations" to gather intelligence from detainees, while carrying out war crimes from systemic rapes to massacres against the Bosniak and Croat populations.

During the Second World War, ultranationalist Croats had executed tens of thousands of Serbs, as well as Roma and Jews, in the same region at the Jasenovac concentration camp, which became known as the "Auschwitz of the Balkans." In a role reversal forty years later, bitterness over the wartime massacres helped fuel extremists and inspire the use of camps once again, with Serb-run facilities adopting deliberate strategies of ethnic cleansing. A judgment from the International Criminal Tribune for the Former Yugoslavia in 2007 declared that the murder of thousands of Muslim Bosniaks in Srebrenica qualified as genocide.[26]

Serbian nationalists around the world continued to dispute that events at Srebrenica fit the category of genocide, while the Croatian minister of culture was revealed to have praised the Fascist leaders of the government that had executed tens of thousands of Serbs at Jasenovac decades before.[27] Multiple communities in the region have been profoundly traumatized as victims of camps and executions, but few want to see themselves as perpetrators.

In the same era, Russia had embraced extensive use of filtration camps for detention and interrogation in Chechnya. Between 1994 and 2003, during the First and Second Chechen Wars, some filtration camps had quasi-legal status; others were rogue creations. The Russian human rights and archival research group Memorial described how, in an attempt to deal with insurgents in the region, Russia progressed quickly to "mass detentions of innocent people," in which "their confession of the crime could be the only accusatory evidence against them. Obtainment of the confession was possible only through intimidation, beatings and tortures."[28] As with the French in Indochina and Algeria, use of field telephones for electrical torture was common.[29] Approximately two hundred thousand people—nearly a quarter of the population of Chechnya itself—were detained at some point.[30]

Declaring whole categories of citizens a threat to the governing power has been a staple of concentration camp strategy, but after the Nazi era, revoking the citizenship of an entire minority fell out of favor. It did not, however, die out entirely. During the apartheid era in the 1960s and 70s, millions of South Africans were forced to move onto Bantustan states—the rough equivalent of reservations—in the government's unsuccessful attempt to transform the non-Bantustan areas of the country into a white nation.[31] The state did eventually manage to strip citizenship from its black population in 1970 via a law that would be reversed more than two decades later, at the end of apartheid.[32] The Afrikaner legacy of dashed independence and martyrdom that were relics of the early concentration camps had cauterized the nation's refusal to bow to norms of global human rights.

4. Yet South Africa was not the last country to combine the loss of citizenship with massive forced relocation. A flight through Korea or Thailand to Yangon in Myanmar and a one-hour hop on a smaller plane can carry anyone to the Bay of Bengal and Sittwe, the capital of Rakhine state. Trees heavy with giant fruit bats line the streets, and what appears to be ten rickshaw drivers and one mini-truck cabbie per capita compete for any foreigner's attention. The town boasted nearly two hundred thousand residents a decade ago, but many of those inhabitants no longer live in Sittwe, having been relegated to detention camps on the outskirts of town.[33]

In the summer of 2012, reports of a gang rape and other violent crimes stirred tensions between Buddhist and Rohingya Muslim communities across Rakhine state. In response to the escalating violence, that October extremists led riots that burned thousands of Rohingya out of their homes. Vandalized mosques were boarded up; one was converted to a police station.

Under the state of emergency declared by the federal government, the Rohingya population throughout the region was loaded onto buses and trucks and dropped off on the outskirts of their hometowns, near Rohingya-only enclaves, or in the middle of nowhere, eventually ending up stuck in the kinds of camps for Internally Displaced Persons (IDPs) typically seen following wars and natural disasters. In some cases armed guards stopped extremists from additional pogroms, but they also kept the Rohingya detainees from leaving.

The only Rohingya permitted to stay in the city of Sittwe have been sealed off in Aung Mingalar, the Muslim Quarter, which has become a kind of extension of the camp system that has risen around the state. Roads leading into the district are blocked at checkpoints by red-and-white sawhorses wrapped in barbed wire, creating a ghetto in the middle of a city filled with Buddhists, Christians, and a panoply of ethnic groups the Rohingya lived among and did business with not long ago. Most residents of the state endured rural poverty even before the advent of the camps, but in the relative prosperity of Sittwe, many Rohingya had assimilated into urban life, working in construction or making eyeglasses and plate-glass windows. Some had attended the city university.

Since the 2012 violence, segregation has been enforced. But the borders of the camps are somewhat permeable. A few Rohingya work as day laborers for the military. As with many prior camp systems, nongovernmental groups enter to coordinate aid to the displaced populations, and journalists sometimes get government permission to visit the camps—or, failing that, are able to bribe their way in, if they do not mind putting their fate in the hands of strangers.

Camp structures vary widely up and down the narrow blade of

the coastal state, as do camp communities, but around Sittwe, hustlers work both sides. Outside drivers cart visitors or goods into the camps, selling the latter at exorbitant rates. Some detainees save their food rations to sell, though they always take a loss, dependent on the mercy of their buyers.

With a little cash, Rohingya entrepreneurs can import comfort foods from town, which they sell to fellow detainees for a profit. In some places longhouse frontage has been converted to small kiosks, with neatly hung rows of packaged goods and stacked canned sodas. A tiny money supply circulates and recirculates in a frenzy, constantly bled off by outsiders. One preteen shopkeeper in Dar Paing Camp in 2015 had taken over the business from his brother, who finally gathered enough money to pay a trafficker to deliver him from Myanmar into another country.

Across the first years of the camps' existence, day-to-day life was unpleasant but more stable than not. A sense of suppressed violence lingered, however, and reports of assaults by extremists haunted the detainees on a regular basis. Spies and informers lurked everywhere.

In 2015 soldiers in the Muslim quarter carried assault rifles, and security police patrolled with pistols. The guards were generally not from Rakhine state, and so lacked some of the local hatred for the Rohingya. Camp detainees were emphatic about wanting detention to be lifted so they could come and go at will, but in 2015 they did not seem to mind the armed protection, and at times expressed gratitude for its presence.

Approximately 4,000 residents live in the quarter itself.[34] Another 120,000 people or so are corralled across the state in camps created for those who lost their homes in the violence. Add in the Rohingya who did not flee their homes but who nonetheless one day found government barricades and checkpoints set up at the outskirts of their villages, and you have more than a million stateless people who live with some form of government segregation or communal detention in Rakhine state.

Early in the process, the then president of Myanmar denounced the 2012 riots and declared that local leaders' role in it would be investigated. But the country was in the first stages of transition from a military dictatorship to democracy. No one was taken to task, and eventually it was understood that the government found the situation to its advantage.

Those who were in Sittwe during what interpreters refer to as "the violence" tell of fire and pursuit, of fleeing homes without time to grab identification papers and family photos, let alone retrieve practical items. They describe the shock of recognizing their neighbors among the attackers, and of seeing law enforcement standing by without intervening. Some residents fled the fire by heading into the small lake bordering the Muslim district of Aung Mingalar, where two women were reported as giving birth in the mud during the riots. Hundreds were killed across the state.

As the camps took shape, international aid organizations negotiated a sometimes bumpy partnership with the government to ensure clean water sources via wells, to provide food and shelters, and to make inroads toward health care and sanitation. Registries of the dispossessed were kept to track the food assistance that was soon forthcoming, but in many cases residents were cut off from fishing, farming, and skilled work.

The poverty in Rakhine state is such that many local extremists have used the food, latrines, and wells provided to the Rohingya camps as a kernel around which to build additional resentment, describing them as luxuries preferentially provided to Muslims by biased outsiders. Most people in Rakhine state do not have access to latrines, let alone plumbing.[35] The town of Sittwe itself was not on an electrical grid until years after the creation of the camps.

The ghetto holds ghosts of an era in which at least some Rohingya managed middle-class lives. The nicest homes—a few still have their glass windowpanes—run slowly to ruin in the blistering humidity. Less sturdy houses fall apart in the ebb and flow of flooding. Plastic sheeting with a UN logo slowly replaces standard repairs, a concession to the ravages of isolation and dependence. Trees and vines grow over early improvised graves behind the mosque, while boys and girls in bright green-and-white uniforms gather outside their school. For those who are able to attend, the open-air path between classrooms lies half buried in muck and standing water. A plaster sign announces that Japan provided for the school's construction in 2005, a reminder that poverty and need for outside help has always existed in Sittwe. But it turns out that things can always get worse.

Outside town, the IDP camps are less vivid, their rows of living quarters arranged in grids, though people try to reclaim any arable inch for growing plants. As in Aung Mingalar, ducks, dogs, goats, and straw-colored hens run everywhere. Children follow strangers, having little else to do. Detainees live in longhouses, eight units to a building, with one roughly ten-by-ten-foot room for each family unit—whether the family has three or eight members. Each family shares a well, a semiprivate space for bathing, and a communal hallway with other longhouse residents.

At first the Rohingya were allowed to pay for temporary travel permits to other parts of the country, but these passes can no longer be had. Residents must use a bus, for which they pay a fare, that will ferry them only to visit other Rohingya in nearby camps. When tensions rise, bus travel is halted.

In 2015, thousands of Rohingya were smuggled by traffickers into other countries in hopes of greater freedom or paying jobs. Some did illegal work; others found only detention or even death at the hands of traffickers. Unless they resort to expensive and dangerous human trafficking, even Rohingya who manage to flee Myanmar are also stuck. Having declared them illegal immigrants, their own country will not take them back, and the ones to which they have fled do not want them.

As the flood of refugees has increased, neighboring countries have worked to block incoming Rohingya. Bangladesh, which counts more than thirty-two thousand registered Rohingya in its official refugee camps just across the border from Myanmar, has regularly threatened to move them to an uninhabitable island.[36] In addition to those officially registered, the country has also been home for decades to hundreds of thousands of unregistered Rohingya, who live in and near the existing camps without legal rights or protection.

Since host countries have not yet forcibly relocated such populations but are saddled with the consequences of another government's decisions, these international refugee camps do not fit the classic model of detention camps. In some cases, however, the willingness to isolate refugees in horrific conditions or the refusal to make any plans to address refugee needs can end up creating detention scenarios indistinguishable from those of concentration camps.

Before it was dismantled and its residents dispersed around the country, the squalid camp at Calais in France lasted a year, holding refugees in increasingly unsafe conditions while many tried to smuggle themselves into the United Kingdom.[37] Australia's more disturbing approach of paying a poverty-stricken third country to take its refugees into island detention at Nauru continued into 2017, despite the more than two thousand case reports of physical abuse and sexual assault recorded by detention staff and leaked to the press.[38]

These camp complexes are cousins to the mammoth camp cities holding Syrian refugees in Jordan, Lebanon, and Turkey—also sometimes funded by outside countries—where in varying degrees of comfort, tens of thousands of people seek asylum or wait for the possibility of return home. The largest refugee camps—such as Dadaab in Kenya, which holds more than 250,000 Somalis—receive comparatively little attention, unless governments threaten to close them down.

But many of these camp cities differ from the Rohingya refugee camps inside Myanmar, in that the former offer protection for populations from other countries, while the latter maintain a vulnerable population still at risk in deliberate segregation from their fellow countrymen. The Rohingya inside Rakhine state continue to live as internal refugees in close proximity to the very people who resorted to violence against them.

The successful effort to label them as foreigners has emboldened those who wish to deny them rights, despite the fact that Rohingya culture has roots going back centuries in the region, with the term even appearing in a 1799 treatise on local Rakhine dialects. In an attempt to tar all Rohingya Muslims as illegal immigrants, the state government has long refused to grant any validity to the word, referring to the group as "Bengali."

Officially, the Rohingya were cut off from full citizenship in 1982, though for many years the law was not enforced, and they had been able to run as candidates and vote during the few opportunities that had arisen on Myanmar's halting, aborted, and resurrected road to democracy. In early 2015, however, anticipating the national elections that November, the government confiscated the temporary ID cards that the Rohingya had held, rendering them stateless.

The Rohingya are the pariah group of Myanmar, but their most enthusiastic jailers, the Rakhine, are also looked down on by the rest of the country. The generals of the dictatorship had no love for Rakhine state, generally treating it as a backwater of hayseeds and traffickers whose natural resources and strategic port were best auctioned off to China for the benefit of those in the capital.[39]

The generals in turn inspired no love in Sittwe, with their surveillance and detentions under the military boot. Before the dictatorship there was British rule, and before that, there was the invading Burmese king Bodawpaya—successive overlords who provided a reasonably accurate unbroken line of grievance stretching back at least to 1784. This grievance helps the Rakhine feel entitled to exert whatever power they can today.

Sitting in a restaurant in Sittwe in 2015, not long before the elections, U Shwe Mg of the Rakhine Nationalist Party says, "We are a peaceful people. We want peace. But we can only take so much."[40] Asked how he still interprets the Rohingya as a threat when it is overwhelmingly the Rohingya who are in camps, he changes the subject. Insisting that he is not speaking for his party, he says that in the face of illegal immigration that threatens to swamp the state, the Rakhine people have a right to determine their own destiny. The Rohingya care nothing for education, he explains; they are religious extremists. He says this without apparent irony, disregarding the slogans of hate that emerged from the 969 Buddhist extremist movement advocating legal restrictions against Muslims.

He says he does not want violence and declares the camps a good solution for now—though deportations should follow. He refers to the citizenship law of 1982 that laid the groundwork for the Rohingya officially being rendered stateless, but does not note any of the reasons it was enacted or extenuating details about its implementation. Borrowing a democracy movement catchphrase, he says that all he wants is for the law to be followed, and asks, "You do believe in the rule of law, don't you?"

Drivers who smuggle journalists or contraband in and out of the camps have their own opinions. One who was born and raised in Sittwe and has never lived anywhere else opens up about the local situation, saying the Rohingya are a problem. Asked about those he grew up with in town—the ones whose parents and grandparents were also born there and ran small businesses or went to school nearby—he expresses mixed feelings. The good ones can stay, he says, but the bad ones must go. He acknowledges that some harm may have been done to those in the camps, but repeats the refrain offered by many in Rakhine: "We have a right to defend ourselves."

Some Rohingya have managed to keep their cell phones in detention, allowing them to share information, call for help in emergencies, and build public awareness around the world. One entrepreneur brought a solar panel into one of the camps that residents can use to recharge cell phones. Links to government announcements are shared, as are privately circulated reports of violent abuse by security forces. Complaints about lack of access to education and emergency medicine proliferate. The Rohingya may be the first group in the history of mass detention to launch their own digital public relations effort from inside their concentration camps.

Conditions remained bad enough in 2015, or hopeless enough, that people continued to resort to dangerous tactics in order to flee. Before rainy season closed off the Bay of Bengal as an escape route, thousands of Rohingya set out with traffickers who charged staggering fees to deliver them to new countries. Myanmar's government would have been happy to see them go, but other countries do not want the refugees. Myanmar learned that it could not empty its camps this way.

In the meantime, the US Holocaust Memorial Museum released a report the same year warning that the Rohingya are "at grave risk for additional mass atrocities and even genocide."[41] Others declared that genocide was already under way, based on reported mass executions that could be hard to confirm.[42] Senior researcher on Burma for Human Rights Watch David Scott Mathieson felt that applying the genocide label in mid-2016 was an overreach for the moment, though he condemned Myanmar's failure to include the Rohingya in an earlier census, as well as their stateless condition.[43] "The government," he says, speaking of the preelection regime, "shouldn't be caving to extremists and their racist agendas."[44]

A visit to the Sittwe-area camps reveals a culture leaching away, with few education and work possibilities, untreated chronic health conditions, and a people turned into scapegoats in order to pacify the demands of another minority, one with its own history of victimization by the government. When presidential elections in November 2015 brought democracy activist Aung San Suu Kyi's party to power, the Rohingya appeared cautiously elated, despite a comment Suu Kyi had made claiming that the media made the situation in Rakhine state worse by exaggerating the problem.[45]

What changes would even be possible remained unclear, since democratic rule was hobbled by the 25 percent of seats in the national legislature reserved by law for the military—a legacy of dictatorship. After no changes appeared in the first one hundred days and little pressure had been exerted on behalf of those detained, even cautious optimism faded.

Former UN secretary general Kofi Annan was named chairman of a committee in Rakhine state to resolve the issue of the Rohingya, and met with citizens and detainees alike. On the day of his arrival in Sittwe, more than a thousand locals gathered at the airport to protest what they saw as outside interference in their affairs. Progress seems unlikely without a non-Rohingya champion for Rohingya rights who is from Myanmar itself. There may not be a leader willing to take up that mantle.

In October 2016, the stasis that had held for years was shattered after an attack on three border posts reportedly left nine police officers dead in the area of Maungdaw, which borders Bangladesh. The government identified the attackers as insurgents. In the days that followed, government troops proceeded to close the region to observers and use automatic weapons and helicopter gunships to kill dozens of Rohingya.[46]

Despite the lack of access to some areas, satellite imagery confirmed the destruction of villages in the region.[47] Reports of a campaign of rape and the deaths of more than one thousand Rohingya were relayed by those seeking refuge on the border with Bangladesh.[48] In February 2017, the Office of the UN High Commissioner for Human Rights confirmed many of these reports, documenting the "devastating cruelty" of summary executions and burning people alive and calling for "a robust reaction" from the international community. The government has repeatedly denied aid groups and journalists access to the areas targeted for military action.

Though some camps in Rakhine state had initially provided protection in the face of 2012 riots against the Rohingya, by normalizing the group's detention and encouraging their demonization for years, the state and national government turned detainees into sitting ducks for a military with an atrocious human rights record—a military that the country's new leadership may not yet be strong enough to defy, if it is even inclined to try.

Standing in Dar Paing Camp in 2015, surveying an open stretch of field just outside Sittwe, it appears that despite sections of heavier fencing, there are places where perimeter security is lax. Even if someone lacked the money to pay traffickers to get to another country, it seems possible to slip away at night and stay clear of the roads—to make an escape. But the ability to leave the camps is not the biggest barrier. Little sympathy exists in the surrounding community for the

Rohingya as citizens, neighbors, or human beings. Dismissing the possibility of departure, an interpreter giving a tour of the camp says, "Where would I go? Everyone would know I am a Rohingya."

Asked what would happen if he were caught outside the camp, he stops to consider the question. "I have no rights. If I am caught, I do not even exist."

5. While the Rohingya found themselves erased from legal existence, the detainees brought to Guantánamo were more thoroughly removed from the world of the living. In January 2002, five days after the arrival of the first prisoners, Bush administration spokesman Ari Fleischer stood behind a podium at 1600 Pennsylvania Avenue and, attributing the description to Defense Secretary Donald Rumsfeld, called the prisoners "the worst of the worst."[49] The phrase would go down in history for its certainty, but the rest of Fleischer's statement lacked specifics. "These are very dangerous people...," he said, "people like them were in a prison uprising...."[50]

If Fleischer sounded vague about the particular crimes committed by the worst of the worst, it was for good reason. Neither the White House nor the jailers at Guantánamo had any clear idea who most of the men were. The soldiers of the Joint Task Force assigned to handle the detainees on their arrival at Guantánamo had been prepared to deal with 9/11 conspirators. They had staffed up with Arab interpreters who were ready to interrogate the new arrivals but wound up with detainees who spoke Pashto, Urdu, or English.[51]

Meanwhile, a photograph of the first prisoners began to circulate. Wearing sensory deprivation gear, their heads shaved, they knelt in two rows, heads bowed, facing away from each other. Some soldiers walked among them, while others stood guard in straight rows outside the fence. A triple strand of barbed wire and spools of razor wire framed the shot. General Lehnert had hoped to avoid running a "penal colony" at Guantánamo, but administration officials seemed intent on making it happen anyway.[52]

Although they lacked details about what was going on, observers recognized the symbolism that seemed deliberately crafted by Washington in that photograph. The image went viral, drawing concern and condemnation.

The British press was blistering in its descriptions of the picture, but along with its outrage there were growing suspicions about what Guantánamo really was. Within a week the *Independent* had used the term "concentration camp" in reference to Guantánamo and linked it to counterinsurgency techniques going back a hundred years. "The parallels between the Boer War and American tactics in Afghanistan are striking," wrote Cahal Milmo, "a large military power using its dominance to tread a narrow line between legality and military necessity."[53]

Julian Borger reported for the *Guardian* from within sight of Camp X-Ray and struggled to interpret what he was seeing. "It may not amount to torture, but the cramped metal cages baking in tropical heat in the US base in Guantanamo Bay seemed to belong to another more brutal era. This is a sort of Caribbean gulag, and without doubt the scene before us would raise concern if it was being run by any other country."[54]

American newspapers were more cautious in their commentary, and in some places strikingly enthusiastic about detention at Guantánamo. In a *Wall Street Journal* editorial published near the end of January, just twelve days after the first prisoners arrived, Claudia Rosett wrote, "The real shame of Guantanamo Bay has nothing to do with US treatment of captured Taliban and Al Qaeda fighters now held there. It has everything to do with the International Committee of the Red Cross rushing to the scene, waving the Geneva Conventions."[55]

By then the prisoner count had risen to 158, and commanders had to suspend transfers because the chain-link cages had filled. New facilities were constructed that spring, and more prisoners arrived. Former US Ambassador-at-Large for War Crimes Issues Pierre-Richard Prosper later described the initial detention pipeline in an interview with the Witness to Guantanamo project. Captives were sometimes rounded up wholesale in Afghanistan, he explained,

then herded to Bagram Theater Internment Facility in Afghanistan
and passed on to Guantánamo.

> Bagram was supposed to be a vetting place. They were
> supposed to be vetted, and those that didn't need to be
> detained were to be let go—and the bad ones to go to [*sic*]
> Guantánamo. But you can see what would happen is, as some
> people, as they reach capacity, are like, "I'm not going to make
> this call. You know...I'm twenty-two years old. I'm not going
> to put my name on the line and say this guy's a cook, and all
> of the sudden it's Bin Laden's lieutenant." Boom. They go to
> Guantánamo.[56]

Operation Enduring Freedom, America's invasion of Afghanistan,
included military action in countries around the world. By January
2002, US forces were carrying out campaigns related to the war on
terror in the Philippines, Kyrgyzstan, and across Africa. Paralleling
the way in which enemy alien camps of the First World War had
taken existing law intended to be applied against specific aliens and
used it to detain whole groups, congressional military authorization
aimed at a specific act—the capture and punishment of those
responsible for 9/11—ballooned into a blank check for antiterror
operations around the globe.

Meanwhile, Vice President Dick Cheney and Donald Rumsfeld
won their campaign to go to war against Iraq as well, citing the suspected existence of weapons of mass destruction there, along with
inexplicable, and ultimately imaginary, links between Iraq and 9/11.

Three weeks after Guantánamo opened, President Bush made
his "axis of evil" speech, indicting Iraq, Iran, and North Korea—
none of which had anything to do with the attack on the World
Trade Center. He used the tragedy to frame a larger battle, claiming
that in the previous six years, Al Qaeda had trained tens of thousands of people for jihad who were "now spread throughout the
world like ticking time bombs—set to go off without warning."[57]

The US Congress authorized the use of military force against Iraq one year after the attacks of September 11.[58] On March 17, 2003, after failing to win approval from the UN Security Council for concerted action against Saddam Hussein, President Bush delivered an ultimatum clearing the way for an independent US campaign in Iraq. One week later, the United States invasion began, and the issue of processing and holding suspects quickly became as big a problem in Iraq as it was in Afghanistan.

6. Who were the first to die in detention in the war on terror? The earliest casualties include Gul Rahman, who was suspected of being a guard for warlord Gulbuddin Hekmatyar. Rahman was subjected to sleep deprivation and roughed up before being chained to a concrete wall at the Salt Pit black site in Afghanistan, where he froze to death.[59]

In December 2002, Dilawar, a twenty-two-year-old taxi driver, was detained at Bagram Collection Point after being arrested with three passengers at a military checkpoint in Afghanistan. He spent his last days with his wrists shackled to the ceiling of his cell. By the night of his final interrogation, he had lost all feeling in his hands, and his legs had been beaten so badly since his arrival that they could no longer bend, even as guards tried to force him to kneel. He was found dead hours later. The military coroner ruled it a homicide.[60]

Just days earlier, Habibullah, another man at Bagram, was reported as having died in detention of natural causes, though his death was also later determined to be a homicide. Records indicate he was turned over to the CIA by Afghan allies who suspected him of being the brother of a former Taliban warlord. Kicked and beaten before his death, he had visible boot marks on his calf and blunt force trauma apparent in dozens of places on his head, neck, and body. It was likely a blow from a boot that killed tissue inside the calf muscle and sent a blood clot to his lungs.[61]

The war in Iraq only brought more detainees. During the invasion army soldiers faced widespread need for detention with no plan in place, so they improvised facilities. In time, prisoners were cleared for release or sent on to more secure detention, often on the basis of vague criteria. Saddam Hussein's former prisons quickly came under US control, and were used by American troops for detainees.

Nagem Sadoon Hatab died in June 2003 after two days in custody at Camp Whitehorse Detention Center near Nasiriyah in Iraq. Soldiers had brought him in on suspicion of selling a rifle captured during an Iraqi ambush of a US Army convoy. When he died, his body was covered with bruises and he had six cracked ribs. A tiny bone at his throat—the hyoid bone—was also broken, which led to death by suffocation when he was dragged by the neck.[62] His body was placed on ice with a fake IV bag strung up beside him in an attempt to hide the homicide.

Manadel al-Jamadi, suspected of supplying explosives to bombers, died forty-five minutes after his arrival at Abu Ghraib in November 2003, during an interrogation in which his handcuffed wrists were hoisted behind him, a position that dislocates the shoulders and causes unbearable pain.[63] More than a hundred people have died in detention thus far during the war on terror.[64]

The most iconic image from twenty-first-century US detention camps, however, did not involve murder at Abu Ghraib. In the photo, Iraqi national Ali Shallal al Qaisi stands on a ready-to-eat-meals cardboard box, an empty sandbag over his head like a hood. He appears to be naked except for a poncho and wires, which a subsequent investigation would note had been attached to his "fingers, toes, and penis to simulate electric torture."[65]

The 2004 Abu Ghraib report revealed that the guard force at the detention camp had been involved in many additional activities to help prepare detainees for interrogation, including sodomy with a chemical light rod and perhaps a broom handle, threats with loaded weapons, guard dog attacks, pouring cold water on detainees, punching prisoners, keeping captives naked for days at a time, putting dog leashes on naked prisoners, arranging groups of naked detainees so that their genitals were touching, and jumping onto piles of naked prisoners. General Geoffrey Miller, who came to Iraq after running the interrogation center at Guantánamo Bay, had at one point announced that he wanted to "Gitmo-ize" treatment of Iraqi detainees as well.[66]

These were just the results found during the military's investigation of itself. Inquiries by human rights groups found many more violations across the board. Forward Operating Base Mercury saw assaults on detainees (in one case with a metal baseball bat) for recreation or "to work out your frustration."[67]

In Afghanistan and Guantánamo, the Bush administration asserted executive privilege in order to permit torture.[68] Secretary of Defense Donald Rumsfeld further announced that detainees in the war on terror were not prisoners of war but "unlawful combatants," arguing that they had no rights under the Geneva Conventions at all. In the face of these arguments, military leaders expressed concerns, with Secretary of State Colin Powell writing to the president to protest that the current course of action would "reverse over a century of US policy and practice in supporting the Geneva Conventions and undermine the protections of the law of war for our troops, both in this specific conflict and in general."[69] Rumsfeld adopted the stance that US forces would "for the most part, treat [detainees] in a manner that is reasonably consistent with the Geneva Conventions."[70] Later, the administration would decide that Taliban members could receive certain Geneva Convention protections (which guarantee rights to humane treatment, food, and medical care), but Al Qaeda members would not.

The policy in Iraq likewise remained muddled for a period of years. Following that example set in Afghanistan, a detainee from the Iraq War was referred to as a "person under control" (PUC) instead of a "prisoner of war" (POW). Use of the PUC designation continued even after Washington officially classified Iraqi detainees as POWs.

Many prisoners were held only for a few days before being cleared for release but were nonetheless tortured during their brief time in detention. Extreme heat and cold, forced exercise to the point of unconsciousness ("smoking a PUC"), and daily pre-interrogation beatings ("fucking a PUC") were standard practice.[71] Testimony about the universal nature of the abuse came directly from soldiers in the unit. "If he [was] a good guy, you know, now he's a bad guy," one sergeant said in an interview with Human Rights Watch, "because of the way we treated him."[72]

Discarding the interrogation methods most often used by federal law enforcement agencies, contractors developed a set of "enhanced interrogation techniques" that was eventually reviewed by top Bush administration officials.[73] The water cure, which had led to courts-martial in the US Army during the conflict in the Philippines a century before, made a reappearance in a form called waterboarding. A confidential Red Cross report noted that one early CIA detainee, Abu Zubaydah, became a guinea pig for every new technique the agency employed.[74]

Zubaydah's detention at a black site in March 2002 was planned even before his capture, in order to keep him invisible.[75] Waterboarded eighty-three times in one month, he was at one point described as "completely unresponsive, with bubbles rising through his open, full mouth."[76] More than a decade later, the Senate Select Committee on Intelligence would use the CIA's own internal documents to show that far from being a senior leader in Al Qaeda, as initially claimed, Abu Zubaydah had been rejected by that organization.[77]

Accounts from former prisoners are even more extensive and show that the deliberate dismantling of human rights protections was felt almost immediately by detainees in every stage of custody overseas and at Guantánamo, which was merely the tip of the iceberg in a network of known and clandestine US detention sites.[78]

An analogue to these black sites could be found in the inmates themselves: along with the many official detainees there were "ghost prisoners," who did not appear on any ledger due to a September 17, 2001, directive signed by President Bush authorizing extrajudicial detention and interrogation.[79] Abu Zubaydah was moved to a clandestine location in a third country by the CIA in order to avoid declaring his presence to Red Cross representatives. The decision to hold in him in a third country was taken without consulting the National Security Council, the State Department, or the CIA station chief in that country.[80] The nature of the techniques planned for use against him were so extraordinary that all "major players" agreed that Abu Zubaydah "should remain incommunicado for the remainder of his life."[81]

The litany of torture that was a key component of US extrajudicial detention in the first decade of the new century quickly blighted the post-9/11 effort to seek justice, compromising testimony and evidence that would become worthless in court. One irony was that the 1975 US Senate's Church Committee hearings had disabled whole sections of the darker side of intelligence operations promoting assassination and human rights violations from the 1960s and 1970s. CIA interrogation manuals still existed, illegal covert operations continued, but across much of government, interrogation methods had moved on. Less illegal and injurious approaches were judged by professional interrogators to be more successful.[82]

As with the questions of detention and military tribunals after 9/11, the White House seemed to want to turn the clock back several decades. Yet many of those programs had been abandoned. If it meant to adopt coercive techniques, the United States would have to reinvent torture for the twenty-first century.

Interrogations overseas and at Guantánamo had begun in the usual way, with modern techniques applied in the wake of a terrorist strike. Mark Fallon, a career agent with the Naval Criminal Investigative Service, was involved from the earliest days at Guantánamo as chief of counterintelligence operations for Europe, Africa, and the Middle East. Even in the beginning, he says, he realized that most of the prisoners were "not just low-value detainees, they were no-value detainees," little more than "bounty babies" who had been turned in by locals for cash.[83]

He also began to notice that strange tactics had been adopted by other interrogation teams. Duct tape and cinder blocks had been left behind in interrogation rooms, which prompted him to bring up the issue of detainee treatment. He was ignored, he says, and frozen out of policy meetings with US Attorney General Alberto Gonzales and a core group of officials he felt had already decided how they wanted things done.

Before he retired, Fallon learned about a host of inexplicable tactics he felt were as alarming as they were pointless. "They had people dressed up like cowboys, in chaps. It was amateur hour," he said. "It was the *F-Troop* version of a concentration camp. I can't even call it *Hogan's Heroes*—that would have been too serious a view of what was going on. Putting a dog leash on detainees. Females were wiping red ink on detainees and pretending it was menstrual blood."[84]

Colonel Britt Mallow, also at Guantánamo in 2002, found the gallery of tactics similarly baffling as he watched coercive interrogation become "low-level people 'freelancing' with it, and high-level [officials] authorizing it."[85] Trying, as Fallon had, to bring attention to the abuses, he found himself rebuffed by commanders who seemed to feel that the detainees were hardened terrorists who merited such treatment although no one, not even the interrogators, knew anything about the identity of several suspects.[86]

Over time, detainee treatment got markedly worse. Two psychologists, James Mitchell and Bruce Jessen, sold the CIA on the idea that using experience gained in helping train personnel to resist interrogation, they could reverse-engineer a coercive interrogation program. Between them, the two men would be paid $81 million.

Asked in 2013 why it had hired men who had never conducted an interrogation, and who furthermore had no language or cultural experience with the population in question, the CIA responded that existing intelligence agencies had no experience with "non-standard means of interrogation."[87] The new interrogation program had been built around the idea of using coercion as its starting premise.[88]

What would lead a psychologist to develop a program designed to mentally demolish suspects and induce total helplessness? Finally acknowledging in 2014 his role as an architect of the program, James

Mitchell explained that on 9/11, he had been at home watching events unfold. "It was horrific that people had to choose between burning to death or jumping off of buildings," he said in an interview. "I don't think that should happen to anybody. And so I called up one of the people who was managing one of my contracts and said, 'I want to be part of the solution.'...I thought back to all those people that died for no reason. And so I was willing to help any way I could."[89]

Mitchell has said that he personally waterboarded Abu Zubay-dah,[90] whose interrogation was later deemed of no value and whose identification as a top lieutenant of Al Qaeda was declared to have been mistaken. He also claims to have waterboarded Khalid Sheikh Mohammed, who is currently facing charges as a defendant in the 9/11 trial.[91] Between them, these men were subjected to water torture in which they sometimes lost consciousness or appeared to drown 266 times.[92]

7. Concentration camps exist to exert control. Torture is a part of that—it breaks resistance and reduces the captive to an utterly dependent body. Under torture, guilt or innocence becomes irrelevant. Whether he was a terrorist or not, Manadel al-Jamadi died in Iraq with his handcuffed wrists hoisted behind him, the same technique that had shattered Resistance fighter Jean Améry when the Gestapo applied it half a century before.

Once a prisoner is tortured, detention becomes a continuation of the torture, and torture becomes an extension of detention, until they are indistinguishable from each other. Summing up her experience of detention in the officers' casino at the Navy Mechanical School in Buenos Aires, survivor Miriam Lewin says, "It was all torture."[93] Years after his abuse, Ali Shallal al Qaisi, the hooded man in the photo from Abu Ghraib, said, "I even have recurring nightmares that I'm in my cell at Abu Ghraib, cell 49 as they called it, being tortured at the hands of the people of a great nation that carries the torch of freedom and human rights."[94]

Along with torture, concentration camps can deliver other, powerful kinds of punishment via the open-ended nature of detention. During the First World War, inmates lingered in internment year after year with no idea how or when they would be freed. Detainees in Guantánamo have the added uncertainty of not knowing whether they will face prosecution on terrorism charges. Some have gone free, some are slated to be held indefinitely, and some may one day go on trial. But in the complicated morass of Guantánamo, even detainees currently facing charges in the military commissions system remain in limbo.

The chief prosecutor in those cases, Brigadier General Mark Martins, was first in his class at West Point, served on the *Harvard Law Review,* and twice received the Bronze Star. Over six feet tall and lean, Martins is a dedicated runner and has the temperament of a competitor who enjoys hills.

After the invasion and the subsequent abuse revelations in Iraq, he spearheaded the Rule of Law campaign for coalition forces there. Moving on to Afghanistan, he led efforts to bring the US detainee operations there into line with international legal norms and supervised the detention camp built at Parwan to replace the mess that had been Bagram. Human rights groups working in Afghanistan praised Martins's willingness to meet with them, and some detainees in custody after this period in Iraq reported more humane conditions.[95]

The facilities Martins helped clean up were turned over to Iraq by 2010 and Afghanistan in 2013. But even then, the transfer was contentious and delayed as the United States tried to retain control over when and if certain detainees would be released, planning to effectively detain some of them indefinitely. Afghan officials balked at the conditions, suggesting that America's demands for extrajudicial detention would violate their country's new constitution.[96]

General Martins believes that the US government can prevail in the pending cases in which it has brought charges against detainees at Guantánamo. Yet uncertainties remain, including a timetable. In mid-2016, Martins acknowledged that even as the fifteenth anniversary of 9/11 approached, "We can't say precisely when this trial will go to trial."[97] He has cultivated the fine art of patience: patience with reporters who show up at Guantánamo for the first time and want to talk about torture that occurred a decade ago, patience with journalists who spar with him year after year in the attempt to get new information on the same case, and patience with judges who sometimes do not accept the government's arguments. He gave up the possibility of promotion and a second star in 2012 in order to keep his role as prosecutor at Guantánamo; he later postponed his retirement to stay on.[98] One way or another, the military commissions at Guantánamo will be his legacy.

Before Martins came on board, the first military commissions at Guantánamo were intended to be a decisive spectacle along the lines of the Nuremberg Trials. But the system is littered with the detritus of failed attempts to conduct them. The earliest efforts to build strong cases had set staff loose among an undifferentiated Guantánamo population in the hope that they could find charges to bring. Scott Lang, the system's first deputy chief prosecutor, recalled a backward arrangement in the commissions' first months: "They gave you the criminals, and said, 'Go find crimes that might fit these criminals.'"[99] The inability to pin specific violations of the law on most of what appeared to be small-fry detainees was remedied by charging detainees with conspiracy.

Internal conflicts over unorthodox methods led to a laundry list of allegations against Colonel Frederic Borch, the first chief prosecutor, in which subordinates submitted written statements directly to him calling the military commissions they had volunteered to be part of "a blight on the reputation of the armed forces," "a fraud on the American people," "a process that appears to be rigged," and a task "I no longer want to be part of."[100]

A prisoner who was not expected to appear in pretrial hearings showed up and derailed his proceedings by pledging allegiance to Al Qaeda and then asking to represent himself. The interpretation provided in the courtroom was riddled with errors, further confusing an already murky process. Despite resignations and growing alarm, ten detainees were brought up on charges in 2004.

Meanwhile, lawsuits were brought on behalf of detainees. Over time, the courts began to assert a stronger role with regard to treatment of detainees. In *Rasul v. Bush,* from 2004, the Supreme Court established that Guantánamo Bay was effectively under US control, and therefore the court had jurisdiction and could rule on matters relating to detainees there.

With *Boumediene v. Bush,* decided in 2008, the court ruled that detainees still had a right to the writ of habeas corpus—to have their claims of unlawful detention heard. "To hold that the political branches may switch the Constitution on or off at will," Justice Anthony Kennedy wrote in his decision, "would lead to a regime in which they, not this Court, say 'what the law is.'"

During its seventh year, Guantánamo was at risk of being purged from the American landscape after the Supreme Court declared a key part of the Military Commissions Act of 2006 unconstitutional. Once Congress stepped in with legislation to revive the military commission system, however, it began the institutionalization of a judicial process that is neither fish nor fowl, neither civilian nor military, thereby creating an impasse that has led to indefinite detention without trial as a feature of American justice.

Along with the difficulty of establishing a military commissions system for use at Guantánamo that is constitutional, attempts to bring suspects to trial have been permanently hobbled by the legacy of torture. Declassified government documents confirm that at least six of the detainees in Martins's pretrial caseload underwent torture at the hands of interrogators.

Mohammed al Qahtani, the sixth defendant originally charged in the 9/11 attacks, was removed from the case in 2009 after Susan Crawford, the military commissions' convening authority, received details of the tactics to which he had been subjected—a combination of solitary confinement, cyclical humiliation, and physical duress that twice sent him to the hospital. In an interview with the

Washington Post, she described the process she went through in deciding that the techniques he had been subjected to could not be squared with subsequently prosecuting him in a court of law.

"You think of torture, you think of some horrendous physical act done to an individual," she said. "This was not any one particular act; this was just a combination of things that had a medical impact on him, that hurt his health. It was abusive and uncalled for. And coercive. Clearly coercive. It was that medical impact that pushed me over the edge."[101]

Even as she dismissed charges against him, Crawford remained convinced, based on the evidence, that Qahtani had planned to be the twentieth hijacker. What was the US government to do with a man they believed to be a failed suicide bomber whom they had tortured? It was decided that he would be detained indefinitely, until the cessation of hostilities in the war on terror.

On January 20, 2009, President Barack Obama took office as the forty-fourth president of the United States. Three of his first five executive orders addressed the concentration camp legacy he had inherited.

He directed steps be taken to close Guantánamo in order to "restore the standards of due process and the core constitutional values that have made this country great even in the midst of war, even in dealing with terrorism." Another order banned torture, and a third set up a task force to look at detention policies.

General Martins was put in charge of reforming the legal process for detainees, which led to the Military Commissions Act of 2009, a measure that expanded rights of due process but defended the nature of detention itself. He went on to become chief prosecutor in the revamped system and brought a fresh case against the five 9/11 defendants.

Under President Obama, the history of torture at Guantánamo was repudiated, but the military commission system and the indefinite detention it allowed were embraced. Although the new system offered more protections for detainees, it was still hamstrung. On the first day of sessions in the new 9/11 case, use of the word "torture" by a defense attorney describing treatment of his client by the CIA led the judge to admonish him for heading into classified territory.[102] The prosecution would later argue that detainees' accounts of their treatment by interrogators were likewise forbidden from discussion in court—that even their memories were classified.[103]

The process soon got mired down in the same morass as before. That year, prisoners started a widespread hunger strike. A handful of minor convictions for "material support for terrorism" (contributing support to those committing violence even if one does not commit it oneself) were jeopardized when one was thrown out by the DC circuit court. A decade after the establishment of Guantánamo, there was little to show but a gallery of tortured detainees and a broken process.

No person interviewed for this book was able to name any other group in the history of democratic nations that has been held without trial as long as the detainees at Guantánamo. In any case, the prosecution has made clear that those prisoners on trial who are considered dangerous, even if they are acquitted, may be held until the end of the conflict. No one knows when that might be.

8. Fourteen years, four months, and twenty-nine days after hijackers brought down the twin towers of the World Trade Center in Manhattan, pretrial hearings for defendants charged in connection with the attacks are called to order at Guantánamo Bay. In preparation, on February 7, 2015, a single plane brings most attendees from the tarmac at Andrews Air Force Base in Maryland to the landing strip at the naval base in Cuba. Flights for these military tribunals carry military prosecutors, along with defense attorneys, journalists, human rights observers, and family members of those killed on 9/11. The passengers resemble the cast of a traveling theater production, which in some ways they are, with the court open for hearings only a handful of weeks each year. A brigadier general, lively student activists, rumpled civilian lawyers, and even

more-rumpled reporters—as constant as the seasons, they all return to Guantánamo.

Except for the beachfront setting and the turkey vultures feeding on the carcasses of banana rats, the naval base is as American as any town in Kansas. Students attend W. T. Sampson Elementary or the base high school. A main road runs through downtown, passing by Subway, McDonalds, and KFC, and free movies are available in an outdoor amphitheater for anyone on the base not in detention. On February 11, 2015, the crowd is invited to see *American Sniper*.[104]

From the ferry landing, a van carries journalists up a hill to the media center, which sits in a decommissioned hangar at Camp Justice. Orientation includes a long list of things that reporters are not allowed to photograph, and even so, the soldiers explain, all images have to be vetted before publication. Each journalist has already signed a thirteen-page list of ground rules, including an injunction against wearing "brightly colored clothing," before receiving permission to visit. A sentence on page four reads, "Attempting to communicate with a detainee and photographing or taking video of a detainee's attempt to communicate with members of the media are also prohibited."[105]

Contact with detainees is generally off-limits, and some among the detention staff do not want to speak to the press, irritated by adversarial reporters or weary of defending the facility against its bad reputation. For a journalist trying to gather news from Gitmo, such conditions make for difficult reporting, but for an observer without a daily deadline, the stage management of these trips is illuminating.

In early 2015, journalists and human rights observers bunk behind the hangar in US Air Force expeditionary tents, while attorneys and 9/11 families sleep in condo units a short drive away. A few miles down the shore, more than a hundred terror suspects are still held in solitary cells or in communal settings behind barbed wire and watchtowers, down from a total of 780.[106] Three current detainees were part of the first group of prisoners brought to Guantánamo in January 2002. Of eight military commission convictions thus far, four have been thrown out. Most of the original convictions were plea bargains in exchange for release to foreign countries. Fifteen years after 9/11, the three cases seen as high-profile are still in pretrial hearings, and the estimate of the average cost per detainee has risen to roughly ten million dollars per year.[107]

On the morning of February 9, 2015, the process of moving prisoners starts early. The detainees known as the 9/11 Five—who are charged with aiding the hijackers' preparation for their suicide flights—are asked after dawn if they will be attending the day's sessions, so that the convoluted process of shackling them and transporting their plastic bins filled with files and personal belongings can begin. Detainees often appear, although the trial has not yet begun. The hearings at this point serve to establish evidence and a framework for the trial that one prosecutor hopes might "take place in the lives of living men."[108]

After pilgrimage through security inspections and surrender of personal devices, observers sit behind glass in the twelve-million-dollar courtroom of the Expeditionary Legal Complex. The facility is theoretically portable in the event that Guantánamo closes and the trial is moved to another venue.[109] Audio and video of the sessions are broadcast to select military facilities on the US mainland, a press room at the hangar next door, and to observers, who sit behind soundproofed panes of glass.

The judge and the court censor have a button they can push to trigger a flashing red light and block the feed coming out of the courtroom. Two years earlier, the red light went off without the judge or the censor pushing the button, which made it apparent that some unseen hand, surely from an intelligence agency, had control over the courtroom. The furious judge addressed the invisible entity aloud, as if speaking to a ghost. "If some external body is turning the commission off based on their own view of what things ought to be, with no reasonable explanation...," he said from the bench, "then we are going to have a little meeting about who turns that light on or off."[110]

Due to the amount of classified material, what can be said aloud in the courtroom is a delicate matter. Attorneys on the case have to have security clearances and additional authorizations in order to access information about specific programs. Not every attorney or staff member can see everything. Occasionally, even the judge has not yet been given permission to be told about a particular item, and will refuse receipt of a document. If attorneys slip up and talk about classified matters, or even refer to the existence of some material, they run the risk of losing the clearances they need to represent their clients.[111]

At a press conference before the hearings begin, it becomes apparent that some of the defense attorneys have been deputized by their colleagues to handle the most delicate references. Everything is euphemism. But on the matter of how soon the trial will actually begin, defense attorney James Connell's prediction echoes the panoramic timetable of the prosecution: "Not only is there no end in sight, there's no middle in sight."[112]

This morning, detainees are brought in by guards. The prosecution, just one team amid the five squads of defense attorneys, sits on the right side of the court facing the judge. Counsel for the defendants sits on the left, each group filling its own row of tables, with each detainee in a chair along the left-hand wall.

Khalid Sheikh Mohammed, often described as the mastermind of 9/11, arrives wearing a Palestinian keffiyeh and takes his seat at the front. Behind him sits Walid bin Attash, accused of selecting and training the hijackers. Third in the row is Ramzi bin al Shibh, whose mental competency has been questioned by his defense team and who has complained of mysterious vibrations rattling his cell. Next is Ammar al Baluchi, accused of funneling money to and acting as concierge for the hijackers. Last comes Mustafa al Hawsawi, whose plastic bin has a prayer mat and a small cushion, which he places on the seat of his chair.

Seated just a few feet from observers, Hawsawi is forty-six years old but looks as tiny as a child. His defense attorneys say he uses the cushion because of rectal damage incurred during interrogation. Declassified government documents support this possibility. He, along with the other defendants, is up on capital charges.

As the courtroom is called to order, chief trial judge James Pohl begins by acknowledging the attorneys present for the February sessions. He moves through Khalid Sheikh Mohammed's counsel, then on to attorneys for bin Attash. As he comes to Ramzi bin al Shibh, he asks a question, but Bin al Shibh brings up another matter. He says aloud the name of the man who is interpreting at the court that day—a new interpreter, in theory a stranger to him—and explains that he knows who the man is. He claims to recognize the man from a torture session at a CIA black site overseas. Amid sudden bustle and confusion in the courtroom, three other defense attorneys chime in to say their clients are also indicating that they have seen the man before.

Judge Pohl declares a brief recess, during which observers try to parse the drama. Had Ramzi bin al Shibh come face-to-face with someone present during his torture? Was he lying? If he is mentally ill, was the idea a product of his mental illness? If so, had the other defendants spontaneously decided to go along with the invention? Was this some coordinated effort on the part of the defendants' counsel? Or if Bin al Shibh was telling the truth, would the CIA plant anyone with a role in torture sessions in the court? Could it have come about through incompetence? It does not take long on the island to learn that Guantánamo raises more questions than it will ever answer.

The judge calls the court back into session. The interpreter is gone, which means that Ramzi bin al Shibh has no one to translate for him. After two brief exchanges, the judge adjourns the court for the day. The first 9/11 pretrial hearings in six months were derailed less than two minutes after they started.

9. General Martins, who worked to improve detention conditions in Iraq and Afghanistan, has made the military commissions hew much closer to democratic principles. He has argued for the legitimacy of the military commissions project with his "five 'uns'" speech, trying

to counter public objections to the legal process unfolding at Guantánamo. Despite these criticisms, he argues, military commissions are not "unfair, unsettled, unknown, unbounded, and unnecessary." Nor are they un-American, he adds, as he details their use by Abraham Lincoln.

Martins exudes honor the way most humans sweat. He also has a brilliant mind, and as one follows the speech point by point, one can almost see the clean elegance of the military commission system that exists in his head: pristine, efficient, and just, rendering legitimate all the years of detention.

The reality of life at Guantánamo drags this vision down to earth. This military commissions process cannot be separated from the detention setting that was created to accommodate it. It is a tragedy for justice that at this point, the trials have become a referendum on the place and the system. They have fallen far short of Nuremberg, and the spectacle has repeatedly been reduced to a show trial—stage-managed, with an invisible authority secretly in control of the courtroom and the FBI infiltrating a defense team in an attempt to investigate possible disclosure of classified information. Such tactics are hardly equivalent to the interrogation and detention atrocities of Soviet Russia, but that is not the bar in a democracy.

The trial at this point has moved beyond the guilt or innocence of the five 9/11 defendants, who wanted to plead guilty in 2008, though the judge was unclear on whether or not he could accept their plea. But determining guilt or innocence is not what the initial Guantánamo system was designed for—it was built for rough justice, which even the revamped military commissions cannot now achieve. Having failed in this, after fifteen years the government has to hold a high-profile trial in order to justify the entire architecture of detention and interrogation out of which the commissions arose.

Across concentration camp history, each country developed its own particular strain of extrajudicial detention and picked up the tools that were accessible, borrowing from the past and inventing new facets of internment as it went along. It was not necessary to directly model Guantánamo tactics on British "deep interrogation" of Irish Republican Army suspects, yet the strategies of prolonged standing postures, noise bombardment, and sleep deprivation worked their way from Europe to the Americas and into international counterinsurgency efforts before ending up at the naval base. No one in the war on terror had to choose to emulate Nazi "night and fog" renditions, when the French, who had been subjected to them, took up the method themselves and brought it into the arsenal of tactics acceptable for use against terror suspects.

In the 1990s, Guantánamo began as a refugee camp and was transformed into a full-fledged detention camp. After 9/11, everything necessary to turn it into a concentration camp—the physical site and a set of permissible tactics—was close at hand. The reinvention of officially sanctioned torture by a democratic nation after other free nations had largely left it behind stands as one of Guantánamo's contributions to concentration camp history. The other is the never-ending bureaucracy of trial by military commission.

Key members of Congress have continued to embrace Guantánamo as a punitive site for detention and torture—such as Arkansas senator Tom Cotton saying in 2015 that the camp's prisoners "can rot in hell."[113]

This embrace of brutal forms of detention does not come solely from political figures but bleeds over into domestic law enforcement as well. In response to a lawsuit, the Federal Bureau of Prisons acknowledged in November 2016 that its employees had visited Guantánamo and a black site—believed to be the Salt Pit in Afghanistan—in 2002 in order to advise the CIA on detention. The employees gave the sites their stamp of approval and reported in their assessment that they "were 'WOW'ed" by the visits, because they had "never been in a facility where individuals are so sensory deprived."[114]

During the 2016 presidential campaign, following terror attacks in Europe and America, several leading candidates advocated not only keeping Guantánamo open but reinstating torture there.[115]

The winning candidate included waterboarding among the top five priorities of the incoming administration and after inauguration quickly moved to bar entry to the US from seven majority-Muslim nations.[116] From vowing to send Islamic militants to Gitmo "to find out everything they know" to promising "a hell of a lot worse than waterboarding," key political figures have continued to advocate using brutal tactics against suspected Muslim terrorists.[117]

Under these circumstances it may be impossible to ever close Guantánamo, yet it may also remain impossible to get the five 9/11 defendants a fair trial, as the insistence on due process collides with the fundamental rejection of human rights that has undergirded the project from its beginning. Guantánamo is antithetical to democracy; the system is choking on itself.

Asked in a roundtable meeting at Camp Justice whether the military commissions, having gone on so long, are likely to set a precedent for how to handle terrorism cases in the future, 9/11 defense attorneys laugh. James Connell, who represents Ammar al Baluchi in the 9/11 case, predicts, "We will not have military commissions for another fifty years—until we forget again."

James Harrington, who represents Ramzi bin al Shibh, the detainee who linked the court interpreter to black-site torture sessions, chimes in: "He's being too optimistic. It'll be more like twenty years." Connell adds, "If you would design a model that would be the worst model you could use, this is it—in part because of the way this is structured, in part because of where we are."[118]

Among the weeds of the now abandoned Camp X-Ray, chain-link cages sit not far from interrogation sheds with no windows as the plywood buildings fall to ruin. At Camp Echo, trailers with mesh metal interior walls offer metal brackets with which to shackle prisoners' ankles to the floor during meetings with their attorneys. Attorneys once found listening devices installed in the overhead smoke detectors there.[119]

Camp Delta, where three captives were discovered hanging in

their cells in 2006, no longer holds prisoners. Camp Iguana, a small set of individual sheds by the sea, first held child detainees and then Uighur prisoners from China while a federal court demanded their release. The clean narrow rooms of Camp 5 are modeled on a prison in Bunker Hill, Indiana. Camp 5's cells held prisoners in solitary confinement for up to twenty-three hours a day, meals and water delivered through a tray in the door to ensure that detainees would have as little human contact as possible with guards—in part because some of them were flinging urine and feces at their jailers.

After a wave of prisoner releases near the end of President Obama's second term, Camp 5 closed in the summer of 2016. At that time Camp 6, a communal-style lockup in which groups of compliant detainees were allowed ongoing access to video games and movies, contained the bulk of the remaining prisoners. They constitute less than 10 percent of all those once housed at Guantánamo. Most of the men who are left, even those cleared for transfer, now have no idea if or when they will be released.

Camp 7 houses the high-value detainees—including the 9/11 five. The United Nations Special Rapporteur on Torture has asked to visit prisoners there but has been denied access.

In its torture report, the Senate Select Committee on Intelligence used the CIA's own records to reveal the massive torture campaign that was deliberately imposed as counterterror strategy. Indefinite detention without trial, even under the hedging category "alien unprivileged enemy belligerent" in use today, is a hallmark of a concentration camp system. To reject torture while trying to salvage the clandestine detention system that made the abuses possible is to try to square a circle.

During a February 2015 meeting in his modest office in a hilltop complex overlooking the war court at Camp Justice, General Martin says that in any book about mass detention, he would hope to see a mention of the tens of thousands of detainees who were cleared for release in post-9/11 American operations overseas. He listens and patiently answers questions about legal precedents for military commissions and explains the need to detain some suspects without trial until hostilities end. He emphasizes that the executive branch is not asking for a blank check when it comes to detention. He discusses President Obama's 2009 remarks at the National Archives framing the legitimacy of this approach. The bright, shining model of how pristine it could be hangs almost visible in the air before him.

10. During a trip back to Guantánamo to tour the detention facilities that March, a group of journalists heads north of the main base to visit the deteriorating remains of Camp X-Ray, preserved by the military after a judge's order requiring the government not to destroy evidence.[120] A brief visit to Camp Echo is followed by a longer tour of Camp 5, including a visit to an empty wing to look at the prisoners' cells.

At Camp 6, guards likewise allow a visit to a vacant section to see the communal living conditions—and a brief peek through a window into an occupied area, though hardly any detainees are visible. At the medical clinic, staff members walk visitors through a mock display of the restraint chair and naogastric tube used for force-feeding detainees on hunger strike, though such strikes have declined precipitously. They explain that many prisoners are on medications for mental disorders. The prison library restricts the material that donors can send but offers printed matter in a wide range of languages, as well as movies and video games. Public affairs staff provide a tour of the galley in which detainees' halal meals are prepared.

Current members of the guard force at the detention complex volunteer to meet for interviews. One had been in grade school on 9/11. He makes clear that whatever bad things might have happened in the past at Guantánamo, they are not going on now. Pointing out that it was a minority of people who were doing harm, he says he hopes that he can change for the better the image of what America stands for in the world.

Yet he does not mention exactly what did happen at Guantá-namo. As is standard practice in the military, soldiers and commanders alike rotate in and out in short tours of duty, from several months to two years. The guard staff moves on, the detention camp warden finishes his tour, and the commander of the detention side of the base leaves, too. Institutional amnesia reigns. Prisoners, though, have always been there; prisoners will always be there.

After only a few days on the island, it is hard to imagine the detention camps disappearing. Asked how quickly he could close the base if the administration somehow found a way to transfer all detainees overseas or to the United States, Rear Admiral Kyle Cozad, in charge of the detention side of Guantánamo, is caught short by his own laughter before he can regain his composure.

Even on the media tour, there seems to be little institutional memory about what was done where and when. A prepared script for the Camp X-Ray trip helps somewhat, but as to the background on buildings still in use — which is most of the detention area — people often don't know the history. At this point, much of it is surely lost.

The Senate Torture Report tracks the skeleton of the interrogation program, publishing the archival record to the degree it was permitted to do so by the CIA. The best overall source of knowledge about Guantánamo turns out to be *Miami Herald* journalist Carol Rosenberg, who was in the press pool on the day the first detainees were brought off the plane and has covered the detention camps and military commissions at the facility almost continuously ever since.

In his expansive *Torture and Democracy*, historian Darius Rejali says, "We live in an age where we substitute movies and storytelling for memory."[121] Rejali also found that while he was researching torture, the biggest challenge was often not unearthing that governments and institutions had done something, but understanding how what was said later about events reframed and blurred what had actually happened. In the absence of the Senate Report, Rosenberg and a few other journalists—along with civil rights organizations that have represented detainees—it is unlikely that we would have any continuous history of what the United States government did in the wake of 9/11.

During the March visit, the rear admiral agrees to do interviews with the press. A TV crew from Jacksonville tries to find a location that might show part of the detention camps without violating censorship rules. At the last minute they are told that the interview will be moved to the exterior of one of the newer buildings, so that viewers will have a chance to see that the captives are held in modern facilities.

As everyone waits for the admiral to arrive, guards appear out of nowhere, walking a detainee toward a camp entrance. They are just yards away. The bearded detainee resembles a shaggy prophet in chains. The soldiers setting up the interview freeze; it's instantly clear that this moment was not supposed to happen. The detainee catches sight of the visitors, or perhaps the TV camera, and calls out a cheery, loud "Hello" as guards hustle him away.

A soldier on the public affairs team says, "Somebody is not going to be happy about that." A journalist expressing a wish to have gotten a photo only prompts a soldier to remind everyone that pictures of detainees trying to communicate with the press would have to be deleted anyway. That a shackled detainee hallooing at visitors in English was a minor crisis underlines the Potemkin nature of the trip. The tour is meant to show off the benign conditions of detention, not to offer a chance to speak with actual detainees.

11. As Hannah Arendt once said of violence as a means to an end, the end sometimes shifts or is never attained.[122] The use of concentration camps changes the world, but going forward, the most predictable outcome of their use is a world with more camps.

Reconcentración under General Weyler in Cuba in the 1890s appeared to be such a dramatic, fierce tactic that it was perhaps inevitable that other imperial powers would turn to it when conflict seemed intractable. In retrospect, it seems almost quaint that in the first decade of the camps' existence, three of the four nations to use them waited until they had tried and failed to put down insurgency by other means.

As for lethal government policies, genocide is possible without camps. By themselves, the massacres of Eastern European Jews outside the Nazi death camp system led to more than a million deaths.[123] Witness Rwanda in 1994, when the Hutu majority slaughtered some eight hundred thousand of its minority Tutsi in their homes, in churches, and on the streets. Concentration camps are not a prerequisite for mass violence.

But Camps have usually served a different purpose than genocide, offering many of the benefits of execution with few of its downsides. And once camps had established themselves as legally acceptable in the First World War, they dominated the rest of the century. Among totalitarian societies, the Gulag was followed by the Holocaust, yet even the democratic British quietly used colonial camps to deal with insurgents and political opponents.

At the height of the Second World War millions were simultaneously on their way to or held in transit camps, German *Konzentrationslager,* punitive Gulag camps, enemy alien camps embracing dozens of nationalities, and Nazi death camps. The second half of the century brought new Communist camp systems. Meanwhile, Cold War rivalries encouraged sophisticated use of camps in anti-Communist or counterterror campaigns at home and abroad.

Over time, counterinsurgency campaigns added new components to concentration camps. Rendition, employed extensively during Operation Condor in South America, in which countries kidnapped and turned over suspects to each other for interrogation or detention, remains an active legacy of the era. After 9/11 the United States relied on its allies to provide black site detention spaces for suspects detained outside the rule of law—a kind of

just-in-time detention. In addition, the business trend of outsourc-
ing found echoes in the US Army's hiring of private contractors to
conduct interrogations at Abu Ghraib.

12. Keeping in mind Hannah Arendt's theory that from a legal
standpoint, concentration camp detainees are generally worse off
than convicted criminals, one question to ask about Guantánamo is
whether most detainees would be better off if convicted. The answer,
since several captives there who entered plea bargains have been
released long before many of their untried fellow prisoners, is a
resounding yes.

The 2014 Senate Torture Report represented a massive attempt,
years in the making, to bring the kind of accountability that has
allowed other nations to leave torture and extrajudicial detention
behind. But it was resisted by the CIA, which managed to block dis-
semination of the full, nearly seven-thousand-page account of the
committee's investigation.

Meanwhile, the House of Representatives voted to prevent Guantánamo prisoners from being relocated to the United States, thus
keeping the camps there open. The country has spent the past ten
years simultaneously systematizing indefinite detention and repudi-
ating it. America is clearly not preparing to build the next Auschwitz, or even Dachau, but it has not yet decided whether it wants a
permanent system of detention without trial, a system almost every
other democracy has rejected or limited to brief chronological
duration.

If these mechanisms of detention are left in place worldwide, an
attorney will always appear with a legal rationale for the impulse to
detain and torture at will. Where abuse is set as policy, someone to
play "the Butcher" can always be found. In the wake of terrorism in
Chattanooga in 2015, a retired American general suggested preemptive detention camps for those believed to be Muslim radicals.[124] In
2016, a former French president proposed internment camps.[125] Dur-

ing the Iraq War, a strategist with the US Army Training and Doctrine Command argued that a policy of internment camps for Sunni Muslims might be the best last-resort choice to defeat the insurgency in Iraq, and could be done benevolently with the cooperation of the Iraqi government.[126] Honorable people can do terrible things.

13. The opaque logic of Guantánamo persists in trying to move forward as if the past had never happened. On February 10, 2015, the day after 9/11 defendant Ramzi bin al Shibh accused his translator of being present at a CIA black site where he was tortured, no public sessions are held at the war court. Defense attorneys are scathing about what they believe to be an additional attempt to infiltrate the defense teams. That afternoon an army spokesman for the Pentagon, Lieutenant Colonel Myles B. Caggins III, tells reporters at Guantánamo that in fact the translator appears to have worked for the CIA. Caggins does not clarify whether the interpreter had been present at a black site or involved in torture sessions.

By the time court reconvenes on February 11, another translator has been flown to Guantánamo. Chief Prosecutor Mark Martins addresses the court to clarify that the prior translator had previously worked for the CIA but is not working for it anymore. That fact is not classified, he notes, but he reminds the attorneys in the room that the translator's name, his physical attributes, his appearance, the issue of whether the man has ever visited that courtroom and whether he has ever even been to Guantánamo remain classified matters and cannot be mentioned.[127]

He suggests that Bin al Shibh's defense team might not have properly vetted the translator and files a motion to obtain the records of how and whether the required paperwork has been submitted. Defense attorneys ask to take a deposition from "the former CIA linguist," as everyone has taken to calling the translator. If he flew out on the plane that brought the other translator in, they might already have missed their chance to talk to him.

On the charge sheet filed for the case, prosecutors assert that Ramzi bin al Shibh received training at an Al Qaeda camp, was a conduit for funds related to the 9/11 plot, and repeatedly tried to get into the United States and attend flight school, which he was unable to do. They allege that he taped a martyr video in preparation for his planned death.

According to the Senate Torture Report, Bin al Shibh was captured in 2002 in Pakistan and turned over to another country for interrogation, then taken back by the CIA in the hopes of getting more information. He was subjected to torture techniques for more than a month, after which detention site personnel recommended an end to the enhanced interrogation. CIA headquarters overruled the request.

Apparently interrogators passed along information gained through these methods as new intelligence, not realizing that Bin al Shibh had already provided the same information to his foreign interrogators before he entered CIA custody.[128]

In the evenings at Guantánamo, prosecutors, defense attorneys, and members of the press end up at the same one or two restaurants. Later, journalists play Cards Against Humanity in the tropical heat. By Friday, the court has staggered through less than eight hours of public pretrial hearings in the first week of what was meant to be a two-week session. Due to other legal crises in the case, the next 9/11 hearings will not take place for eight months.

At the tiny Guantánamo Bay airport, waiting to leave that Saturday, everyone gathers to fly back to Andrews Air Force Base. At the crowded gate, the traveling show assembles again—the defense attorneys, the activists, the prosecutors, and the 9/11 families—their grief in some cases as fresh as it was in 2001.

Almost everyone heads home together on one plane, courtroom adversaries and allies alike. Near departure, the flight attendant turns on the public address system and asks the last passenger for the DC flight to please report to the gate for departure.

Then, unaware that attorneys are not supposed to mention his presence let alone his name, the flight attendant broadcasts the name of the translator, the last passenger out of Guantánamo we are all waiting on. It would be a breach of security in the courtroom, where his name and his presence are classified. But Guantánamo's reality, the reality of the black sites and the camps, applies only in detention or in special courts and has nothing to do with the world of the living.

The translator eventually appears. When the time comes, he walks to the tarmac. Whatever he may have witnessed, whatever he knows, he is free to go home. He climbs the stairs and gets on the plane with everyone else.

14. Even isolated from the world, covered up, and left behind, all the camps for more than a century were filled with bodies: bodies that failed the detainees, bodies that saved them, bodies that hounded them. Elie Wiesel was so plagued by hunger he felt his entire self had been reduced to just a stomach.

Argentinian prisoners who had their eyes covered nonetheless were able to identify detention sites by the physical geography of their camps—a kind of forensics of the body. In accounts shared before the Senate Torture Report emerged, many suspected terrorists reported accurately the damage inflicted on their bodies in interrogation chambers despite being told that the government owned even their memories of their torture.

In almost every case, documentary proof or witness testimony emerges at some point. With outside help, Mohamedou Ould Slahi managed to publish *Guantanamo Diary,* his account of interrogation and detention, while still trapped behind barbed wire. "This stuff will eventually come out," says Mark Fallon. "It's just a matter of when." He believes the United States would be better off biting the bullet and getting it over with.

We have detainees in indefinite detention. It's not about what they did to us. It's about what we did to them. If we're supposed to live up to our values as Americans, at some point, we have to say, "We fucked up." With the internment of Japanese Americans, we fucked up. Native Americans, women couldn't vote, slavery—we fucked up. The only way you get by these shameful things as a country is to own up to them.[129]

Whether America is ready for that reckoning is unclear. The presidential impunity granted in 2009 emboldened rather than shamed those who had advocated coercive interrogation, and torture has since become a rallying cry.

Without accountability, no dividing line can separate the past from the future. It is a hopeful sign that years, decades, or even a century later, many governments have been called to account for their actions. Along with the Nuremberg Trials and parallel proceedings at other camps, legal cases restoring property and money to Jews and other survivors of Nazi camps continue today. In this century, Germany has apologized for its actions against the Herero and Nama people a hundred years after its original extermination order. Japanese Americans who brought cases during internment were later able to prove in court that the US solicitor general had not followed ethical guidelines in presenting evidence. Japan continues to be brought to the table for resolution of the question of "comfort women" in Korea and China. The British government has agreed to pay settlements to the Mau Mau survivors it once demonized. Argentinian courts continue to prosecute members of the juntas for torture and murder, and to work with grandmothers of the babies stolen from mothers who were killed. Chile has spent years bringing its generals to justice.

And even Guantánamo, troubling as it remains, has surrendered most of its prisoners. Mass releases in its first several years have been followed since by more measured departures. Established by executive order in 2011, periodic review board hearings now give prisoners the opportunity to make a case for their release. But dozens of "forever prisoners"—those the government still believes are dangerous but for whom no evidence or only evidence tainted by torture is available—remain.

Policy planners will always return to mass detention, because it seems as if it should work, and it feels as if it could be done humanely. The damage done by concentration camps has never stopped the reflexive enthusiasm for their use. As Justice Antonin Scalia said of Japanese American internment, "You are kidding yourself if you think the same thing will not happen again."[130]

15. Twenty miles from the Spanish border, in a canopy of emerald trees, the entrance to the camp at Gurs deep in southern France seems like a path into a dark fairy tale. A single narrow road lined with identical stele on each side leads into the camp, but it is impossible to see through the trees where it goes.

Gurs is large. The road through its middle extends two-thirds of a mile or more, though most of it has fallen to ruin amid the trees and undergrowth that have been allowed to swallow much of the former camp site. Small signs mark where buildings stood, and walking past marker after marker for another island of barracks that has gone to ghost, it is strange to think of the world filled with these cities of death.

Many permanent Nazi camps were even larger, great metropolises and closed universes, here a machine shop, in this corner the rabbit hutches and the uniform factory, along that path whole warehouses for the clothing of the murdered, over there a crematorium. At several camps, buildings for detainees were burned shortly after liberation because of unburied corpses and the risk of disease. At others, such as Treblinka, everything was destroyed by the retreating Nazis in an attempt to hide their crimes: buildings razed, train tracks taken up, earth plowed, and sand from a nearby quarry used to cover what was left.[131]

At the death camp of Auschwitz-Birkenau, however, the shoddy barracks deteriorated on their own, slowly collapsing to ruin. Today, a reconstruction of the foundation of Crematorium IV, which was set on fire by prisoners during an uprising, now sits open to the elements, uneven piles of bricks scattered like broken teeth across the earth. Everywhere—on tombstones in the Jewish cemetery at Gurs, along the cracked bricks of Birkenau, amid dirt and debris—little piles of stones rise, tiny memorials to the dead.

At Neuengamme, in northern Germany, where gypsy boxer Johann Trollmann labored before he was murdered, a hush prevails. Most of the original buildings for prisoners have been leveled, little more than their foundations remaining. The long rectangular shapes stretching on and on resemble the graveyard for an institution, but one that refuses to stay dead.

In California, and at other Japanese American internment sites, the thousands of barracks are gone. After the war ended and the camps at Tule Lake closed, the longhouses that held families were split in half, loaded onto an improvised flatbed trailer, and hauled off by homesteaders. Today some remain outside town, with one still in use as a storage shed by a farmer, its interior lined with Japanese graffiti scribbled up and down the walls.

Leaving Guantánamo on a clear day, it is possible to see much of the naval base from above. As the plane climbs and banks north, the landmarks that visitors are forbidden from photographing for security reasons grow small and indistinct. The tents of Camp Justice blur with the media hangar and the courtroom complex. The detention sites fade from view. Rising higher, the plane arcs over open water, leaving behind the base and then the island altogether, along with the vanished remains of the first Cuban concentration camps from a century before.

Half a world away sit the burned-out villages of the Rohingya, the camps of North Korea, and black sites for systems yet to be discovered. The last moment in time when no concentration camp existed was more than a century ago; that moment seems unlikely to come again. The face of the planet is riddled with camps and the ruins of camps. Even from the vantage of outer space, it is still impossible to take it all in. There is always a location out of view, on the far side of the globe, where the innocent and the guilty and those in between have been trapped together for a time, for now, or forever. Old camps reopen, new ones are born. No final chapter can be written yet for the chronic spectacle of the camps.

Acknowledgments

THE WONDERFUL THING ABOUT ACKNOWLEDGMENTS is being able to give credit to those who made it possible to bring something new into the world. The terrible thing about acknowledgments is not having enough room to thank everyone who deserves it, since the list would be long enough to make this a two-volume book.

I am indebted most of all to the former detainees and concentration camp survivors who were willing to tell me their stories. This book would likewise not exist without the many camp memorial staff members and archivists in the United States and abroad who were patient and helpful far beyond the obligations of duty—not to mention the strangers who gave me rides and food, or made calls on my behalf during the inevitable crises that arose overseas.

My agent, Katherine Boyle of Veritas Literary Agency, has now managed to sell two unusual books on my behalf, for which I will always be grateful. My editor, John Parsley at Little, Brown and Company, did not bat an eye at the suggestion that a century of detention, death, and torture had the makings of a compelling story. Many others at Little, Brown, including Maggie Southard, Vanessa Mobley, Malin von Euler-Hogan, Gabriella Mongelli, Michael Noon, Chris Jerome, Claire Gibbs, Nicole Dewey, and the whole publicity team were also of tremendous assistance. I'm honored by their work on this book.

I would also like to thank the following people for their advice or assistance over the past five years: Beth Macy, Megan and Rick Prelinger (and their marvelous Prelinger Library), Delphine Schrank,

Jack Shafer, Laurie Hertzel, Michelle Legro, Alejandra Matus, Alberto Barrera, Beatriz Miranda, Toomas Hendrik Ilves, Saed, Martha Bridegam, Anne Applebaum, Nikolaus Wachsmann, Paul Lombardo, Ben Yagoda, Carol Rosenberg, Kevin Forder, W. Joseph Campbell, Haydee Oberreuter, Carla Avenia, Jess Bravin, Arun Rath, John Lawrence Tone, Brodie Bettandorff, John Ptak, Roger Repplinger, Tina Whang Solak, Jonathan Coleman, Patricia Ricapa, Tom Schumacher, Kayleigh Long, and Gabrielle Paluch.

Family, friends, and neighbors outside the writing world likewise helped in immeasurable ways, from letting me commandeer a spare room during writing marathons to helping with children or pets when I was out of the country. I also owe a permanent debt to my children, who have grown accustomed to my strange hours and odd topics of conversation when I am writing. I owe even more to my husband, who consistently believes in me long after my own hope gives out.

Notes

INTRODUCTION *Sailing to Guantánamo*

1. Jean Améry, *At the Mind's Limits: Contemplations by a Survivor on Auschwitz and Its Realities* (Bloomington: Indiana University Press, 1980), 34.
2. Ian R. Smith and Andreas Stucki, "The Colonial Development of Concentration Camps (1868–1902)," *Journal of Imperial and Commonwealth History* 39, no. 3 (2011): 417–37.
3. Fergus Millar, "Condemnation to Hard Labour in the Roman Empire, from the Julio-Claudians to Constantine," *Papers of the British School at Rome*, vol. 2 (1984), 125 and 128.
4. For more on this idea, see part three ("Discipline") of Michel Foucault's *Discipline and Punish: The Birth of the Prison* (New York: Vintage, 1995).
5. Walter Scheidel, "Slavery and Forced Labor in Early China and the Roman World," *Princeton/Stanford Working Papers in Classics*, April 2013, 8. These offenses are in some cases not ones we would accept as crimes today, but they were part of the existing legal code at the time.
6. Ibid., 9.
7. Quoted in Alexander Solzhenitsyn's *Gulag Archipelago, 1918–1956: An Experiment in Literary Investigation, Volume 3* (New York: Harper & Row, 1978), 36.
8. The institution of chattel slavery has much in common with forced labor and also predates concentration camps. While related in its global reach and its destruction of life and liberty, the international slave trade functioned along different lines, with the bedrock purpose of the suffering beginning in the economic sphere. Slavery did not develop around detention; detention was just one horrific element of using human beings as salable commodities to fuel national economies.
9. Lewis Hanke, *Aristotle and the American Indians: A Study of Race Prejudice in the Modern World* (Bloomington: Indiana University Press, 1959), 58–59.
10. John Ehle, *Trail of Tears: The Rise and Fall of the Cherokee Nation* (New York: Knopf, 2001), 340.

11. Ibid., 333.

12. Kevin Smith, ed., *Strange Visitors: Documents in Indigenous-Settler Relations in Canada from 1876* (Toronto: University of Toronto Press, 2014), 81–82.

13. See Article 155 of the Lieber Code (General Orders No. 100, "Instructions for the Government of Armies of the United States in the Field").

14. See Article 156 of the Lieber Code.

15. Jonathan Fabian Witt, *Lincoln's Code: The Laws of War in American History* (New York: Free Press, 2012), 343.

16. Percy Bordwell, *The Law of War Between Belligerents: A History and Commentary* (Chicago: Callaghan & Co., 1908), 78.

17. Joseph T. Glatthaar, *The March to the Sea and Beyond: Sherman's Troops in the Savannah and Carolinas Campaigns* (Baton Rouge: LSU Press, 1995), 142.

18. "Eyes To Weep With," *Foreign Affairs*, June 1923, 246.

19. Jonathan Hyslop, "The Invention of the Concentration Camp: Cuba, South Africa and the Philippines, 1896–1907," *South African Historical Journal* 63, no. 2, 262.

20. Leona Toker, *Return from the Archipelago: Narratives of Gulag Survivors* (Bloomington: Indiana University Press, 2000), 122.

21. Giorgio Agamben, *Homo Sacer: The Camp as Biopolitical Paradigm of the Modern* (Palo Alto, CA: Stanford University Press, 1998). "Today it is not the city but rather the camp that is the fundamental biopolitical paradigm of the West."

CHAPTER ONE *Born of Generals*

1. John Lawrence Tone, *War and Genocide in Cuba, 1895–1898* (Chapel Hill: University of North Carolina Press, 2006), 154.

2. "Weyler Is at His Post," *New York Times*, February 11, 1896, 5.

3. Tone, 189.

4. Ibid., 43 and 53.

5. Ibid., 80.

6. Arsenio Martínez Campos, letter to Spanish prime minister Antonio Cánovas del Castillo, July 25, 1895.

7. Ibid.

8. Philip S. Foner, *The Spanish-Cuban-American War and the Birth of American Imperialism, vol. I: 1895–1898* (New York: Monthly Review Press, 1972), 22.

9. Valeriano Weyler, *Memorias de un General* (Barcelona: Altaya, 2008), 21–29.

10. Tone, 157. In his post at the latter, Weyler developed a brutal plan to force locals off their land, a plan that foreshadowed the forced relocation aspects of *reconcentración*.

11. Tone, 158.

12. "Cruelties for Cubans," *New York Times*, January 18, 1896, 16. The insurgents' representatives attributed this quote to Martínez Campos, but endorsed its accuracy.

13. Murat Halstead, *The Story of Cuba: Her Struggles for Liberty* (Akron, OH: Werner, 1897), 124.

14. "Weyler in Cuba," *New York Times*, February 12, 1896, 4.

15. "Spain Recalls Weyler," *New York Times*, October 3, 1897, 1. This article quotes Weyler on arrival in Cuba the year before.

16. "Weyler's Draconic Laws," *New York Times*, February 18, 1896, 5.

17. "Gen. Weyler Denounced," *New York Times*, February 18, 1896, 16.

18. *New York World*, March 8, 1896.

19. Charles Jay Taylor, "The Cuban Melodrama," *Puck* (cover), June 3, 1896.

20. Frederick Funston, *Memories of Two Wars: Cuban and Philippine Experiences* (Lincoln: University of Nebraska Press, 2009), 10.

21. "The Debate in the Senate," *New York Times*, February 21, 1896, 2.

22. John Tyler Morgan, *Belligerent Rights for Cuba: Speeches of Hon. J. T. Morgan, of Alabama, in the Senate of the United States* (Washington, DC: Library of Congress, 1897), 130.

23. Ibid.

24. Tone, 155.

25. See Foner, Chapter 10, "The American People and Cuban Independence."

26. "Spain Is Full of Wrath," *New York Times*, March 1, 1896, 1.

27. Ibid.

28. Tone, 164.

29. "Gen. Weyler's Command," *New York Times*, May 16, 1896, 5.

30. "No Rations for Rebels," *New York Times*, May 31, 1896 (datelined May 20), 5.

31. "Spain's Press Censorship," *New York Times*, January 2, 1897, 1.

32. "Barbed Wire for Cuba," *New York Times*, February 25, 1897, 2.

33. Foner, 114.

34. Ibid., quoting William Calhoun, 117.

35. Tone, 207.

36. Stephen Bonsal, "The Real Condition of Cuba To-Day," *The Review of Reviews* 15 (1897): 103.

37. Marouf Hasian Jr., *Restorative Justice, Humanitarian Rhetorics, and Public Memories of Colonial Camp Cultures* (Basingstoke, UK: Palgrave Macmillan, 2014), 43.

38. Bonsal, 571.

39. W. Joseph Campbell, *The Year that Defined American Journalism: 1897 and the Clash of Paradigms* (New York: Routledge, 2006), 22.

40. Richard Harding Davis, "The Fate of the Pacificos," *Cuba in War Time* (New York: R. H. Russell, 1898). This volume of Cuba stories collected Davis's reporting from the prior year.

41. James Creelman, *On the Great Highway* (Boston: Lothrop, 1901), 158.

42. "Baffled Weyler Rages at the Journal," *New York Journal*, October 10, 1897.

43. James Creelman, *New York World*, May 17, 1896.

44. Creelman, *On the Great Highway*, 160.

45. "How Spain is Calumniated," *New York Times*, March 8, 1896, 1–2.

46. "Americans Dying of Hunger," *New York Times*, May 14, 1897, 4.

47. Valeriano Weyler, *Mi Mando en Cuba (10 febrero 1896 a 31 octubre 1897): historia militar y política de la última guerra separatista durante dicho mando por el General Weyler* (Madrid: Litogr. y Casa Editorial de Felipe González Rojas, 1910–11), vol. V, 11–19.

48. Such as those that ran in the Havana newspaper *El Comercio* in September 1897, included in the press clippings appendix of Weyler's *Mi Mando en Cuba,* vol. V, 197–98.

49. "Spain Recalls Weyler," *New York Times,* October 2, 1897, 1.

50. "Havana, Oct. 6," *New York Times,* October 7, 1897, 1.

51. Foner, 130.

52. "Cubans Dying of Hunger," *New York Times,* January 12, 1898, 4.

53. "Distress in Cuba Great," *New York Times,* December 28, 1897, 7.

54. "Miss Barton Gives Alms," February 13, 1898, 2.

55. Fannie Ward, "Our Cuban Letter: Part Two," *Deseret News,* March 4, 1898, 1.

56. "Capt. Sigsbee Toasts Autonomy," *New York Times,* February 13, 1898, 2. Captain Dwight Sigsbee, "Personal Narrative of the Maine," *Century Magazine,* December 1898.

57. "Incidents of the Funeral," *New York Times,* February 18, 1898, 2. Sigsbee, 259.

58. From a March 21, 1898, letter to Brooks Adams in Joseph Bucklin Bishop's *Theodore Roosevelt in His Time* (New York: Scribner, 1920), 87.

59. Captain Dwight Sigsbee, *The "Maine": An Account of Her Destruction in Havana Harbor* (New York: Century, 1899), 55.

60. No. 775, "Cuban Correspondence," United States Congressional serial set, Issue 3610 (Washington, DC: U.S. Government Printing Office), 25.

61. Foner, 243.

62. President William McKinley, "Message to Congress Requesting a Declaration of War with Spain," April 11, 1898.

63. "Ready for the Volunteers," *New York Times,* May 11, 1898, 3.

64. Frank Keeler with Carolyn Tyson, ed., *The Journal of Frank Keeler,* 1898 (Washington, DC: Marine Corps Letters Series, No. 1, Training and Education Command, 1967), 7.

65. "Cuba and the War Revenue Bill: Speech of Hon. Amos J. Cummings of New York in the House of Representatives" (Washington, DC), April 29, 1898.

66. Tone, 150.

67. Foner, 17.

68. Tone, 224.

69. Ibid., 234.

70. George Kennan, "The Regeneration of Cuba," *The Outlook* 63 (1899): 152.

71. Brian McAllister Linn, *The Philippine War, 1899–1902* (Lawrence: University Press of Kansas, 2000), 5–6.

72. Walter Millis, *The Martial Spirit* (Cambridge, MA: The Riverside Press, 1931), 383.

73. Linn, *Philippine War,* 32.

74. Moorfield Storey, Secretary Root's record. *"Marked severities" in Philippine warfare. An analysis of the law and facts bearing on the action and utterances of President Roosevelt and Secretary Root* (Boston: G. H. Ellis, 1902), 32.

75. "Political Affairs in the Philippine Islands," *Congressional Edition* 4235 (Washington, DC: U.S. Government Printing Office, 1902), 33, quoting *Manila News*, November 4, 1901.

76. "Political Affairs in the Philippine Islands," 33.

77. Storey, 33.

78. From the *Portsmouth Daily Times*, August 12, 1902. Quoted by Andrew Lee Feight in the *Portsmouth Free Press*, 2nd Series, vol. 1, no. 2 (November–December 2005).

79. "Gen. Bell's Spectacular Charge," *New York Times*, March 1, 1903, SM5.

80. Gen. J. Franklin Bell's address to Batangas officers, December 1, 1901. He noted that it was possible to implement more severe measures without resorting to excessive force to compel the extraction of information from a suspect, and that solitary confinement on bread and water was permitted, but only under the supervision of a doctor.

81. Linn, *Philippine War*, 224.

82. General J. Franklin Bell, General Order No. 3, December 9, 1901. The order continued: "for when inflicting merited punishment upon a guilty class it is unfortunately at times impossible to avoid the doing of damage to some who do not individually deserve it."

83. Report of Brigadier General J. Franklin Bell, U.S. Army, Commanding, Appendix C, *Annual Reports of the War Department for the Fiscal Year Ended June 30, 1902, Volume IX* (Washington, DC: U.S Government Printing Office, 1902), 270.

84. "Affairs in the Philippines Islands: Hearings before the Committee," *Hearings Before the Committee on the Philippines of the United States Senate in Relation to Affairs in the Philippine Islands (January 31–June 28, 1902)*, Volume 3 (Washington, DC: U.S. Government Printing Office), 2877–78.

85. *Buffalo Courier*, January 21, 1902.

86. *Baltimore American*, January 21, 1902.

87. *Detroit Free Press*, January 21, 1902.

88. *Columbus Evening Press*, January 27, 1902.

89. *Indianapolis Journal*, January 27, 1902, 1.

90. "Spooner and Tillman Have a Spirited Tilt," *New York Times*, January 29, 1902, 1.

91. "Turner Calls Smith Monster," *Spokesman-Review*, May 8, 1902, 2.

92. "Glenn Court-Martial Ended," *Chicago Tribune*, June 7, 1902, 3. However the water cure had been used in other times and places by other armies and rebels, it was in the Philippines—as with reconcentration—that it became a tool of the US military.

93. Louise Barnett, *Atrocity & American Military Justice in Southeast Asia* (London: Routledge, 2010), 132.

94. "Gen. Jacob H. Smith Is Seriously Ill," *New York Times*, August 14, 1902, 1.

95. "Policy of Reconcentration," *New York Times*, June 20, 1902, 3.

96. "New Chief of Staff Will Be Gen. Bell," *New York Times*, February 2, 1906, 6.

97. Rule 8, Rules of the Spanish Treaty Claims Commission, November 24, 1902, Senate Document 25, 58th Congress, 2nd session, 7.

98. Glenn Anthony May, "Was the Philippine-American War a 'Total War'?", *Anticipating Total War: The German and American Experiences, 1871–1914* (Cambridge: Cambridge University Press, 1999), 452.

99. "Intervention at Any Moment," *New York Times*, September 22, 1906, 2.

100. Richard Gott, *Cuba: A New History* (New Haven, CT: Yale University Press, 2005), 117.

101. Weyler, *Memorias*, 236.

102. "Embassy Lauds Weyler," *New York Times*, October 21, 1930, 25.

103. "Military experts have professed," *New York Times*, September 14, 1898, 6.

CHAPTER TWO *Death and Genocide in Southern Africa*

1. John Laband, *Daily Lives of Civilians in Wartime Africa* (Westport, CT: Greenwood, 2007), 92.

2. Robert Thurston Hopkins, *Rudyard Kipling: A Literary Appreciation* (London: Frederick A. Stokes, 1916), 253. Excerpt re: cup of milk is from "A Soldier's Diary," by M. C. Jackson. For details on the slaughter of animals (run down, burned alive, etc.) see John Boje's *An Imperfect Occupation* (Champaign: University of Illinois Press, 2015), 98–99.

3. John Bryn Roberts, Speech in House of Commons, HC Deb 28 May 1900, vol. 83, 1587–88.

4. Ibid., 1589.

5. Emily Hobhouse, *Boer War Letters* (Cape Town: Human & Rousseau, 1984), 18–22.

6. Ibid., 28–33.

7. "Liberals Checkmated by Mr. Chamberlain," *New York Times*, December 8, 1900, 7.

8. David Lloyd George, Speech in House of Commons, HC Deb 25 July 1900, vol. 86, 1212.

9. Samuel Smith, Speech in House of Commons, HC Deb 11 December 1900, vol. 88, 573.

10. Walker Barth and Roland Cvetkovski, *Imperial Co-operation and Transfer, 1870–1930* (London: Bloomsbury, 2015), 221.

11. Ibid., 221–22.

12. Ibid., 222.

13. Hobhouse, *Boer War Letters*, 32–33.

14. Ibid., 37.

15. Ibid.

16. Ibid., 38.
17. Ibid., 48.
18. Elizabeth Van Heyningen, *The Concentration Camps of the Anglo-Boer War: A Social History* (Cape Town: Jacana Media, 2013), 115.
19. Hobhouse, *Boer War Letters,* 50.
20. Ibid., 51.
21. Ibid., 55.
22. Ibid., 57.
23. Ibid., 60.
24. Ibid., 61–62.
25. Ibid., 59, 116, and 266.
26. Ibid., 49, 53, and 71.
27. Ibid., 83.
28. Van Heyningen, 151.
29. Warwick, 148–49.
30. Van Heyningen, 154.
31. Warwick, 156.
32. Ibid., 149.
33. Nomboniso Gasa, *Women in South African History: They Remove Boulders and Cross Rivers* (Cape Town: HSRC Press, 2007), 105.
34. Warwick, 155.
35. Van Heyningen, 153.
36. Gasa, *Women,* 104.
37. Anthony Marx, *Making Race and Nation: A Comparison of South Africa, the United States, and Brazil* (Cambridge: Cambridge University Press, 1998), 91.
38. Van Heyningen, 150.
39. Letter from Captain F. Wilson Fox to Joseph Chamberlain, Secretary of State for the Colonies, as part of report on the Orange River Colony, January 2, 1902.
40. Van Heyningen, xiii.
41. Warwick, 145.
42. Van Heyningen, 151.
43. Hobhouse, *Boer War Letters,* 68.
44. Ibid., 78–79.
45. Ibid., 82.
46. Ibid., 79.
47. "A Lady Missioner," *Bloemfontein Post,* February 21, 1901.
48. Hobhouse, *Boer War Letters,* 91.
49. Ibid., 92.
50. Ibid., 104.
51. Ibid., 111.
52. John Ellis, Speech in House of Commons, HC Deb 17 June 1901, vol. 95, 548.

53. William Brodrick, Secretary of State for War, Reply before House of Commons, HC Deb 5 March 1901, vol. 90, 557.

54. House of Commons Debate, 21 June 1901, vol. 95, 1053–54.

55. House of Commons Debate, 17 June 1901, vol. 95, 574.

56. William Thomas Stead, ed., *The Review of Reviews* 24 (July–December 1901): 282.

57. Ibid., 578.

58. Allen Welsh Dulles, *The Boer War* (New York: Gordon Press, 1974 reprint of 1902 original), 18.

59. Stead, 282.

60. Written account of Lieutenant David Miller, September 1901, as quoted in Keith Surridge's essay in *British Ways of Counterinsurgency: A Historical Perspective* (London: Routledge, 2016), 38.

61. Ian R. Smith and Andreas Stucki, "The Colonial Development of Concentration Camps (1868–1902)," *Journal of Imperial and Commonwealth History* 39, no. 3 (2011): 427.

62. Telegram from Lord Milner to Mr. Chamberlain, December 1, 1901.

63. Letter from John Percival, Bishop of Hereford to the *Times* of London, October 22, 1901.

64. D. C. Lathbury, ed. "The Week," *The Pilot: A Weekly Review of Politics, Literature, & Learning* 4, no. 87 (October 26, 1901): 462.

65. Emily Hobhouse, *The Brunt of the War and Where It Fell* (London: Methuen, 1902), 136.

66. Jane Waterson, "A Letter on the Camps," *Cape Times*, July 22, 1901.

67. Emily Hobhouse letter to St. John Brodrick, July 26, 1901. Reply from Brodrick to Hobhouse, July 27, 1901.

68. Birgit Susanne Seibold, *Emily Hobhouse and the Reports on the Concentration Camps during the Boer War, 1899–1902* (Stuttgart: Ibidem, 2011), 88.

69. Alexander Downes, *Targeting Civilians in War* (Ithaca, NY: Cornell University Press, 2011), 174.

70. "Report on the Concentration Camps in South Africa, by the Committee of Ladies Appointed by the Secretary of State for War: Containing Reports on the Camps in Natal, the Orange River Colony, and the Transvaal" (London: Eyre & Spottiswood, 1902), paragraph 33.

71. Letter from Lucy Deane dated December 23, 1901. Quoted in van Heyningen, 197.

72. Peter Warwick, *Black People and the South African War: 1899–1902* (Cambridge: Cambridge University Press, 1983), 145.

73. Horst Drechsler, *Let Us Die Fighting: the Struggle of the Herero and Nama against German Imperialism, 1884–1915* (London: Zed Press, 1980), 144.

74. BAB Reichs-Kolonial-Amts, Nr. 2113, 89–90, "Leutwein to Kolonial-abteilung," February 23, 1904. Cited in Drechsler's *Fighting*, 148.

75. Isabel Hull, *Absolute Destruction: Military Culture and the Practices of War in Imperial Germany* (Ithaca, NY: Cornell University Press, 2006), 63.

76. Jan-Bart Gewald, "The Great General of the Kaiser," *Botswana Notes and Records* 26, 68.

77. Drechsler, *Fighting*, 154.

78. Hull, *Destruction*, 60.

79. Casper Erichsen, "The Angel of Death Has Descended Violently among Them," African Studies Centre Research Report 79, 2005, 22.

80. Diary of Lothar von Trotha, August 11, 1904, as quoted in Erichsen's "The Angel of Death," 29.

81. Jan-Bart Gewald, *Herero Heroes: A Socio-political History of the Herero of Namibia, 1890–1923* (Columbus: Ohio State University Press, 1999), 195.

82. Ibid.

83. Ibid., 186.

84. Ibid., 195–96.

85. *Cape Argus*, September 28, 1905. As quoted in Erichsen's "The Angel of Death," 58.

86. Erichsen, 49.

87. Bartrop et al., eds., *Modern Genocide: The Definitive Resource and Document Collection* (Santa Barbara, CA: ABC-Clio, 2014), 1031.

88. Hull, 83.

89. Erichsen, 140.

90. Testimony of Edward Frederiks to the British, *Parliamentary Papers, House of Commons and Command, Volume 17* (London: HM Stationery Office, 1918), 99.

91. M. Bayer, Mit dem Hauptquartier in Siadwestafrika, 236. Cited in Drechsler's *Fighting*, 219.

92. Erichsen, 143.

93. Ibid., 76.

94. Ibid., 153.

95. "Kaiser's Commander in Africa Denounced," *New York Times*, August 27, 1905, 4.

96. George Steinmetz, "The First Genocide of the 20th Century and Its Postcolonial Afterlives: Germany and the Namibian Ovaherero," *Journal of the International Institute* 12, no. 2, Winter 2005.

97. Bayer, Hauptquartier, 236. Cited in Drechsler's *Fighting*, 222.

98. Herero deaths: Jeremy Sarkin, *Colonial Genocide and Reparations Claims in the 21st Century: The Socio-Legal Context of Claims under International Law by the Herero against Germany for Genocide in Namibia, 1904–1908* (Santa Barbara, CA: ABC-Clio, 2008), 5. Nama deaths: Dominik Schaller, "Every Herero Will Be Shot," *Forgotten Genocides: Oblivion, Denial, and Memory* (Philadelphia: University of Pennsylvania Press, 2011), 52.

99. Warwick, 145.

100. David Lloyd George, Speech in House of Commons, HC Deb 17 June 1901, vol. 95, 620–21.

101. Letter from Alfred Milner to Joseph Chamberlain, December 7, 1901.

102. Donald Shriver, *Honest Patriots: Loving a Country Enough To Remember Its Misdeeds* (Oxford: Oxford University Press, 2008), 88.

CHAPTER THREE *The First World War and the War on Civilians*

1. Paul Cohen-Portheim, *Time Stood Still: My Internment in England* (London: Duckworth, 1931), 6.
2. Ibid., 7.
3. Alien Registration and British Nationality Act, enacted August 5, 1914.
4. Cohen-Portheim, 9.
5. Letter to the Editor, *Daily Mail*, August 20, 1914, 4.
6. E. S. Turner, *Dear Old Blighty* (London: Faber & Faber, 2012).
7. Sophie de Schaepdrijver, "The 'German Atrocities' of 1914," Papers for *World War One* collection, British Library.
8. *A Documentary History of the War* (London: Times Publishing, 1917), 263.
9. Cohen-Portheim, 15.
10. William Blackstone et al., *Commentaries on the Laws of England, Volume 1* (New York: E. Duyckinck, 1827), 279.
11. David Cesarani, "An Alien Concept? The Continuity of Anti-Alienism in British Society before 1940," *The Internment of Aliens in Twentieth Century Britain* (London: Frank Cass, 1993), 32.
12. Ibid., 33.
13. Bryan Cheyette, *Constructions of 'the Jew' in English Literature and Society* (Cambridge: Cambridge University Press, 1995), 170.
14. Stefan Manz, "Civilian Internment in Scotland during the First World War," *"Totally Un-English" Britain's Internment of Enemy Aliens in Two World Wars* (Amsterdam: Rodopi, 2005), 94.
15. Reginald McKenna, House of Commons Debate, 26 November 1914, vol. 68, 1394.
16. Cohen-Portheim, 13.
17. Ibid., 21.
18. Ibid., 26–27.
19. Many of the numbers related to World War I concentration camps and detention come from historian Matthew Stibbe's excellent work on the subject. His essays "The Internment of Civilians by Belligerent States during the First World War" (from the *Journal of Contemporary History* 41, no. 1 (January 2006) and "Enemy Aliens and Internment" (in the equally useful *International Encyclopedia of the First World War*) are both invaluable resources.
20. Stibbe, "The Internment of Civilians," 4.
21. M. Talha Çiçek, *War and State Formation in Syria: Cemal Pasha's Governate During World War I, 1914–1917* (New York: Routledge, 2014), 144.
22. Stibbe, "Enemy Aliens and Internment."
23. Curt Gentry, *J. Edgar Hoover: The Man and the Secrets* (New York: W. W. Norton, 2001), 69.

24. Stibbe, "The Internment of Civilians," 10.
25. Review of First World War archival material at the International Committee of the Red Cross headquarters in Geneva, Switzerland, conducted by the author in May 2015.
26. B. E. Sargeaunt, *The Isle of Man and the Great War* (Isle of Man: Brown & Sons, 1922), 61.
27. Cohen-Portheim, 43.
28. Ibid., 65.
29. Stibbe records 4,273 British prisoners in German camps in May 1917, and 15,773 Germans and Austro-Hungarians in British detention, a ratio of roughly four to one.
30. Israel Cohen, *The Ruhleben Prison Camp: A Record of Nineteen Months' Internment* (London: Methuen, 1917), 1.
31. Ibid., 24.
32. Ibid., 27.
33. Stibbe, "Enemy Aliens and Internment."
34. Ibid.
35. Cohen, xiii.
36. James Gerard, *My Four Years in Germany* (New York: Grosset & Dunlap, 1917), 131–32.
37. Nancy Gentile Ford, *Americans All!: Foreign-born Soldiers in World War I* (College Station: Texas A&M University Press, 2002), 62.
38. William Murphy, *Political Imprisonment and the Irish, 1912–1921* (Oxford: Oxford University Press, 2014), 60.
39. Ibid., 59.
40. Ibid., 60.
41. "Interned Prisoners," debate between Lieutenant-Commander Joseph Kenworthy and Sir Robert Lynn, HC Deb 14 April 1921, vol. 140, 1270.
42. See, for example, Brazil's National Truth Commission Report, the "Relatório da Comissão Nacional da Verdade" referenced in endnotes for chapter 9.
43. Geoffrey Robertson, *An Inconvenient Genocide: Who Now Remembers the Armenians?* (London: Biteback Press, 2014), 36 and 38.
44. Joint declaration of France, Great Britain, and Russia, May 24, 1915. Forwarded via the American Embassy in Washington on May 29.
45. Hilmar Kaiser, *At the Crossroads of Der Zor: Death, Survival, and Humanitarian Resistance in Aleppo, 1915–1917* (London: Gomindas Institute, 2002), 2.
46. Joël Kotek and Pierre Rigoulot, *Le Siècle des Camps* (Paris: JC Lattès, 2000), 110.
47. Henry Morgenthau, *Ambassador Morgenthau's Story: A Personal Account of the Armenian Genocide* (New York: Cosimo, 2010), 233.
48. Robertson, 16.
49. Adolf Lukas Vischer, *Barbed Wire Disease: A Psychological Study of the Prisoner of War* (London: John Bale, Sons & Danielsson, 1919).

50. Cohen-Portheim, 85.
51. Ibid., 81.
52. Ibid., 86.
53. Ibid., 47–49.
54. Ibid., 94.
55. Conrad Hoffman, *In the Prison Camps of Germany* (New York: Association Press, 1920), 45.
56. Cohen-Portheim, 85.
57. Manz, 94.
58. Don Gifford and Robert Seldman, *Ulysses Annotated: Notes for James Joyce's Ulysses* (Stanford: University of California Press, 2008), 202.
59. Tammy Proctor, *Civilians in a World at War, 1914–1918* (New York: NYU Press, 2010), 230.
60. See, for example, the Aborigines Protection Act of New South Wales, 1909.
61. Peter Read, *Settlement: A History of Australian Indigenous Housing* (Canberra: Aboriginal Studies Press, 2000), 61.
62. "Anti-German Scare," Robert Bartholomew and Peter Hassall, *A Colorful History of Popular Delusions* (Amherst, NY: Prometheus Books, 2015), 224.
63. Cohen-Portheim, 3.
64. Stibbe, "The Internment of Civilians," 8.

CHAPTER FOUR *Gulag Rising*

1. Alexander Rabinowich, *The Bolsheviks Come to Power: The Revolution of 1917 in Petrograd* (London: Pluto Press, 2004), 276.
2. The Socialist Revolutionaries won over 40 percent of the vote, but had schismed in the interim, with one side of the split throwing its support to the Bolsheviks, bolstering their claim to leadership but only as a coalition.
3. Steven Main, "The Creation and Development of the Library System in the Red Army During the Russian Civil War (1918–1920)," *Library Quarterly* 65, no. 3 (July 1995): 326.
4. Anne Applebaum, *Gulag* (New York: Doubleday, 2003), 8. From Mikhail Geller's *Le monde concentrationnaire et la littérature soviétique*.
5. Edward Acton, *Critical Companion to the Russian Revolution, 1914–1921* (Bloomington: Indiana University Press, 1997), 317.
6. Applebaum, 8.
7. Richard Pipes, *The Russian Revolution* (New York: Knopf, 2011), 833.
8. Leona Toker, *Return from the Archipelago: Narratives of Gulag Survivors* (Bloomington: Indiana University Press, 2000), 16.
9. "On the Organization of the Solovetsky Forced-Labor Camp," Sovnarkom decree, November 2, 1923.
10. Dmitri Likhachev, *Reflections on the Russian Soul: A Memoir* (Budapest: CEU Press, 2000), 82.

11. Ibid., 80.

12. Ibid., 87.

13. "Soviet Will Start Prisoners Air Service to Take Prisoners to Lonely Solovetsky Islands," *New York Times*, January 24, 1926, 62.

14. "Rolland Denounces Abuse of His Name," *New York Times*, June 8, 1924, 66.

15. Likhachev, 91.

16. Ibid., 97.

17. Ibid., 99.

18. The first reference I found to the mosquito torture in Russia is from "Emma Goldman Denounces Rule of Soviet," *New York Times*, April 5, 1925, 4. Specific references to mosquito torture at Solovki appear later in memoirs, such as Anton Klinger's *Solovetskaia katorga*.

19. Aleksandr Solzhenitsyn, *The Gulag Archipelago, Volume 2: An Experiment in Literary Investigation* (New York: HarperCollins, 2007), 36.

20. Likhachev, 104.

21. Jaroslav Leontiev, "Pravozastupniki," *Novaya Gazeta*, October 31, 2002.

22. Solzhenitsyn, *Gulag Archipelago, Volume 2*, 53.

23. Boris Cederholm, *In the Clutches of the Tcheka* (Boston: Houghton Mifflin, 1929).

24. "Protest on Barring Soviet Lumber Here," *New York Times*, July 8, 1930, 10.

25. Cristina Vatulescu, *Police Aesthetics: Literature, Film, and the Secret Police in Soviet Times* (Stanford: Stanford University Press, 2010), 124.

26. Marina Goldovskaya, *Woman with a Movie Camera: My Life as a Russian Filmmaker* (Austin: University of Texas Press, 2010), 143–44.

27. Natalia Kuziakina, *Theater in the Solovki Prison Camp* (Abingdon, UK: Routledge, 2014), 89.

28. Likhachev, 111.

29. Tova Yedlin, *Maxim Gorky: A Political Biography* (Santa Barbara, CA: Greenwood, 1999), 188.

30. Likhachev, 119.

31. Applebaum, 23.

32. Likhachev, 110.

33. Solzhenitsyn, *Gulag Archipelago, Volume 2*, 36.

34. Applebaum, *Gulag*, 52.

35. Timothy Snyder, *Bloodlands: Between Hitler and Stalin* (New York: Basic Books, 2010), 25.

36. Ibid., 27.

37. Applebaum, 45.

38. Solzhenitsyn, *Gulag Archipelago, Volume 1*, 60.

39. In a short story re-creating his Gulag experiences at Kolyma, Varlam Shalamov quotes *The Notes of Maria Volkonskaya* for the nineteenth-century figure, and compares it to his own quota (Varlam Shalamov, *Kolyma Tales* (London: Penguin,

1994), 301. Solzhenitsyn later used this figure when discussing quotas in *Gulag Archipelago, Volume 2*, 200–201.

40. Likhachev, 179.
41. Applebaum, 62.
42. Nick Baron, "Conflict and Complicity: The Expansion of the Karelian Gulag, 1923–1933," Cahiers du Monde Russe 2/2001, vol. 22, 643.
43. Julie Draskoczy, "A Body of Work: Building Self and Society at Stalin's White Sea–Baltic Canal," 2010 dissertation for Philosophy PhD at the University of Pittsburgh, 77–78.
44. Likhachev, 183.
45. Walter Duranty, "Soviet Releases 12,484 in Record Amnesty," *New York Times*, August 5, 1933, 1.
46. Draskoczy, 13.
47. H. P. Smolka, "Taming the Arctic: A Visit to Russia's New Empire," *New York Times*, November 1, 1936, SM12.
48. Henry Wallace, *Soviet Asia Mission* (New York: Reynal & Hitchcock, 1946), 35.
49. Elinor Lipper, *Eleven Years in Soviet Prison Camps* (Chicago: Regnery, 1951), 112.
50. Prisoner interviews from Mikhail Mikheev's 1995 documentary *Kolyma*.
51. Ibid.
52. Walter Duranty, "Million Are Held in Russian Camps, 200,000 in Forests," *New York Times*, February 3, 1931, 1.
53. Margarete Buber-Neumann, *Under Two Dictators: Prisoner of Stalin and Hitler* (London: Pimlico, 2009), 22.
54. Ibid., 13.
55. Harold Denny, "Soviet Arrests 71 in War on 'Terror,'" *New York Times*, December 4, 1934, 1.
56. "Killings Justified, Soviet Envoy Says," *New York Times*, February 12, 1935, 17.
57. Harold Denny, "Soviet Executes 66 As Terrorists," *New York Times*, December 6, 1934, 1.
58. Buber-Neumann, *Dictators*. From Nikolaus Wachsmann's introduction, xi.
59. Walter Duranty, "Red Square: Russia's Pulsing Heart," *New York Times*, September 18, 1932, 134.
60. Nicholas Werth, "The Mechanism of a Mass Crime," *The Specter of Genocide: Mass Murder in Historical Perspective* (Cambridge: Cambridge University Press, 2003), 217.
61. Buber-Neumann, 23.
62. Ibid., 27.
63. Darius Rejali, *Torture and Democracy* (Princeton, NJ: Princeton University Press, 2007), 83.
64. Buber-Neumann, 41–42.
65. Ibid., 86.
66. Ibid, 87.

67. Ibid., 71.

68. Snyder, *Bloodlands*, 124.

69. Ibid., 138.

70. Ibid., 126.

71. Alan Barenberg, *Gulag Town, Company Town: Forced Labor and Its Legacy in Vorkuta* (New Haven, CT: Yale University Press), 3.

72. "Newly developed mines at Vorkuta, on the southern tip of Novaya Zemlya..." from "Russians Said to Get Coal from New Arctic Mines," *New York Times*, February 14, 1947, 3.

73. Snyder, 128.

74. Buber-Neumann, 120.

75. Ibid., 141.

76. Steven Barnes, *Death and Redemption: The Gulag and the Shaping of Soviet Society* (Princeton, NJ: Princeton University Press, 2011), 111.

77. Ibid., 113.

78. Michael Scammell, *Alexander Solzhenitsyn: A Biography* (New York: W. W. Norton, 1984), 108.

79. Ibid., 110.

80. Ibid., 112.

81. Solzhenitsyn, *Gulag Archipelago, Volume 1*, 17–18.

82. Barnes, 114.

83. Ibid., 116–17.

84. Ibid., 109.

85. Anna Reid, *Leningrad: The Epic Siege of World War II* (New York: Bloomsbury, 2011), 418.

86. Mark Edele, *"A 'Generation of Victors'?": Soviet Second World War Veterans from Demobilization to Organization, Volume 3* (Chicago: University of Chicago Press, 2004), 75.

87. Seth Bernstein, "Burying the Alliance: Interment, Repatriation, and the Politics of the Sacred in Occupied Germany," *Journal of Contemporary History* (2017), 11.

88. Applebaum, 579.

89. Daniela Agostino et al., *Panic and Mourning: The Cultural Work of Trauma* (Berlin: Walter de Gruyter, 2013), 212.

90. "Soviet Frees 2 Americans Long Held in Labor Camps," *New York Times*, January 9, 1955, 1.

91. Scammell, 202.

92. Solzhenitsyn, *Gulag Archipelago, Volume 2*, 265.

93. Scammell, 314.

94. Nikita Khrushchev, speech before the 20th congress of the Communist party of the USSR, Moscow, February 25, 1956.

95. Solzhenitsyn, *Gulag Archipelago, Volume 1*, 177.

96. Snyder, 27.

97. Solzhenitsyn, *Gulag Archipelago, Volume 1*, 145.

CHAPTER FIVE *The Architecture of Auschwitz*

1. Udo Wohlfeld, "NOHRA" camp entry in *The United States Holocaust Memorial Museum Encyclopedia of Camps and Ghettos, 1933–1945*, ed. Geoffrey P. Megargee (Bloomington: Indiana University Press, 2009), 139–40.

2. Adam Seipp, *The Ordeal of Peace: Demobilization and the Urban Experience in Britain and Germany, 1917–1921* (London: Routledge, 2016), 94.

3. *The Dachau Concentration Camp 1933 to 1945* (Brussels: International Dachau Committee, 2003), 60.

4. Richard Evans, *The Coming of the Third Reich* (New York: Penguin, 2005), 347.

5. Peter Hoffman, *Hitler's Personal Security* (Cambridge, MA: Da Capo Press, 2000), 5. Harold Marcuse, *Legacies of Dachau* (Cambridge: Cambridge University Press, 2001), 19–20.

6. See Stibbe, "Enemy Aliens and Internment" and Jean-Claude Farcy, *Les camps de concentration français de la première guerre mondiale: 1914–1920* (Paris: Anthropos, 1995), 126.

7. "Ebert Dismisses Armistice Terms at Convention," *New York Times*, February 8, 1919.

8. See for instance "Germans at Work in Lille," *New York Times*, February 1, 1919, 3.

9. "Eisner Says Plague Swept German Camps," *New York Times*, February 12, 1919, 3.

10. Harold Marcuse, "The Idea of a Concentration Camp," course notes, October 2005: http://www.history.ucsb.edu/faculty/marcuse/classes/33d/33d05/33d05L05Camps.htm.

11. Marcuse, *Dachau*, 20.

12. Leni Yahil, *The Holocaust: The Fate of European Jewry: 1932–45* (Oxford: Oxford University Press, 1991), 44.

13. Hans Beimler, *Four Weeks in the Hands of Hitler's Hell-Hounds: The Nazi Murder Camp of Dachau* (London: Modern Books Limited, 1933), 12.

14. Ibid., 14–15.

15. Ibid., 21.

16. Ibid., 26.

17. Stanislav Zámečník, *That Was Dachau, 1933–1945* (Brussels: International Dachau Committee), 28. Quoting an article from the *Münchner Neueste Nachtrichten*.

18. Max Weinreich, *Hitler's Professors: The Part of Scholarship in Germany's Crimes against the Jewish People* (New Haven, CT: Yale University Press, 1946), 28.

19. Zámečník, 44.

20. *Dachau Concentration Camp 1933 to 1945*, 63.

21. Beimler, 27.

22. Ibid., 35.

23. Zámečník, 32.

24. Ibid.

25. Ibid.

26. "Nazis Shoot Down Fleeing Prisoners," *New York Times*, April 23, 1933, 22.

27. Ibid. The reporter for the unbylined article wrote, "Many of the prisoners looked as if the community would not suffer from their exclusion."

28. *Times* of London correspondent quoted by Frederick Birchall in "Nazis Hold 80,000, Camp Study Shows," *New York Times*, August 29, 1933, 1 and 4.

29. Nikolaus Wachsmann, *The Nazi Concentration Camps, 1933–1939* (Lincoln: University of Nebraska Press, 2012), 40.

30. George Browder, *Foundations of the Nazi Police State* (Lexington: University Press of Kentucky, 2015 reissue), 154.

31. Wachsmann, *Nazi Concentration Camps*, 39.

32. Zámečník, 34.

33. Wachsmann, *Nazi Concentration Camps*, 113.

34. Adolf Hitler's speech before the Reichstag, July 13, 1934. See also Browder, 154, and Wachsmann, 89.

35. Timothy Ryback, "The First Killings of the Holocaust," *New York Times*, January 2, 2012.

36. *Dachau Concentration Camp 1933 to 1945*, 91.

37. Zámečník, 71. In *The Nazi Concentration Camps*, Wachsmann notes that these lines were deleted from the manuscript, likely to avoid criticizing his peers (74).

38. Letter from Heinrich Himmler to Reich Minister of Justice Franz Gürtner, November 6, 1935. Cited in Zámečník, 76.

39. N. H. Baynes, ed., *The Speeches of Adolf Hitler* (Oxford: Oxford University Press, 1942), 731.

40. Victor Klemperer, *I Will Bear Witness, Volumes 1–2* (New York: Modern Library, 2001), 65–66.

41. "Persecution of Roma (Gypsies) in Prewar Germany, 1933–39," U.S. Holocaust Memorial Museum: https://www.ushmm.org/wlc/en/article.php?ModuleId=10005482.

42. "Measures taken against the Gypsy Nuisance" and the establishment of a "Concentration Camp on Friedberger Landstrasse," a record created in 1929 by the Frankfurt Council. Institute of Municipal History, Frankfurt am Main, Germany.

43. The Johann Trollmann account is largely based on the published work of Roger Repplinger, author of *Leg dich, Zigeuner: Die Geschichte von Johann Trollmann und Tull Harder*, and e-mail exchanges with him conducted in the second half of 2016.

44. Samuel Cavert, "Olympic Boycott Urged by Cavert," *New York Times*, September 22, 1935, 104–5.

45. "Nazis Urge Exhibit on Olympic Guests," *New York Times*, April 23, 1936, 8.

46. "Reich Curbs Drive on 'Foes' of State to Halt Criticism," *New York Times*, July 30, 1935, 1.

47. Bettina Greiner, *Suppressed Terror: History and Perception of Soviet Special Camps in Germany* (Lanham, MD: Lexington Books, 2014), 147.

48. Zámečník, 85.
49. Wachsmann, *Nazi Concentration Camps,* 86–87.
50. Ibid., 88.
51. Nikolaus Wachsmann, *KL* (New York: Farrar, Straus and Giroux, 2015), 665.
52. Richard Wetzell, *Inventing the Criminal: A History of German Criminology, 1880–1945* (Chapel Hill: University of North Carolina Press, 2003), 223.
53. Baynes, ed., *Speeches of Adolf Hitler, Volume I,* 731–32.
54. Richard Breitman, *The Architect of Genocide: Himmler and the Final Solution* (New York: Knopf, 1991), 53.
55. Uta Gerhardt and Thomas Karlauf, *The Night of Broken Glass: Eyewitness Accounts of Kristallnacht* (New York: Wiley, 2012), 8 and 24.
56. "Paris Press Scores Nazis," *New York Times,* November 11, 1938, 4.
57. "Netherlands Acts to Take Refugees," *New York Times,* November 16, 1938, 7.
58. Wachsmann, *KL,* 186.
59. Ibid.
60. Margarete Buber-Neumann, *Under Two Dictators: Prisoner of Stalin and Hitler* (London: Pimlico, 2009), 153.
61. Ibid., 161.
62. Ibid., 166.
63. Ibid., 167.
64. Ibid., 169.
65. Wachsmann, *KL,* 191.
66. Otto Tolischus, "Hitler Gives Word," *New York Times,* September 1, 1939, 1.
67. Alfred Helmut Naujocks, Testimony taken at Nuremberg, Germany, September 11, 1945.
68. *Buchenwald Concentration Camp, 1937–1945: A Guide to the Permanent Exhibition* (Goettingen: Wallstein, 2004), 115.
69. Buber-Neumann, 209.
70. Adolf Hitler, *Mein Kampf* (New York: Reynal & Hitchcock, 1941), 939.
71. Matthew Cooper, *The Nazi War against Soviet Partisans* (New York: Stein and Day, 1979), 79.
72. Timothy Snyder, *Bloodlands: Between Hitler and Stalin* (New York: Basic Books, 2010), 144.
73. Wachsmann, *KL,* 201.
74. Michael Fleming, *Auschwitz, the Allies and Censorship of the Holocaust* (Cambridge: Cambridge University Press, 2014), 17.
75. Buber-Neumann, 174.
76. Ibid., 194–95 and 203.
77. Ibid., 215.
78. Sarah Helm, *Ravensbrück: Life and Death in Hitler's Concentration Camp for Women* (New York: Doubleday/Nan Talese, 2014), 216.

79. Buber-Neumann, 261.

80. Ibid., 271.

81. Wachsmann, *KL*, 295.

82. Martin Gilbert, *The Holocaust: A History of the Jews of Europe during the Second World War* (New York: Macmillan, 1987), 191.

83. Wachsmann, *KL*, 288.

84. Krystyna Żywulska, *I Survived Auschwitz* (Warsaw: tCHu, 2011), 15.

85. Ibid., 16.

86. Ibid., 19.

87. Ibid., 63.

88. Ibid., 103.

89. Ibid., 142–43.

90. Philippe Bourgois, "Missing the Holocaust: My Father's Account of Auschwitz from August 1943 to June 1944," *Anthropological Quarterly* 78, no. 1 (Winter 2005): 113.

91. Elie Wiesel, *Night, Dawn, Day* (New York: Hill and Wang, 2008), 74 and 80.

92. Żywulska, 155.

93. Ibid., 165.

94. Ibid., 178.

95. "Extermination Camp Gassed 5 Million Jews, Survivor Says," *Washington Post*, April 12, 1945, 1. "French Planes Fly Food to Liberated Prisoners," *New York Times*, April 3, 1945, 10.

96. "Allies Are Urged to Execute Nazis," *New York Times*, July 2, 1942, 6.

97. "Polish Executions Put at 3,200,000," *New York Times*, July 27, 1942, 9.

98. Elie Wiesel, remarks at the opening of the U.S. Holocaust Museum, Washington, DC, April 22, 1993.

99. Wiesel, *Night*, 45.

100. Buber-Neumann, xix–xxi.

101. Details taken from a 2015 visit to Auschwitz and "Designing the Exhibition: The Challenges and the Solutions," an interview with exhibition designer Chanan de Lange.

CHAPTER SIX *Increments of Evil*

1. "German Jurist and Wife, Exiled, Suicides in Paris," *New York Times*, July 19, 1933, 5.

2. Arthur Koestler, *Scum of the Earth* (London: Eland, 2007), ebook, location 989.

3. Jon Nixon, *Hannah Arendt and the Politics of Friendship* (London: Bloomsbury, 2015), 139.

4. Elisabeth Young-Bruehl, *Hannah Arendt: For the Love of the World* (New Haven, CT: Yale University Press, 2004), 152.

5. Ibid., 153.

6. Much of the information about the detainees held at Gurs and the conditions of their detention was gathered from a 2015 visit to the former campsite and access to camp history provided there through research gathered by the Amicale du Camp de Gurs.

7. George Axelsson, "Majorca Gripped by Spy Fever," *New York Times*, November 3, 1937, 2.

8. Joël Kotek and Pierre Rigoulot, *Le Siècle des Camps* (Paris: JC Lattès, 2000), 255.

9. Jean-François Berdah, "The Devil in France: The Tragedy of Spanish Republicans and French Policy after the Civil War (1936–1945)" in *Discrimination and Tolerance in Historical Perspective* (Pisa: Plus Pisa University Press, 2009), 302.

10. Young-Bruehl, 105–6.

11. Ibid., 107.

12. Hannah Arendt, Television Interview with Günter Gaus, *Zur Person*, October 28, 1964.

13. Pierre Birnbaum, *Leon Blum: Prime Minister, Socialist, Zionist* (New Haven, CT: Yale University Press, 2015), 3.

14. Gurs Camp memorial visit, 2015.

15. Jürgen Matthäus, *Jewish Responses to Persecution: 1941–1942* (Lanham, MD: AltaMira Press, 2013), 34.

16. Koestler, location 3182.

17. Koestler, location 941.

18. Young-Bruehl, 155.

19. Hannah Arendt, "We Refugees," in *Altogether Elsewhere: Writers on Exile*, Marc Robinson, ed. (London: Faber and Faber, 1994), 111.

20. Roger Kershaw, "Collar the lot! Britain's policy of internment during the Second World War," British National Archives, July 2, 2015.

21. W. F. Leysmith, "Britons in Dispute over Enemy Aliens," *New York Times*, April 7, 1940, 33.

22. James Reston, "Arrests in Britain," *New York Times*, May 13, 1940, 1.

23. François Lafitte, *The Internment of Aliens* (London: Libris, 1988), xiv.

24. Eric Koch, *Deemed Suspect: A Wartime Blunder* (London: Methuen, 1980), 17.

25. Mario Cacciottolo, "The Dunera Boys: 70 years on after notorious voyage," BBC News, July 10, 2010.

26. R. A. W. Rhodes, ed., *The Australian Study of Politics* (New York: Springer, 2009), 44.

27. Martin Auger, *Prisoners of the Home Front: German POWs and 'Enemy Aliens' in Southern Quebec, 1940–46* (Vancouver: UBC Press, 2005), Appendix A: 153.

28. Leysmith, 33.

29. Richard Dove, ed., *"'Totally Un-English'?: Britain's Internment of 'Enemy Aliens' in Two Wars* (Amsterdam: Rodopi, 2005), 12.

30. Kotek and Rigoulot, 241.

31. Amedeo Osti Guerrazzi, *The Italian Army in Slovenia: Strategies of Antipartisan Repression, 1941–1943* (New York: Springer, 2013), 58.

32. Claudia Rome, "59 Years Ago, They Fled to an Internment Camp," *New York Times,* July 21, 2003.

33. Paul Bartrop and Steven Leonard Jacobs, *Modern Genocide: The Definitive Resource and Document Collection* (Santa Barbara, CA: ABC-CLIO, 2014), 1268.

34. Shaul Ferrero, "Switzerland and the Refugees Fleeing Nazism: Documents on the German Jews Turned Back at the Basel Border in 1938–1939," *Yad Vashem Studies* XXVII, Jerusalem (1999): 203–34.

35. Donna Ryan, *The Holocaust and the Jews of Marseille: The Enforcement of Anti-Semitic Policies in Vichy France* (Champaign: University of Illinois, 1996), 146.

36. Young-Bruehl, 112.

37. Hannah Arendt, *The Origins of Totalitarianism* (San Diego: Harvest, 1968), 443.

38. Gavan Daws, *Prisoner of the Japanese* (New York: Pocket Books, 2007), 128.

39. "Captain's Log," Episode 559, *This American Life,* June 26, 2015.

40. Patrica Pui Huen Lim and Diana Wong, eds., *War and Memory in Malaysia and Singapore* (Singapore: Institute of Southeast Asian Studies, 2000), 54.

41. In 2016, Mitsubishi became the latest firm to settle with wartime workers, apologizing for using more than 3,500 forced laborers in its wartime facilities, and agreeing to compensate the victims. See Chun Han Wong's "Mitsubishi Materials Strikes Deal with Chinese over WWII Forced Labor," *Wall Street Journal,* June 1, 2016.

42. Tanaka Toshiyuki, *Japan's Comfort Women: Sexual Slavery and Prostitution During World War II and the US Occupation* (London: Routledge, 2002), 32.

43. "Recent Policy of the Government of Japan on the Issue Known As 'Wartime Comfort Women,'" Ministry of Foreign Affairs of Japan, June 2001.

44. "Report on the mission to the Democratic People's Republic of Korea, the Republic of Korea and Japan on the issue of military sexual slavery in wartime," United Nations Economic and Social Council, January 4, 1996.

45. Ibid.

46. Jake Adelstein and Angela Kubo, "'Gesture of healing': South Korea and Japan Reconcile on World War II Sex Slaves," *Los Angeles Times,* December 28, 2015.

47. Leslie Hatayama, *Righting a Wrong: Japanese Americans and the Passage of the Civil Liberties Act of 1988* (Stanford CA: Stanford University Press, 1994), 11. More than 270 were arrested in the Los Angeles field office alone. Memo from Los Angeles office to DC Headquarters, Federal Bureau of Investigation, December 8, 1941, 12:58 a.m.

48. For example, Carl Junghans, former Soviet propaganda filmmaker turned documentarian for the Nazis; he had arrived in New York before the United States joined the war and started feeding information of dubious accuracy to the FBI. See Junghans's US Immigration file A-7595300.

49. "Overview of the World War II Enemy Alien Control Program," United States National Archives: http://www.archives.gov/research/immigration/enemy-aliens-overview.html (accessed June 10, 2016).

50. Jan Jarboe Russell, *The Train to Crystal City: FDR's Secret Prisoner Exchange Program and America's Only Family Internment Camp During World War II* (New York: Scribner, 2015), xvi.

51. J. L. DeWitt, "Public Proclamation No. 1," Headquarters Western Defense Command and Fourth Army, Presidio of San Francisco, California, March 2, 1942.

52. *Congressional Record,* March 19, 1942, 2726.

53. "How to Vote by Absentee Ballot," *Denson Communique No. 1,* Jerome War Relocation Center, Arkansas, October 23, 1942, 1.

54. Elaine Briseño, "Project explores New Mexico prison camps for Japanese-Americans during WWII," *Albuquerque Journal,* December 20, 2015.

55. *Korematsu v. United States,* 323 U.S. 214 (1944).

56. *Ex Parte Mitsuye Endo,* 323 US 283 (December 18, 1944).

57. Arendt, *Origins,* 286–87 and 287 n42.

58. "Décès au Camp: Liste Alphabétique," Amicale du camp de Gurs.

59. Bella Gutterman and Naomi Morgernstern, *The Gurs Haggadah: Passover in Perdition* (Jerusalem: Devorah Publishing, 2003), 25.

60. "Misery and Death in French Camps," *New York Times,* January 26, 1941, 24.

61. Figures based on calculating average number of deaths in the second half of November 1940, based on data from "Décès au Camp: Liste Alphabétique," Amicale du camp de Gurs.

62. Renée Poznanski, *Jews in France in World War II* (Hanover, NH: University Press of New England, 2001), 188.

63. Warren Lansing, "Camps for Aliens in France Squalid," *New York Times,* March 30, 1941, 25.

64. Poznanski, 208.

65. Ibid., 209.

66. Ibid., 212.

67. Ibid., 261.

68. Ibid., 264.

69. Ibid., 217.

70. Ibid., 222.

71. Daniel Brigham, "Liquidation Day Set For France's Jews," *New York Times,* January 27, 1943, 10.

72. Kenneth Ringle, "Ringle Report on Japanese Internment," January 20, 1942. Written in response to a request from the Chief of Naval Operations that Lieutenant K. D. Ringle write a report on his views of the Japanese.

73. Neal Kumar Katyal, "The Solicitor General and Confession of Error," *Fordham Law Review* 81, no. 3033.

74. Peter Irons, *Justice at War* (Stanford: University of California Press, 1983), 67.

75. Ibid., 46.

76. Ibid., 371.

77. Hannah Arendt and Karl Jaspers, *Correspondence: 1926–1969* (New York: Harcourt Brace Jovanovich, 1992), 417.

78. Ibid., 418.

79. Hannah Arendt, *Eichmann in Jerusalem* (New York: Penguin, 2006), 278.

80. Ibid., xx.

81. David Frum interview with Bettina Stangneth, "The Lies of Adolf Eichmann," *The Atlantic,* October 8, 2014.

82. Arendt, *Eichmann,* 117.

83. See, for example, Isaiah Trunk's *Judenrat* (Lincoln, NE: University of Nebraska Press, 1972).

CHAPTER SEVEN *Stepchildren of the Gulag*

1. Gladwin Hill, "Poles Found Cowed by Fear into Submission to Regime," *New York Times,* October 22, 1945, 1.

2. Giles MacDonogh, *After the Reich: The Brutal History of the Allied Occupation* (New York: Basic Books, 2009), 183.

3. Hill, "Poles," 3.

4. "Poland: Free election," *Time,* January 13, 1947.

5. Kevin McDermott, *Communist Czechoslovakia, 1945–89: A Political and Social History* (London: Palgrave Macmillan, 2015), 65.

6. Joël Kotek and Pierre Rigoulot, *Le Siècle des Camps* (Paris: JC Lattès, 2000), 542.

7. *Estonia Since 1944,* Estonian International Commission for the Investigation of War Crimes and Crimes against Humanity, (Tallinn: Tallinna Raamatutrükikoda, 2009), 448.

8. "The New Totalitarians" (editorial), *New York Times,* August 8, 1947, 16.

9. Mao Zedong, "Report on an Investigation of the Peasant Movement in Hunan, March 1927," *Selected Works of Mao Tse-tung, Volume I* (Peking: Foreign Languages Press, 1975), 29.

10. Mao, "Report on an Investigation," 28.

11. Philip Williams and Yenna Wu, *The Great Wall of Confinement: The Chinese Prison Camp through Contemporary Fiction and Reportage* (Berkeley: University of California Press, 2004), 19.

12. Ibid., 49.

13. Ibid., 46.

14. Harry Wu, *Laogai: The Chinese Gulag* (Boulder, CO: Westview Press, 1992), 57.

15. Klaus Mühlhahn, *Criminal Justice in China: A History* (Cambridge, MA: Harvard University Press, 2009), 132–34.

16. Williams and Wu, *The Great Wall,* 48.

17. Harry Wu, *Bitter Winds* (New York: John Wiley & Sons, 1994), 15.

18. Ibid., 45.

19. Jean-Luc Domenach, *Chine: L'archipel oublié* (Paris: Fayard, 1992), 71–72.

20. Wu, *Bitter Winds*, 63.

21. Bradley Martin, *Under the Loving Care of the Fatherly Leader* (New York: Thomas Dunne, 2004), 48.

22. Ibid., 8.

23. Ibid., 1–2.

24. "Huge File Lists War Prisoners," *New York Times,* July 13, 1958, 44.

25. Family account of Dr. Tae Byung Whang, whose father, Do Ik Whang, was arrested on June 24, 1950, in Pyongyang—from correspondence January 7, 2013.

26. "Report of the detailed findings of the Commission of Inquiry on Human Rights in the Democratic People's Republic of Korea," United Nations Human Rights Council, 7 February 2014, 222.

27. Kang Chol-Hwan, *The Aquariums of Pyongyang: Ten Years in the North Korean Gulag* (New York: Basic Books, 2001), 43–44.

28. Ibid., 49.

29. See, for example, the account of Kim Young-Soon, who was sent to Yodok with her family, losing both parents and one son in the camp. "Report of the detailed findings of the Commission of Inquiry," 230.

30. "Report of the detailed findings of the Commission of Inquiry," 224.

31. Ibid., 233.

32. Ibid., 226.

33. Ibid., 208.

34. Martin, *Loving Care*, 302–4.

35. "Report of the detailed findings of the Commission of Inquiry," 30.

36. Blaine Harden, *Escape from Camp 14: One Man's Remarkable Odyssey from North Korea to Freedom in the West* (New York: Penguin, 2012).

37. Hyeonseo Lee, "North Korean Truths," *New York Times*, February 6, 2015.

38. Williams and Wu, *Great Wall*, 133–34.

39. Wu, *Bitter Winds*, 92.

40. Ibid., 118.

41. Fidel Castro, *My Life: A Spoken Autobiography* (New York: Simon & Schuster, 2007), 220–21.

42. Hart Phillips, "Cuban Show Trial of Batista Aides Opens in Stadium," *New York Times,* January 23, 1959, 1.

43. Daniel Solomon, *Breaking Up with Cuba: The Dissolution of Friendly Relations between Washington and Havana, 1956–1961* (Jefferson, NC: McFarland, 2011), 229.

44. Samuel Farber, *The Politics of Che Guevara: Theory and Practice* (Chicago: Haymarket, 2016), xi.

45. Jorge Castañeda, *Compañero: The Life and Death of Che Guevara* (New York: Knopf, 2009), 178. Castañeda quotes Guevara from Ministry of Industries meeting minutes of January 20, 1962.

46. Paco Ignacio Taibo, *Guevara, Also Known As Che* (London: Macmillan, 1999), 379.

47. Jon Lee Anderson, *Che Guevara: A Revolutionary Life* (New York: Grove/Atlantic, 2010), 567.

48. Thomas Paterson, *Contesting Castro: The United States and the Triumph of the Cuban Revolution* (Oxford: Oxford University Press, 1995), 88.

49. Paul Kidd, "The Price of Achievement Under Castro," *Saturday Review,* May 3, 1969, 23.

50. "Lista Parcial de Prisiones y Centros Correccionales," *Comisión Cubana de Derechos Humanos y Reconciliación Nacional* (Cuban Commission of Human Rights and National Reconciliation), Havana, December 31, 1996.

51. "Cuba: Events of 2015," Human Rights Watch World Report 2016.

52. Wu, *Bitter Winds*, 149.

53. Ibid., 210.

54. Ibid., 167.

55. Ibid., 175.

56. Ibid., 180.

57. Ibid., 184.

58. Charles Antoine de Nerciat, "Saigon Today Is Less Fun, Less Corrupt and Cheaper," *New York Times*, September 21, 1975, 88.

59. Kevin Buckley, "The Expected Blood Bath Did Not Happen," *New York Times*, May 16, 1976, 208.

60. Max Austerlitz, "Vietnamizing South Vietnam," *New York Times*, April 25, 1976.

61. Buckley, "Blood Bath," 208.

62. Ginetta Sagan and Stephen Denney, "Reeducation in Unliberated Vietnam: Loneliness, Suffering, and Death," *Indochina Newsletter*, (Berkeley: Institute of East Asian Studies, University of California), October–November 1982.

63. Doan van Toai and David Chanoff, *Vietnamese Gulag* (New York: Simon and Schuster, 1986), 207.

64. Ibid., 249.

65. Khmer Rouge saying from "Cambodia, 1975–1979" exhibition, US Holocaust Memorial Museum, May 2015.

66. Samantha Power, *"A Problem From Hell": America and the Age of Genocide* (New York: Basic Books, 2013), 109.

67. Elizabeth Becker, "Reporting massive human rights abuses behind a façade," *Columbia Journalism Review,* October 3, 2016.

68. David Chandler, *Voices from S-21: Terror and History in Pol Pot's Secret Prison* (Berkeley: University of California Press, 1999), 66.

69. Ibid., 68.

70. Cambodia Tribunal Monitor: http://www.cambodiatribunal.org/history/cambodian-history/khmer-rouge-history/; accessed April 23, 2016.

71. "Special to the JTA: Elie Wiesel; A Journey to Cambodia," Jewish Telegraphic Agency, February 29, 1980.

72. Dith Pran, ed., *Children of Cambodia's Killing Fields: Memoirs by Survivors* (New Haven, CT: Yale University Press, 1999), 1–4.

73. Sydney Schanberg, *Beyond the Killing Fields: War Writings* (Lincoln, NE: Potomac Books, 2002), 2.

74. Wu, *Bitter Winds*, 199.

75. Ibid., 227.

76. Ibid., 250.

77. "Made in China," *60 Minutes*, September 15, 1991.

78. Simon Denyer, "China's Labor Camps Close, But Human Rights Groups Say Grim Detention Conditions Linger," *Washington Post*, December 6, 2013.

79. "China: Events of 2015," *World Report*, Human Rights Watch, 2016.

80. Sarah Henry, "Harry Wu, a Prisoner in Chinese Labor Camps for 19 Years, is Now Your Basic American Suburbanite and an All-Around Pain in the You-Know-What for China," *Los Angeles Times Magazine*, November 17, 1996.

81. Andrew Jacobs, "Champion of Human Rights in China Leaves a Tarnished Legacy," *New York Times*, August 13, 2016.

CHAPTER EIGHT *Echoes of Empire*

1. Jane Muthoni Mara, "Witness Statement of Jane Muthoni Mara," *Jane Muthoni Mara vs. The Foreign and Commonwealth Office*, Claim No.: HQ09X02666, paragraph 4.

2. Caroline Elkins, *Britain's Gulag* (New York: Pimlico, 2005), 15.

3. David Anderson, *Histories of the Hanged* (New York: W. W. Norton, 2011), 62–63.

4. "New Trial for Kenyatta," *Sydney Morning Herald,* July 16, 1953, 1.

5. Mara, "Witness Statement," paragraph 7.

6. In the cyclical history that detention camps often have, the Deoli camp was converted to a detention camp for Chinese Indians after independence. In 1962, after the Sino-Indian Border Conflict, a mass relocation of Indians with Chinese ancestry to Deoli resulted in years of hardship for thousands of adults and children, some of whom did not survive the ordeal. See James Griffiths's "India's Forgotten Chinese Internment Camp," *The Atlantic*, August 9, 2013.

7. Purba Banerjee, "A Biographical Sketch of Tagore," *India Perspectives* 24, no. 2 (August 22, 2013): 129.

8. *Calcutta Review,* July–September 1963, 179. Interestingly, during the early days of World War II, Anderson became home secretary, and advocated restraint in the detention of enemy aliens, recognizing that many of the German and Austrian aliens were in fact Jewish refugees from the Nazis. His advice was not heeded.

9. "Destroyers Assist Surabaya Advance," *New York Times*, November 13, 1945, 1.

10. Mara, "Witness Statement," paragraph 18.

11. Elkins, *Gulag*, xiiv.

12. Kenya Legislative Council Debates, vol. 55, May 7, 1953, as quoted in Elkins, 59.

13. Mara, "Witness Statement," paragraph 15.

14. Ibid., paragraph 22.

15. Huw Bennett, "'A Very Salutary Effect': The Counter-Terror Strategy in the Early Malayan Emergency, June 1948 to December 1949," *Journal of Strategic Studies* 32 (2009): 3.

16. Mark Townsend, "New documents reveal cover-up of 1948 British 'massacre' of villagers in Malaya," *Guardian*, April 9, 2011.

17. CO 537/4753: Statement by Henry Gurney, the High Commissioner for Malaya, Annex 'A' to minutes of the 16th meeting of the BDCC (FE), January 28, 1949. Gurney was killed in October 1951 during a roadside ambush by Malayan Communist guerrillas.

18. For photos, and witness and survivor accounts, see the 1993 BBC production *In Cold Blood: The Truth of the Batang Kali Massacre.*

19. Paulo Muoka Nzili, "Witness Statement of Paulo Muoka Nzili," *Paulo Muoka Nzili vs. The Foreign and Commonwealth Office*, Claim No.: HQ09X02666, paragraph 22.

20. Olivier de Frouville, "The Committee on Enforced Disappearances," 2008, 1. Frouville was Chair and Rapporteur of the United Nations Working Group on Enforced or Involuntary Disappearances.

21. Interview with Paul Teitgen, prefect of police for Algiers in 1956 and 1957. From the Yves Boisset documentary *La Bataille d'Alger.*

22. In 1954, Algeria's population was approximately 9,577,000. United Nations, Department of Economic and Social Affairs, Population Division. World Population Prospects: The 2015 Revision.

23. Alistair Horne, *A Savage War of Peace: Algeria 1954–1962* (New York: New York Review of Books, 2011), 338.

24. Simone de Beauvoir, *Hard Times: Force of Circumstance—The Autobiography of Simone de Beauvoir, 1952–1962, Volume 2* (New York: Basic Books, 1994), 179–80.

25. Darius Rejali, *Torture and Democracy* (Princeton, NJ: Princeton University Press, 2007), 486–87.

26. Donald Reid, *Germaine Tillion, Lucie Aubrac, and the Politics of Memories of the French Resistance* (Newcastle upon Tyne: Cambridge Scholars Publishing, 2009), 76.

27. Kathy Kadane, "Ex-agents say CIA compiled death lists for Indonesians," *San Francisco Examiner*, May 20, 1990.

28. Kathy Kadane, Letter to the Editor, *New York Review of Books*, April 10, 1997.

29. Kadane, "Ex-agents."

30. Taufik Ahmad, "Survival through Slavery," *Inside Indonesia*, Edition 99, January–March 2010.

31. Robert Cribb and Michelle Ford, "The Killings of 1965–66," *Inside Indonesia*, Edition 99, January–March 2010.

32. Thomas Fuller, "Suharto's Gulag / The Buru Island 'Humanitarian Project': Former Prisoners Look Back on a Remote Tropical Hell," *International Herald Tribune*, March 15, 2000.

33. Elkins, *Gulag*, xi.
34. Ngugi wa Thiong'o, *In the House of the Interpreter* (New York: Random House, 2012), 36.
35. Ibid., 202.
36. Ibid., 237.
37. Ibid., 38.
38. Mara, "Witness Statement," paragraph 44.
39. Ibid., paragraph 56.
40. Wambugu Wa Nyingi, "Witness Statement of Wambugu Wa Nyingi," *Wambugu Wa Nyingi vs. The Foreign and Commonwealth Office*, Claim No.: HQ09X02666, paragraph 43.
41. Ibid., paragraph 62.
42. Elkins, *Gulag*, 281.
43. Ibid., 282.
44. Enoch Powell, "Hola Camp, Kenya (Report)," HC Deb 27 July 1959, vol. 610, 237.
45. Fabian Klose, *Human Rights in the Shadow of Colonial Violence: The Wars of Independence in Kenya and Algeria* (Philadelphia: University of Pennsylvania Press, 2013), 114.
46. Klose, *Human Rights*, 115.
47. Bernard Fall, *The Two Viet-nams: A Political and Military Analysis* (New York: Praeger, 1966), 362.
48. "Origins of the Insurgency in South Vietnam, 1954–1960," *Pentagon Papers, Gravel Edition, Volume 1* (Boston: Beacon Press, 1971), 253.
49. John Donnell and Gerald Hickey, *The Vietnamese 'Strategic Hamlets': A Preliminary Report* (Santa Monica, CA: RAND, 1962), 11.
50. Mai Elliott, *Rand in Southeast Asia: A History of the Vietnam War Era* (Santa Barbara, CA: RAND, 2010), 28.
51. Fall, *Two Viet-nams*, 362.
52. "Red Cross Inspects Prisons in Vietnam," *New York Times*, February 4, 1968, 14. The Red Cross estimated some 20,000 prisoners held in prisons and reeducation camps, without clear distinctions between criminals, POWs, and political prisoners.
53. "Internal Security Act of 1950," U.S. Statutes at Large, 81st Cong., II Sess., Chp. 1024, 987–1031, section 103(a).
54. "Text of President's Message Vetoing the Communist-Control Bill," *New York Times*, September 23, 1950, 6.
55. The Non-Detention Act of 1971 invalidated emergency detention provisions of the Internal Security Act of 1950.
56. Frank Furedi, *The Mau Mau War in Perspective* (London: James Currey, 1989), 3.
57. David McBeath Anderson, "Witness Statement of David McBeath Anderson," *Ndiku Mutua & Others vs. The Foreign and Commonwealth Office*, Claim No: HQ09X02666, 8.

58. Letter from British attorney general in Kenya Eric Griffith-Jones to Governor Sir Evelyn Baring, June 1957.

59. Mara, "Witness Statement," paragraph 74.

60. Wa Nyingi, "Witness Statement," paragraph 90.

61. William Hague, "Statement to Parliament on settlement of Mau Mau claims," Foreign & Commonwealth Office, June 6, 2013.

62. "British colonial 'cover up' in Mau Mau camp revealed in new secret document release," *Telegraph*, November 30, 2012.

63. Mara, "Witness Statement," paragraph 67.

CHAPTER NINE *Bastard Children of the Camps*

1. Unless otherwise noted, the account of Felipe Agüero Piwonka's experience with detention and its aftermath are primarily taken from an interview conducted by the author in Santiago, on January 11, 2016.

2. Marvine Howe, "Opposition Intensifies in Chile as Legislators Vote to Denounce Allende Government and Its Policies," *New York Times*, August 24, 1973, 10.

3. "Military Junta in Chile Orders Break with Cuba," *New York Times*, September 14, 1973, 1.

4. Seymour Hersh, "Censored Matter in Book about CIA Said To Have Related Chile Activities," *New York Times*, September 11, 1974, 14.

5. Handwritten notes of CIA director Richard Helms from meeting with President Richard Nixon on Chile, September 15, 1970.

6. Tim Weiner, *Legacy of Ashes: The History of the CIA* (New York: Anchor, 2007), 361.

7. Marc Ensalaco, *Chile Under Pinochet: Recovering the Truth* (Philadelphia: University of Pennsylvania Press, 2000), 27.

8. Ensalaco, *Chile*, 27.

9. Katherine Hite, "Chile's National Stadium As Monument, As Memorial," *ReVista*, Spring 2004.

10. "Thousands in Europe Protest the Chilean Coup," *New York Times*, September 13, 1973, 18.

11. "Chilean and Saudi Delegates Shout and Shove Each Other at U.N.," *New York Times*, October 4, 1973, 2.

12. In yet another example of the perennial nature of the detention impulse, Dawson Island had previously been used in the late nineteenth century to intern the Selk'nam, an indigenous people whose land was taken by ranchers with the complicity of the government and who faced almost complete extermination.

13. "Chile Junta Offers Tour of 'Prison'," *Washington Post*, September 23, 1973, A20. "Chilean Junta Frees Suspected Right-Wing Terrorists," *Washington Post*, September 27, 1973, A26.

14. "Mass Executions Reported," *New York Times*, September 24, 1973, 4.

15. "Junta Denies Executions," *New York Times*, September 24, 1973, 4.

16. Marvine Howe, "A Silence Broken Only by Rifle Shots," *New York Times*, "Week in Review," October 7, 1973, 6.

17. "Chile: An Amnesty International Report," Amnesty International, 1974, 12–14.

18. Jonathan Kandell, "Chile's Junta Tells, in 264 Pages, Why It Staged Coup," *New York Times*, October 31, 1973, 3.

19. Telegram From the Department of State to the Embassy in Brazil, Washington, DC, March 31, 1964, 2:29 p.m., National Archives and Records Administration, RG 59, Central Files 1964–66, POL 23–9 BRAZ.

20. White House Audiotape, President Lyndon B. Johnson discussing the impending coup in Brazil with Undersecretary of State George Ball, March 31, 1964, US National Archives.

21. A. J. Langguth, *Hidden Terrors: The Truth about U.S. Police Operations in Latin America* (New York: Pantheon, 1978), 91.

22. J. Patrice McSherry, *Predatory States: Operation Condor and Covert War in Latin America* (Lanham, MD: Rowman & Littlefield, 2005), 53. Langguth, 138.

23. Brazilian National Truth Commission, December 2014 report, Part 1, 232: "According to DOPS concierge books...diplomats Claris Rowley Halliwell, Frederic Chapin Lincoln and C. Harlow Duffin frequented the DOPS building in São Paulo. Halliwell, political officer of the American consulate, made 49 visits to the DOPS between 1971 and 1974. In 1971 alone, there were 31 visits to the building." See also "Comissão da Verdade quer ouvir Fiesp e consulado americano sobre possível ligação com a repressão," from the commission, February 18, 2013.

24. Confidential Memorandum of Conversation, dated October 7, 1970, "Conditions in DEOPS Prison as Told by Detained American Citizen," page 2 of Document 6 of the packet given to the government of Brazil by Vice President Joe Biden on June 20, 2014: http://www.cnv.gov.br/index.php/outros-destaques/498 -documentos.

25. "Relatório da Comissão Nacional da Verdade," December 10, 2014.

26. Marvine Howe, "Chilean Refugees Denied Passes to Leave Country," *New York Times*, September 24, 1973, 1.

27. Agüero interview with author, January 11, 2016.

28. See Jorge Escalante Hidalgo's *"La Misión era Matar: El Juicio a la Caravana Pinochet-Arellano"* (Santiago: LOM Ediciones, 2000) and Adam Bernstein's "Sergio Arellano Stark, driver of the 'Caravan of Death' under Pinochet, dies at 94," *Washington Post*, March 10, 2016.

29. Interview with Jorge Escalante by the author, Santiago, January 9, 2016.

30. Ibid.

31. Ensalaco, 60–61.

32. Report of the Chilean National Commission on Truth and Reconciliation ("Valech Report"), 520, 631, 632.

33. Wolfgang S. Heinz and Hugo Frühling, *Determinants of Gross Human Rights Violations by State and State Sponsored Actors in Brazil, Uruguay, Chile and Argentina: 1960–1990* (The Hague: Martinus Nijhoff, 1999), 506.

34. Interview with Ana Becerra by the author, Santiago, January 9, 2016.

35. Valech Report, 526.

36. Ensalaco, 90.

37. Author interview with Haydee Oberreuter, January 9, 2015. See also *Iberoamericana* (Madrid: Iberoamericana/Editorial Vervuert, 2005), 14.

38. Maria Ugarte exhibition on site at Villa Grimaldi memorial, Santiago.

39. Interview with Haydee Oberreuter.

40. Alex Yannis, "Soccer Storm Brewing in Soviet Bloc," *New York Times*, Sports section, November 4, 1973, 11. Use of the term continued for some time. See also "No Rubles for Chile Soccer," *New York Times*, January 14, 1974, 68; Marvine Howe, "Top Allende Men Held on Isle: Says They Are Held in 'Concentration Camp,'" *New York Times*, February 27, 1974.

41. "15 Political Deaths in Argentina Laid to Rightist Groups," *New York Times*, April 4, 1976, 9.

42. Michael Humphrey, *The Politics of Atrocity and Reconciliation* (London: Routledge, 2013), 40.

43. Material obtained during a January 2016 visit to the ESMA detention site in Buenos Aires.

44. "Nunca Más," Report of Conadep (National Commission on the Disappearance of Persons), 1984. Part I, Repression, Anti-Semitism.

45. Entry for "Tabique," Marguerite Feitlowitz, *A Lexicon of Terror: Argentina and the Legacies of Torture* (Oxford: Oxford University Press, 2011).

46. Author interview with Miriam Lewin in Buenos Aires, January 15, 2016.

47. Secretary of State Henry Kissinger to Foreign Minister Guzzetti in a June 10, 1976, meeting, US State Department Memorandum of Conversation, Santiago, Chile, June 10, 1976, 8:10–9:15 a.m.

48. As McSherry notes, Kissinger specifically told Pinochet not to worry about the speech on human rights, because it "was not aimed at Chile." During the same conference, he expressed support for other Operation Condor states, McSherry, *Predatory*, 111–12.

49. Ibid., 112.

50. Secretary of State Henry Kissinger to Foreign Minister Guzzetti in a June 10, 1976, meeting, US State Department Memorandum of Conversation, Santiago, Chile, June 10, 1976, 8:10–9:15 a.m. Attempts were made by the author to contact Kissinger to discuss his diplomatic role during this period, but no response was received.

51. "Comments on Operation Condor, prepared by the CIA on April 18, 1977, partially declassified...reveals a working meeting held in Buenos Aires between 13 and 16 December 1976. It was attended by representatives of

Brazil's intelligence services along with representatives of Chile, Bolivia, Paraguay and Uruguay, in addition to the host country, Argentina."

52. Peter Kornbluh, *The Pinochet File: A Declassified Dossier on Atrocity and Accountability* (New York: New Press, 2013), 345.

53. Notes from Vichey Cevallos detention site visit, Buenos Aires, January 14, 2016.

54. "Pinochet Arrested in London: Former Dictator Held on Murder Charges," *Evening Mail* (Birmingham), October 17, 1998, 2.

55. Escalante interview with author, January 9, 2016.

CHAPTER TEN *Guantánamo Bay and the World*

1. Details of Masri's account not otherwise sourced come from the "Declaration of Khaled El-Masri," *Khaled El-Masri v. George Tenet, et al.,* Civil Action No. 1:05cv1417-TSE-TRJ, and from "America Kidnapped Me," his account of his rendition published in the *Los Angeles Times* on December 18, 2005.

2. For information on shell company ownership of and overall flight history of aircraft N313P-N4476S, see the jet's profile at "The Rendition Project": https://www.therenditionproject.org.uk/flights/aircraft/N313P.html. For flight logs, see Exhibit A, "Declaration of Khaled El-Masri," *Khaled El-Masri v. George Tenet, et al.,* Civil Action No. 1:05cv1417-TSE-TRJ.

3. Don Van Natta, "Germany Weighs If It Played Role in Seizure by U.S.," *New York Times,* February 21, 2006, 1.

4. Lisa Myers and Aram Roston, "CIA Accused of Detaining Innocent Man," MSNBC.com, April 21, 2005.

5. Amy Davidson, "Torturing the Wrong Man," *The New Yorker,* December 13, 2012.

6. David Cole, *Enemy Aliens: Double Standards and Constitutional Freedoms in the War on Terrorism* (New York: New Press, 2003), 188.

7. Chris Rickerd, "Homeland Security Suspends Ineffective, Discriminatory Immigration Program," ACLU Washington Legislative Office (press release), May 6, 2011.

8. President George W. Bush address to the United States Congress, September 20, 2001.

9. Carol Rosenberg, "Prisoners Arrive in Cuba," *Miami Herald,* January 12, 2002.

10. Details of Camp X-Ray come from a four-day March 2015 tour of the Guantánamo detention camps.

11. Rosenberg, "Prisoners arrive in Cuba."

12. See Miles Fischer's "Applicability of the Geneva Conventions to 'Armed Conflict' in the War on Terror," *Fordham Law Journal* 30, no. 3 (2006), Article 4.

13. "Documents Related to the Former Detention and Interrogation Program," CIA FOIA Reading Room, Document No. 6552082.

14. President George W. Bush, "Presidential Memorandum," February 7, 2002.

15. Jess Bravin, *The Terror Courts* (New Haven, CT: Yale University Press, 2013), 363. In discussing court-mandated changes to the military commission, Bravin

includes a list of "the principal attributes that first inspired them: providing convictions based on coerced statements, concealing government misconduct in obtaining evidence, and speeding executions by prohibiting appeals." Much of the book is an explanation of these motivations and how they played out.

16. John Yoo, Memorandum for William J. Haynes II, General Counsel of the Department of Defense, March 14, 2003, 38.

17. Ibid., 80.

18. Bravin, *Terror Courts*, 31.

19. *Ex parte Quirin* was discussed by the court July 29 and 30, 1942, with a decision on July 31; an extended opinion was filed October 29 of the same year. See also Jess Bravin's *The Terror Courts*, 35.

20. The operation to interdict the Haitian refugees and bring them to Guantánamo, named Sea Signal, was run by General Lehnert, who was brought back in to reopen the Guantánamo facility in 2002.

21. Bravin, *Terror Courts*, 75.

22. Mary Tabor, "Judge Orders the Release of Haitians," *New York Times*, June 9, 1993.

23. Charlie Savage, *Takeover: The Return of the Imperial Presidency and the Subversion of American Democracy* (New York: Back Bay Books, 2008), 374 n53.

24. Jess Bravin, "Lawyers Question Holding Suspected Terrorists Without Offering Legal Case Against Them," *Wall Street Journal*, July 3, 2002.

25. Karen Greenberg, *The Least Worst Place: Guantanamo's First 100 Days* (Oxford: Oxford University Press, 2010), 62–63.

26. "The Court finds that Serbia has violated its obligation under the Genocide Convention to prevent genocide in Srebrenica and that it has also violated its obligations under the Convention by having failed fully to co-operate with the International Criminal Tribunal for the former Yugoslavia (ICTY)."

27. Sven Milekic, "Croatian Culture Minister Wrote for Pro-Fascist Journal," Balkan Transitional Justice, February 11, 2016.

28. "Filtration System," Memorial, April 9, 2008: www.memo.ru/2008/09/04/040908leng/part61.htm. Accessed July 5, 2016.

29. French Indochina and Algeria: Darius Rejali describes the French as having the most critical role in the development of electrical tortures in *Torture and Democracy* (Princeton, NJ: Princeton University Press, 2007), 191. Russian forces in Chechnya: from "Filtration System," Memorial.

30. "Filtration System," Memorial.

31. South Africa's Bantustan states for black Africans predated the war, but with new legislation their strategic use to limit the powers of black Africans increased exponentially.

32. The Black Homeland Citizenship Act of 1970 was the culmination of many years' work toward depriving black people of South African citizenship.

33. Descriptions of Yangon and Sittwe are from a June and July 2015 trip to Myanmar.

34. Hard-liners are so worried about widespread illegal immigration that they complained that vast numbers of unauthorized persons were sneaking across the border and into the Muslim Quarter, posing a threat to Sittwe itself. The quarter was placed on lockdown in May 2016 in order to conduct a census, which revealed the same number of residents as before.

35. In a 2003 survey done well before the riots, 70 percent of Rakhine state residents interviewed exhibited resistance to the idea of latrines, raising significant concerns about sanitation and hygiene in the region. See D. Bajracharya's "Myanmar Experiences in Sanitation and Hygiene Promotion: Lessons Learned and Future Directions," *International Journal of Environmental Health Research* 13 (June 2003): S148.

36. "Bangladesh Plans to Move Rohingya Refugees to Island in the South," *The Guardian*, May 27, 2015.

37. Mauricio Lima and Adam Nossiter, "'We Are Ready to Leave': France Clears Out Calais 'Jungle,'" *New York Times*, October 24, 2016.

38. Paul Farrell et al., "The Nauru Files: Cache of 2,000 Leaked Reports Reveal Scale of Abuse of Children in Australian Offshore Detention," *The Guardian*, August 10, 2016.

39. Conversations with assorted locals in Sittwe about the Sino-Myanmar oil and gas pipelines revealed the anger that fueled protests after the federal government signed a lucrative thirty-year energy deal that led to Sittwe being the conduit for the output from offshore fields going straight to China's Yunnan province with little regard for the needs of the region.

40. Interview by author with U Shwe Mg in Sittwe, July 2, 2016.

41. "They Want Us All To Go Away: Early Warning Signs of Genocide in Burma," US Holocaust Memorial Museum Report, May 2015.

42. Azeem Ibrahim's *The Rohingyas: Inside Myanmar's Hidden Genocide* (London: Hurst, 2016) is one of the more recent works to embrace the term "genocide" in describing events in Rakhine state.

43. Interview with David Scott Mathieson, July 20, 2016.

44. David Scott Mathieson, e-mail exchange, October 1, 2016.

45. "Don't Exaggerate the Problems: Suu Kyi on Myanmar's Persecuted Rohingya," Reuters World News, November 5, 2015.

46. Jonah Fisher, "Myanmar Army Kills 25 in Rohingya Villages," BBC News, Yangon, November 14, 2016.

47. "Burma: Satellite Images Show Fire-Damaged Villages," Human Rights Watch, October 31, 2016.

48. Wa Lone and Simon Lewis, "Exclusive: Rohingya Women Say Myanmar Soldiers Raped Them amid Crackdown on Militants," Reuters, October 28, 2016. Antoni Slodkowski, "Exclusive: More than 1,000 feared killed in Myanmar army crackdown on Rohingya - U.N. officials," Reuters, February 8, 2017.

49. "These are, as Secretary Rumsfeld said, among some of the worst of the worst of the Al Qaeda with whom we have fought." Ari Fleischer, "White House Briefing: Press Pushes Enron Questions," CNN Live Event, aired January 16, 2002, 12:52 ET.

50. Ibid.

51. Greenberg, *Least Worst Place*, 82.

52. Greenberg, *Least Worst Place*, 86.

53. Cahal Milmo, "Guantanamo Bay: Camp X-Ray's Origins Can Be Traced Back to Boer War," *The Independent* [UK], January 18, 2002, 4.

54. Julian Borger, "In a Sniper's Sights: Life in Camp X-Ray," *The Guardian*, January 25, 2002.

55. Claudia Rosett, "The Red Cross Needs to Get Real," *Wall Street Journal*, January 23, 2002.

56. Interview with Pierre-Richard Prosper by the Witness to Guantánamo Project, recorded in San Francisco on March 4, 2015.

57. President George W. Bush, "State of the Union Address," printed in the *New York Times*, January 30, 2002, 22.

58. "Authorization for Use of Military Force Against Iraq Resolution of 2002," US Public Law No: 107-243.

59. Senate Select Committee on Intelligence, *Report on Torture* (New York: Melville House, 2014).

60. Tim Golden, "In U.S. Report, Brutal Details of 2 Afghan Inmates' Deaths," *New York Times*, May 20, 2005. Alex Gibney, "Killing Wussification," *The Atlantic*, May 21, 2009.

61. "Final Report of Postmortem Examination" for Mullah Habibullah, Autopsy dated December 6–8, 2002. The name was redacted from this autopsy, but the ACLU has compared documents from the subsequent court-martial to match it with Habibullah's name.

62. "Autopsy Report: Nadem Sadoon Hatab, 52 y/o Iraqi Male Whitehorse Detainment Facility, Nasiriyah, Iraq June 3, 2003." Also Deborah Hastings, "Long before Abu Ghraib, Nasiriyah Death Ruled a Homicide," *Houston Chronicle*, August 1, 2004.

63. Jane Mayer, "A Deadly Interrogation," *The New Yorker*, November 14, 2005.

64. John Sifton, "Bush Administration Homicides," *Salon*, May 5, 2009.

65. "Findings and Recommendations, Part One," *The 'Taguba Report' on Treatment of Abu Ghraib prisoners in Iraq*, Findings of Fact, Section 6.

66. James Kuhnhenn, "General Who Investigated Prisoner Abuse Blames Military Leadership," McClatchy DC, May 11, 2004. The U.S. military's own Taguba Report of 2004 concluded that Miller was successful in doing so.

67. "Leadership Failure: Firsthand Accounts of Torture of Iraqi Detainees by the US Army's 82nd Airborne Division," Human Rights Watch, September 25, 2005, 1.

68. Charlie Savage, *Power Wars: Inside Obama's Post-9/11 Presidency* (New York: Little, Brown, 2015), 13.
69. Memorandum from Colin Powell to President George W. Bush, January 26, 2002.
70. "Geneva Convention Doesn't Cover Detainees," Reuters, January 11, 2002.
71. "Leadership Failure," 5.
72. Ibid., 12.
73. Mark Mazzetti, "Bush Aides Linked to Talks on Interrogations," *New York Times*, September 24, 2008.
74. "ICRC Report on the Treatment of Fourteen 'High-Value Detainees' in CIA Custody," February 2007, 9. The techniques listed were suffocation by water, prolonged stress standing position, beatings by use of a collar (used to bang the detainee's head against the wall), beating and kicking, confinement in a box, prolonged nudity, sleep deprivation, exposure to cold temperature (including cold cells and cold water poured over a detainee), prolonged shackling, threats against the detainee or his family, forced shaving, and deprivation of food.
75. Senate Select Committee, *Torture*, 36.
76. Ibid., 54.
77. Ibid., 313.
78. Secretary Rumsfeld's eventual rejection of some techniques was not effectively communicated. Torture tactics made their way into Afghanistan and then to Iraq and continued. "Documents and interviews also indicate that the influence of the Secretary's approval of aggressive interrogation techniques survived their January 15, 2003, rescission." See "The Treatment of US Detainees in Custody," Hearings before the Committee on Armed Services, United States Senate, 10th Congress, Second Session, June 17 and September 25, 2008, 44.
79. Ariane de Vogue, "Classified Detainee Memos at Center of Legal War," ABC News, April 9, 2008.
80. Senate Select Committee, *Torture*, 22.
81. Ibid., 47.
82. Interview by the author with Mark Fallon, career Naval Criminal Investigative Service agent and former chief of Counterintelligence Operations for Europe, Africa and the Middle East, September 15, 2016.
83. Ibid.
84. Ibid.
85. Joshua E. S. Phillips, *None of Us Were Like This Before: American Soldiers and Torture* (New York: Verso Books, 2012), 80.
86. Jesse Tuel, "Tried and True: Alumnus leads criminal investigations after 9/11," *Virginia Tech Magazine* 35, no. 3 (Spring 2013). Ret. Army Colonel Britt Mallow: "Most of [the suspects] were captured with just scraps of paper, or nothing....You're given somebody, and you don't know what their name is. You don't know with whom they were involved."
87. Senate Select Committee, *Torture*, 32.

88. Ibid., 44.

89. "The Architect: VICE News Interviews James Mitchell," Vice News, December 11, 2014.

90. Jason Leopold, "Psychologist James Mitchell Admits He Waterboarded al Qaeda Suspects," Vice News, December 15, 2014.

91. Mitchell made this claim after his interview with Vice News aired in 2014.

92. Senate Select Committee, *Torture*, 48.

93. Author interview with Miriam Lewin, Buenos Aires, January 15, 2016.

94. Joby Warrick, "Exams Back Up Reports of Detainee Abuse, Group Says," *Washington Post*, June 19, 2008.

95. Peter Finn, "Brig. Gen. Mark Martins, Lead Prosecutor in 9/11 Case, in Fight of his Career," *Washington Post*, May 4, 2012. See also Sameer Yacoub and Barbara Surk, "Many Say Iraqi Government Has Learned Few Positive Lessons from Past Abuses," *Salt Lake Tribune*, July 14, 2010.

96. Rob Nordland and Charlie Savage, "U.S. Again Delays Transfer of Bagram Prison to Afghan Forces," *New York Times*, March 9, 2013.

97. Brig. Gen. Mark Martins, "Post Commissions Press Briefing for Week of July 18 Thru July 29, 2016," Office of Military Commissions, July 28, 2016.

98. Finn, "Brig. Gen. Mark Martins."

99. Bravin, *Terror Courts*, 116.

100. Ibid., 136–37.

101. Bob Woodward, "Guantanamo Detainee Was Tortured, Says Official Overseeing Military Trials," *Washington Post*, January 14, 2009.

102. *United States v. Khalid Shaikh Mohammad et al. (2)*, court transcript, Arraignments and Motions Hearing, May 5, 2012, 9:23 a.m. session, 19.

103. Carol Rosenberg, "Guantánamo Defense Attorneys Want to Accuse U.S. of Torture—but Can't," *Miami Herald*, October 22, 2013.

104. Most of the physical observations of the Guantánamo Bay base and detention site are from two visits made in February and March 2015.

105. "Department of Defense Media Ground Rules for Guantanamo Bay, Cuba (GTMO)," dated September 10, 2010.

106. There is some debate over the total number of detainees who have been held on the base post-9/11, and of course, there may be detainees the public does not know about. The number provided by Carol Rosenbaum of the *Miami Herald* is 780.

107. "Guantanamo: By the Numbers," *Miami Herald*, October 25, 2016.

108. Clay Trivett, one of the 9/11 case prosecutors, speaking in Guantánamo pretrial hearings on February 18, 2016.

109. Carol Rosenberg, "New Court Can Silence Captives Who Tell Secrets," *Miami Herald*, February 4, 2008.

110. *United States v. Khalid Shaikh Mohammad et al. (2)*, court transcript of hearing dated January 28, 2013, 13:31, 1446.

111. For a detailed look at the challenges, see Shayana Kadidal's "Confronting Ethical Issues in National Security Cases: The Guantánamo Habeas Litigation," *Seton Hall Law Review* 41, no. 4, 1397–1426.

112. James Connell statement to author at press conference of defense attorneys, Camp Justice, Guantánamo Bay Naval Base, Cuba, February 8, 2015.

113. Martin Matishak, "Senator Says Gitmo Detainees Can 'Rot in Hell,'" *The Hill*, February 5, 2015.

114. Carl Takei, "Bureau of Prisons Covered Up Its Visit to the CIA's Torture Site," ACLU National Prison Project, November 22, 2016. This information was also previously disclosed in the Senate Torture Report.

115. During the 2016 campaign, Donald Trump and Chris Christie explicitly embraced waterboarding and/or more severe tactics. Marco Rubio suggested that all ISIS members should be taken to Guantánamo for the kind of interrogations that would make them tell everything they knew. (For Trump, see "Trump On Waterboarding: 'I Love It, I Think It's Great'" from the Daily Caller, April 20, 2016. For Christie see "On Torture, Cruz Stands Alone," from Politico, January 21, 2016. For Rubio see "Rubio: Captured Terrorists Will Get 'One-Way Ticket to Guantanamo Bay, Cuba,'" from *Free Beacon*, January 14, 2016.)

116. Sammy Nickalls, "Waterboarding Is One of Trump's Top Five Presidential Priorities," *Esquire*, November 9, 2016.

117. Rebecca Kaplan, "Marco Rubio: My Gun a 'Last Line of Defense' against ISIS," CBSNews.com, January 17, 2016; Jonathan Swan, "Trump Calls for 'Hell of a Lot Worse Than Waterboarding,'" *The Hill*, February 6, 2016.

118. From pre-session meeting with defense attorneys, February 5, 2015, Camp Justice, Guantánamo Bay Naval Base.

119. Carol Rosenberg, "FBI Hid Microphones in Guantánamo, But No One Listened, Prison Commander Testifies," *Miami Herald*, February 13, 2013.

120. Charlie Savage, "Camp X-Ray: A Ghost Prison," *New York Times*, September 1, 2014.

121. Rejali, *Torture*, 25.

122. Hannah Arendt, *On Violence* (New York: Harcourt, 1970), 80.

123. See Greg Cashman's *An Introduction to the Causes of War: Patterns of Interstate Conflict* (Lanham, MD: Rowman and Littlefield, 2007), 2.

124. Interview of Wesley Clark by Thomas Roberts, MSNBC, July 17, 2015.

125. Mark Deen, "Sarkozy Declares He's Running to Win Back France's Presidency," *Bloomberg Businessweek*, August 22, 2016.

126. Wade Markel, "Draining the Swamp: The British Strategy of Population Control," *Parameters*, Spring 2006, 46.

127. By the time Martins addressed attorneys regarding their obligations in the courtroom, stories about the drama over the former CIA translator's presence at Guantánamo had already been reported around the world. See, for example, "Guantánamo hearing halted by supposed CIA 'black site' worker serving

as war court linguist," from the *Miami Herald*, February 9, 2015, and "Pentagon says Guantanamo interpreter worked for CIA," from the Associated Press, February 10, 2015.

128. "The Detention and Interrogation of Ramzi Bin Al-Shibh," *Senate Select Committee on Intelligence: Committee Study of the Central Intelligence Agency's Detention and Interrogation Program*, Executive Summary version declassified December 3, 2014, 75–79.

129. Fallon interview, September 15, 2016.

130. Audrey McAvoy, "Scalia: 'Kidding Yourself' If You Think Internment Camps Won't Return," *Washington Times*, February 3, 2014.

131. Paul Bogard, *The Ground Beneath Us: From the Oldest Cities to the Last Wilderness, What Dirt Tells Us About Who We Are* (New York: Little, Brown, 2017), 170.

Index

Campbell-Bannerman, Henry, 75
Canada, 10, 115, 117, 118–19
  WWI enemy aliens, 101–2, 114, 115
  WWII enemy aliens, 233
Cánovas del Castillo, Antonio, 32
Caravan of Death, 341, 344, 353, 354
Cards Against Humanity, 404
Castle, Barbara, 315
Castro, Fidel, 276, 278–79, 280
Castro, Raúl, 279
Cavert, Samuel, 184
Cederholm, Boris, 128
censorship, 28, 31, 62, 70–71, 147, 184–85,
  400
Central Cuban Relief Committee, 34–35
Central Utah War Relocation Center, 244
Ceylon, prisoner-of war camps in, 61
Chadwick, James, 113
Chaffee, Adna, 41–43, 42–43
Chagall, Marc, 238
Chamberlain, Joseph, 58, 75, 77, 86
Chamberlain, Neville, 232
Chechnya, 364–65
Cheney, Dick, 377
Chen Ming, 276
Chhe, Siet, 288
Chiang Kai-Shek, 260
Chile, 324–44, 347, 351–53, 352–53, 406
China, 8, 259–67, 261–67, 274–76,
  279–84, 290–92, 293
Churchill, Winston, 232, 233
CIA, 308, 338, 356–57, 381–83, 402
citizenship, 106, 182, 270, 365–75
Civilian Exclusion Orders, 243–44
civilizing mission, 9, 47, 65, 75–78, 170, 305
Clinton, Bill, 363
Code of Ur-Nammu, 8
Cohen, Israel, 99–102
Cohen-Portheim, Paul, 88–91, 93–95,
  97–99, 102, 110–14, 114–16
Cold War, 297–98, 307–9, 316–19, 324–37,
  337–39, 401
collaboration, 67, 143–44, 272–73
Columbus, Christopher, 3
Columbus Evening Press, 48
comfort women, 241–42, 406

Commentaries on the Law of England
  (Blackstone), 91
Committee for Cooperation for Peace in
  Chile, 342
Committee for the Defense of Revolutionists
  Imprisoned in Russia, 124
The Communist Manifesto (Marx & Engels), 119
Compiègne, 229
concentration camps, 5
  accountability for, 252–54, 350–53, 402,
    405–6
  apparent simplicity of, 14
  blaming victims in, 67, 71, 252, 253–55
  boredom in, 111
  bureaucracy in, 87, 102–4
  characteristics of, 5–6, 87
  civilizations within, 98–99, 111–12, 128,
    151, 229
  classifications of prisoners, 12, 81,
    359–61, 380
  cultural life in, 111, 126–27, 134–35,
    176–77, 207
  definition of, 5
  future of, 400–402
  hidden sites, 330–33, 349–50
  incomprehensibility of, 215
  increasing severity of, 53
  indefinite internment in, 102, 385–87,
    397–98
  international law on, 39–40
  lack of resistance to, 215–17, 252, 253–55
  memorialization of the dead from, 85–87
  mental illness in, 97, 110–14, 176
  naming, 73–74
  normalization of, 219–20, 374–75
  origins of, 10–13
  in peacetime, 159–60
  precursors to, 8–10
  public opinion against, 22–23, 26–27,
    31–32, 36–38, 56–59, 74–75, 85–87,
    215, 343, 375–76
  as punishment, 169–70
  remains of, 407–9
  results of, 8, 15–16, 154–55, 250–52
  spread of, 16
  standardization of in WWI, 115–16

About the Author

ANDREA PITZER is the author of *The Secret History of Vladimir Nabokov*. Her writing has appeared in *USA Today*, Slate, *Lapham's Quarterly*, and McSweeney's, among other publications. In 2009, she founded Nieman Storyboard, the narrative nonfiction site of the Nieman Foundation for Journalism at Harvard University. She lives in northern Virginia.

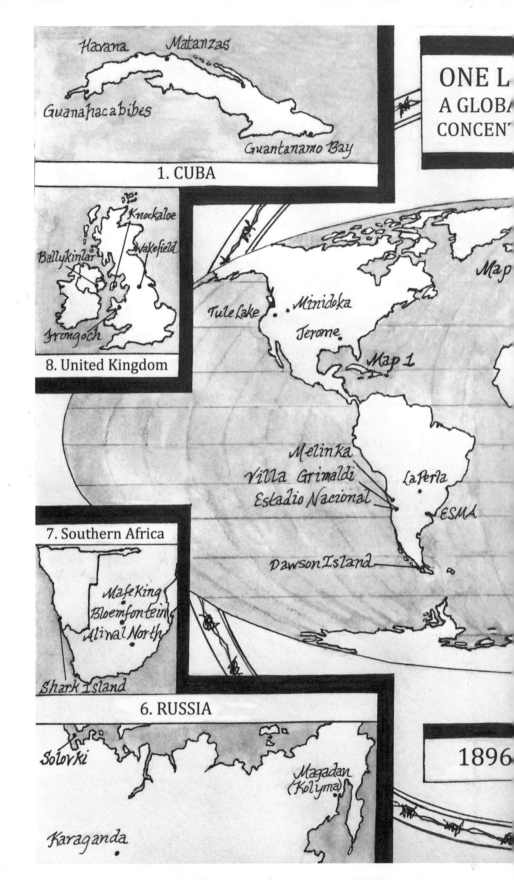

1. CUBA
- Havana
- Matanzas
- Guanahacabibes
- Guantanamo Bay

8. United Kingdom
- Knockaloe
- Wakefield
- Ballykinlar
- Frongoch

7. Southern Africa
- Mafeking
- Bloemfontein
- Aliwal North
- Shark Island

6. RUSSIA
- Solovki
- Magadan (Kolyma)
- Karaganda

ONE L
A GLOBA
CONCENT

Map

- Tule Lake
- Minidoka
- Jerome

Map 1

- Melinka
- Villa Grimaldi
- Estadio Nacional
- La Perla
- ESMA
- Dawson Island

1896